THE LOOK OF THE WEST, 1860

THE LOOK OF THE WEST, 1860

Across the Plains to California

by

Sir Richard Burton

Foreword by Robert G. Athearn

UNIVERSITY OF NEBRASKA PRESS
Lincoln and London

The text and appendix of this book originally comprised part of *The City of the Saints and Across the Rocky Mountains to California* published by Longman, Green, Longman, and Roberts in London in 1862. The present text is reproduced from the Second Edition.

Library of Congress Catalog Card Number 63–17030
International Standard Book Number 0–8032–5029–0
Manufactured in the United States of America

First Bison Book printing: 1963
Most recent printing indicated by the first digit below:
    3   4   5   6   7   8   9   10

FOREWORD

The American West was a source of never-ending fascination for Britons of the Victorian era. In their expansive mood these people covered the globe, developing their empire, investing capital, and exploring for new locations to place even more money. Out along the high plains that sloped upward to the towering Rockies, these successors of the Elizabethan seadogs found a land that was ready for exploitation and it attracted them in a powerful way. An endless expanse of grazing land, a high, dry climate, limitless possibilities for fishing and hunting in and along the mountains, and a warm welcome to those with investment money painted a bright picture for the young men of wealthy British families blessed with surplus funds.

The unveiling of a vast western cattle domain shortly after the close of the American Civil War erased the well-established image of the Great American Desert and it was principally British capital that provided the means of utilizing this grassy empire. "Second sons" came West to look after father's or uncle's investment and perhaps to dry out their systems before the effects of a self-indulgent life at home threatened their livers. Some failed in both attempts, but a good many others succeeded and sent home handsome dividends. Others enjoyed the best of two worlds and lived a comfortable life in the new land without sacrificing many of the comforts available at home. The guest register of the Frewen brothers' ranch in Wyoming was said to have resembled Burke's Peerage.

More than one Briton came West, laden with pounds sterling with which to buy a "ranche," armed only with the knowledge he had acquired through his reading. There was much to be read concerning the West because America as a whole had been under inspection by British travelers for some decades, and after the Civil War, in particular, they came in great numbers. As soon as any kind of transportation facilities were available visitors appeared, curious to see all they could of the new land. Some were members of the idle rich, anxious to shoot down a buffalo or two, others were preachers, journalists, army officers on leave, or independent adventurers—incorrigible travelers who were constitutionally unable to stay at home. A good many of them swore up and down that they just wanted to see the country, had absolutely no intention of writing a single word about what they had seen, but at the insistence of close friends who read their fascinating letters, they reluctantly agreed to share the treasure with the reading public. Others frankly admitted that they went out to see and to hurry home to write about it.

One of those inveterate wanderers, who was ever restless at home and who therefore was annually pregnant with a new travel book, was Sir Richard Francis Burton. This "explorer and scholar," as the *Dictionary of National Biography* labeled him, was nearly forty years old and a seasoned observer when he made his quick trip across the American continent in 1860. Until that time he was an army officer by profession, having held a commission in the Indian Army, and it was in this service that he learned considerable about the East. His understanding of Mohammedan customs was of great value to him in later years when he undertook his famous annotation of *The Arabian Nights.* He began his literary career in 1849 and in the next few years was extremely prolific, writing on such subjects as India, Goa, falconry, bayonet exercises, and the sword. The mid-fifties saw him convalescing in England after having been wounded on an exploration trip to Somaliland, during which time he wrote another book and became acquainted with his future wife. After his return to health he volunteered for service in the Crimea (1855) where he spent a year. The next few years saw him at the head of an exploration of Central Africa sponsored by the Royal Geographical Society, from which he returned in 1859.

His trip across the plains, with a visit at Salt Lake City, must have arisen largely out of restlessness. "Burton's plan of life was now entirely unsettled," the *Dictionary* tells us, explaining that in addition to uncertainty over his professional future, his engagement to Isabel Arundell was not sanctioned by her parents. The latter problem was cleared up when the couple defied the family and were secretly married not long after his return from America, in January, 1861. In his marriage year he entered the consular service and served at successive posts in West Africa, South America, and later at Damascus. These assignments—indeed, nearly every activity he pursued—resulted in books. His last post was at Trieste where he lived until his death in 1890. Throughout his consular career he seems to have been granted a good deal of leave for his explorations, for the resultant books continued at a steady pace and his total bibliography amounted to more than fifty volumes.

The City of the Saints, from which the present volume is drawn, is in many ways typical of descriptions of the West left by his fellow Britons. As an outsider he had no patriotic axe to grind and he was free to assess what he saw with a candor that frequently annoyed Americans. His countrywoman, Frances Trollope, had figuratively fired from the hip a generation earlier, much to the vexation of her readers on this side of the Atlantic. It is this kind of assessment, however, that is of value today as a helpful antidote for the "puffing" of the country of which promotional writers often were guilty.

Sir Richard's book on America's West suffers the same limitations of any travel work by a foreigner in that it is impressionistic and not always completely accurate. But his slips of the pen are minor and if one makes allowance for his complaints about the plainness of western cooking—the British, of all people!—a good picture may be gained of the austere conditions of travel that prevailed prior to the coming of the transcontinental railroad. Of his fellow Britons who ventured westward before the advent of rail service, few viewed the scene with a keener or more cosmopolitan eye, and Burton's account of his journey is one of the fuller and more interesting.

Robert G. Athearn
University of Colorado

CONTENTS

LIST OF ILLUSTRATIONS

ERRATUM

Page 226, line 8 from bottom, for '*Pyrios*' read '*Kyrios*'

A Note on the Text

As the title suggests, *The City of the Saints and Across the Rocky Mountains to California* dealt with two main topics: Burton's visit to Salt Lake City—"The City of the Saints"—and his journey across the continent from St. Joseph, Missouri, to Sacramento, California. In the approximately 350 pages (Chapters IV through X, Appendixes II through V) which Burton devoted to "descriptive geography, ethnology, and statistics of Utah Territory," to Salt Lake City, and to the Mormon religion there is relatively little information of interest to the present-day reader. Consequently, the present volume is confined to those portions of the account which are concerned with Burton's journey: Chapters I, II, III, XI, XII, XIII, Conclusion, and Appendix I. Chapter numbers and pagination have been altered after Chapter III, but with the exception of one brief paragraph deleted at the opening of Chapter IV (Chapter XI in the original), the text is reproduced exactly as it appeared in the second edition, published in 1862.

THE LOOK OF THE WEST, 1860

DEDICATION

TO

RICHARD MONCKTON MILNES

I HAVE PREFIXED YOUR NAME,

DEAR MILNES,

TO

" THE CITY OF THE SAINTS : "

THE NAME OF A LINGUIST, TRAVELLER, POET,

AND ABOVE ALL

A MAN OF INTELLIGENT INSIGHT INTO THE THOUGHTS AND

FEELINGS OF HIS BROTHER MEN

PREFACE.

UNACCUSTOMED, of late years at least, to deal with tales of twice-told travel, I cannot but feel, especially when, as in the present case, so much detail has been expended upon the trivialities of a Diary, the want of that freshness and originality which would have helped the reader over a little lengthiness. My best excuse is the following extract from the Lexicographer's "Journey to the Western Islands," made in company with Mr. Boswell during the year of grace 1773, and upheld even at that late hour as somewhat a feat in the locomotive line.

"These diminutive observations seem to take away something from the dignity of writing, and therefore are never communicated but with hesitation and a little fear of abasement and contempt. But it must be remembered that life consists not of a series of illustrious actions or elegant enjoyments; the greater part of our time passes in compliance with necessities, in the performance of daily duties, in the removal of small inconveniences, in the procurement of petty pleasures, and we are well or ill at ease, as the main stream of life glides on smoothly or is ruffled by small obstacles and frequent interruptions."

True! and as the novelist claims his right to elaborate, in the "domestic epic," the most trivial scenes of household routine, so the traveller may be allowed to enlarge, when copying nature in his humbler way, upon the subject of his little drama, and, not confining himself to the Great, the Good, and the Beautiful, nor suffering himself to be wholly engrossed by the claims of Cotton, Civilisation, and Christianity, Useful Knowledge and

Missionary enterprise, to *desipere in loco* by expatiating upon
his bed, his meat, and his drink.

The notes forming the groundwork of this volume were
written — on Patent Improved Metallic Pocket-books — in
sight of the objects which attracted my attention. The old
traveller is again right when he remarks : " There is yet another
cause of error not always easily surmounted, though more
dangerous to the veracity of itinerary narratives than imperfect
mensuration. An observer deeply impressed by any remarkable spectacle does not suppose that the traces will soon vanish
from his mind, and having commonly no great convenience for
writing,"— Penny and Letts are of a later date — " defers the
description to a time of more leisure and better accommodation.
He who has not made the experiment, or is not accustomed to
require rigorous accuracy from himself, will scarcely believe
how much a few hours take from certainty of knowledge and
distinctness of imagery ; how the succession of objects will be
broken, how separate parts will be confused, and how many
particular features and discriminations will be found compressed
and conglobated with one gross and general idea." Brave
words, somewhat pompous and diffused, yet worthy to be written
in letters of gold. But though of the same opinion with M.
Charles Didier, the Miso-Albion (Séjour chez le Grand-Chérif
de la Mekkeh, Preface, p. vi.), when he characterises " un
voyage de fantaisie " as " le pire de tous les romans ; " and with
Admiral Fitzroy (Hints to Travellers, p. 3), that the descriptions
should be written with the objects in view, I would avoid the
other extreme, viz. that of publishing, as our realistic age is apt
to do, mere photographic representations. Byron could not write
verse when on Lake Leman, and the traveller who puts forth his
narrative without after-study and thought, will produce a kind
of Persian picture, pre-Raphaelitic enough, no doubt, but lacking
distance and perspective — in artists' phrase, depth and breadth
— in fact, a narrative about as pleasing to the reader's mind as the
sage and saleratus prairies of the Far West would be to his ken.

In working up this book I have freely used authorities well

known across the water, but more or less rare in England. The books principally borrowed from are "The Prairie Traveller," by Captain Marcy; "Explorations of Nebraska," by Lt. G. A. Warren; and Mr. Bartlett's "Dictionary of Americanisms." To describe these regions without the aid of their first explorers, Messrs. Frémont and Stansbury, would of course have been impossible. If I have not always specified the authority for a statement, it has been rather for the purpose of not wearying the reader by repetitions, than with the view of enriching my pages at the expense of others.

In commenting upon what was seen and heard, I have endeavoured to assume — whether successfully or not the public will decide — the cosmopolitan character, and to avoid the capital error, especially in treating of things American, of looking at them from the fancied vantage-ground of an English point of view. I hold the Anglo-Scandinavian * of the New World to be in most things equal, in many inferior and in many superior, to his cousin in the Old; and that a gentleman, that is to say, a man of education, probity, and honour — not, as I was once told, one who must get *on onner* and *onnest* — is everywhere the same, though living in separate hemispheres. If in the present transition state of the Far West, the broad lands lying between the Missouri River and the Sierra Nevada have occasionally been handled somewhat roughly, I have done no more than I should have permitted myself to do whilst treating of rambles beyond railways through the semi-civilised parts of Great Britain, with their "pleasant primitive populations;" Wales, for instance, or Cornwall.

I need hardly say that this elaborate account of the Holy

* The word is proposed by Dr. Norton Shaw, Secretary to the Royal Geographical Society, and should be generally adopted. Anglo-Saxon is to Anglo-Scandinavian what Indo-Germanic is to Indo-European; both serve to humour the absurd pretensions of claimants whose principal claim to distinction is pretentiousness. The coupling England with Saxony suggests to my memory a toast once proposed after a patriotic and fusional political feed in the Isle of the Knights — "Malta and England united can conquer the world."

City of the West and its denizens would not have seen the light so soon after the appearance of a " Journey to Great Salt Lake City," by M. Jules Remy, had there not been much left to say. The French naturalist passed through the Mormon Settlements in 1855, and five years in the Far West are equal to fifty in less conservative lands; the results of which are, that the relation of my experiences will in no way clash with his, or prove a tiresome repetition to the reader of both.

If in parts of this volume there appear a tendency to look upon things generally in their ludicrous or absurd aspects — from which nothing sublunary is wholly exempt — my excuse must be *sic me natura fecit.* Democritus was not, I believe, a whit the worse philosopher than Heraclitus. The Procreation of Mirth should be a theme far more sympathetic than the Anatomy of Melancholy, and the old Roman gentleman had a perfect right to challenge all objectors with

> ridentem dicere verum
> Quid vetat ?

Finally, I would again solicit forbearance touching certain errors of omission and commission which are to be found in these pages. Her Most Gracious Majesty has been pleased to honour me with an appointment as Consul at Fernando Po, in the Bight of Biafra, and the necessity of an early departure has limited me to a single revise.

14, St. James' Square :
    1st July, 1861.

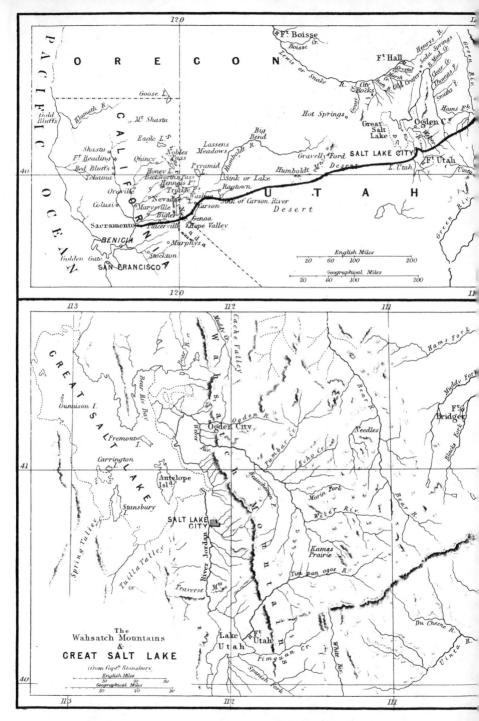

The Wahsatch Mountains & GREAT SALT LAKE

(from Capt.ⁿ Stansbury)

Londo

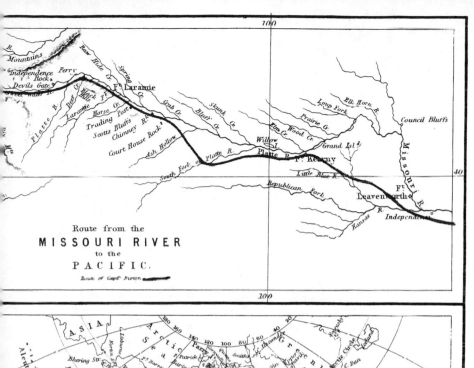

Route from the
MISSOURI RIVER
to the
PACIFIC.

Route of Cap.ᵗ Burton

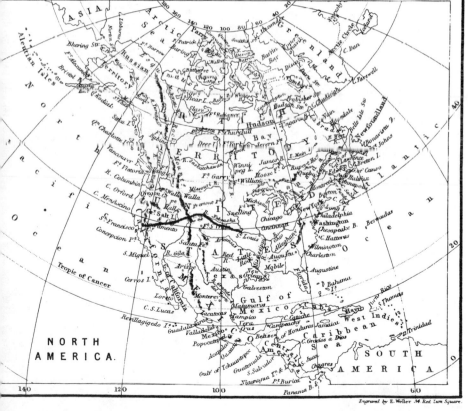

NORTH
AMERICA.

Engraved by E. Weller, 34 Red Lion Square.

CHAPTER I.

WHY I WENT TO GREAT SALT LAKE CITY.   THE VARIOUS ROUTES.
THE LINE OF COUNTRY TRAVERSED.   DIARIES AND DISQUISITIONS.

A TOUR through the domains of Uncle Samuel without visiting
the wide regions of the Far West, would be, to use a novel simile,
like seeing Hamlet with the part of Prince of Denmark, by desire,
omitted.   Moreover, I had long determined, to add the last
new name to the list of " Holy Cities ; " to visit the young rival,
soi-disant, of Memphis, Benares, Jerusalem, Rome, Meccah ;
and after having studied the beginnings of a mighty empire " in
that New World which is the Old," to observe the origin and the
working of a regular go-ahead Western and Columbian revelation.   Mingled with the wish of prospecting the City of the Great
Salt Lake in a spiritual point of view, of seeing Utah as it is,
not as it is said to be, was the mundane desire of enjoying a
little skirmishing with the savages, who in the days of Harrison
and Jackson had given the pale faces tough work to do,
and that failing, of inspecting the line of route which Nature,
according to the general consensus of guide-books, has pointed
out as the proper, indeed the only practical direction for a railway between the Atlantic and the Pacific.   The commerce of the
world, the Occidental Press had assured me, is undergoing its
grand climacteric : the resources of India and the nearer orient
are now well nigh cleared of " loot," and our sons, if they would
walk in the paths of their papas, must look to Cipangri and the
parts about Cathay for *their* annexations.

The Man was ready, the Hour hardly appeared propitious for other than belligerent purposes. Throughout the summer of 1860 an Indian war was raging in Nebraska; the Comanches, Kiowas, and Cheyennes were " out ; " the Federal Government had despatched three columns to the centres of confusion; intestine feuds amongst the aborigines were talked of ; the Dakota or Sioux had threatened to " wipe out " their old foe the Pawnee, both tribes being possessors of the soil over which the road ran. Horrible accounts of murdered postboys and cannibal emigrants, greatly exaggerated, as usual, for private and public purposes, filled the papers, and that nothing might be wanting the following positive assertion (I afterwards found it to be, as Sir Charles Napier characterised one of a Bombay editor's sayings, " a marked and emphatic lie ") was copied by full half the press :

" Utah has a population of some fifty-two or fifty-three thousand — more or less — rascals. Governor Cumming has informed the President exactly how matters stand in respect to them. Neither life nor property is safe, he says, and bands of depredators roam unpunished through the territory. The United States judges have abandoned their offices, and the law is boldly defied everywhere. He requests that 500 soldiers may be retained at Utah to afford some kind of protection to American citizens who are obliged to remain here."

" Mormon " had in fact become a word of fear; the Gentiles looked upon the Latter Day Saints much as our crusading ancestors regarded the " Hashshashiyun," whose name indeed was almost enough to frighten them. Mr. Brigham Young was the Shaykh-el-Jebel, the Old Man of the Hill redivivus, Messrs. Kimball and Wells were the chief of his Fidawin, and " Zion on the tops of the mountains" formed a fair representation of Alamut.

" Going amongst the Mormons ! " said Mr. M—— to me at New Orleans; " they are shooting and cutting one another in all directions—how can *you* expect to escape ? "

Another general assertion was that " White Indians "—those Mormons again !—had assisted the " Washos," " Pah Utes " and " Bannacks" in the fatal affair near Honey Lake, where Major Ormsby, of the militia, a military frontier-lawyer, and his forty men lost the numbers of their mess.

But sagely thus reflecting that " dangers which loom large from afar generally lose size as one draws near," that rumours of wars might have arisen, as they are wont to do, from the political necessity for another " Indian botheration," as editors call it; that Governor Cumming's name might have been used in vain, that even the President might not have been a Pope, infallible; and that the Mormons might turn out somewhat less black then they were painted: moreover, having so frequently and wilfully risked the chances of an " I told you so " from the lips of friends, those " prophets of the past;" and, finally, having been so much struck with the discovery by some western man of an enlarged truth, viz. that the bugbear approached has more affinity to the bug than to the bear, I resolved to risk the chance of the " red nightcap " from the bloodthirsty Indian and the poisoned bowie-dagger—without my Eleonora or Berengaria—from the jealous Latter Day Saints. I forthwith applied myself to the audacious task with all the recklessness of a " party " from Town precipitating himself for the first time into " foreign parts" about Calais.

And first a few words touching routes.

As all the world knows, there are three main lines proposed for a " Pacific R. R.," between the Mississippi and the Western Ocean, the Northern, Central, and Southern *

The first, or British, was in my case not to be thought of; it involves semi starvation, possibly a thorough plundering by the Bedouins, and what was far worse five or six months of slow travel. The third, or Southern, known as the Butterfield or American Express, offered to start me in an ambulance from St. Louis, and to pass me through Arkansas, El Paso, Fort Yuma on the Gila River, in fact through the vilest and most desolate portion of the West. Twenty-four mortal days and nights—twenty-five being schedule time—must be spent in that ambulance; passengers becoming crazy by whiskey, mixed with want of sleep, are often obliged to be strapped to their seats; their meals, despatched during the ten minute halts, are simply abominable, the heats are excessive, the climate malarious; lamps may not be used at night for fear of un-existing Indians:

* The following Table showing the lengths, comparative costs, &c., of the several routes explored for a railroad from the Mississippi to the Pacific, as extracted from the Speech of the Hon. Jefferson Davis, of Mississippi, on the Pacific

briefly, there is no end to this Via Mala's miseries. The line received from the United States Government upwards of half a million of dollars per annum for carrying the mails, and its contract had still nearly two years to run.

There remained therefore the central route, which has two branches. You may start by stage to the gold regions about Denver City or Pike's Peak, and thence, if not accidentally or purposely shot, you may proceed by an uncertain ox-train to Great Salt Lake City, which latter part cannot take less than thirty-five days. On the other hand there is " the great emi-

Railway Bill in the United States Senate, January 1859, and quoted by the Hon. Sylvester Maury in the "Geography and Resources of Arizona and Sonora."

ROUTES.	Distance by proposed railroad route.	Sum of ascents and descents.	Comparative cost of different routes.	No. of miles of route through arable lands.	No. of miles of route through land generally uncultivable, arable soil being found in small areas.	Altitude above the sea of the highest point on the route.
	Miles.	Feet.	Dollars.			Feet.
Route near forty-seventh and forty-ninth parallels, from St. Paul to Seattle .	1,955	18,654	135,871,000	535	1,490	6,044
Route near forty-seventh and forty-ninth parallels, from St. Paul to Vancouver .	1,800	17,645	425,781,000	374	1,490	6,044
Route near forty-first and forty-second parallels, from Rock Island, viâ South Pass, to Benicia	2,299	29,120*	122,770,000	899	1,400	8,373
Route near thirty-eighth and thirty-ninth parallels, from St. Louis, viâ Coo-che-to-pa and Tah-ee-chay-pah passes, to San Francisco	2,325	49,985†	Impracticable.	865	1,460	10 032
Route near thirty-eighth and thirty-ninth parallels, from St. Louis, viâ Coo-che-to pa and Madelin Passes, to Benicia . .	2,535	56,514‡	Impracticable.	915	1,620	10,032
Route near thirty-second parallel, from Memphis to San Francisco	2,366	48,521†	113,000,000	916	1,450	7,550
Route near thirty-second parallel, from Memphis to San Pedro	2,090	48,862†	99,000,000	690	1,400	7,550
Route near thirty-second parallel, near Gaines' Landing to San Francisco by coast route	2.174	38,200§	94,000,000	984	1,190	5,717
Route near thirty-second parallel, from Gaines' Landing to San Pedro . .	1,748	30,181§	72,000,000	558	1,190	5,717
Route near thirty-second parallel, from Gaines' Landing to San Diego . . .	1,683	33,454§	72,000,000	524	1,159	5,717

* The ascents and descents between Rock Island and Council Bluffs are not known, and therefore not included in this sum.
† The ascents and descents between St. Louis and Westport are not known, and therefore not included in this sum.
‡ The ascents and descents between Memphis and Fort Smith are not known, and therefore not included in this sum.
§ The ascents and descents between Gaines' Landing and Fulton are not known, and therefore not included in this sum.

gration route from Missouri to California and Oregon, over which
so many thousands have travelled within the past few years.
I quote from a useful little volume, " The Prairie Traveller,"*
by Randolph B. Marcy, Captain U.S. Army. " The track is
broad, well worn, and cannot be mistaken. It has received the
major part of the Mormon emigration, and was traversed by
the army in its march to Utah in 1857."

The mail coach on this line was established in 1850, by
Colonel Samuel H. Woodson, an eminent lawyer, afterwards an
M.C., and right unpopular with Mormondom, because he sacrile-
giously owned part of Temple Block, in Independence, Mo., which
is the old original New Zion. The following are the rates of
contract and the phases through which the line has passed.

1. Colonel Woodson received for carrying a monthly mail,
$19,500 (or $23,000 ?): length of contract 4 years.

2. Mr. F. M'Graw, $13,500, besides certain considerable
extras.

3. Messrs. Heber Kimball & Co. (Mormons), $23,000.

4. Messrs. Jones & Co., $30,000.

5. Mr. J. M. Hockaday, weekly mail, $190,000.

6. Messrs. Russell, Majors, & Waddell, army contractors :
weekly mail, $190,000.†

Thus it will be seen that in 1856 the transit was in the hands
of the Latter Day Saints : they managed it well, but they lost
the contracts during their troubles with the Federal Government
in 1857, when it again fell into Gentile possession. In those
early days it had but three changes of mules, at Forts Bridger,
Laramie, and Kearny. In May 1859 it was taken up by the
present firm, which expects, by securing the monopoly of the
whole line between the Missouri River and San Francisco, and
by canvassing at head-quarters for a bi-weekly—which they
have now obtained—and even a daily transit, which shall constitutionally extinguish the Mormon community, to insert the
fine edge of that wedge which is to open an aperture for the

* Printed by Messrs. Harper Brothers, New York, 1859, and Messrs. Sampson
Low, Son, and Co., Ludgate Hill, and amply meriting the honours of a second edition.

† In the American Almanac for 1861 (p. 196), the length of routes in Utah
Territory is 1450 miles, 533 of which have no specified mode of transportation, and
the remainder, 977, in coaches ; the total transportation is thus, 170,872 miles, and
the total cost $144,638.

Pacific R. R. about to be.   At Saint Joseph (Mo.), better
known by the somewhat irreverend abbreviation of St. Jo., I
was introduced to Mr. Alexander Majors, formerly one of the
contractors for supplying the army in Utah—a veteran mountaineer, familiar with life on the prairies.   His meritorious
efforts to reform the morals of the land have not yet put
forth even the bud of promise.   He forbad his drivers and
employés to drink, gamble, curse, and travel on Sundays; he
desired them to peruse Bibles distributed to them gratis; and
though he refrained from a lengthy proclamation commanding
his lieges to be good boys and girls, he did not the less expect it
of them.   Results : I scarcely ever saw a sober driver; as for pro-
fanity—the Western equivalent for hard swearing—they would
make the blush of shame crimson the cheek of the old Isis
bargee; and, rare exceptions to the rule of the United States, they
are not to be deterred from evil talking even by the dread presence
of a "lady."   The conductors and road-agents are of a class
superior to the drivers; they do their harm by an inordinate
ambition to distinguish themselves.   I met one gentleman who
owned to three murders, and another individual who lately attempted to ration the mules with wild sage.   The company was
by no means rich; already the papers had prognosticated a
failure, in consequence of the Government withdrawing its
supplies, and it seemed to have hit upon the happy expedient of
badly entreating travellers that good may come to it of our
evils.   The hours and halting-places were equally vilely selected :
for instance, at Forts Kearny, Laramie, and Bridger, the only
points where supplies, comfort, society, are procurable, a few
minutes of grumbling delay were granted as a favour, and the
passengers were hurried on to some distant wretched ranch*,
apparently for the sole purpose of putting a few dollars into the
station-master's pockets.   The travel was unjustifiably slow, even
in this land, where progress is mostly on paper.   From St. Jo.
to Great Salt Lake City, the mails might easily be landed during
the fine weather, without inconvenience to man or beast, in ten

* "Rancho" in Mexico means primarily a rude thatched hut where herdsmen
pass the night; the "rancharia" is a sheep walk or cattle run, distinguished
from a "hacienda" which must contain cultivation.   In California it is a large
farm with grounds often measured by leagues, and it applies to any dirty hovel in
the Mississippian valley.

days ; indeed, the agents have offered to place them at Placerville in fifteen. Yet the schedule time being twenty-one days, passengers seldom reached their destination before the nineteenth— the sole reason given was, that snow makes the road difficult in its season, and that if people were accustomed to fast travel and if letters were received under schedule time, they would look upon the boon as a right.

Before proceeding to our preparations for travel, it may be as well to cast a glance at the land to be travelled over.

The United States territory lying in direct line between the Mississippi River and the Pacific Ocean is now about 1200 miles long from north to south, by 1500 of breadth, in 49° and 32°, N. Lat. about equal to Equatorial Africa, and 1800 in N. Lat. 38°. The great uncultivable belt of plain and mountain region through which the Pacific R. R. must run, has a width of 1100 statute miles near the northern boundary ; in the central line, 1200 ; and through the southern, 1000. Humboldt justly ridiculed the "maddest natural philosopher," who compared the American Continent to a female figure — long, thin, watery, and freezing at the 58th°, the degrees being symbolic of the year at which woman grows old. Such description manifestly will not apply to the 2,000,000 of square miles in this section of the Great Republic—she is everywhere broader than she is long.

The meridian of 105° north longitude (G.)— Fort Laramie lies in 104° 31′ 26″—divides this vast expanse into two nearly equal parts. The eastern half is a basin or river valley rising gradually from the Mississippi to the Black Hills, and the other outlying ranges of the Rocky Mountains. The average elevation near the northern boundary (49°) is 2500 feet, in the middle latitude (38°) 6000 feet, and near the southern extremity (32°), about 4000 feet above sea level. These figures explain the complicated features of its water-shed. The western half is a mountain region whose chains extend, as far as they are known, in a general N. and S. direction.

The 99th meridian (G.)—Fort Kearny, lies in 98° 58′ 11″ — divides the western half of the Mississippian valley into two unequal parts.

The eastern portion, from the Missouri to Fort Kearny—400 to 500 miles in breadth—may be called the "Prairie land." It is true that passing westward of the 97° meridian, the *mauvaises terres,* or Bad Grounds, are here and there met with, especially near the 42nd parallel, in which latitude they extend further to the east, and that upward to 99° the land is rarely fit for cultivation, though fair for grazing. Yet along the course of the frequent streams there is valuable soil, and often sufficient wood to support settlements. This territory is still possessed by settled Indians, by semi-nomads and by powerful tribes of equestrian and wandering savages, mixed with a few white men, who, as might be expected, excel them in cunning and ferocity.

The western portion of the valley, from Fort Kearny to the base of the Rocky Mountains — a breadth of 300 to 400 miles —is emphatically " the desert," sterile and uncultivable, a dreary expanse of wild sage (artemisia) and saleratus. The surface is sandy, gravelly and pebbly ; cactus carduus and aloes abound ; grass is found only in the rare river bottoms where the soils of the different strata are mixed, and the few trees along the borders of streams — fertile lines of wadis, which laborious irrigation and coal mining might convert into oases — are the cottonwood, and willow, to which the mezquite * may be added in the southern latitudes. The desert is mostly uninhabited, unendurable even to the wildest Indian. But the people on its eastern and western frontiers, namely, those holding the extreme limits of the fertile prairie, and those occupying the desirable regions of the western mountains, are, to quote the words of Lieut. Gouverneur K. Warren, U. S. Topographical Engineers, whose valuable reconnaissances and explanations of Nebraska in 1855-56 and '57, were published in the Reports of the Secretary of War, " on the shore of a sea, up to which population and agriculture may advance and no further. But this gives these outposts much of the value of places along the Atlantic frontier, in view of the future settlements to be formed in the mountains, between which and the present frontier a most valuable trade would exist. The western frontier has always been looking to the east for a market, but as soon as the

---

* Often corrupted from the Spanish to muskeet (*Algarobia glandulosa*), a locust inhabiting Texas, New Mexico, California, &c., bearing, like the carob generally, a long pod full of sweet beans, which pounded and mixed with flour are a favourite food with the S.-Western Indians.

wave of emigration has passed over the desert portion of the plains, to which the discoveries of gold have already given an impetus that will propel it to the fertile valleys of the Rocky Mountains, then will the present frontier of Kansas and Nebraska become the starting point for all the products of the Mississippi Valley, which the population of the mountains will require. We see the effects of it in the benefits which the western frontier of Missouri has received from the Santa Fé tract, and still more plainly in the impetus given to Leavenworth by the operations of the army of Utah in the interior region. This flow of products has, in the last instance, been only in one direction, but when those mountains become settled, as they eventually must, then there will be a reciprocal trade materially beneficial to both."

The mountain region westward of the sage and saleratus desert, extending between the 105th and 111th meridian (G.)— a little more than 400 miles — will in time become sparsely peopled. Though in many parts arid and sterile, dreary and desolate, the long bunch grass (*Festuca*), the short curly buffalo grass (*Sisleria dactyloides*), the mesquit grass (*Stipa spata*), and the Gramma, or rather as it should be called "Gamma" grass (*Chondrosium fœneum*)* which clothe the slopes west of Fort Laramie, will enable it to rear an abundance of stock. The fertile valleys, according to Lieut. Warren, "furnish the means of raising sufficient quantities of grain and vegetable for the use of the inhabitants, and beautiful healthy and desirable locations for their homes. The remarkable freedom here from sickness is one of the attractive features of the region, and will in this respect go far to compensate the settler from the Mississippi valley for his loss in the smaller amount of products that can be taken from the soil. The great want of suitable building material, which now so seriously retards the growth of the west will not be felt there." The heights of the Rocky Mountains rise abruptly from 1000 to 6000 feet over the lowest known passes, computed by the Pacific R. R. surveyors to vary from 4000 to 10,000 feet above sea level. The two chains forming the eastern and western rims of the Rocky

---

* Some of my informants derived the word from the Greek letter; others make it Hispano-Mexican.

Mountain basin, have the greatest elevation, walling in as it were the other subranges.

There is a popular idea that the western slope of the Rocky Mountains is smooth and regular; on the contrary, the land is rougher, and the ground is more complicated than on the eastern declivities. From the summit of the Wasach range to the eastern foot of the Sierra Nevada, the whole region, with exceptions, is a howling wilderness, the sole or bed of an inland sweetwater sea, now shrunk into its remnants — the Great Salt and the Utah Lakes. Nothing can be more monotonous than its regular succession of high grisly hills, cut perpendicularly by rough and rocky ravines, and separating bare and barren plains. From the seaward base of the Sierra Nevada to the Pacific — California — the slope is easy, and the land is pleasant, fertile and populous.

After this *aperçu* of the motives which sent me forth, once more a pilgrim, to young Meccah in the west, of the various routes, and of the style of country wandered over, I plunge at once into personal narrative.

Lieut. Dana (U. S. Artillery), my future *compagnon de voyage*, left St. Louis *, " the turning-back place of English sportsmen," for St. Jo. on the 2nd of August, preceding me by two days. Being accompanied by his wife and child, and bound on a weary voyage to Camp Floyd, Utah Territory, he naturally wanted a certain amount of precise information concerning the route, and one of the peculiarities of this line is that no one knows anything about it. In the same railway car which carried me from St. Louis were five passengers, all bent upon making Utah with the least delay — an unexpected cargo of officials: Mr. F********, a federal judge with two sons; Mr. W*****, a State secretary; and Mr. G****, a State marshal. As the sequel may show, Dana was doubly fortunate in securing places before the list could be filled up by the unusual throng: all we thought of at the time was our good luck in escaping a septidium at St. Jo., whence the stage started on Tuesdays only. We hurried therefore to pay for our tickets — $175 each

---

* St. Louis (Mo.) lies in N. L. 28° 37′ and W. long. (G.) 90° 16′ : its elevation above tide water is 461 feet: the latest frost is in the frst week of March, the earliest is in the middle of November, giving some 115 days of cold. St. Joseph (Mo.) lies about N. L. 39° 40′, and W. long. (G.) 34° 54′.

being the moderate sum — to reduce our luggage to its minimum approach towards 25lbs. the price of transport for excess being exorbitantly fixed at $1 per lb., and to lay in a few necessaries for the way, tea and sugar, tobacco and cognac. I will not take liberties with my company's "kit"; my own, however, was represented as follows :

One indian-rubber blanket pierced in the centre for a poncho, and garnished along the longer side with buttons, and corresponding elastic loops with a strap at the short end, converting it into a carpet-bag,— a " sine quâ non " from the Equator to the Pole. A buffalo-robe ought to have been added as a bed : ignorance however prevented, and borrowing did the rest. With one's coat as a pillow, a robe, and a blanket, one may defy the dangerous "bunks " of the stations.

For weapons I carried two revolvers : from the moment of leaving St. Jo. to the time of reaching Placerville or Sacramento the pistol should never be absent from a man's right side — remember it is handier there than on the other — nor the bowie knife from his left. Contingencies with Indians and others may happen, when the difference of a second saves life : the revolver should therefore be carried with its butt to the fore, and when drawn it should not be levelled as in target practice, but directed towards the object, by means of the right fore-finger laid flat along the cylinder whilst the medius draws the trigger. The instinctive consent between eye and hand, combined with a little practice, will soon enable the beginner to shoot correctly from the hip; all he has to do, is to think that he is pointing at the mark, and pull. As a precaution, especially when mounted upon a kicking horse, it is wise to place the cock upon a capless nipple, rather than trust to the intermediate pins. In dangerous places the revolver should be discharged and reloaded every morning, both for the purpose of keeping the hand in, and to do the weapon justice. A revolver is an admirable tool when properly used ; those, however, who are too idle or careless to attend to it, had better carry a pair of " Derringers." For the benefit of buffalo and antelope, I had invested $25 at St. Louis, in a " shooting iron " of the " Hawkins" style,—that enterprising individual now dwells in Denver City,— it was a long top-heavy rifle, it weighed 12lbs., and it carried the smallest ball — 75 to the pound — a combination highly conducive to good practice.   Those, however, who can use light weapons, should prefer the Maynard breechloader, with an extra barrel for small shot ; and if Indian fighting is in prospect, the best tool without any exception, is a ponderous double-barrel, 12 to the pound, and loaded as fully as it can bear with slugs.   The last of the battery was an air-gun to astonish the natives, and a bag of various ammunition.

Captain Marcy outfits his prairie traveller with a " little blue mass, quinine, opium, and some cathartic medicine put up in doses for adults."   I limited myself to the opium, which is invaluable when one expects five consecutive days and nights in a prairie wagon, quinine, and Warburg's drops, without which no traveller should ever face fever, and a little citric acid, which, with green tea drawn off the moment the leaf has sunk, is perhaps the best substitute for milk and cream.   The " holy weed Nicotian " was not forgotten; cigars must be bought in extraordinary quantities, as the driver either receives or takes the lion's share : the most satisfactory outfit is a *quantum sufficit* of Louisiana Pirique and Lynchburg goldleaf, — cavendish without its abominations of rum and honey or molasses, — and two pipes, a meerschaum for luxury and a briar-root to fall back upon when the meer-schaum shall have been stolen.   The Indians will certainly pester for matches; the best lighting apparatus, therefore, is the Spanish mechero, the Oriental sukhtah — agate and cotton match — besides which it offers a pleasing exercise, like billiards, and one at which the British soldier greatly excels, surpassed only by his exquisite skill in stuffing the pipe.

For literary purposes, I had, besides the two books above quoted, a few of the great guns of exploration, Frémont, Stansbury, and Gunnison, with a selection of the most violent Mormon and Anti-Mormon polemicals, sketching materials,— I prefer the " improved metallics " five inches long, and serving for both diary and drawing book — and a tourist's writing case of those sold by Mr. Field (Bible Warehouse, The Quadrant), with but one alteration, a snap lock, to obviate the use of that barbarous invention called a key.   For instruments I carried a pocket sextant with a double face, invented by Mr. George, of the R. Geographical Society, and beautifully made by Messrs. Cary, an artificial horizon of black glass, and bubble tubes to level it, night and day compasses, with a portable affair attached to a watch chain,—a traveller feels nervous till he can "orienter" himself,—a pocket thermometer, and a B. P. ditto. The only safe form for the latter would be a strong neck-less tube, the heavy pyriform bulbs in general use never failing to break at the first opportunity. A Stanhope lens, a railway whistle, and instead of the binocular, useful for things of earth, a very valueless telescope — (warranted by the maker to show Jupiter's satellites, and by utterly declining so to do, reading a lesson touching the non-advisability of believing an instrument maker)—completed the outfit.

The prairie traveller is not particular about toilette : the easiest dress is a dark flannel shirt, worn over the normal article; no braces, — I say it, despite Mr. Galton, — but broad leather belt for "six-shooter" and for "Arkansas tooth-pick," a long clasp-knife, or for the rapier of the Western world, called after the hero who perished in the "red butchery of the Alamo." The nether garments should be forked with good buckskin, or they will infallibly give out, and the lower end should be tucked into the boots, after the sensible fashion of our grand-fathers, before those ridiculous Wellingtons were dreamed of by our sires. In warm weather, a pair of moccasins will be found easy as slippers, but they are bad for wet places, they make the feet tender, they strain the back sinews and they form the first symptom of the savage mania. Socks keep the feet cold ; there are however those who should take six pair The use of the pocket-handkerchief is unknown in the plains, some people however, are uncomfortable without it; not liking "se emungere" after the fashion of Horace's father.

In cold weather—and rarely are the nights warm—there is nothing better than the old English tweed shooting-jacket made with pockets like a poacher's, and its similar waistcoat, a "stomach warmer" without a roll collar, which prevents com-fortable sleep, and with flaps as in the Year of Grace 1760 when men were too wise to wear our senseless vests, whose only pro-perty seems to be that of disclosing after exertions a lucid inter-val of linen or longcloth. For driving and riding, a large pair of buckskin gloves, or rather gauntlets, without which even the teamster will not travel, and leggings — the best are made in the country, only the straps should be passed through and sewn on to the leathers — are advisable, if at least

the man at all regards his epidermis : it is almost unnecessary
to bid you remember spurs, but it may be useful to warn you
that they will, like riches, make to themselves wings.   The
head covering by excellence is a brown felt, which, by a little
ingenuity, boring, for instance, holes round the brim to admit a
ribbon, you may convert into a riding hat or night cap, and
wear alternately after the manly slouch of Cromwell and his
Martyr, the funny three-cornered spittoon-like " shovel " of the
Dutch Georges, and the ignoble cocked-hat, which completes the
hideous metamorphosis.

And above all things, as you value your nationality — this is
written for the benefit of the home reader — let no false shame
cause you to forget your hat-box and your umbrella.   I purpose,
when a moment of inspiration waits upon leisure and a mind at
ease, to invent an elongated portmanteau, which shall be perfec-
tion,— portable — solid leather of two colours, for easy distin-
guishment,— snap-lock — in length about three feet, in fact
long enough to contain without creasing, " small clothes,"
a lateral compartment destined for a hat, and a longitudinal
space where the umbrella can repose : its depth —— but I
must reserve that part of the secret until this benefit to British
humanity shall have been duly made by Messrs. Bengough
Brothers and patented by myself.

The dignitaries of the mail coach, acting upon the principle
" first come first served," at first decided, maugre all our attempts at " moral suasion," to divide the party by the interval
of a week.   Presently reflecting, I presume, upon the unadvisa-
bility of leaving at large five gentlemen, who being really in
no particular hurry might purchase a private conveyance and
start leisurely westward, they were favoured with a revelation of
" 'cuteness."   On the day before departure, as, congregated in
the Planter's House Hotel, we were lamenting over our " morning
glory," the necessity of parting, — in the prairie the more the
merrier, and the fewer the worse cheer, — a youth from the office
was introduced to tell, Hope-like, a flattering tale and a tremen-
dous falsehood.   This juvenile delinquent stated with unblush-
ing front, over the hospitable cock-tail, that three coaches
instead of one had been newly and urgently applied for by the
road-agent at Gt. S. L. city, and therefore that we could not
only all travel together, but also all travel with the greatest com-

fort. We exulted. But on the morrow only two conveyances appeared, and not long afterwards the two dwindled off to one. "The Prairie Traveller" doles out wisdom in these words, "information concerning the route coming from strangers living or owning property near them, from agents of steamboats and railways, or from other persons connected with transportation companies,"—how carefully he piles up the heap of sorites, —" should be received with great caution and never without corroboratory evidence from disinterested sources." The main difficulty is to find the latter—to catch your hare—to know whom to believe.

I now proceed to my Diary.

THE START.

Tuesday, 7th August, 1860.

Precisely at 8 A.M. appeared in front of the Patee House— the Fifth Avenue Hotel of St. Jo.—the vehicle destined to be our home for the next three weeks. We scrutinised it curiously.

The mail is carried by a "Concord coach," a spring wagon, comparing advantageously with the horrible vans which once dislocated the joints of men on the Suez route. The body is shaped somewhat like an English tax-cart considerably magnified. It is built to combine safety, strength, and lightness, without the slightest regard to appearances. The material is well-seasoned white oak—the western regions and especially Utah, are notoriously deficient in hard woods—and the manufacturers are the well-known coachwrights, Messrs. Abbott of Concord, N. Hampshire; the colour is sometimes green, more usually red, causing the antelopes to stand and stretch their large eyes whenever the vehicle comes in sight. The wheels are five to six feet apart, affording security against capsising, with little "gather" and less "dish;" the larger have fourteen spokes and seven felloes; the smaller twelve and six. The tyres are of unusual thickness, and polished like steel by the hard dry ground, and the hubs or naves and the metal nave-bands are in massive proportions. The latter not unfrequently fall off as the wood shrinks, unless the wheel is allowed to stand in water; attention must be paid to resetting them, or in the frequent and heavy "sidlins" the spokes may snap off all round like pipe stems. The wagon bed is supported by iron bands or perpendiculars

abutting upon wooden rockers, which rest on strong leather
thoroughbraces : these are found to break the jolt better than the
best steel springs, which moreover, when injured, cannot readily
be repaired.   The whole bed is covered with stout osnaburg
supported by stiff bars of white oak; there is a sun-shade or
hood in front, where the driver sits, a curtain behind which can
be raised or lowered at discretion, and four flaps on each side
either folded up or fastened down with hooks and eyes. In heavy
frost the passengers must be half dead with cold, but they care
little for that if they can go fast.   The accommodations are as
follows:—In front sits the driver with usually a conductor or
passenger by his side ; a variety of packages, large and small, is
stowed away under his leather cushion ; when the break must
be put on, an operation often involving the safety of the vehicle,
his right foot is planted upon an iron bar which presses by a
leverage upon the rear wheels,— and in hot weather a bucket for
watering the animals hangs over one of the lamps, whose companion is usually found wanting.   The inside has either two or
three benches fronting to the fore or placed *vis-à-vis ;* they are
moveable and reversible, with leather cushions and hinged
padded backs ; unstrapped and turned down they convert the
vehicle into a tolerable bed for two persons or two and a half.
According to Cocker, the mail bags should be safely stowed
away under these seats, or if there be not room enough, the
passengers should perch themselves upon the correspondence ;
the jolly driver, however, is usually induced to cram the light
literature between the wagon bed and the platform, or running
gear beneath, and thus when ford-waters wash the hubs, the
letters are pretty certain to endure ablution.   Behind, instead of
dicky, is a kind of boot where passengers' boxes are stored beneath a stout canvas curtain with leather sides.   The comfort
of travel depends upon packing the wagon ; if heavy in front or
rear, or if the thoroughbraces be not properly "fixed" the
bumping will be likely to cause nasal hæmorrhage.   The description will apply to the private ambulance, or as it is called in
the west " avalanche," only the latter, as might be expected, is
more convenient ; it is the drosky in which the vast steppes of
Central America are crossed by the government employés.

On this line mules are preferred to horses as being more
enduring.   They are all of legitimate race, the breed between

the horse and the she-ass is never heard of, and the mysterious jumard is not believed to exist. In dry lands where winter is not severe—they inherit the sire's impatience of cold — they are invaluable animals ; in swampy ground this American dromedary is the meanest of beasts, requiring when stalled to be hauled out of the mire before it will recover spirit to use its legs. For sureness of foot (during a journey of more than 1000 miles, I saw but one fall and two severe stumbles), sagacity in finding the road, apprehension of danger, and general cleverness, mules are superior to their mothers : their main defect is an unhappy obstinacy derived from the other side of the house. They are great in hardihood, never sick nor sorry, never groomed nor shod even where ice is on the ground ; they have no grain, except five quarts per diem when snow conceals the grass ; and they have no stable save the open corral. Moreover, a horse once broken down requires a long rest : the mule, if hitched up or ridden for short distances, with frequent intervals to roll and repose, may still, though "*resté*," get over 300 miles in tolerable time. The rate of travel on an average is five miles an hour ; six is good : between seven and eight is the maximum, which sinks in hilly countries to three or four. I have made behind a good pair, in a light wagon, forty consecutive miles at the rate of nine per hour, and in California a mule is little thought of if it cannot accomplish 250 miles in forty-eight hours. The price varies from $100 to $130 per head when cheap, rising to $150 or $200, and for fancy animals from $250 to $400. The value, as in the case of the Arab, depends upon size ; "rats," or small mules, especially in California, are not esteemed. The "span"— the word used in America for beasts well matched — is of course much more expensive. At each station on this road, averaging twenty-five miles apart — beyond the forks of the Platte they lengthen out by one-third —are three teams of four animals, with two extra, making a total of fourteen, besides two ponies for the express riders. In the East they work beautifully together, and are rarely mulish beyond a certain ticklishness of temper which warns you not to meddle with their ears when in harness, or to attempt encouraging them by preceding them upon the road. In the West, where they run half wild and are lassoed for use once a week, they are fearfully handy with their heels ; they flirt out with the hind legs, they rear like goats, breaking the harness and

casting every strap and buckle clean off the body, and they bite
their replies to the chorus of curses and blows : the wonder is that
more men are not killed.   Each fresh team must be ringed half
a dozen times before it will start fairly ; there is always some
excitement in change ; some George or Harry, some Julia or
Sally disposed to shirk work or to play tricks, some Brigham
Young or General Harney—the Trans-Vaal republican calls his
worst animal " England "— whose stubbornness is to be corrected by stone-throwing or the lash.

But the waggon still stands at the door.   We ought to start
at 8.30 A.M. ; we are detained an hour whilst last words are said,
and adieu — a long adieu—is bidden to joke and julep, to ice
and idleness.   Our " plunder " * is clapped on with little ceremony ; a hat-case falls open—it was not mine, gentle reader—
collars and other small gear cumber the ground, and the owner
addresses to the clumsy-handed driver the universal G— d—,
which in these lands changes from its expletive or chrysalis
form to an adjectival development.   We try to stow away as
much as possible ; the minor officials, with all their little faults,
are good fellows, civil and obliging ; they wink at non-payment
for bedding, stores, weapons, and they rather encourage than
otherwise the multiplication of whiskey-kegs and cigar-boxes.
We now drive through the dusty roads of St. Jo., the observed
of all observers, and presently find ourselves in the steam ferry
which is to convey us from the right to the left bank of the
Missouri River.   The " Big Muddy," as it is now called,—the
Yellow River of old writers, — venerable sire of snag and
sawyer, displays at this point the source whence it has drawn
for ages the dirty brown silt which pollutes below their junction
the pellucid waters of the " Big Drink."†   It runs, like the lower
Indus, through deep walls of stiff clayey earth, and, like that
river, its supplies when filtered (they have been calculated to contain one-eighth of solid matter) are sweet and wholesome as its
brother streams.   The Plata of this region, it is the great sewer
of the prairies, the main channel and common issue of the water-
courses and ravines which have carried on the work of denudation
and degradation for days dating beyond the existence of Egypt.

According to Lieutenant Warren, who endorses the careful ex-

---

* In Canada they call personal luggage *butin*.
† A " Drink " is any river : the Big Drink is the Mississippi.

aminations of the parties under Governor Stevens in 1853, the Missouri is a superior river for navigation to any in the country, except the Mississippi below their junction. It has, however, serious obstacles in wind and frost. From the Yellowstone to its mouth the breadth when full varies from one-third to half a mile: in low water the width shrinks, and bars appear. Where timber does not break the force of the winds, which are most violent in October, clouds of sand are seen for miles, forming banks, which, generally situated at the edges of trees on the islands and points, often so much resemble the Indian mounds in the Mississippi Valley, that some of them — for instance, those described by Lewis and Clark at Bonhomme Island — have been figured as the works of the ancient Toltecs. It would hardly be feasible to correct the windage by foresting the land. The bluffs of the Missouri are often clothed with vegetation as far as the debouchure of the Platte River. Above that point the timber, which is chiefly cotton wood, is confined to ravines and bottom lands, varying in width from ten to fifteen miles above Council Bluffs, which is almost continuous to the mouth of the James River. Everywhere, except between the mouth of the Little Cheyenne and the Cannon Ball rivers, there is a sufficiency of fuel for navigation ; but, ascending above Council Bluffs, the protection afforded by forest growth on the banks is constantly diminishing. The trees also are injurious; imbedded in the channel by the " caving-in " of the banks, they form the well-known sawyers, or floating timbers, and snags, trunks standing like *chevaux de frise* at various inclinations, pointing down the stream. From the mouth of the James River down to the Mississippi, it is a wonder how a steamer can run : she must lose half her time by laying to at night, and is often delayed for days, as the wind prevents her passing by bends filled with obstructions. The navigation is generally closed by ice at Sioux City on the 10th of November, and at Fort Leavenworth by the 1st of December. The rainy season of the spring and summer commences in the latitude of Kansas, Missouri, Iowa, and Southern Nebraska, between the 15th of May and the 30th of June, and continues about two months. The floods produced by the melting snows in the mountains come from the Platte, the Big Cheyenne, the Yellowstone, and the Upper Missouri, reaching the lower river about the 1st of July, and lasting a month. Rivers like this, whose navigation depends upon temporary floods, are greatly inferior for ascent than for descent. The length of the inundation much depends upon the snow on the mountains : a steamer starting from St. Louis on the first indication of the rise would not generally reach the Yellowstone before low water at the latter point, and if a miscalculation is made by taking the temporary rise for the real inundation, the boat must lay by in the middle of the river till the water deepens.

Some geographers have proposed to transfer to the Missouri, on account of its superior length, the honour of being the real head of the Mississippi; they neglect, however, to consider the direction and the course of the stream, an element which must enter largely in determining the channels of great rivers. It will, I hope, be long before this great ditch wins the day from the glorious Father of Waters.

The reader will find in Appendix No. I. a detailed itinerary, showing him the distance between camping places, the several mail stations where mules are changed, the hours of travel, and the facilities for obtaining wood and water,—in fact, all things required for the novice, hunter or emigrant. In these pages I shall consider the route rather in its pictorial than in its geographical aspects, and give less of diary than of dissertation upon the subjects which each day's route suggested.

Landing in Bleeding Kansas — she still bleeds *— we fell at once into " Emigration Road," a great thoroughfare, broad and well worn as a European turnpike or a Roman military route, and undoubtedly the best and the longest natural highway in the world. For five miles the line bisected a bottom formed by a bend in the river, with about a mile's diameter at the neck. The scene was of a luxuriant vegetation. A deep tangled wood — rather a thicket or jungle than a forest — of

* And no wonder !—

"I advise you, one and all, to enter every election district in Kansas and vote at the point of the bowie-knife and revolver. Neither give nor take quarter, as our case demands it."

"I tell you, mark every scoundrel among you that is the least tainted with freesoilism or abolitionism, and exterminate him. Neither give nor take quarter from them."

(Extracts from speeches of Gen. Stringfellow — happy name ! — in the Kansas Legislature.)

oaks and elms, hickory, bass-wood*, and black walnut, poplar
and hackberry (*Celtis crassifolia*), box-elder, and the common
willow (*Salix longifolia*), clad and festooned, bound and an-
chored by wild vines, creepers, and huge llianas, and shelter-
ing an undergrowth of white alder and red sumach, whose
pyramidal flowers were about to fall, rested upon a basis of deep
black mire, strongly suggestive of chills,—fever and ague. After
an hour of burning sun and sickly damp, the effects of the late
storms, we emerged from the waste of vegetation, passed through
a straggling " neck o' the woods," whose yellow inmates reminded me of Mississippian descriptions in the days gone by,
and after spanning some very rough ground we bade adieu to the
valley of the Missouri, and emerged upon the region of the
Grand Prairie †, which we will pronounce " perrairey."

Differing from the card-table surfaces of the formation in
Illinois and the lands east of the Mississippi, the Western
Prairies are rarely flat ground. Their elevation above sea-level
varies from 1000 to 2500 feet, and the plateau's aspect impresses
the eye with an exaggerated idea of elevation, there being no
object of comparison — mountain, hill, or sometimes even a tree
— to give a juster measure. Another peculiarity of the prairie is,
in places, its seeming horizontality, whereas it is never level : on
an open plain, apparently flat as a man's palm, you cross a long
ground-swell which was not perceptible before, and on its further incline you come upon a chasm wide and deep enough to
contain a settlement. The aspect was by no means unprepossessing. Over the rolling surface, which, however, rarely breaks
into hill and dale, lay a tapestry of thick grass already turning

---

* The bass-wood (*Tilia americana*) resembles our linden : the trivial name is
derived from " bast," its inner bark being used for mats and cordage. From the
pliability of the bark and wood, the name of the tree is made synonymous with
" dough-face " in the following extract from one of Mr. Brigham Young's sermons :—
" I say, as the Lord lives, we are bound to become a sovereign State in the Union,
or an independent nation by ourselves ; and let them drive us from this place if
they can — they cannot do it. I do not throw this out as a banter. You Gentiles, and hickory and *bass-wood* Mormons, can write it down, if you please ; but
write it as I speak it." The above has been extracted from a " Dictionary of
Americanisms " by John Russell Bartlett (London, Trübner and Co., 1859), a
glossary which the author's art has made amusing as a novel.

† The word is somewhat indefinite. Hunters apply it generally to the bare lands
lying westward of the timbered course of the Mississippi : in fact, to the whole
region from the southern Rio Grande to the Great Slave Lake.

to a ruddy yellow under the influence of approaching autumn.
The uniformity was relieved by streaks of livelier green in the
rich soils of the slopes, hollows, and ravines, where the water
gravitates, and, in the deeper "intervales" and bottom lands on
the banks of streams and courses, by the graceful undulations and
the waving lines of mottes or prairie islands, thick clumps and
patches simulating orchards by the side of cultivated fields.
The silvery cirri and cumuli of the upper air flecked the surface of earth with spots of dark cool shade, surrounded by a blaze
of sunshine, and by their motion, as they trooped and chased one
another, gave a peculiar liveliness to the scene; while here and
there a bit of hazy blue distance, a swell of the sea-like land upon
the far horizon, gladdened the sight — every view is fair from
afar.   Nothing, I may remark, is more monotonous, except
perhaps the African and Indian jungle, than those prairie tracts,
where the circle of which you are the centre has but about a
mile of radius; it is an ocean in which one loses sight of land.
You see as it were the ends of the earth, and look around in vain
for some object upon which the eye may rest: it wants the sublimity of repose so suggestive in the sandy deserts, and the
perpetual motion so pleasing in the aspect of the sea.   No
animals appeared in sight where, thirty years ago, a band of
countless bisons dotted the plains; they will, however, like the
wild aborigins, their congeners, soon be followed by beings
higher in the scale of creation.   These prairies are preparing to
become the great grazing grounds which shall supply the un-
populated East with herds of civilised kine, and perhaps with
the yak of Tibet, the llama of South America, and the koodoo
and other African antelopes.

As we sped onwards we soon made acquaintance with a tradi-
tionally familiar feature, the "pitch-holes," or "chuck-holes"
— the ugly word is not inappropriate — which render travelling
over the prairies at times a sore task.   They are gullies and
gutters, not unlike the Canadian "cahues" of snow formation:
varying from 10 to 50 feet in breadth, they are rivulets in
spring and early summer, and — few of them remain perennial —
they lie dry during the rest of the year. Their banks are slightly
raised, upon the principle, *in parvo*, that causes mighty rivers,
like the Po and the Indus, to run along the crests of ridges, and
usually there is in the sole a dry or wet cunette, steep as a step,

and not unfrequently stony; unless the break be attended to, it threatens destruction to wheel and axletree, to hound and tongue. The pitch-hole is more frequent where the prairies break into low hills; the inclines along which the roads run then become a network of these American nullahs.

Passing through a few wretched shanties * called Troy—last insult to the memory of hapless Pergamus—and Syracuse (here we are in the third, or classic stage of U. S. nomenclature), we made, at 3 P.M., Cold Springs, the junction of the Leavenworth route. Having taken the northern road to avoid rough ground and bad bridges, we arrived about two hours behind time. The aspect of things at Cold Springs, where we were allowed an hour's halt to dine and to change mules, somewhat dismayed our fine-weather prairie travellers. The scene was the *rale* " Far West." The widow body to whom the shanty belonged lay sick with fever. The aspect of her family was a "caution to snakes:" the ill-conditioned sons dawdled about, listless as Indians, in skin tunics and pantaloons fringed with lengthy tags such as the redoubtable " Billy Bow-legs " wears on tobacco labels; and the daughters, tall young women, whose sole attire was apparently a calico morning-wrapper, colour invisible, waited upon us in a protesting way. Squalor and misery were imprinted upon the wretched log-hut, which ignored the duster and the broom, and myriads of flies disputed with us a dinner consisting of dough-nuts, green and poisonous with saleratus, suspicious eggs in a massive greasy fritter, and rusty bacon, intolerably fat. It was our first sight of squatter life, and, except in two cases, it was our worst. We could not grudge 50 cents a head to these unhappies; at the same time we thought it a dear price to pay — the sequel disabused us — for flies and bad bread, worse eggs and bacon.

The next settlement, Valley Home, was reached at 6 P.M. Here the long wave of the ocean land broke into shorter seas, and for the first time that day we saw stones, locally called rocks (a Western term embracing everything between a pebble and a boulder), the produce of nullahs and ravines. A well 10 to 12 feet deep supplied excellent water. The ground was in places so far reclaimed as to be divided off by posts and rails; the scanty crops of corn (Indian corn), however, were wilted and

---

* American authors derive the word from the Canadian *chienté*, a dog-kennel. It is, however, I believe, originally Irish.

withered by the drought, which this year had been unusually long. Without changing mules we advanced to Kennekuk, where we halted for an hour's supper under the auspices of Major Baldwin, whilome Indian agent; the place was clean, and contained at least one charming face.

Kennekuk derives its name from a chief of the Kikapoos, in whose reservation we now are.   This tribe, in the days of the Baron la Hontan (1689), a great traveller, but " aiblins," as Sir Walter Scott said of his grandmither, " a prodigious story-teller," then lived on the Rivière des Puants, or Fox River, upon the brink of a little lake supposed to be the Winnebago, near the Sakis (Osaki, Sawkis, Sauks, or Sacs)*, and the Pout-eoustamies (Potowottomis).   They are still in the neighbour-hood of their dreaded foes, the Sacs and Foxes †, who are described as stalwart and handsome bands, and they have been accompanied in their southern migration from the waters west-ward of the Mississippi, through Illinois, to their present southern seats by other allies of the Winnebagos ‡, the Iowas, Nez Percés

* In the days of Major Pike, who, in 1805-6-7, explored, by order of the Government of the U. S., the western territories of N. A., the Sacs numbered 700 warriors and 750 women; they had four villages, and hunted on the Mississippi and its confluents from the Illinois to the Iowa River, and on the western plains that bordered on the Missouri.   They were at peace with the Sioux, Osages, Poto-wottomies, Menomenes or Folles Avoines, Iowas, and other Missourian tribes, and were almost consolidated with the Foxes, with whose aid they nearly exterminated the Illinois, Cahokias, Kaskasias, and Peorians.   Their principal enemies were the Ojibwes.   They raised a considerable quantity of maize, beans, and melons, and were celebrated for cunning in war rather than for courage.

† From the same source we learn that the Ottagamies, called by the French Les Renards, numbered 400 warriors and 500 women ; they had three villages near the confluence of the Turkey River with the Mississippi, hunted on both sides of the Mississippi from the Iowa stream below the Prairie du Chien to a river of that name above the same village, and annually sold many hundred bushels of maize.   Conjointly with the Sacs the Foxes protected the Iowas, and the three people, since the first treaty of the two former with the U. S., claimed the land from the entrance of the Jauflione on the western side of the Mississippi, up the latter river to the Iowa above the Prairie du Chien, and westward to the Mis-souri.   In 1807 they had ceded their lands lying south of the Mississippi to the U. S., reserving to themselves, however, the privileges of hunting and residing on them.

‡ The Winnebagos, Winnepegs (turbid water), or Ochangras, numbered, in 1807, 450 warriors and 500 women, and had seven villages on the Wisconsin, Rock, and Fox rivers, and Green Bay : their proximity enabled the tribe to muster in force within four days.   They then hunted on the Rock River, and the eastern side of the Mississippi, from Rock River to the Prairie du Chien, on Lake Michigan, on Black River, and in the countries between Lakes Michigan, Huron, and

Ottos, Omahas, Kansas, and Osages.   Like the great nations of
the Indian territory, the Cherokees, Creeks, Choktaws, and
Chikasaws, they form intermediate social links in the chain of
civilisation between the outer white settlements and the wild
nomadic tribes to the west, the Dakotas and Arapahos, the
Snakes and Cheyennes.   They cultivate the soil, and rarely
spend the winter in hunting buffalo upon the plains.   Their
reservation is twelve miles by twenty-four ; as usual with land
set apart for the savages, it is well watered and timbered, rich
and fertile : it lies across the path and in the vicinity of civilisation ; consequently the people are greatly demoralised.   The
men are addicted to intoxication, and the women to unchastity ;
both sexes and all ages are inveterate beggars, whose principal
industry is horse-stealing.   Those Scottish clans were the most
savage that vexed the Lowlands ; it is the case here : the tribes
nearest the settlers are best described by Col. B ——'s phrase,
" great liars and dirty dogs."   They have wellnigh cast off the
Indian attire, and rejoice in the splendours of boiled and ruffled
shirts, after the fashion of the whites.   According to our host,
a stalwart son of that soil which for generations has sent out her
best blood westward, Kain-tuk-ee, the Land of the Cane, the
Kikapoos number about 300 souls, of whom one-fifth are braves.
He quoted a specimen of their facetiousness ; when they first saw
a crinoline, they pointed to the wearer and cried, " There walks
a wigwam."   Our "vertugardin" of the 19th century has run the
gauntlet of the world's jests, from the refined impertinence of
Mr. Punch to the rude grumble of the American Indian and the
Kafir of the Cape.

Beyond Kennekuk we crossed the first Grasshopper Creek.
Creek, I must warn the English reader, is pronounced " crik,"
and in these lands, as in the jargon of Australia, means not " an
arm of the sea," but a small stream of sweet water, a rivulet ; the
rivers of Europe, according to the Anglo-American of the West,
are " criks."   On our line there are many grasshopper creeks ; they
anastomose with, or debouch into, the Kansas River, and they

Superior.   Lieutenant Pike is convinced, "from a tradition among themselves, and
their speaking the same language as the Ottos of the Platte River," that they are a
tribe who about 150 years before his time had fled from the oppression of the Mexican
Spaniards, and had become clients of the Sioux.   They have ever been distinguished
for ferocity and treachery.

reach the sea *viâ* the Missouri and the Mississippi. This particular Grasshopper was dry and dusty up to the ankles; timber clothed the banks, and slabs of sandstone cumbered the sole. Our next obstacle was the Walnut Creek, which we found, however, provided with a corduroy bridge; formerly it was a dangerous ford, rolling down heavy streams of melted snow, and then crossed by means of the "bouco" or coracle, two hides sewed together, distended like a leather tub with willow rods, and poled or paddled. At this point the country is unusually well populated; a house appears after every mile. Beyond Walnut Creek a dense nimbus, rising ghostlike from the northern horizon, furnished us with a spectacle of those perilous prairie storms which make the prudent lay aside their revolvers and disembarrass themselves of their cartridges. Gusts of raw, cold, and violent wind from the west whizzed overhead, thunder crashed and rattled closer and closer, and vivid lightning, flashing out of the murky depths around, made earth and air one blaze of living fire. Then the rain began to patter ominously upon the carriages; the canvas, however, by swelling, did its duty in becoming water-tight, and we rode out the storm dry. Those learned in the weather predicted a succession of such outbursts, but the prophecy was not fulfilled. The thermometer fell about 6° (F.), and a strong north wind set in, blowing dust or gravel, a fair specimen of "Kansas gales," which are equally common in Nebraska, especially during the month of October. It subsided on the 9th of August.

Arriving about 1 A.M. at Locknan's Station, a few log and timber huts near a creek well feathered with white oak and American elm, hickory and black walnut, we found beds and snatched an hourful of sleep.

8th August, to Rock Creek.

Resuming, through air refrigerated by rain, our now weary way, we reached at 6 A.M. a favourite camping ground, the "Big Nemehaw" Creek, which, like its lesser neighbour, flows after rain into the Missouri River, *viâ* Turkey Creek, the Big Blue, and the Kansas. It is a fine bottom of rich black soil, whose green woods at that early hour were wet with heavy dew, and scattered over the surface lay pebbles and blocks of quartz, and porphyritic granites. "Richland," a town mentioned in guide books, having disappeared, we drove for breakfast to Seneca, a city consisting of a few shanties, mostly garnished with tall square lumber fronts, ineffectually, especially when the houses stand one by one, masking the diminutiveness of the buildings behind them. The land, probably in prospect of a Pacific R. R., fetched the exaggerated price of $20 an acre, and already a lawyer has " hung out his shingle " there.

Refreshed by breakfast and the intoxicating air, brisk as a bottle of *veuve Clicquot*,—it is this that gives one the " prairie fever,"— we bade glad adieu to Seneca, and prepared for another long stretch of twenty-four hours. That day's chief study was of wagons, those ships of the great American Sahara which, gathering in fleets at certain seasons, conduct the traffic between the eastern and the western shores of a waste which is every-where like a sea and which presently will become salt. The white-topped wain,—banished by railways from Pennsylvania, where, drawn by the " Conestoga horse," it once formed a marked feature in the landscape,—has found a home in the far West. They are not unpicturesque from afar, these long winding trains, in early morning like lines of white cranes trooping slowly over the prairie, or in more mysterious evening resembling dim sails crossing a rolling sea. The vehicles are more simple than our Cape wagons, huge beds like punts mounted on solid wheels, with logs for breaks, and contrasting strongly with the emerald plain, white tilts of twilled cotton or osnaburg, supported by substantial oaken or hickory bows. The wain is literally a " prairie ship;" its body is often used as a ferry, and when hides are unprocurable the covering is thus converted into a " bull boat." Two stakes driven into the ground, to mark the length, are connected by a longitudinal keel and ribs of willow rods : cross-sticks are tied with thongs to prevent " caving in," and the canvas is strained over the framework. In this part of the country the wagon is unnecessarily heavy ; made to carry 4000 lbs., it rarely carries 3000 : westward I have seen many a load of $3\frac{1}{2}$ tons of 2000 lbs. each, and have heard of even 6 tons. The wheels are of northern white oak, well seasoned under pain of perpetual repairs, the best material, "bow-dark" Osage orange wood (*bois d'arc*, or *Maclura aurantiaca*), which shrinks but little, being rarely procurable about Concord and Troy, the great centres of wagon manufacture. The neap or tongue (pole) is jointed where it enters the hounds, or these will be broken by the heavy jolts; and the perch is often made moveable, so that after accidents a temporary conveyance can be made out of the débris. A long covered wooden box hangs behind: on the road it carries fuel; at the halt it becomes a trough, being preferred to nose-bags, which prevent the animals breathing comfortably; and in the hut, where every part of the wagon is utilised, it acts as a chest for valuables. A bucket swings beneath the vehicle, and it is generally provided with an extra chain for "coralling." The teams vary in number from six to thirteen yoke; they are usually oxen, an "old-country" prejudice operating against the use of cows.* The yoke, of pine or other light wood, is, as everywhere in the States, simple and effective, presenting a curious contrast to the uneasy and uncertain contrivances which still prevail in the antiquated Campagna and other classic parts of Europe. A heavy cross-piece, oak or cotton wood, is bevelled out in two places, and sometimes lined with sheet-lead, to fit the animals' necks, which are held firm in bows of bent hickory passing through the yoke and pinned above. The several pairs of cattle are connected by strong chains and rings projecting from the under part of the woodwork.

THE WESTERN YOKE.

The " ripper," or driver, who is bound to the gold regions of Pike's Peak, is a queer specimen of humanity. He usually hails from one of the old Atlantic cities, — in fact, from settled America,— and, like the civilised man generally, he betrays a remarkable aptitude for facile descent into savagery. His

* According to Mormon rule, however, the full team consists of one wagon (12 ft. long, 3 ft. 4 in. wide, and 18 in. deep), two yoke of oxen, and two milch cows. The Saints have ever excelled in arrangements for travel by land and sea.

dress is a harlequinade, typical of his disposition. Eschewing
the chimney-pot or stove-pipe tile of the bourgeois, he affects the
" Kossuth," an Anglo-American version of the sombrero, which
converts felt into every shape and form, from the jaunty little
head-covering of the modern sailor to the tall steeple-crown
of the old puritan. He disregards the trichotomy of St. Paul,
and emulates St. Anthony and the American aborigines in
the length of his locks, whose ends are curled inwards, with a
fascinating sausage-like roll not unlike the cockney " aggra-
wator." If a young hand, he is probably in the buckskin mania,
which may pass into the squaw mania, a disease which knows
no cure : the symptoms are, a leather coat and overalls to match,
embroidered if possible, and finished along the arms and legs
with fringes cut as long as possible, whilst a pair of gaudy
moccasins, resplendent with red and blue porcelain beads, fits his
feet tightly as silken hose. I have heard of coats worth $250,
vests $100, and pants $150 : indeed, the poorest of buckskin
suits will cost $75, and if hard-worked it must be renewed
every six months. The successful miner or the gambler — in
these lands the word is confined to the profession — will add
$10 gold buttons to the attractions of his attire. The older
hand prefers to buckskin a " wamba " or round-about, a red or
rainbow-coloured flannel over a check cotton shirt; his lower
garments, garnished *a tergo* with leather, are turned into Hes-
sians by being thrust inside his cowhide Wellingtons, and, when
in riding gear, he wraps below each knee a fold of deer, antelope, or cow skin, with edges scalloped where they fall over the
feet, and gartered tightly against thorns and stirrup thongs,
thus effecting that graceful elephantine bulge of the lower leg
for which " Jack ashore " is justly celebrated. Those who suffer
from sore eyes wear huge green goggles, which give a crab-like
air to the physiognomy, and those who cannot procure them
line the circumorbital region with lamp-black, which is supposed
to act like the Surma or Kohl of the Orient. A broad leather
belt supports on the right a revolver, generally Colt's Navy or
medium size (when Indian fighting is expected, the large dragoon
pistol is universally preferred); and on the left, in a plain black
sheath, or sometimes in the more ornamental Spanish scabbard,
is a buckhorn or ivory handled bowie-knife. In the East the
driver partially conceals his tools; he has no such affectation in

the Far West: moreover, a glance through the wagon-awning shows guns and rifles stowed along the side. When driving he is armed with a mammoth fustigator, a system of plaited cow-hides cased with smooth leather; it is a knout or an Australian stock-whip, which, managed with both hands, makes the sturdiest ox curve and curl its back. If he trudges along an ox-team, he is a grim and grimy man, who delights to startle your animals with a whip-crack, and disdains to return a salutation: if his charge be a muleteer's you may expect more urbanity; he is then in the "upper-crust" of teamsters, he knows it, and demeans himself accordingly. He can do nothing without whiskey, which he loves to call tarantula-juice, strychnine, red-eye, corn-juice, Jersey-lightning, leg-stretcher, "tangle-leg,"* and many other hard and grotesque names; he chaws tobacco like a horse; he becomes heavier "*on* the shoulder" or "*on* the shyoot," as, with the Course of Empire, he makes his way westward; and he frequently indulges in a "spree," which in these lands means four acts of drinking-bout, with a fifth of rough-and-tumble. Briefly, he is a post-wagon driver exaggerated.

Each train is accompanied by men on horse or mule back — oxen are not ridden after Cape fashion in these lands.† The equipment of the cavalier excited my curiosity, especially the saddle, which has been recommended by good authorities for military use. The coming days of fast warfare, when "heavies," if not wholly banished to the limbo of things that were, will be used as mounted "beefeaters," only for show, demand a saddle with as little weight as is consistent with strength, and one equally easy to the horse and the rider. In no branch of improvement, except in hat-making for the army, has so little been done as in saddles. The English military or hunting implement still endures without other merit than facility to the beast, and, in the man's case, faculty of falling uninjured with his horse. Unless the rider be copper-lined and iron-limbed,

---

* For instance, "whiskey is now tested by the distance a man can walk after tasting it. The new liquor called 'Tangle-leg' is said to be made of diluted alcohol, nitric acid, pepper, and tobacco, and will upset a man at a distance of 400 yards from the demijohn."

† Captain Marcy, in quoting Mr. Anderson's remarks on ox-riding in South-Western Africa, remarks that "a ring instead of a stick put through the cartilage of the animal's nose would obviate the difficulty of managing it." As in the case of the camel, a ring would soon be torn out by an obstinate beast; a stick resists.

it is little better in long marches than a rail for riding. As far as convenience is concerned, an Arab pad is preferable to Peat's best. But the Californian saddle cannot supply the deficiency, as will, I think, appear in the course of description.

The native Indian saddle is probably the degenerate offspring of the European packsaddle: two short forks, composing the pommel and cantle, are nailed or lashed to a pair of narrow sideboards, and the rude tree is kept in shape by a green skin or hide allowed to shrink on. It remarkably resembles the Abyssinian, the Somal, and the Circassian saddle, which, like the "dug-out" canoe, is probably the primitive form instinctively invented by mankind. It is the sire of the civilised saddle, which in these lands varies with every region. The Texan is known by its circular seat; a string passed round the tree forms a ring: provided with flaps after the European style it is considered easy and comfortable. The Californian is rather oval than circular; borrowed and improved from the Mexican, it has spread from the Pacific to the Atlantic slope of the Rocky Mountains, and the hardy and experienced mountaineer prefers it to all others: it much resembles the Hungarian, and in some points recalls to mind the old French cavalry demi-pique. It is composed of a single tree of light strong wood, admitting a freer circulation of air to the horse's spine — an immense advantage — and, being without iron, it can readily be taken to pieces, cleaned or mended, and refitted. The tree is strengthened by a covering of raw hide carefully sewed on; it rests upon a "sweat-leather," a padded sheet covering the back, and it is finished off behind with an "anchero" of the same material protecting the loins. The pommel is high, like the crutch of a woman's saddle, rendering impossible, under pain of barking the knuckles, that rule of good riding which directs the cavalier to keep his hands low. It prevents the inexperienced horseman being thrown forward, and enables him to "hold on" when likely to be dismounted; in the case of a good rider, its only use is to attach the lariat, riata, or lasso. The great merit of this "unicorn" saddle is its girthing: with the English system, the strain of a wild bull or of a mustang "bucker" would soon dislodge the riding gear. The "sincho" is an elastic horsehair cingle, five to six inches wide, connected with "lariat straps," strong thongs passing round the pommel and cantle; it is girthed well back from the horse's shoulder, and can be drawn till the animal suffers pain: instead of buckle, the long terminating strap is hitched two or three times through an iron ring.   The whole saddle is covered with a machila, here usually pronounced *macheer*, two pieces of thick leather handsomely and fancifully worked or stamped, joined by a running thong in the centre, and open to admit the pommel and cantle. If too long, it draws in the stirrup leathers, and cramps the ankles of any but a bowlegged man.   The machila is sometimes garnished with pockets, always with straps behind to secure a valise, and a cloak can be fastened over the pommel, giving purchase and protection to the knees.   The rider sits erect, with the legs in a continuation of the body line, and the security of the balance-seat enables him to use his arms freely: the *pose* is that of the French schools in the last century, heels up and toes down.   The advantages of this equipment are obvious; it is easier to horse and man probably than any yet invented.   On the other hand, the quantity of leather renders it expensive: without silver or other ornaments, the price would vary from $25 at San Francisco to $50 at Gt. S. L. City, and the highly got-up rise to $250 = 50*l*. for a saddle! If the saddle-cloth slips out, and this is an accident which frequently occurs, the animal's back will be galled.   The stirrup-leathers cannot be shortened or lengthened without dismounting, and without leggings the board-like leather *macheer* soon makes the *mollets* innocent of skin.   The pommel is absolutely dangerous: during my short stay in the country I heard of two accidents, one fatal, caused by the rider being thrown forward on his fork.   Finally, the long seat, which is obligatory, answers admirably with the Californian pacer or canterer, but with the high-trotting military horse it would inevitably lead — as has been proved before the European stirrup-leather was shortened — to hernias and other accidents.

To the stirrups I have but one serious objection—they cannot be made to open in case of the horse falling; when inside the stiff leathern *macheer*, they cramp the legs by bowing them inwards, but habit soon cures this.   Instead of the light iron contrivances which before recovered play against the horse's side, which freeze the feet in cold, and which toast them in hot weather, this stirrup is sensibly made of wood.   In the

Eastern states it is a lath bent somewhat in the shape of the dragoon form, and has too little weight: the Californian article is cut out of a solid block of wood, mountain mahogany being the best, then maple, and lastly the softer pine and cotton-wood. In some parts of the country it is made so narrow that only the toe fits in, and then the instep is liable to be bruised. For riding through bush and thorns, it is provided in front with zapateros or leathern curtains, secured to the straps above, and to the wood on both sides; they are curiously made, and the size, like that of the Turk's lantern, denotes the owner's fashionableness; dandies may be seen with the pointed angles of their stirrup-guards dangling almost to the ground. The article was borrowed from Mexico — the land of character dresses. When riding through prickly chapparal, the leathers begin higher up, and protect the leg from the knee downwards. I would not recommend this stirrup for Hyde Park, or even Brighton: but in India and other barbarous parts of the British empire, where, on a cold morning's march, men and officers may be seen with wisps of straw defending their feet from the iron, and on African journeys where the bush is more than a match for any texture yet woven, it might, methinks, be advantageously used.

The same may be said of the spurs, which, though cruel in appearance, are really more merciful than ours. The rowels have spikes about two inches long; in fact, are the shape and size of a small starfish; but they are never sharpened, and the tinkle near the animal's sides serves to urge it on without a real application. The two little bell-like pendants of metal on each side of the rowel-hinge serve to increase the rattling, and when a poor rider is mounted upon a tricksy horse, they lock the rowels, which are driven into the sincho, and thus afford another *point-d'appui*. If the rider's legs be long enough, the spurs can be clinched under the pony's belly. Like the Mexican, they can be made expensive: $25 a pair would be a common price.

The bridle is undoubtedly the worst part of the horse's furniture. The bit is long, clumsy, and not less cruel than a Chifney. I have seen the Arab ring which, with sufficient leverage, will break a horse's jaw, and another, not unlike an East Indian invention, with a sharp triangle to press upon the animal's palate, apparently for the purpose of causing it to rear

and fall backwards.   It is the offspring of the Mexican manége,
which was derived, through Spain, from the Moors.

Passing through Ash-point at 9.30 A.M., and halting for water
at Uncle John's Grocery, where hang-dog Indians, squatting,
standing, and stalking about, showed that the forbidden luxury
— essence of corn — was, despite regulations, not unprocurable
there, we spanned the prairie to Guittard's Station.   This is a
clump of board houses on the far side of a shady, well-wooded
creek — the Vermilion, a tributary of the Big Blue River, — so
called from its red sandstone bottom, dotted with granitic and
porphyritic boulders.

Our conductor had sprained his ancle, and the driver, being
in plain English drunk, had dashed like a Phaeton over the
" chuck-holes ; " we willingly, therefore, halted at 11.30 A.M. for
dinner.   The host was a young Alsatian, who, with his mother
and sister, had emigrated under the excitement of Californian
fever, and had been stopped, by want of means, half way.   The
improvement upon the native was palpable : the house and
kitchen were clean, the fences neat ; the ham and eggs, the hot
rolls and coffee, were fresh and good, and although drought had
killed the salad we had abundance of peaches and cream, an
offering of French to American taste which, in its simplicity,
luxuriates in the curious mixture of lacteal with hydrocyanic
acid.

At Guittard's I saw, for the first time, the Pony Express rider
arrive.   In March 1860, " the great dream of news transmitted
from New York to San Francisco (more strictly speaking from
St. Joseph to Placerville, California), in eight days, was tested."
It appeared, in fact, under the form of an advertisement in the
St. Louis " Republican," * and threw at once into the shade the

---

* The following is the first advertisement : —

" *To San Francisco in eight days, by the Central Overland California and Pike's
Peak Express Company.*

" The first courier of the ' Pony Express ' will leave the Missouri river on Tuesday,
April the 3rd, at — o'clock, P.M., and will run regularly weekly hereafter, carrying
a letter mail only.   The point on the Missouri river will be in telegraphic communication with the East, and will be announced in due time.

" Telegraphic messages from all parts of the United States and Canada, in connection with the point of departure, will be received up to 5 o'clock, P.M., of the
day of leaving, and transmitted over the Placerville and St. Joseph Telegraph
wire to San Francisco, and intermediate points, by the connecting Express, in eight

great Butterfield Mail, whose expedition had been the theme
of universal praise. Very meritoriously has the contract been
fulfilled. At the moment of writing (Nov. 1860), the distance
between New York and San Francisco has been further reduced
by the advance of the electric telegraph — it proceeds at the
rate of six miles a day — to Fort Kearny from the Mississippi
and to Fort Churchill from the Pacific side. The merchant thus
receives his advices in six days. The contract of the government with Messrs. Russell, Majors, and Co., to run the mail from
St. Joseph to Gt. S. L. City, expired the 30th of November,
and it was proposed to continue it only from Julesburg on the
crossing of the South Platte, 480 miles west of St. Joseph.
Mr. Russell, however, objected, and so did the Western
States generally, to abbreviating the mail-service as contem-
plated by the post-office department. His spirit and energy
met with supporters whose interest it was not to fall back on the
times when a communication between New York and California
could not be secured short of twenty-five or thirty days; and,
aided by the newspapers, he obtained a renewal of his contract. The riders are mostly youths, mounted upon active and
lithe Indian nags. They ride 100 miles at a time — about eight
per hour — with four changes of horses, and return to their
stations the next day—of their hardships and perils we shall hear
more anon. The letters are carried in leathern bags, which are
thrown about carelessly enough when the saddle is changed, and
the average postage is $5 = 1l.$ per sheet.

days. The Letter Mail will be delivered in San Francisco in ten days from the
departure of the Express. The Express passes through Forts Kearny, Laramie and
Bridger, Great Salt Lake City, Camp Floyd, Carson City, the Washoe Silver Mines,
Placerville, and Sacramento. And letters for Oregon, Washington Territory,
British Columbia, the Pacific Mexican Ports, Russian Possessions, Sandwich
Islands, China, Japan, and India, will be mailed in San Francisco.

"Special messengers, bearers of letters, to connect with the Express of the 3rd
April, will receive communications for the Courier of that day at No. 481 Tenth
street, Washington City, up to 2.45 P.M. on Friday, March 30th; and in New
York, at the office of J. B. Simpson, Room No. 8, Continental Bank Building,
Nassau street, up to 6.50 A.M., of 31st March.

"Full particulars can be obtained on application at the above places, and Agents
of the Company.

                                                "W. H. RUSSELL, President.
    "Leavenworth City, Kansas, March, 1860.
    "*Office, New York.*—J. B. Simpson, Vice-President: Samuel and Allen, Agents,
St. Louis, Mo.: H. J. Spaulding, Agent, Chicago."

Beyond Guittard's the prairies bore a burnt-up aspect.   Far
as the eye could see the tintage was that of the Arabian
Desert, sere and tawny as a jackal's back.   It was still, however, too early; October is the month for those prairie fires
which have so frequently exercised the western author's pen.
Here, however, the grass is too short for the full development
of the phenomenon, and beyond the Little Blue River there is
hardly any risk.   The fire can easily be stopped, *ab initio*, by
blankets, or by simply rolling a barrel; the African plan of
beating down with boughs might also be used in certain places;
and when the conflagration has extended, travellers can take
refuge in a little Zoar by burning the vegetation to windward.
In Texas and Illinois, however, where the grass is tall and rank,
and the roaring flames leap before the wind with the stride of
maddened horses, the danger is imminent, and the spectacle
must be one of awful sublimity.

In places where the land seems broken with bluffs, like an
iron-bound coast, the skeleton of the earth becomes visible;
the formation is a friable sandstone, overlying fossiliferous lime,
which is based upon beds of shale.   These undergrowths show
themselves at the edges of the ground-waves and in the dwarf
precipices, where the soil has been degraded by the action of
water.   The yellow-brown humus varies from forty to sixty
feet deep in the most favoured places, and erratic blocks of
porphyry and various granites encumber the dry watercourses
and surface drains.   In the rare spots where water then lay, the
herbage was still green, forming oases in the withering waste,
and showing that irrigation is its principal if not its only want.

Passing by Marysville, in old maps Palmetto City, a county-
town which thrives by selling whiskey to ruffians of all descriptions, we forded before sunset the "Big Blue," a well-known
tributary of the Kansas River.   It is a pretty little stream,
brisk and clear as crystal, about forty or fifty yards wide by 2·50
feet deep at the ford.   The soil is sandy and solid, but the
banks are too precipitous to be pleasant when a very drunken
driver hangs on by the lines of four very weary mules.   We then
stretched once more over the "divide"— the ground, generally
rough or rolling, between the fork or junction of two streams,
in fact, the Indian Doab — separating the Big Blue from its
tributary the Little Blue.   At 6 P.M. we changed our fagged

animals for fresh, and the land of Kansas for Nebraska, at Cottonwood Creek, a bottom where trees flourished, where the ground
had been cleared for corn, and where we detected the prairie
wolf watching for the poultry. The fur of our first coyote was
light yellow brown, with a tinge of red, the snout long and sharp,
the tail bushy and hanging, the gait like a dog's, and the
manner expressive of extreme timidity; it is a far more cowardly
animal than the larger white buffalo-wolf and the black wolf of
the woods, which are also far from fierce. At Cottonwood Station
we took " on board " two way-passengers, "lady" and "gentleman," who were drafted into the wagon containing the judiciary.
A weary drive over a rough and dusty road, through chill night
air and clouds of mosquitoes, which we were warned would
accompany us to the Pacific slope of the Rocky Mountains,
placed us about 10 P.M. at Rock, also called Turkey Creek—
surely a misnomer, no turkey ever haunted so villainous a spot!
Several passengers began to suffer from fever and nausea; in
such travel the second night is usually the crisis, after which a
man can endure for an indefinite time. The "ranch" was a
nice place for invalids, especially for those of the softer sex.
Upon the bedded floor of the foul " doggery " lay, in a seemingly
promiscuous heap, men, women, children, lambs, and puppies,
all fast in the arms of Morpheus, and many under the influence
of a much jollier god. The *employés,* when aroused pretty
roughly, blinked their eyes in the atmosphere of smoke and
mosquitoes, and declared that it had been "merry in hall" that
night—the effects of which merriment had not passed off.
After half an hour's dispute about who should do the work,
they produced cold scraps of mutton and a kind of bread which
deserves a totally distinct generic name. The strongest stomachs
of the party made tea, and found some milk which was not more
than one quarter flies. This succulent meal was followed by
the usual douceur. On this road, however mean or wretched the
fare, the station-keeper, who is established by the proprietor of
the line, never derogates by lowering his price.

The Valley of the Little Blue, 9th August.

A little after midnight we resumed our way, and in the state
which Mohammed described when he made his famous night
journey to heaven,—*bayni 'l naumi wa 'l yakzán,*—we crossed

the deep shingles, the shallow streams, and the heavy vegetation
of the Little Sandy, and five miles beyond it we forded the
Big Sandy. About early dawn we found ourselves at another
station, better than the last only as the hour was more propitious.
The colony of Patlanders rose from their beds without a dream
of ablution, and clearing the while their lungs of Cork brogue,
prepared a neat *déjeûner à la fourchette* by hacking "fids"
off half a sheep suspended from the ceiling, and frying them in
melted tallow. Had the action occurred in Central Africa,
among the Esquimaux, or the Araucanians, it would not have
excited my attention : mere barbarism rarely disgusts; it is the
unnatural cohabitation of civilisation with savagery that makes
the traveller's gorge rise.

Issuing from Big Sandy Station at 6.30 A.M., and resuming
our route over the divide that still separated the valleys of the
Big Blue and the Little Blue, we presently fell into the line of
the latter and were called upon by the conductor to admire it.
It is pretty, but its beauties require the cosmetic which is said
to act unfailingly in the case of fairer things,—the viewer should
have lately spent three months at sea, out of sight of rivers
and women. Averaging two miles in width, which shrinks to
one quarter as you ascend, the valley is hedged on both sides
by low rolling bluffs or terraces, the boundaries of its ancient
bed and modern debordements. As the hills break off near the
river, they show a diluvial formation ; in places they are washed
into a variety of forms, and being white, they stand out in bold
relief. In other parts they are sand mixed with soil enough to
support a last-year's growth of wheat-like grass, weed-stubble,
and dead trees, that look like old cornfields in new clearings.
One could not have recognised, at this season, Col. Frémont's
description written in the month of June — the "hills with
graceful slopes looking uncommonly green and beautiful."
Along the bluffs the road winds, crossing at times a rough projecting spur, or dipping into some gully washed out by the rains
of ages. All is barren beyond the garden-reach which runs
along the stream ; there is not a tree to a square mile,—in these
regions the tree, like the bird in Arabia and the monkey in
Africa, signifies water,— and animal life seems well nigh extinct.
As the land sinks towards the river bottom it becomes less
barren. The wild sun-flower (*Helianthus*)— it seldom, however,

turns towards the sun—now becomes abundant; it was sparse
near the Missouri; it will wax even -more plentiful around
Gt. S. L. City, till walking through the beds becomes difficult. In size it greatly varies according to the quality of
the soil ; 6 feet is perhaps the maximum. It is a growth of
some value. The oleaginous seeds form the principal food of
half-starved Indians, while the stalks supply them with a scanty
fuel : being of rapid growth, it has been used in the States to
arrest the flow of malaria, and it serves as house and home to
the rattlesnake. Conspicuous by its side is the sumach, whose
leaf, mixed with kinnikinki, the peel of the red willow,
forms the immemorial smoking material of the Wild Man of
the North. Equally remarkable for their strong odour, are
large beds of wild onions; they are superlatively wholesome,
but they affect the eater like those of Tibet. The predominant colours are pink and yellow, the former a lupine,
the latter a shrub, locally called the rabbit-bush. The blue
lupine also appears with the white mallow, the eccentric putoria, and the taraxacum (dandelion), so much used as salad in
France and in the Eastern States. This land appears excellently
adapted for the growth of manioc or cassava. In the centre
of the bottom flows the brownish stream, about twenty yards
wide, between two dense lines of tall sweet cottonwood. The
tree which was fated to become familiar to us during our wanderings, is a species of poplar (*P. monilifera*), called by the
Americo-Spaniards, and by the people of Texas and New Mexico,
" Alamo ı" resembling the European aspen, without its silver
lining, the colour of the leaf, in places, appears of a dull
burnished hue, in others bright and refreshingly green. Its
trivial name is derived, according to some, from the fibrous
quality of the bark, which, as in Norway, is converted into food
for cattle and even man ; according to others, from the cotton-
like substance surrounding the seeds. It is termed " sweet" to
distinguish it from a different tree with a bitter bark, also called
a cottonwood or narrow-leaved cottonwood (*Populus angusti-
folia*), and by the Canadians *liard amère*. The timber is soft
and easily cut; it is in many places the only material for
building and burning, and the recklessness of the squatters has
already shortened the supply.

This valley is the Belgium of the adjoining tribes, the once terrible Pawnees, who here met their enemies, the Dakotas and the Delawares: it was then a great buffalo ground; and even twenty years ago it was well stocked with droves of wild horses, turkeys, and herds of antelope, deer, and elk. The animals have of late migrated westward, carrying off with them the " bones of contention." Some details concerning the present condition of these bands and their neighbours may not be uninteresting—these poor remnants of nations which once kept the power of North America at bay, and are now barely able to struggle for existence.

In 1853, the government of the United States, which has ever acted paternally towards the Indians, treating with them — Great Britain did the same with the East Indians—as though they were a civilised people, availed itself of the savages' desire to sell lands encroached upon by the whites, and set apart for a general reservation 181,171 square miles. Here, in the far west, were collected into what was then believed to be a permanent habitation, the indigenes of the land, and the various bands once lying east of the Mississippi. This " Indian's home " was bounded, in 1853, on the north by the North-western Territory and Minnesota; on the south by Texas and New Mexico; to the east lay Iowa, Missouri, and Arkansas; and to the west, Oregon, Utah, and New Mexico.

The savages' reservation was then thus distributed. The eastern portion nearest the river was stocked with tribes removed to it from the eastern states, namely, the Iowas, Sacs and Foxes, Kikapoos, Delawares, Potowottomis, Wyandots, Quapaws, Senecas, Cherokees, Seminoles, Creeks, Choctaws, Chikasaws, Miamis, and Ottawas. The west and part of the north-east—poor and barren lands—were retained by the aboriginal tribes, Ponkahs, Omahas or Mahas, Pawnees, Ottos, Kansas or Konzas, and Osages. The central and the remainder of the western portion—wild countries abounding in buffalo—were granted to the Western Pawnees, the Arikaris, Arapahos, Cheyennes, Kiowas, Comanches, Utahs, Grosventres, and other nomads.

It was somewhat a confusion of races. For instance, the Pawnees form an independent family, to which some authors join the Arikari; the Sacs (Sauk) and Foxes, Winnebagos, Ottos, Kaws, Omahas, Cheyennes, Mississippi Dakotas, and Missouri Dakotas, belong to the Dakotan family; the Choctaws, Creeks, and Seminoles are Appalachians; the Wyandots, like the Iroquois, are Hodesaunians : and the Ottawas, Delawares, Shawnees, Potowottomis, Peorians, Mohekuneuks, Kaskasias, Piankashaws, Weaws, Miamis, Kikapoos, and Menomenes, are, like the Ojibwes, Algonquins.

The total number of Indians on the prairies and the Rocky Mountains was estimated roughly at 63,000.

Still the resistless tide of emigration swept westward : the Federal Government was as powerless to stem it, as was General Fitzroy of New South Wales to prevent, in 1852, his subjects flocking to the "gold diggings." Despite all orders, reckless whites would squat upon, and thoughtless reds, bribed by whiskey, tobacco, and gunpowder, would sell off, the lands. On the 20th May, 1854, was passed the celebrated " Kansas-Nebraska Bill," an act converting the greater portion of the "Indian Territory," and all the "North-Western Territory," into two new territories Kansas, north of the 37th parallel, and Nebraska, north of the 40th. In the passage of this bill, the celebrated " Missouri Compromise " of 1828, prohibiting negro slavery north of 36° 30′, was repealed, under the presidency of General Pearce.* It provided that the rights and properties of

---

* The "Missouri Compromise" is an important event in Anglo-American history ; it must be regarded as the great parent of the jangles and heart burnings which have disunited the United States. The great Jefferson prophesied in these words, "the Missouri question is a breaker on which we lose the Missouri country by revolt, and what more God only knows. From the battle of Bunker's Hill to the treaty of Paris, we never had so ominous a question."

The origin of the trouble was this. In 1817 the Eastern half of the Mississippi territory became the territory of Alabama, and – in those days events had wings—. the 14th Dec. 1819 witnessed the birth of Alabama as a free sovereign and independent slave State. The South, strong in wealth and numbers, thereupon moved towards legalising slavery in the newly acquired territory of Missouri, and when Mo. claimed to be admitted as a State, demanded that it should be admitted as a slave State. The Free-soilers, or opposite party, urged two reasons why Missouri should be a free State. Firstly, Since the date of the union eight new States had been admitted, four slave and four free. Alabama the last, was a slave State, therefore it was the turn for a free State. Secondly,—and here was the rub,— that " Slavery ought not to be permitted in any State or territory where it could be prohibited." This very broad principle involved, it is manifest, the ruin of the slave-ocracy. From the days of Mr. Washington to those of Mr. Lincoln, the northern or labour states have ever aimed at the ultimate abolition of servitude by means of non-extension. The contest about Missouri began in 1818, and raged for three years, complicated by a new feature, namely, Maine separating herself from

the Indians, within their shrunken possessions, should be respected. By degrees the Indians sold their lands for whiskey, as
of old, and retired to smaller reservations. Of course, they suffered in the bargain; the savage ever parts with his birth-right
for the well-known mess of pottage. The Osages, for instance,
cancelled $4000, claimed by unscrupulous traders, by a cession
of two million acres of arable land. The Potowottomis fared
even worse ; under the influence of liquor, ὡς λέγουσι, their
chiefs sold 100,000 acres of the best soil on the banks of the
Missouri for a mere song. The tribe was removed to a bald
smooth prairie, sans timber and consequently sans game; many
fled to the extreme wilds, and the others, like the Acadians of
yore, were marched about till they found homes—many of
them six feet by two—in Fever Patch, on the Kaw or Kansas
River. Others were more fortunate. The Ottos, Omahas, and
Kansas, had permanent villages near the Missouri and its two
tributaries, the Platte and the Kansas. The Osages, formerly a
large nation in Arkansas, after ceding 10,000,000 of acres for a
stipend of $52,000 for thirty years, were settled in a district on
the west bank of the Neosho or White-water—the Grand River.
They are described as the finest and largest men of the semi-
nomad races, with well-formed heads and symmetrical figures,
brave, warlike, and well disposed to the whites. Early in June,
after planting their maize, they move in mounted bands to the
prairies, feast upon the buffalo for months, and bring home
stores of smoked and jerked meat. When the corn is in milk

Massachusetts, and balancing the admission of Alabama, by becoming a free
State. The lower House several times voted to exclude the "peculiar institution" from the new State, and the conservative Senate—in which the southern
element was ever predominant—as often restored it. Great was the war of words
amongst the rival legislators ; at length, after repeated conferences, both Senate
and House agreed upon a bill admitting Missouri, after her constitution should be
formed, free of restriction, but prohibiting slavery north of 36° 30'. Missouri acknowledged the boon by adopting a constitution which denied the rights of citizens even
to free negroes. She was not finally admitted until the 10th August, 1821, when
her legislature had solemnly covenanted to guarantee the rights of citizenship
to "the citizens of either of the States." Such is an outline of the far-famed
"Missouri Compromise." The influence of the southern slave-holders caused it to
be repealed, as a slip of Texas happened to lie north of the prohibitative latitude,
and the late Mr. S. A. Douglas did it to death in 1854. The free-soilers of course
fought hard against the "sad repeal," and what they now fight about, forty years
afterwards, is to run still further south the original line of limitation. *Hinc illæ
lachrymæ !*

they husk and sun-dry it; it is then boiled, and is said to be better flavoured and more nutritious than the East Indian " hutah," or the American hominy. After the harvest in October, they return to the game country, and then pass the winter under huts or skin lodges. Their chief scourge is small-pox: apparently, all the tribes carry some cross. Of the settled races the best types are the Choctaws and the Cherokees; the latter have shown a degree of improvability, which may still preserve them from destruction; they have a form of government, churches, theatres, and schools; they read and write English; and George Guess, a well-known chief, like the negro inventor of the Vai syllabarium in West Africa, produced an alphabet of sixty-eight characters, which, improved and simplified by the missionaries, is found useful in teaching the vernacular.

Upon the whole, however, the philanthropic schemes of the government have not met with brilliant success. The chiefs are still bribed, and the people cheated, by white traders, and poverty, disease, and debauchery, rapidly thin the tribesmen. Sensible heads have proposed many schemes for preserving the race. Apparently the best of these projects is to introduce the Moravian discipline. Of all missionary systems, I may observe, none have hitherto been crowned with important results, despite the blood and gold so profusely expended upon them, except two — those of the Jesuits and the United Brethren. The fraternity of Jesus spread the gospel by assimilating themselves to the heathen; the Unitas Fratrum by assimilating the heathen to themselves. The day of Jesuit-ism, like that of protection, is going by. The advance of Moravianism, it may safely be prophesied, is to come. These civilisation-societies have as yet been little appreciated, because they will not minister to that ignorant enthusiasm which extracts money from the pockets of the many. Their necessarily slow progress is irksome to ardent propagandists. We naturally wish to reap as well as to sow; and man rarely invests capital in schemes of which only his grandson will see the results.

The American philanthropist proposes to wean the Indian savage from his nomad life by turning his lodge into a log tent, and by providing him with cattle instead of buffalo, and the domestic fowl instead of grasshoppers. The hunter become a herdsman would thus be strengthened for another step—the agricultural life, which necessarily follows the pastoral. Factors would be appointed instead of vicious traders—*coureurs des bois,* as the Canadians call them ; titles to land would be granted in fee simple, practically teaching the value of property in severalty, alienation into white hands would be forbidden, and, if possible, a cordon militaire would be stretched between the races. The agricultural would lead to the mechanical stage of society. Agents and assistant craftsmen would teach the tribes to raise mills and smithies (at present there are mills without millers, stock without breeders, and similar attempts to make civilisation run before she can walk), and a growing appreciation for the peace, the comfort, and the luxuries of settled life would lay the nomad instinct for ever.

The project labours only under one difficulty—the one common to philanthropic schemes. In many details it is somewhat visionary — utopian. It is, like peace on earth, a " dream of the wise." Under the present system of Indian agencies, as will in a future page appear, it is simply impossible. It has terrible obstacles in the westward gravitation of the white race, which, after sweeping away the aborigines — as the grey rat in Europe expelled the black rat — from the east of the Mississippi in two centuries and a half, threatens, before a quarter of that time shall have elapsed, to drive in its advance towards the Pacific, the few survivors of now populous tribes either into the inhospitable regions north of the 49th parallel, or into the anarchical countries south of the 32nd. And where, I may ask, in the history of the world do we read of a people learning civilisation from strangers instead of working it out for themselves, through its several degrees of barbarism, feudalism, monarchy, republicanism, despotism ? Still it is a noble project : mankind would not willingly see it die.

The Pawnees were called by the French and Canadian traders Les Loups, that animal being their totem, and the sign of the tribe being an imitation of the wolf's ears, the two fore fingers of the right hand being stuck up on the side of the head. They were in the last generation a large nation, containing many clans — Minnikajus, the Sans Arc, the Loup Fork, and others. Their territory embraced both sides of the Platte River, especially the northern lands; and they rendered these grounds terrible to the trapper, trader and traveller. They were always well mounted. Old Mexico was then, and partially is still, their stable, and a small band has driven off horses by hundreds. Of late years they have become powerless. The influenza acts as a plague amongst them, killing off 400 or 500 in a single season, and the nation now numbers little more than 300 braves, or rather warriors, the latter, in correct parlance, being inferior to the former, as the former are subservient to the chief. A treaty concluded between them and the United States, in the winter of 1857, sent them to a reserve on the Loup Fork, where their villages were destroyed by the Sioux. They are Ishmaelites, whose hand is against every man. They have attempted, after the fashion of declining tribes, to strengthen themselves by alliances with their neighbours, but have always failed in consequence of their propensity to plunder developing itself even before the pow-wow was concluded. They and the northern Dakotas can never be trusted. Most Indian races, like the Bedouin Arabs, will show hospitality to the stranger who rides into their villages, though no point of honour deters them from robbing him after he has left the lodge-shade. The Pawnees, African-like, will cut the throat of a sleeping guest. They are easily distinguished from their neighbours by the scalp-lock protruding from a shaven head. After killing white men, they have insulted the corpse in a manner familiar to those who served in the Affghan war. They have given up the practice of torturing prisoners, saying that the " Great Spirit," or rather, as the expression should be translated, the " Great Father " no longer wills it. The tradition is, that a few years ago a squaw of a hostile tribe was snatched from the stake by a white trader, and the action was interpreted as a decree of heaven. It is probably a corruption of the well-known story of the rescue of the Itean woman by Petalesharoo, the son of the " Knife Chief." Like the southern and western Indians generally, as is truly remarked by Captain Mayne Reid *, " They possess more of that cold continence and chivalrous delicacy than characterise the red men of the forest." They are too treacherous to be used as soldiers. Like most

* The Scalp-hunters, chap. xlii.

pedestrian Indians, their arms and bodies are light and thin,
and their legs are muscular and well developed. They are
great in endurance. I have heard of a Pawnee who, when
thoroughly "stampeded" by his enemies, "loped" from Fort
Laramie to Kearny — 300 miles — making the distance as fast
as the mail. This bad tribe is ever at war with their hereditary enemies the Sioux. They do not extend westward of Fort
Kearny. The principal subtribe is the Arikari, or Ree, called
Pedani by the Dakota, who attacked and conquered them.
Their large villages, near the mouth of the Grand River, were
destroyed by the expedition sent in 1825-26, under Colonel
Leavenworth, to chastise the attack upon the trading party of
General Ashley.

A more interesting people than the Pawnee is the Delaware,
whose oldest tradition derives him from the region west of the
Mississippi. Thence the tribe migrated to the Atlantic shores,
where they took the title of Lenne Lenape, or men, and
the neighbouring races in respect called them " uncle." Wil-
liam Penn and his followers found this remnant of the great
Algonquin confederacy in a depressed state : subjugated by the
Five Nations, they had been compelled to take the name of
" Iroquois Squaws." In those days they felt an awe of the
white man, and looked upon him as a something godlike. Since
their return to the west their spirit has revived, their war-path
has reached through Utah to the Pacific Ocean, to Hudson's
Bay on the north, and southwards to the heart of Mexico.
Their present abodes are principally near Fort Leavenworth
upon the Missouri, and in the Choctaw territory near Fort
Arbuckle, upon the eastern Colorado or Canadian river. They
are familiar with the languages, manners, and customs of their
pale-faced neighbours ; they are so feared as rifle shots, that a
host of enemies will fly from a few of their warriors, and they
mostly lead a vagrant life, the wandering Jews of the west,
as traders, hunters, and trappers amongst the other Indian
tribes. For 185 years the Shawnees have been associated with
them in intermarriage, yet they are declining in numbers ; here
and there some are lost, one by one, in travel or battle ; they
have now dwindled to about a hundred warriors, and the extinction of the tribe appears imminent. As hunters and guides,
they are preferred to all others by the whites, and it is believed

that they would make as formidable partisan soldiers as any on this continent. When the government of the United States, after the fashion of France and England, begins to raise " Irregular Native Corps," the loss of the Delawares will be regretted.

Changing mules at Kiowa, about 10 A.M., we pushed forward through the sun, which presently was mitigated by heavy nimbi, to Liberty Farm, where a station supplied us with the eternal eggs and bacon of these *mangeurs de lard*. It is a dish constant in the great West, as the omelet and pigeon in the vetturini days of Italy, when, prompted by the instincts of self-preservation, the inmates of the dovecot, unless prevented in time, are said to have fled their homes at the sight of Milordo's travelling carriage, not to return until the portent had disappeared. The Little Blue ran hard by, about fifty feet wide by three or four deep, fringed with emerald-green oak groves, cotton-wood, and long-leaved willow : its waters supply catfish, suckers, and a soft shelled turtle, but the fish are full of bones, and taste, as might be imagined, much like mud. The country showed vestiges of animal life, the prairie bore signs of hare and antelope : in the valley coyotes, wolves, and foxes, attracted by the carcasses of cattle, stared us in the face, and near the stream, plovers, jays, the blue bird (sialia), and a kind of starling called the swamp or redwinged blackbird, twittered a song of satisfaction. We then resumed our journey over a desert, waterless save after rain, for twenty-three miles ; it is the divide between the Little Blue and the Platte rivers, a broken table land rising gradually towards the west, with, at this season, a barren soil of sand and clay. As the evening approached, a smile from above lit up into absolute beauty the homely features of the world below. The sweet commune with nature in her fairest hours denied to the sons of cities—who must contemplate her charms through a vista of brick wall, or over a foreground of chimney-pots—consoled us amply for all the little hardships of travel. Strata upon strata of cloud-banks, burnished to golden red in the vicinity of the setting sun, and polished to dazzling silvery white above, lay piled half way from the horizon to the zenith, with a distinct strike towards a vanishing point in the west, and dipping into a gateway through which the orb of day slowly retired. Overhead floated in a sea of amber and yellow, pink and green, heavy purple nimbi, ap-

parently turned upside down, — their convex bulges below, and
their horizontal lines high in the air,—whilst, in the East, black
and blue were so curiously blended, that the eye could not distinguish whether it rested upon darkening air or upon a lowering
thundercloud.   We enjoyed these beauties in silence, not a soul
said "look there !" or " how pretty !"

At 9 P.M., reaching " Thirty-two Mile Creek," we were pleasantly surprised to find an utter absence of the Irishry.   The
station-master was the head of a neathanded and thrifty family
from Vermont ; the rooms, such as they were, looked cosy and
clean, and the chickens and peaches were plump and well
" fixed."   Soldiers from Fort Kearny loitered about the adjoining store, and from them we heard past fights and rumours
of future wars which were confirmed on the morrow.   Remounting at 10.30 P.M., and before moonrise, we threaded the
gloom without other accident than the loss of a mule that was
being led to the next station.   The amiable animal, after breaking loose, coquetted with its pursuers for a while, according to
the fashion of its kind, and when the cerne or surround was
judged complete, it dashed through the circle and gave leg-
bail, its hoofs ringing over the stones till the sound died away
in the distant shades.

The Platte River and Fort Kearny, August 10.

After a long and chilly night, — extensive evaporation making
40° F. feel excessively cold, — lengthened by the atrocity of
the mosquitoes, which sting even when the thermometer stands
below 45°, we awoke upon the hill sands divided by two miles
of level green savannah, and at 4 A.M. reached Kearny station,
in the valley of La Grande Platte, seven miles from the fort of
that name.   The first aspect of the stream was one of calm and
quiet beauty, which, however, it owed much to its accessories :
some travellers have not hesitated to characterise it as " the
dreariest of rivers."   On the south is a rolling range of red
sandy and clayey hillocks, sharp towards the river — the " coasts
of the Nebraska."   The valley, here two miles broad, resembles
the ocean deltas of great streams, it is level as a carpet, all short
green grass without sage or bush.   It can hardly be called a
bottom, the rise from the water's edge being, it is calculated,
about 4 feet per 1000.   Under a bank, from half a yard to a

yard high, through its two lawns of verdure, flowed the stream straight towards the slanting rays of the rising sun, which glittered upon its broad bosom and shed rosy light over half the heavens. In places it shows a sea horizon, but here it was narrowed by Grand Island, which is fifty-two miles long, with an average breadth of one mile and three quarters, and sufficiently elevated above the annual flood to be well timbered.

Without excepting even the Missouri, the Platte is doubtless the most important western influent of the Mississippi. Its valley offers a route scarcely to be surpassed for natural gradients, requiring little beyond the superstructure for light trains; and by following up its tributary—the Sweetwater—the engineer finds a line laid down by nature to the foot of the South Pass of the Rocky Mountains, the dividing ridge between the Atlantic and the Pacific water-beds. At present the traveller can cross the 300 or 400 miles of desert between the settlements in the east and the populated parts of the western mountains by its broad highway, with never-failing supplies of water, and, in places, fuel. Its banks will shortly supply coal to take the place of the timber that has thinned out.

The Canadian voyageurs first named it La Platte, the Flat River, discarding, or rather translating after their fashion, the musical and picturesque aboriginal term, "Nebraska," the "shallow stream:" the word has happily been retained for the territory. Springing from the eastern slope of the Rocky Mountains, it has, like all the valley streams westward of the Mississippi, the Niobrara, or Eau qui court*, the Arkansas, and the Canadian River, a declination to the south-east. From its mouth to the junction of its northern and southern forks, the river valley is mostly level, and the scenery is of remarkable sameness: its singularity in this point affects the memory. There is not a tributary, not a ravine, in places not a tree to distract attention from the grassy intermediate bottom, which, plain as a prairie, extends from four to five and even twelve miles in width, bounded on both sides by low, rolling, sandy hills, thinly vegetated, and in few places showing dwarf bluffs. Between the Forks and Fort Laramie the ground is more accented, the land near its banks often becomes precipitous, the road must

---

* For an accurate geographical description of this little-known river, the reader is referred to Lieut. Warren's report, published by the Secretary of War, U. S.

sometimes traverse the tongues and ridges which project into the valley, and in parts the path is deep with sand. The stream averages about a mile in breadth, and sometimes widens out into the semblance of an estuary, flowing in eddies where holes are, and broken by far-reaching sand-bars and curlew shallows. In places it is a labyrinth of islets, variously shaped and of all sizes, from the long tongue which forms a vista to the little bouquet of cool verdure, grass, young willows, and rose bushes. The shallowness of the bed causes the water to be warm in summer; a great contrast to the clear, cool springs on its banks. The sole is treacherous in the extreme, full of quicksands and gravel shoals, channels and cuts, which shift, like those of the Indus, with each year's flood; the site being nearly level, the river easily swells, and the banks, here of light there of dark-coloured silt, based, like the floor, on sand, are, though vertical, rarely more than two feet high. It is a river wilfully wasted by nature. The inundation raises it to about six feet throughout: this freshet, however, is of short duration, and the great breadth of the river causes a want of depth which renders it unfit for the navigation of a craft more civilised than the Indian's birch or the Canadian fur-boat. Col. Frémont failed to descend it in September with a boat drawing only four inches. The water, like that of the Missouri, and for the same reason, is surcharged with mud drained from the prairies; carried from afar, it has usually a dark tinge; it is remarkably opaque after floods, if a few inches deep, it looks bottomless, and finally, it contains little worth fishing for. From the mouth to Fort Kearny, beyond which point timber is rare, one bank, and one only, is fringed with narrow lines of well-grown cottonwood, red willows, and cedars, which are disappearing before the emigrant's axe. The cedar now becomes an important tree. It will not grow on the plains, owing to the dryness of the climate and the excessive cold; even in the sheltered ravines the wintry winds have power to blight all the tops that rise above prairie level, and where the locality is better adapted for plantations, firs prevail. An interesting effect of climate upon the cedar is quoted by travellers on the Missouri River. At the first Cedar Island (43° north latitude) large and straight trees appear in the bottom lands, those on the bluffs being of inferior growth; higher up the stream they diminish, seldom being seen in any

number together above the mouth of the Little Cheyenne
(45° north latitude), and there they are exceedingly crooked
and twisted. In the lignite formations above the Missouri and
the Yellowstone, the cedar, unable to support itself above
ground, spreads over the hill sides and presents the appearance
of grass or moss.

Beyond the immediate banks of the Platte the soil is either
sandy, quickly absorbing water, or it is a hard, cold, unwhole-
some clay, which long retains muddy pools, black with decayed
vegetation, and which often in the lowest levels becomes a mere
marsh. The wells deriving infiltration from the higher lands beyond are rarely more than three feet deep; the produce is somewhat saline, and here and there salt may be seen efflorescing from
the soil around them. In the large beds of prêle (an equisetum),
scouring rush, and other aquatic plants which garnish the banks,
myriads of mosquitoes find a home. Flowers of rich, warm colour
appear, we remark, in the sandy parts: the common wild helianthus
and a miniature sunflower like chamomile, a thistle *(carduus leu-
cographus)*, the cactus, a peculiar milkplant *(asclepias syrivea)*,
a spurgewort *(asclepias tuberosa)*, the amorpha, the tradescantia,
the putoria and the artemisia or prairie sage. The richer soils
and ravines produce in abundance the purple aster — violet of
these regions — a green plant, locally known as "Lamb's
Quarters," a purple flower with bulbous root, wild flax with
pretty blue blossoms, besides mallow, digitalis, anemone, etre
ptanthis, and a honeysuckle. In parts the valley of the Platte
is a perfect parterre of wild flowers.

After satisfying hunger with vile bread and viler coffee,— how
far from the little forty-berry cup of Egypt! — for which we
paid $0·75, we left Kearny Station without delay. Hugging the
right bank of our strange river, at 8 A.M. we found ourselves at
Fort Kearny, so called, as is the custom, after the gallant officer,
now deceased, of that name.

Every square box or blockhouse in these regions is a fort;
no misnomer, however, can be more complete than the word
applied to the military cantonments on the frontier. In former
times the traders to whom these places mostly belonged erected
quadrangles of sundried brick with towers at the angles; their
forts still appear in old books of travels: the War Department,
however, has been sensible enough to remove them. The

position usually chosen is a river bottom, where fuel, grass, and water are readily procurable. The quarters are of various styles; some, with their low verandahs, resemble Anglo-Indian bungalows or comfortable farmhouses, others are the storied houses with the "stoop" or porch of the Eastern States in front, and low, long, peat-roofed tenements are used for magazines and outhouses. The best material is brown adobe or unburnt brick; others are of timber, whitewashed and clean-looking, with shingle roofs, glass windows, and gay green frames,— that contrast of colours which the New Englander loves. The habitations surround a cleared central space for parade and drill; the ground is denoted by the tall flagstaff, which does not, as in English camps, distinguish the quarters of the commanding officer. One side is occupied by the officers' bungalows, the other, generally that opposite, by the adjutant's and quartermaster's offices, and the square is completed by low ranges of barrack and commissariat stores, whilst various little shops, stables, corrals for cattle, a chapel, perhaps an artillery park, and surely an ice-house — in this point India is far behind the wilds of America — complete the settlement. Had these cantonments a few more trees and a far more brilliant verdure, they would suggest the idea of an out-station in Guzerat, the Deccan, or some similar Botany Bay for decayed gentlemen who transport themselves.

Whilst at Washington I had resolved — as has already been in-timated— when the reports of war in the West were waxing loud, to enjoy a little Indian fighting. The meritorious intention — for which the severest "wig," concluding with something personally offensive about volunteering in general, would have been its sole result in the "fast-anchored isle"—was most courteously received by the Hon. John B. Floyd, Secretary of War, who provided me with introductory letters addressed to the officers commanding various "departments "*— "divisions," as

* The following is a list of the military departments into which the United States are divided:—

MILITARY COMMANDS.

Department of the East. — The country east of the Mississippi River; headquarters at Troy, N. Y

Department of the West. — The country west of the Mississippi River, and east of the Rocky Mountains, except that portion included within the limits of the departments of Texas and New Mexico; head quarters at St. Louis, Mo.

they would be called by Englishmen — in the West. The first tidings that saluted my ears on arrival at Fort Kearny acted as a quietus: an Indian action had been fought, which signified that there would be no more fighting for some time. Captain Sturgis, of the 1st Cavalry, U.S., had just attacked, near the Republican Fork of Kansas River, a little south of the fort, with six companies (about 350 men) and a few Delawares, a considerable body of the enemy, Comanches, Kiowas, and Cheyennes, who apparently had forgotten the severe lesson administered to them by Colonel — now Brigadier-General — Edwin V. Sumner, 1st Cavalry, in 1857, and killed twenty-five with only two or three of his own men wounded. According to details gathered at Fort Kearny, the Indians had advanced under a black flag, lost courage, as wild men mostly will, when they heard the *pas de charge*, and, after making a running fight, being well mounted as well as armed, had carried off their " cripples " lashed to their horses. I had no time to call upon Captain Sully, who remained in command at Kearny with two troops (here called companies) of dragoons, or heavy cavalry, and one of infantry; the mail wagon would halt there but a few minutes. I therefore hurriedly chose the alternative of advancing, with the hope of seeing " independent service " on the road. Intelligence of the fight had made even the conductor look grave; fifty or sixty miles is a flea-bite to a mounted war party, and disappointed Indians upon the war path are especially dangerous — even the most friendly cannot be trusted when they have lost, or have not succeeded in taking, a few scalps. We subsequently heard that they had crossed our path,

Department of Texas.—The State of Texas, and the territory north of it to the boundaries of New Mexico, Kansas, and Arkansas, and the Arkansas River, including Fort Smith. Fort Bliss, in Texas, is temporarily attached to the department of New Nexico; head-quarters at San Antonio, Texas.

Department of New Mexico. — The territory of New Mexico; head-quarters at Santa Fé, New Mexico.

Department of Utah. — The territory of Utah, except that portion of it lying west of the 117th degree of west longitude; head-quarters, Camp Floyd, U. T.

Department of the Pacific. — The country west of the Rocky Mountains, except those portions of it included within the limits of the departments of Utah and New Mexico, and the district of Oregon; head-quarters at San Francisco, California.

District of Oregon. — The territory of Washington and the State of Oregon, excepting the Rogue River and Umpqua districts in Oregon; head-quarters at Fort Vancouver, Washington Territory.

but whether the tale was true or not is an essentially doubtfu
matter. If this chance failed, remained the excitement of the
buffalo and the Mormon, both were likely to show better sport
than could be found in riding wildly about the country after
runaway braves.

We all prepared for the "gravity of the situation" by discharging and reloading our weapons, and bade adieu, about
9·30 A.M., to Fort Kearny. Before dismissing the subject of
forts, I am disposed to make some invidious remarks upon the
army system of outposts in America.

The War Department of the United States has maintained
the same system which the British, much to their loss, — I need
scarcely trouble the reader with a list of evils done to the soldier
by outpost duty,—adopted and pertinaciously kept up for so long
a time in India; nay, even maintain to the present day, despite
the imminent danger of mutiny. With the Anglo-Scandinavian
race, the hate of centralisation in civil policy extends to military
organisation, of which it should be the vital principle. The
French, gifted with instinct for war, and being troubled with
scant prejudice against concentration, civil as well as military,
soon abandoned, when they found its futility, the idea of defending their Algerian frontier by extended lines, blockhouses, and
feeble entrenched posts. They wisely established, at the centres
of action, depôts, magazines, and all the requisites for supporting large bodies of men, making them pivots for expeditionary
columns, which by good military roads could be thrown in
overwhelming numbers, in the best health and in the highest
discipline, wherever an attack or an insurrectionary movement
required crushing.

The necessity of so doing has long occurred to the American
Government, in whose service at present "a regiment is stationed to-day on the borders of tropical Mexico; to-morrow the
war whoop, borne on a gale from the north-west, compels its
presence to the frozen latitudes of Puget's Sound." The objections to altering their present highly objectionable system are
two: the first is a civil consideration, the second a military one.

As I have remarked about the centralisation of troops, so it is
with their relation to civilians; the Anglo-Scandinavian blood
shows similar manifestations in the old and in the new country.
The French, a purely military nation, pet their army, raise it to
the highest pitch, send it in for glory, and when it fails are to its

faults a little blind. The English and Anglo-Americans, essentially a commercial and naval people, dislike the red coat; they look upon, and from the first they looked upon, a standing army as a necessary nuisance; they ever listen open-eared to projects for cutting and curtailing army expenditure; and when they have weakened their forces by a manner of atrophy, they expect them to do more than their duty, and if they cannot command success, abuse them. With a commissariat, transport and hospitals — delicate pieces of machinery, which cannot run smoothly when roughly and hurriedly put together — unaccustomed to and unprepared for service, they land an army 3000 miles from home, and then make the world ring with their disappointment, and their complainings anent fearful losses in men and money. The fact is that, though no soldiers in the world fight with more bravery and determination, the Anglo-Scandinavian race, with their present institutions, are inferior to their inferiors in other points, as regards the art of military organisation. Their fatal wants are order and economy, combined with the will and the means of selecting the best men — these belong to the emperor, not to the constitutional king or the president — and most of all, the habit of implicit subjection to the commands of an absolute dictator. The end of this long preamble is that the American Government apparently thinks less of the efficiency of its troops than of using them as escorts to squatters, as police of the highway. Withal they fail, emigrants will not be escorted, women and children will struggle when they please, even in an Indian country, and every season has its dreadful tales of violence and starvation, massacre and cannibalism. In France the emigrants would be ordered to collect in bodies at certain seasons to report their readiness for the road to the officers commanding stations, to receive an escort, as he should deem proper, and to disobey at their peril.

The other motive of the American outpost system is military, but also of civilian origin. Concentration would necessarily be unpalatable to a number of senior officers, who now draw what in England would be called command allowances, at the several stations.* One of the principles of a republic is to pay a man

---

* The aggregate of the little regular army of the United States in 1860 amounted to 18,093. It was dispersed into eighty military posts, viz. thirteen in the Department of the east, nine in the west, twenty in Texas, twelve in the Depart-

only whilst he works; pensions, like sinecures, are left to governments less disinterested. The American army — it would hardly be believed — has no pensions, sale of commissions, off-reckonings, nor retiring-list. A man hopelessly invalided, or in his second childhood, must hang on by means of furloughs and medical certificates to the end. The colonels are mostly upon the sick-list,—one died lately aged ninety-three, and dating from the days of Louis XVI.,—and I heard of an officer who, though practising medicine for years, was still retained upon the cadre of his regiment. Of course, the necessity of changing such an anomaly has frequently been mooted by the legislature; the scandalous failure, however, of an attempt at introducing a pension-list into the United States navy so shocked the public that no one will hear of the experiment being renewed, even *in corpore vili*, the army.

To conclude the subject of outpost system. If the change be advisable in the United States, it is positively necessary to the British in India. The peninsula presents three main points, not to mention the detached heights that are found in every province, as the great pivots of action, the Himalayas, the Deccan, and the Nilgherry Hills, where, until wanted, the Sepoy and his officer, as well as the white soldier — the latter worth 100*l.* a head — can be kept in health, drilled, disciplined, and taught the hundred arts which render an " old salt " the most handy of men. A few years ago the English soldier was fond of Indian service; hardly a regiment returned home without leaving hundreds behind it. Now, long, fatiguing marches, scant fare, the worst accommodation, and the various results of similar hardships, make him look upon the land as a Golgotha; it is with difficulty that he can be prevented from showing his disgust. Both in India and America, this will be the greatest benefit of extensive railroads: they will do away with single stations, and enable the authorities to carry out a system of concentration most beneficial to the country and to the service which, after many years of sore drudgery, may at last discern the good time coming.

In the United States, two other measures appear called for by circumstances. The Indian race is becoming desperate, wild-

---

ment of New Mexico, two in Utah (Fort Bridger and Camp Floyd), eleven in Oregon, and thirteen in the Department of California. They each would have an average of about 225 men.

beast like, hemmed in by its enemies that have flanked it on the east and west, and are gradually closing in upon it. The tribes can no longer shift ground without inroads into territories already occupied by neighbours, who are, of course, hostile; they are, therefore, being brought to final bay.

The first is a camel corps. At present, when disturbances on a large scale occur in the far West—the spring of 1862 will probably see them — a force of cavalry must be sent from the East, perhaps also infantry. "The horses, after a march of 500 or 600 miles, are expected to act with success"—-I quote the sensible remarks of a "late captain of infantry" (Captain Patterson, U.S. army)—against scattered bands of mounted hunters, with the speed of a horse and the watchfulness of a wolf or antelope, whose faculties are sharpened by their necessities; who, when they get short of provisions, separate and look for something to eat, and find it in the water, in the ground, or on the surface; whose bill of fare ranges from grass-seed, nuts, roots, grasshoppers, lizards, and rattlesnakes, up to the antelope, deer, elk, bear, and buffalo, and who having a continent to roam over, will neither be surprised, caught, conquered, overawed, or reduced to famine by a rumbling, bugle-blowing, drum-beating town passing through their country on wheels, at the speed of a loaded waggon." But the camel would in these latitudes easily march sixty miles per diem for a week or ten days, amply sufficient to tire out the sturdiest Indian pony; it requires water only after every fifty hours, and the worst soil would supply it with ample forage in the shape of wild sage, rabbit bush, and thorns. Each animal would carry two men, with their arms and ammunition, rations for the time required, bedding and regimental necessaries, with material to make up a *tente d'abri* if judged necessary. The organisation should be that of the Sindh Camel Corps, which, under Sir Charles Napier, was found so efficient against the frontier Beloch. The best men for this kind of fighting would be the Mountaineers, or Western Men, of the caste called "Pikes;" properly speaking, Missourians, but popularly any "rough" between St. Louis and California. After a sound flogging, for the purpose of preparing their minds to admit the fact that all men are *not* equal, they might be used by sea or land, whenever hard, downright fighting is required. It is

understood that hitherto the camel, despite the careful selection
by Mr. De Leon, the excellent Consul-General of the United
States in Egypt, and the valuable instructions of Hekekyan
Bey, has proved a failure in the western world. If so, want
of patience has been the sole cause ; the animal must be acclimatised, by slow degrees, before heavy loading to test its powers
of strength and speed.   Some may deem this amount of delay
impossible.   I confess my belief that the Anglo-Americans can,
within any but the extremest limits, accomplish anything they
please — except unity.

The other necessity will be the raising of native regiments.
The French in Africa have their Spahis, the Russians their
Cossacks, and the English their Sepoys. The American Government has often been compelled, as in the case of the creek
battalion, which did good service during the Seminole cam-
paign, indirectly to use their wild aborigines ; but the public
sentiment, or rather prejudice, which fathers upon the modern
Pawnee the burning and torturing tastes of the ancient Mohawk,
is strongly opposed to pitting Indian against Indian in battle.
Surely this is a false as well as a mistaken philanthropy. If
war must be, it is better that Indian instead of white blood
should be shed.   And invariably the effect of enlisting savages
and barbarians, subjecting them to discipline, and placing
them directly under the eye of the civilised man, has been
found to diminish their ferocity.   The Bashi Buzuk, left to
himself, roasted the unhappy Russian ; in the British service he
brought his prisoner alive into camp with a view to a present
or promotion.   When talking over the subject with the officers
of the United States regular army, they have invariably con-
curred with me in the possibility of the scheme, provided
that the public animus could be turned pro instead of con ;
and I have no doubt but that they will prove as leaders of
Irregulars,— it would be invidious to quote names, — equal to
the best of the Anglo-Indians, Skinner, Beatson, and Jacob.
The men would receive about ten dollars per man, and each
corps number 300.   They would be better mounted and better
armed than their wild brethren, and they might be kept,
when not required for active service, in a buffalo country, their
favourite quarters, and their finest field for soldierlike exercises.

The main point to be avoided is the mistake committed by the British in India, that of appointing too many officers to their Sepoy corps.

We left Kearny at 9·30 A.M., following the road which runs forty miles up the valley of the Platte. It is a broad prairie, plentifully supplied with water in wells two to four feet deep; the fluid is cool and clear, but it is said not to be wholesome. Where the soil is clayey pools abound; the sandy portions are of course dry. Along the southern bank near Kearny are few elevations; on the opposite or northern side appear high and wooded bluffs. The road was rough with pitchholes, and for the first time I remarked a peculiar gap in the ground like an East Indian sun-crack,— in these latitudes you see none of the deep fissures which scar the face of mother earth in tropical lands,— the effect of rain streams and snow water acting upon the clay. Each succeeding winter lengthens the head and deepens the sole of this deeply gashed water-cut, till it destroys the road. A curious mirage appeared, doubling to four the strata of river and vegetation on the banks. The sight and song of birds once more charmed us after a desert where animal life is as rare as upon the plains of Brazil. After fifteen miles of tossing and tumbling, we made "Seventeen Mile Station," and halted there to change mules. About twenty miles above the fort the southern bank began to rise into mounds of tenacious clay, which, worn away into perpendicular and precipitous sections, composes the columnar formation called O'Fallon's Bluffs. At 1·15 P.M. we reached Plum Creek, after being obliged to leave behind one of the conductors, who had become delirious with the "shakes." The establishment, though new, was already divided into three; the little landlady, though she worked so manfully, was, as she expressed it, "enjoying bad health," in other words, suffering from a "dumb chill." I may observe that the Prairie Traveller's opinions concerning the power of encamping with impunity upon the banks of the streams in this country must not be applied to the Platte. The whole line becomes with early autumn a hotbed of febrile disease. And generally throughout this season the stranger should not consider himself safe on any grounds save those defended from the southern trade wind, which, sweeping directly from the Gulf of Mexico, bears with it noxious exhalations.

About Plum Ranch the soil is rich, clayey, and dotted with swamps and " slews," by which the English traveller will understand sloughs. The drier portions were a Gulistan of bright red blue and white flowers, the purple aster, and the mallow, with its parsnip-like root, eaten by the Indians, the gaudy yellow helianthus — we remarked at least three varieties — the snowy mimulus, the graceful flax, sometimes four feet high, and a delicate little euphorbia, whilst in the damper ground appeared the polar plant, that prairie compass, the plane of whose leaf ever turns towards the magnetic meridian. This is the " weed-prairie," one of the many divisions of the great natural meadows; grass prairie, rolling prairie, motte prairie, salt prairie, and soda prairie. It deserves a more poetical name, for

> " These are the gardens of the desert, these
> The unshorn fields, boundless and beautiful,
> For which the speech of England has no name."

Buffalo herds were behind the hills, but we were too full of sleep to follow them. The plain was dotted with blanched skulls and bones, which would have made a splendid bonfire. Apparently the expert voyageur has not learned that they form good fuel; at any rate, he has preferred to them the " chips" of which it is said that a steak cooked with them requires no pepper.*

We dined at Plum Creek on buffalo, probably bull beef, the worst and driest meat, save elk, that I have ever tasted; indeed, without the assistance of pork fat, we found it hard to swallow. As every one knows, however, the two-year old cow is the best eating, and at this season the herds are ever in the worst condition. The animals calve in May and June, consequently they are in August completely out of flesh. They are fattest about Christmas, when they find it difficult to run. All agree in declaring that there is no better meat than that of the young buffalo: the assertion, however, must be taken *cum grano salis*. Wild flesh was never known to be equal to tame, and that monarch did at least one wise thing

---

* The chip corresponds with the bois de vache of Switzerland, the tezek of Armenia, the arghol of Thibet, and the gobar of India. With all its faults, it is at least superior to that used in Sindh.

who made the loin of beef Sir Loin. The voyageurs and travellers who cry up the buffalo as so delicious, have been living
for weeks on rusty bacon and lean antelope; a rich hump with
its proper menstruum, a cup of *café noir* as strong as possible,
must truly be a "tit bit." They boast that the fat does not
disagree with the eater; neither do three pounds of heavy pork
with the English ploughboy, who has probably taken less
exercise than the Canadian hunter. Before long, buffalo flesh
will reach New York, where I predict it will be held as inferior
to butcher's meat as is the antelope to park-fed venison.
Whilst hunting, Indians cut off the tail to test the quality of
the game, and they have acquired by habit a power of judging
on the run between fat and lean.

Resuming our weary ride, we watered at "Willow Island
Ranch," and then at "Cold Water Ranch,"—drinking shops all
—five miles from Midway Station, which we reached at 8 P.M.
Here, whilst changing mules, we attempted with sweet speech
and smiles to persuade the landlady, who showed symptoms of
approaching maternity, into giving us supper. This she sturdily
refused to do, for the reason that she had not received due
warning. We had, however, the satisfaction of seeing the
employés of the line making themselves thoroughly comfortable
with bread and buttermilk. Into the horrid wagon again,
and "a rollin:" lazily enough the cold and hungry night
passed on.*

To the Forks of the Platte. 11*th August.*

Precisely at 1·35 in the morning we awoke, as we came to
a halt at Cotton Wood Station. Cramped with a four days' and
four nights' ride in the narrow van, we entered the foul tenement,
threw ourselves upon the mattresses, averaging three to each,
and ten in a small room, every door, window, and cranny being
shut,—after the fashion of these western folks, who make up for

---

* According to Colonel Frémont, the total amount of buffalo robes purchased
by the several companies, American, Hudson's Bay, and others, was an annual
total of 90,000, from the eight or ten years preceding 1843. This is repeated by
the Abbé Domenech, who adds, that the number does not include those slaughtered
in the southern regions by the Comanches and other tribes of the Texan frontier,
nor those killed between March and November, when the skins are unfit for
tanning. In 1847, the town of St. Louis received 110,000 buffalo robes, stags',
deer, and other skins, and twenty-five salted tongues.

a day in the open air by perspiring through the night in un-
ventilated log-huts, — and, despite mosquitoes, slept.

The morning brought with it no joy.   We had arrived at the
westernmost limit of the "gigantic Leicestershire" to which
buffalo at this season extend, and could hope to see no trace of
them between Cotton Wood Station and the Pacific.   I cannot,
therefore, speak *ex cathedrâ* concerning this, the noblest "ve-
nerie" of the West: almost every one who has crossed the
prairies, except myself, can.   Captain Stansbury* will enlighten
the sportsman upon the approved méthod of bryttling the beasts,
and elucidate the mysteries of the "game-beef," marrow-bone
and depuis, tongue and tenderloin, bass and hump, hump-
rib and liver, which latter, by-the-bye, is not unfrequently
eaten raw, with a sprinkling of gall†, by the white hunter
emulating his wild rival, as does the European in Abyssinia.   The Prairie Traveller has given, from experience, the
latest observations concerning the best modes of hunting the
animal.   All that remains to me, therefore, is to offer to the
reader a few details collected from reliable sources, and which
are not to be found in the two works above alluded to.

The bison (*bison Americanus*) is trivially known as the
Prairie Buffalo, to distinguish it from a different and a larger
animal, the Buffalo of the Woods, which haunts the Rocky
Mountains.   The "Monarch of the Prairies," the "most gigantic
of the indigenous mammalia of America," has, it is calculated,
receded westward ten miles annually for the last 150 years.
When America was discovered, the buffalo extended down to
the Atlantic shore.   Thirty years ago, bands grazed upon the
banks of the Missouri River.   The annual destruction is variously computed at from 200,000 to 300,000 head—the American Fur Company receive per annum about 70,000 robes, which
are all cows,— and of these not more than 5000 fall by the
hands of white men.   At present there are three well-known
bands, which split up, at certain seasons, into herds of 2000 and
3000 each.   The first family is on the head-waters of the Mississippi; the second haunts the vast crescent-shaped valley of
the Yellowstone; whilst the third occupies the prairie country

* Exploration and Survey, &c., chap. ix.
† "Prairie bitters" — made of a pint of water and a quarter of a gill of buffalo gall — are considered an *elixir vitæ* by old voyageurs.

between the Platte and the Arkansas. A fourth band, westward of the Rocky Mountains, is quite extinct. Fourteen to fifteen years ago, buffalo was found in Utah Valley, and later still upon the Humboldt River : according to some, they emigrated northwards, through Oregon and the lands of the Blackfeet. It is more probable, however, that they were killed off by the severe winter of 1845, their skulls being still found scattered in heaps, as if a sudden and general destruction had come upon the doomed tribe.

The buffalo is partially migratory in its habits : it appears to follow the snow, which preserves its food from destruction. Like the antelope of the Cape, when on the "trek," the band may be reckoned by thousands. The grass, which takes its name from the animal, is plentiful in the valley of the Big Blue; it loves the streams of little creeks that have no bottom land, and shelters itself under the sage. It is a small, moss-like gramen, with dark seed, and, when dry, it has been compared by travellers to twisted grey horsehair. Smaller herds travel in Indian file; their huge bodies, weighing 1500 lbs., appear, from afar, like piles erected to bridge the plain. After calving, the cows, like the African koodoo and other antelopes, herd separately from the males, and for the same reason, timidity and the cares of maternity. As in the case of the elephant and the hippopotamus, the oldsters are driven by the young ones, *en chari-vari*, from the band, and a compulsory bachelorhood souring their temper, causes them to become "rogues." The albino, or white buffalo, is exceedingly rare; even veteran hunters will confess never to have seen one. The same may be said of the glossy black accident called the "silk robe," supposed by western men to be a cross between the parent and the offspring. The buffalo calf has been tamed by the Flatheads and others: I have never, however, heard of its being utilised.

The Dakotas and other prairie tribes will degenerate, if not disappear, when the buffalo is "rubbed out." There is a sympathy between them, and the beast flies not from the barbarian and his bow as it does before the face of the white man and his hotmouthed weapon. The aborigines are unwilling to allow travellers, sportsmen, or explorers to pass through the country whilst they are hunting the buffalo, that is to say, preserving the game till their furs are ready for robes. At these times no one is permitted to kill any but stragglers, for fear of stampeding the band; the animal not only being timid, but also in the habit of hurrying away cattle and stock, which often are thus irretrievably lost. In due season the savages surround one section, and destroy it; the others remaining unalarmedly grazing within a few miles of the scene of slaughter. If another tribe interferes, it is a *casus belli*, death being the punishment for poaching. The white man, whose careless style of *battue* is notorious, will be liable to the same penalty, or, that failing, to be plundered, by even " good Indians;" and I have heard of an English gentleman who, for persisting in the obnoxious practice, was very properly threatened with prosecution by the Government agent.

What the cocoa-nut is to the East Indian, and the plantain and the calabash to various tribes of Africans, such is the "boss" to the carnivorous son of America. No part of it is allowed to waste. The horns and hoofs make glue for various purposes, especially for feathering arrows; the brains and part of the bowels are used for curing skins; the hide clothes the tribes from head to foot; the calf-skins form their apishamores, or saddle-blankets; the sinews make their bowstrings, thread, and finer cord ; every part of the flesh, including the fœtus and placenta, is used for food. The surplus hides are reserved for market. They are prepared by the squaws, who, curious to say, will not touch a bearskin till the age of maternity has passed; and they prefer the spoils of the cow, as being softer than those of the bull. The skin, after being trimmed with an iron or bone scraper — this is not done in the case of the " parflèche," or thick sole-leather — and softened with brain or marrow, is worked till thoroughly pliable with the hands. The fumigation, which gives the finishing touch, is confined to buckskins intended for garments. When the hair is removed, the hides supply the place of canvas, which they resemble in whiteness and facility of folding. Dressed with the hair, they are used, as their name denotes, for clothing; they serve also for rugs and bedding. In the prairies, the price ranges from $1 to $1·50 in kind; in the Eastern States, from $5 to $10. The fancy specimens, painted inside, decorated with eyes, and otherwise adorned with split porcupine-quills dyed a gamboge-yellow, fetch from $8 to $35. A " buffalo " (*subaudi* robe) was shown to me, painted with curious figures, which, according to my Canadian informant, were a kind of hieroglyph or *aide-mémoire*, even ruder than the Mexican picture-writing.

The Indians generally hunt the buffalo with arrows. They are so expert in riding, that they will, at full speed, draw the missile from the victim's flank before it falls. I have met but one officer, Captain Heth, of the 10th Regiment, who ever acquired the art. The Indian hog-spear has been used to advantage. Our predecessors in Eastern conquest have killed with it the tiger and nylgau; there is, therefore, no reason why it might not be efficiently applied to the buffalo. Like the Bos Caffre, the bison is dull, surly, and stupid, as well as timid and wary; it requires hard riding, with the chance of a collar-bone broken by the horse falling into a prairie-dog's home; and when headed or tired an old male rarely fails to charge.

The flies chasing away the mosquitoes—even as Aurora routs the lingering shades of night—having sounded our *reveillée* at Cotton Wood station, we proceeded by means of an "eye-opener," which even the abstemious judge could not decline, and the use of the "skillet," to prepare for a breakfast composed of various abominations, especially cakes of flour and grease, molasses and dirt, disposed in pretty equal parts. After paying the usual $0.50, we started in the high wind and dust, with a heavy storm brewing in the north, along the desert valley of the dark, silent Platte, which here spread out in broad basins and lagoons, picturesquely garnished with broad-leafed dock and beds of *prêle*, flags and water-rushes, in which, however, we saw nothing but traces of Monsieur Maringouin. On our left was a line of subconical buttes, red, sandy-clay pyramids, semi-detached from the wall of the rock behind them, with smooth flat faces fronting the river, towards which they slope at the natural angle of 45°. The land around, dry and sandy, bore no traces of rain; a high wind blew, and the thermometer stood at 78° (F.), which was by no means uncomfortably warm. Passing Junction House Ranch and Frémont Slough—whiskey-shops both—we halted for "dinner," about 11 A. M., at Frémont Springs, so called from an excellent little water behind the station. The building is of a style peculiar to the south, especially Florida,—two huts connected by a roof-work of thatched timber, which acts as the best and coolest of verandahs. The station-keeper, who receives from the proprietors of the line $30 per month, had been there only three weeks; and his wife, a comely young person, uncommonly civil and smiling for a " lady," supplied us with the luxuries of pigeons, onions, and light bread, and declared her intention of establishing a poultry-yard.

An excellent train of mules carried us along a smooth road at a slapping pace, over another natural garden even more flowery than that passed on the last day's march.   There were beds of lupins, a brilliant pink and blue predominating, the green plant locally known as "Lamb's Quarters" (*Chenopodium album*); the streptanthis; the milk-weed, with its small white blossoms; the anemone; the wild flax, with its pretty blue flowers, and growths which appeared to be clematis, chamomile and digitalis.   Distant black dots — dwarf cedars, which are yearly diminishing,— lined the bank of the Platte and the long line of River Island ; they elicited invidious comparisons from the Pennsylvanians of the party.   We halted at Half-way House, near O'Fallon's Bluffs, at the quarters of Mr. M——, a *compagnon de voyage* who had now reached his home of twenty years, and therefore insisted upon "standing drinks."   The business is worth $16,000 per annum ; the contents of the store somewhat like a Parsee's shop in Western India—everything from a needle to a bottle of champagne.   A sign-board informed us that we were now distant 400 miles from St. Jo., 120 from Fort Kearny, 68 from the upper, and 40 from the lower crossing of the Platte.   As we advanced the valley narrowed, the stream shrank, the vegetation dwindled, the river islands were bared of timber, and the only fuel became buffalo chip and last year's artemisia.   This hideous growth which is to weary our eyes as far as central valleys of the Sierra Nevada, will require a few words of notice.

The artemisia, absinthe, or wild sage, differs much from the panacea concerning which the Salernitan school rhymed :

" Cur moriatur homo cui Salvia crescit in horto."

Yet it fills the air with a smell that caricatures the odour of the garden plant, causing the traveller to look round in astonishment; and when used for cooking it taints the food with a taste between camphor and turpentine.   It is of two kinds.   The smaller or white species (*A. filifolia*) rarely grows higher than a foot.   Its fetor is less rank, and at times of scarcity it forms tolerable fodder for animals. The Western men have made of it, as of the " red root," a tea, which must be pronounced decidedly inferior to corn coffee. The Indians smoke it, but they are not particular about what they inhale : like that perverse p——n of Ludlow, who smoked the bell-ropes rather than not smoke at all, or like schoolboys who break themselves in upon rattan, they use even the larger sage as well as a variety of other graveolent growths. The second kind (*A. tridentata*) is to the family of shrubs what the prairie-cedar is to the trees — a gnarled, crooked, rough-barked deformity. It has no pretensions to beauty except in earliest youth and in the dewy hours when the breeze turns up its leaves that glitter like silver in the sun, and its constant presence in the worst and most desert tracks teaches one to regard it, like the mangrove in Asia and Africa, with aversion. In size it greatly varies ; in some places it is but little larger than the white species ; near the Red Buttes its woody stem often attains the height of a man and the thickness of his waist. As many as fifty rings have been counted in one wood, which, according to the normal calculation, would bring its age up to half a century. After its first year, stock will eat it only when threatened with starvation. It has, however, its use ; the tra-veller, despite its ugliness, hails the appearance of its stiff, wiry clumps at the evening halt ı it is easily uprooted, and by virtue of its essential oil it makes a hot and lasting fire, and ashes over. According to Colonel Frémont, " it has a small fly accompanying it through every change of elevation and lati-tude." The same eminent authority also suggests that the re-spiration of air so highly impregnated with aromatic plants, may partly account for the favourable effect of the climate upon consumption.

At 5 P.M., as the heat began to mitigate, we arrived at Alkali Lake Station and discovered some "exiles from Erin," who supplied us with antelope meat and the unusual luxury of ice taken from the Platte. We attempted to bathe in the river, but found it flowing liquid mire. The Alkali Lake was out of sight ; the driver, however, consoled me with the reflection that I should "glimpse " alkali lakes till I was sick of them.

Yesterday and to-day we have been in a line of Indian " re-moves." The wild people were shifting their quarters for grass ; when it becomes a little colder they will seek some winter abode

on the banks of a stream which supplies fuel and where they
can find meat, so that with warmth and food, song and chat —
they are fond of talking nonsense as African negroes — and smoke
and sleep, they can while away the dull and dreary winter.
Before describing the scene, which might almost serve for a picture of Bedouin or gipsy life — so similar are the customs of all
savages — I have something to say about the Red Man.

This is a country of misnomers. America should not, according to the school books, have been named America, consequently
the Americans should not be called Americans. A geographical
error, pardonable in the fifteenth century, dubbed the old
tenants of these lands Indians*, but why we should still call
them the Red Men cannot be conceived. I have now seen
them in the north, south, east and west of the United States,
yet never, except under the influence of ochre or vermilion, have
I seen the Red Man red. The real colour of the skin, as may be
seen under the leggings, varies from a dead pale olive to a dark
dingy brown. The parts exposed to the sun are slightly burnished,
as in a Tartar or an Affghan after a summer march. Between
the two extremes above indicated there are, however, a thousand shades of colour, and often the skin has been so long
grimed in with pigment, grease, and dirt that it suggests a
brickdust tinge which a little soap or soda would readily remove.
Indeed the colour and the complexion, combined with the lank
hair, scant beard, and similar peculiarities, renders it impossible
to see this people for the first time without the strongest im-
pression that they are of that Turanian breed which in præhistoric
ages passed down from above the Himalayas as far south as
Cape Comorin.

Another mistake touching the Indian is the present opinion
concerning him and his ancestors. He now suffers in public
esteem from the reaction following the highflown descriptions
of Cooper and the herd of minor romancers, who could not

---

* Columbus and Vespucius both died in the conviction that they had only discovered portions of Asia. Indeed, as late as 1533, the astronomer Schöner maintained that Mexico was the Quinsai of Marco Polo. The early navigators called
the aborigines of the New World "Indians," believing that they inhabited the
eastern portion of "India," a term then applied to the extremity of Oriental
Asia. Until the present century the Spaniards applied the names India and Indies
to their possessions in America.

but make their heroes heroes. Moreover, men acquainted only with the degenerate Pawnees or Diggers, extend their evil opinions to the noble tribes now extinct — the Iroquois and Algonquins, for instance, whose remnants, the Delawares and Ojibwes, justify the high opinion of the first settlers. The exploits of King Philip, Pontiac, Gurister Sego, Tecumseh Keokuk, Ietan, Captain J. Brant, Black Hawk, Red Jacket, Osceola, and Billy Bowlegs, are rapidly fading away from memory, whilst the failures of such men as Little Thunder, and those like him, stand prominently forth in modern days. Besides the injustice to the manes and memories of the dead, this depreciation of the Indians tends to serious practical evils. Those who see the savage lying drunk about stations, or eaten up with disease, expect to beat him out of the field by merely showing their faces; they fail, and pay the penalty with their lives — an event which occurs every year in some parts of America.

The remove of the village presented an interesting sight, — an animated, shifting scene of bucks and braves, squaws and papooses, ponies dwarfed by bad breeding and hard living, dogs and puppies straggling over the plains westward. In front, singly or in pairs, rode the men, not gracefully, not according to the rules of Mexican *manège*, but like the Abyssinian eunuch, as if born upon and bred to become part of the animal. Some went barebacked, others rode, like the ancient chiefs of the Western Islands, upon a saddle-tree, stirrupless, or provided with hollow blocks of wood: in some cases the saddle was adorned with bead hangings, and in all a piece of buffalo hide with the hair on was attached beneath to prevent chafing. The cruel ringbit of the Arabs is not unknown. A few had iron curbs, probably stolen; for the most part they managed their nags with a hide thong lashed round the lower jaw and attached to the neck. A whip, of various sizes and shapes, sometimes a round and tattooed ferule, more often a handle like a butcher's tally-stick, flat, notched, one foot long, and provided with two or three thongs, hung at the wrist. Their nags were not shod with parflêche, as amongst the horse-Indians of the south. Their long, lank, thick, brownish-black hair, ruddy from the effects of weather, was worn parted in the middle, and depended from the temples confined with a long twist of otter or beaver's skin in two queues, or pig-tails reaching to the breast: from the poll, and distinct from the remainder of the hair, streamed the scalp-lock. This style of hair-dressing, doubtless, aids in giving to the coronal region that appearance of depression which characterises the North American Indians as a race of " Flat heads," and which probably being considered a beauty, led to the artificial deformities of the Peruvian and the Aztec. The parting in men, as well as in women, was generally coloured with vermilion, and plates of brass or tin, with beveled edges, varying in size from a shilling to half-a-crown, were inserted into the front hair. The scalp-lock — in fops the side-locks also — was decorated with tin or silver plates often twelve in number, beginning from the head and gradually diminishing in size as they approached the heels; a few had eagle's, hawk's, and crow's feathers stuck in the hair, and sometimes, grotesquely enough, crownless Kossuth hats, felt broadbrims, or old military casquettes, surmounted all this finery. Their scanty beard was removed ; they compare the bushy-faced European to a dog running away with a squirrel in its mouth. In their ears were rings of beads, with pendants of tin plates or mother o' pearl, or huge circles of brass wire not unlike a Hindu tailor's ; and their fore-arms, wrists, and fingers were, after an African fashion, adorned with the same metals, which the savage ever prefers to gold or silver. Their other decorations were cravats of white or white and blue, oval beads, and necklaces of plates like those worn in the hair. The body dress was a tight sleeved waistcoat of dark drugget, over an American cotton shirt; others wore tattered flannels, and the middle was wrapped round with a common blanket, presented by the government agent, — scarlet and blue being the colours preferred, white rare : — a better stuff is the coarse broadcloth manufactured for the Indian market in the United States. The leggings were a pair of pantaloons without the body part — in their palmy days the Indians laughed to scorn their future conquerors for tightening the hips so as to impede activity — looped up at both haunches with straps to a leathern girdle, and all wore the breech cloth, which is the common Hindu languti or T-bandage. The cut of the leggings is a parallelogram, a little too short and much too broad for the limb ; it is sewn so as to fit tight, and the projecting edges, for which the light coloured list or bordering is usually preserved, answers the effect of a military stripe. When buckskin leggings are made the outside edges are fringed, producing that feathered appearance which distinguishes in our pictures the nether limbs of the Indian brave. The garb ends with moccasins*, the American brogues, which are made in two ways. The simplest are of one piece, a cylinder of skin cut from above and below the hock of some large animal — moose, elk, or buffalo — and drawn on before shrinking, the joint forming the heel, whilst the smaller end is sewn together for a toe. This rough contrivance is little used but as a *pis-aller*. The other kind is made of tanned hide in two pieces; a sole and an upper leather, sewn together at the junction; the last is a bit of board rounded off at the end. They are open over the instep, where also they can be laced or tied, and they fit as closely as the Egyptian mizz or under-slipper, which they greatly resemble. They are worn by officers in the far West as the expatriated Anglo-Indian adopts the " Juti." The greatest inconvenience to the novice is the want of heel; moreover, they render the feet uncomfortably tender, and unless soled with parflêche or thick leather, they are scant defence against stony ground; during dry weather they will last fairly, but they become, after a single wetting, even worse than Bombay-made Wellingtons. A common pair will cost $2 ; when handsomely embroidered with bead-work by the squaws they rise to $15.

The braves were armed with small tomahawks or iron hatchets, which they carried with the powder horn, in the belt, on the right side, while the long tobacco-pouch of antelope skin hung by the left. Over their shoulders were leather targes, bows and arrows, and some few had rifles; both weapons were defended from damp in deerskin cases, and quivers with the inevitable bead-work, and the fringes which every savage seems to love. These articles reminded me of those in use amongst the Bedouins of El Hejaz. Their nags were lean and ungroomed; they treat them as cruelly as do the Somal ; yet nothing — short of whiskey — can persuade the Indian warrior, like the man of Nejd, to part with a favourite steed. It is his all in all, his means of livelihood, his profession, his pride : he is an excellent judge of horseflesh, though ignoring the mule and ass; and if he offers an animal for

* This Algonquin word is written *moccasson* or *mocasin*, and is pronounced *moksin*.

which he has once refused to trade, it is for the reason that an
Oriental takes to market an adult slave — it has become useless. Like the Arab he considers it dishonourable to sell a
horse ; he gives it to you, expecting a large present, and if disappointed he goes away grumbling that you have " swallowed "
his property. He is fond of short races, — spurts they are
called, — as we had occasion to see ; there is nothing novel nor
interesting in the American as there is in the Arabian hippo-
logy ; the former learnt all its arts from Europeans, the latter
taught them.

Behind the warriors and braves followed the baggage of the
village. The lodge-poles, in bundles of four and five, had been
lashed to pads or packsaddles, girthed tight to the ponies' backs,
the other ends being allowed to trail along the ground, like the
shafts of a truck ; the sign easily denotes the course of travel.
The wolf-like dogs were also harnessed in the same way ; more
lupine than canine, they are ready when hungry to attack
man or mule ; and, sharp-nosed and prick-eared, they not a little
resemble the Indian pariah dog. Their equipments, however,
were of course on a diminutive scale, a little pad girthed round
the barrel, with a breastplate to keep it in place, enabled them
to drag two short light lodge-poles tied together at the smaller
extremity. One carried only a hawk on its back — yet falconry
has never, I believe, been practised by the Indian. Behind the
ponies the poles were connected by cross sticks, upon which
were lashed the lodge covers, the buffalo robes, and other bulkier
articles. Some had strong frames of withes or willow basket-
work, two branches being bent into an oval, garnished below
with a network of hide thongs for a seat, covered with a light
wicker canopy, and opening, like a cage, only on one side ; a
blanket or a buffalo role defends the inmate from sun and rain.
These are the litters for the squaws when weary, the children,
and the puppies, which are part of the family till used for feasts.
It might be supposed to be a rough conveyance ; the elasticity of
the poles, however, alleviates much of that inconvenience. A very
ancient man, wrinkled as a last year's walnut, and apparently
crippled by old wounds, was carried, probably by his great-grand-
sons, in a rude sedan. The vehicle was composed of two pliable
poles, about ten feet long, separated by three cross bars, twenty
inches or so apart ; a blanket had been secured to the foremost

and hindermost, and under the centre-bit lay Senex secured
against falling out. In this way the Indians often bear the
wounded back to their villages; apparently they have never
thought of a horse-litter, which might be made with equal
facility and would certainly save work.

Whilst the rich squaws rode the poorer followed their pack-
horses on foot, eyeing the more fortunate as the mercer's wife
regards what she terms the "carriage lady." The women's dress
not a little resembles their lords'; the unaccustomed eye often
hesitates between the sexes. In the fair, however, the waistcoat
is absent, the wide-sleeved shift extends below the knees, and the
leggings are of somewhat different cut. All wore coarse shawls,
or white, blue, and scarlet cloth-blankets round their bodies. Upon
the upper Platte we afterwards saw them dressed in cotton gowns,
after a semi-civilised fashion, and with bowie knives by their
sides. The grandmothers were fearful to look upon, horrid ex-
crescences of nature, teaching proud man a lesson of humility,
and a memento of his neighbour in creation, the "humble ape;"
— it is only civilisation that can save the aged woman from resembling the gorilla. The middle-aged matrons were homely bodies,
broad and squat like the African dame after she has become *mère
de famille;* their hands and feet were notably larger from work
than those of the men, and the burdens upon their backs caused
them to stoop painfully. The young squaws — pity it is that
all our household Indian words, papoose, for instance, toma
hawk, wigwam, and powwow, should have been naturalised out
of the Abenaki and other harsh dialects of new England — deserved a more euphonious appellation. The belle savage of the
party had large and languishing eyes and dentists' teeth that
glittered, with sleek, long black hair like the ears of a Blenheim
spaniel, justifying a natural instinct to stroke or pat it, drawn
straight over a low broad Quadroon-like brow. Her figure
had none of the fragility which distinguishes the higher race,
who are apparently too delicate for human nature's daily food —
porcelain, in fact, when pottery is wanted; — nor had she the
square corpulency which appears in the negro woman after
marriage. Her ears and neck were laden with tinsel ornaments,
brass wire rings adorned her wrists and fine arms, a bead-work
sash encircled her waist, and scarlet leggings, fringed and tas-
selled, ended in equally costly moccasins. When addressed by

the driver in some terms to me unintelligible, she replied with a
soft clear laugh — the principal charm of the Indian as of the
smooth-throated African woman — at the same time showing
him the palm of her right hand as though it had been a looking-
glass.   The gesture would have had a peculiar significance in
Sindh ; here, however, I afterwards learned, it simply conveys a
refusal.   The maidens of the tribe, or those under six, were
charming little creatures, with the wildest and most piquant expression, and the prettiest doll-like features imaginable; the
young coquettes already conferred their smiles as if they had
been of any earthly value.   The boys once more reminded me of
the East; they had black beady eyes, like snakes, and the wide
mouths of young caymans.   Their only dress, when they were not
in " birth-day suit," was the Indian languti.   None of the braves
carried scalps, finger bones, or notches on the lance, which serve
like certain marks on saw-handled pistols further east, nor had
any man lost a limb.   They followed us for many a mile, peering into the hinder part of our travelling wigwam, and ejaculating " How!   How!" the normal salutation.   It is supposed to
mean " good," and the Western man, when he drinks to your
health, says " Here, how!" and expects a return in kind.   The
politeness of the savages did not throw us off our guard; the
Dakota of these regions are expert and daring kleptomaniacs;
they only laughed, however, a little knowingly as we raised the
rear curtain, and they left us after begging pertinaciously —
Bakhshish is an institution here as on the banks of the Nile —
for tobacco, gunpowder, ball, copper caps, lucifers and what not?
The women, except the pretty party, looked, methought, somewhat scowlingly, but one can hardly expect a smiling countenance from the human biped trudging ten or twenty miles under
a load fit for a mule.   A great contrast with these Indians was a
train of " Pikespeakers," who, to judge from their grim looks,
were returning disappointed from the new gold-diggings.   I
think that if obliged to meet one of the two troops by moonlight
alone, my choice would have fallen upon "messieurs les sauvages."

     At 6 P.M. we resumed our route, with a good but fidgetty train,
up the Dark Valley, where mosquitoes and sultry heat combined to worry us.   Slowly travelling and dozing the while, we
arrived about 9·15 P.M. at Diamond Springs, a bright little
water much frequented by the " lightning-bug" and the big-eyed

"Devil's darning-needle,"* where we found whiskey and its usual accompaniment, soldiers. The host related an event which he said had taken place but a few days before. An old mountaineer, who had married two squaws, was drinking with certain Cheyennes, a tribe famous for ferocity and hostility to the whites. The discourse turning upon topics stoical, he was asked by his wild boon-companions if he feared death? The answer was characteristic: "You may kill me if you like!" Equally characteristic was their acknowledgment; they hacked him to pieces, and threw the corpse under a bank. In these regions the opposite races regard each other as wild beasts; the white will shoot an Indian as he would a coyote. He expects to go under whenever the "all-fired, red-bellied varmints"—I speak, O reader, occidentally—get the upper hand, and *vice versâ.*

The Platte river divides at N. lat. 40° 05′ 05″, and W. long. (G.) 101° 21′ 24″. The northern, by virtue of dimensions, claims to be the main stream. The southern, which is also called in obsolete maps Padouca, from the Pawnee name for the Ictans, whom the Spaniards term Comanches †, averages 600 yards, about 100 less than its rival in breadth, and according to the prairie people affords the best drinking. Hunters often ford the river by the Lower Crossing, twenty-eight miles above the bifurcation. Those with heavily-loaded wagons prefer this route, as by it they avoid the deep loose sands on the way to the Upper Crossing. The mail coach must endure the four miles of difficulty, as the road to Denver City branches off from the western ford.

At 10 P.M., having "caught up" the mules, we left Diamond Springs and ran along the shallow river which lay like a thin sheet of shimmer broken by clumps and islets that simulated under the imperfect light of the stars, houses and towns, hulks and ships, wharfs and esplanades. On the banks large bare spots

---

* The first is the fire fly, the second is the dragon-fly, called in country parts of England "the Devil's needle."

† The Kaumainsh (Comanche) a warlike and independent race, who, with the Apaches, have long been the bane of New Spain, were in the beginning of this century entirely erratic, without any kind of cultivation, subsisting, in fact, wholly by the chase and plunder. They were then bounded westward by New Mexico, where they have laid waste many a thriving settlement: eastward by the Pawnees and Osages; northwards by the Utahs, Kiowas, and Shoshones; and southwards by the nations on the Lower Red River.

white with salt glistened through the glooms, the land became so
heavy that our fagged beasts groaned, and the descents, watercuts
and angles were so abrupt that holding on constituted a fair
gymnastic exercise. The air was clear and fine. My companions
snored whilst I remained awake enjoying a lovely aurora, and
Epicurean-like reserving sleep for the Sybaritic apparatus,
which, according to report, awaited us at the grand *établissement*
of the Upper Crossing of La Grande Platte.

This was our fifth night in the mail wagon. I could not but
meditate upon the difference between travel in the pure prairie
air, despite an occasional " chill," and the perspiring miseries of
an East Indian dawk, or of a trudge in the miasmatic and pes-
tilential regions of Central Africa. Much may be endured when,
as was ever the case, the highest temperature in the shade does
not exceed 98° F.

12th August.—We cross the Platte.

Boreal aurora glared brighter than a sunset in Syria. The
long streamers were intercepted and mysteriously confused by
a massive stratum of dark cloud, through whose narrow rifts and
jagged chinks the splendours poured in floods of magic fire.
Near the horizon the tint was an opalline white,— a broad
band of calm steady light,— supporting a tender rose colour,
which flushed to crimson as it scaled the upper firmament. The
mobility of the spectacle was its chiefest charm. The streamers
either shot out or shrank from full to half-length ; now they
flared up, widening till they filled the space between Lucifer
rising in the east and Aries setting in the west, then they narrowed to the size of a span; now they stood like a red arch
with steadfast legs and oscillating summit, then, broadening
at the apex, they apparently revolved with immense rapidity ;
at times the stars shone undimmed through the veil of light,
then they were immersed in its exceeding brilliancy. After
a full hour of changeful beauty, paling in one place and blushing in another, the northern lights slowly faded away with a
blush which made the sunrise look colder than its wont.
It is no wonder that the imaginative Indian, looking with love
upon these beauties, connects them with the ghosts of his
ancestors.

Cramped with cold and inaction,—at 6 A.M. the thermometer

showed only 56° F. in the sun;—hungry, thirsty, and by no means in the mildest of humours, we hear with a gush of joy, at 3·15 A.M. the savage Yep! yep! yep! with which the driver announces our approach.   The plank lodgings soon appear; we spring out of the ambulance, a qualm comes over us, all is dark and silent as the grave; nothing is prepared for us; the wretches are all asleep.   A heavy kick opens the door of the soon-found restaurant, when a pheesy, drowsy voice from an inner room asks us, in German-English, — so strong is the causality, the crapulousness of why and wherefore in this "divided, erudite race:" — "And how ze komen in?"   Without attempting to gratify his intellectual cravings, we ordered him out of bed, and began to talk of supper, refreshment, and repose.   But the "critter" had waxed surly after securing for himself a compound epithet, of which "hunds—" is the first syllable, and his every negative answer concluded with a faint murmur of "petampt."   I tried to get his bed for Mrs. Dana, who was suffering severely from fatigue.   He grumbled out that his "lady and bebbé" were occupying it.   At length I hit upon the plan of placing the cushions and cloaks upon the table, when the door opened for a second dog-Teuton, who objected to that article of furniture being used otherwise than for his morning meal.   *Excédés*, and mastering with pain our desire to give these villain "sausage-eaters" "particular fits," we sat down, stared at the fire, and awaited the vile food.   For a breakfast cooked in the usual manner, coffee boiled down to tannin (ever the first operation), meat subjected to half sod, half stew, and lastly, bread raised with sour milk corrected with soda, and so baked that the taste of the flour is ever prominent, we paid these German rascals $0·75, a little dearer than at the Trois Frères.

At the Upper Crossing of the South Fork there are usually tender adieux; the wenders towards Mormonland bidding farewell to those bound for the perilous gold regions of Denver City and Pike's Peak.   If "fresh," they take leave of one another with sincere commiseration for one another's dooms, each deeming of course his own the brighter.   The wagons were unloaded, thus giving us the opportunity of procuring changes of raiment and fresh caps—our felts had long disappeared under the influence of sleeping on the perch.   By some means we retained our old ambulance, which after five days and nights we had learned to look upon as a home; the Judiciary, however, had to exchange theirs for one much lighter and far less comfortable. Presently those bound to Denver City set out upon their journey. Conspicuous among them was a fair woman who had made her first appearance at Cotton Wood Creek—fit place for the *lune de mélasse*—with an individual, apparently a well-to-do drover, whom she called "Tom" and "husband." She had forgotten her "fixins" which, according to a mischievous and scandalous driver, consisted of a reticule containing a "bishop," a comb, and a pomatum pot, a pinchbeck watch, and a flask of "Bawme,"—not of Meccah. Being a fine young person of Scotch descent, she had, till dire suspicions presented themselves, attracted the attentions of her fellow travellers, who pronounced her to be "all sorts of a gal." But virtue is rabid in these lands, and the purity of the ermine must not be soiled. It was fortunate for Mr. and Mrs. Mann, the names were *noms de voyage*, that they left us so soon. In a certain southern city I heard of a high official, who during a trip upon one of the floating palaces of the Mississippi, had to repeat "deprendi miserum est;" the fond, frail pair was summarily ejected with bag and baggage to furnish itself with a down stream passage on board a lumber raft.

We crossed the "Padouca" at 6·30 A.M., having placed our luggage and the mails for security in an ox cart. The South Fork is here 600 to 700 yards broad; the current is swift, but the deepest water not exceeding 250 feet the teams are not compelled to cross diagonally. The channel was broken with sandbanks and islets, the bed was dark, and gravelly, the water, though dark as hotel coffee, was clear, not as described by Captain Stansbury "perfectly opake, with thick yellow mud," and the earthbanks which rise to five feet are never inundated. The half-broken mules often halted, and seemed inclined to lie down; a youth waded on the lower side of the team, shouting and swinging his arms to keep them from turning their heads down stream; the instinct of animals to find an easy ford ended with a few desperate struggles up the black oozy mire. Having reloaded on the left bank, and cast one last look of hatred upon the scene of our late disappointment, we set out at 7 A. M. to cross the divide separating the Northern and Southern Forks of the Platte.

We had now entered upon the outskirts of the American wilderness, which has not one feature in common with the deserts of the Old World. In Arabia and Africa there is majesty in its monotony: those awful wastes so brightly sunburnished that the air above them appears by contrast black: one vast and burning floor, variegated only by the mirage-reek, with nothing below the firmament to relieve or correct the eye. Here it is a brown smooth space, insensibly curving out of sight, wholly wanting " second distance," and scarcely suggesting the idea of immensity; we seem in fact to be travelling for twenty miles over a convex, treeless hill-top. The air became sultry, white clouds shut in the sky, and presently arose the high south wind, which at this season blows a gale between 10 A.M. and 3 P.M. The ground, bleached where sandy, was thinly scattered here and there with wiry grass, dun and withered, and with coarse and sunburnt shrubs, amongst which the " leadplant" (*Amorphe canescens*) was the characteristic. A dwarf aloetic vegetation became abundant; vegetation was fast going the way of all grass; after rain, however, it is doubtless fresh and copious. The buffalo grass sought the shade of the wild sage. A small euphorbia, the cottonweed, a thistle haunted by the Cynthia cardua, that butterfly common to the eastern and western hemispheres, and a bright puloria mingled with mushrooms, like huge bulbs. The cactus was of two kinds; the flat leaved species is used by white men to filter water, and by the savages, who peel and toast it, as provaunt *: there is another globular variety (an *echinocactus*) lying stalkless, like a half melon, with its brilliant flowers guarded by a panoply of spines. We pursued a sandy tract, broken by beds of nullahs and fiumaras, between two ridges of hillocks, draining to the right into a low bottom denoted by a

* There is another kind of cactus called by the whites " whiskey-root," and by the Indian " peioke," used like the intoxicating mushroom of Siberia. " It grows in Southern Texas, in the range of sand-hills bordering on the Rio Grande, and in gravelly, sandy soil. The Indians eat it for its exhilarating effect on the system, producing precisely the same excitement as alcoholic drinks. It is sliced as you would a cucumber, the small piece is chewed and swallowed, and in about the same time as comfortably tight cocktails would ' stir the divinity within ' you, this indicates itself; only its effects are what I might term a little *k-a-v-o-r-t-i-n-g*, giving rather a wilder scope to the imagination and actions." (A Correspondent of the *New Orleans Picayune*, quoted by Mr. Bartlett).

lively green, with bays and bends of lush, reedlike grass. This
is the well known Lodge Pole Creek or Fork, a mere ditch, the
longest and narrowest of its kind, rising from a mountain
lakelet near the " New Bayou " or " Park," in the Black Hills,
and falling into the South Fork of the Platte, about seventy
miles west of the bifurcation. By following up this water
along the Cherokee trail to its head in the Cheyenne Pass of
the Rocky Mountains, instead of describing the arc *viâ* Fort
Laramie, the mail would gain 61 miles : emigrants, indeed,
often prefer the short cut. Moreover, from the Cheyenne Pass
to Gt. S. L. City, there is, according to accounts, a practicable
road south of the present line which, as it would also save time
and labour, has been preferred for the mail line.

In the American Sahara animal life began to appear. The
coyote turned and stared at us as though we were trespassing
upon his property. This is the jackal of the western world,
the small prairie-wolf, the *canis latrans*, and the old Mexican
coyotl, best depicted by the old traveller, Abbé Clavigero, in
these words : " It is a wild beast, voracious like the wolf, cunning
like the fox, in form like the dog, and in some qualities like the
jackal." The animal has so often been described that there is
little new to say about it. The mountain men are all agreed
upon one thing, namely, that the meat is by no means bad ;
most of them have tried " wolf-mutton " in hard times, and
may expect to do so again. The civilizee shudders at the idea
of eating wolf from a food-prejudice, whose consideration forms
a curious chapter in human history. It is not very easy, says
Dr. Johnson, to fix the principles upon which mankind have
agreed to eat some animals and reject others ; and as the principle is not evident, so it is not uniform. Originally invented for
hygienic purposes, dietetic laws soon became tenets of religion,
and passed far beyond their original intention : thus pork,
for instance, injurious in Syria, would not be eaten by a Jew in
Russia. An extreme arbitrariness marks the modern systems of
civilised people : the Englishman, for instance, eats oysters,
periwinkles, shrimps, and frogs, whilst he is nauseated by the
snails, robins, and crows which the Frenchman uses ; the Italian
will devour a hawk, whilst he considers a rabbit impure, and has
refused to touch potatoes even in a famine ; and all delight in
that foul feeder, the duck, whilst they reject the meat of the

cleanly ass. The Mosaic law seems still to influence the European world, causing men to throw away much valuable provision because unaccustomed to eat it or to hear of its being eaten. The systems of China and Japan are far more sensible for densely populated countries, and the hippophagists have shown, at least, that one animal has been greatly wasted. The terrible famines, followed by the equally fearful pestilences, which have scourged mankind, are mainly owing to the prevalence of these food-prejudices, which, as might be expected, are the most deeply rooted in the poorer classes, who can least afford them.

I saw to-day, for the first time, a prairie-dog village. The little beast, hardly as large as a guinea-pig, belongs to the family of squirrels and the group of marmots — in point of manner it somewhat resembles the monkey. "Wish-ton-Wish"* — an Indian onomatoplasm — was at home, sitting posted like a sentinel upon the roof, and sunning himself in the mid-day glow. It is not easy to shoot him; he is out of doors all day; but, timid and alert, at the least suspicion of danger he plunges with a jerking of the tail, and a somersault, quicker than a shy young rabbit's, into the nearest hole, peeping from the ground, and keeping up a feeble little cry (wish! ton! wish!), more like the note of a bird than a bark. If not killed outright, he will manage to wriggle into his home. The villages are generally on the brow of a hill, near a creek or pond, thus securing water without danger of drowning. The earth burrowed out whilst making the habitations is thrown up in heaps, which serve as sitting places in the wet season, and give a look-out upon the adjacent country; it is more dangerous to ride over them than to charge a field of East Indian "T'hur," and many a broken leg and collar-bone have been the result. The holes, which descend in a spiral form, must be deep, and they are connected by long galleries, with sharp angles, ascents and descents, to puzzle the pursuer. Lieutenant Pike had 140 kettles of water poured into one, without dislodging the occupant. The village is always cleared of grass, probably by the necessities of the tenants, who, though

* The name will recall to mind one of Mr. Fennimore Cooper's admirable fictions, the "Wept of Wish-ton-Wish," which was, however, a bird, the "Whippoor-Will," or American night hawk.

they enjoy insects, are mainly graminivorous, and rarely venture half a mile from home. The limits are sometimes three miles square, and the population must be dense, as a burrow will occur every few paces. The *Cynomys Ludovicianus* prepares for winter by stopping the mouth of its burrow, and constructing a deeper cell, in which it hybernates till spring appears. It is a graceful little animal, dark brown above and white below, with teeth and nails, head and tail somewhat like the grey sciurus of the States. The Indians and trappers eat this American marmot, declaring its flesh to be fatter and better than that of the squirrel. Some travellers advise exposing the meat for a night or two to the frost, by which means the rankness of subterranean flavour is corrected. It is undoubted that the rattlesnake — both of the yellow and black species — and the small white burrowing-owl (*Strix cunicularia*) are often found in the same warren with this rodent, a curious happy family of reptile, bird, and beast, and in some places he has been seen to associate with tortoises, rattlesnakes, and horned frogs (*Phrynosoma*). According to some naturalists, however, the fraternal harmony is not so perfect as it might be : the owl is accused of occasionally gratifying his carnivorous lusts by laying open the skull of Wish-ton-Wish with a smart stroke of the beak. We sighted, not far from the prairie-dog village, an animal which I took to be a lynx ; but the driver, who had often seen the beast in Minnesota and Old " Ouisconsinc," declared that they are not to be found here.

At 12.45 P.M., travelling over the uneven barren, and in a burning Scirocco, we reached Lodge-pole Station, where we made our " noonin." The hovel fronting the creek was built like an Irish shanty, or a Beloch hut, against a hill side, to save one wall, and it presented a fresh phase of squalor and wretchedness. The mud walls were partly papered with " Harper's Magazine," " Frank Leslie," and the " New York Illustrated News ;" the ceiling was a fine festoon-work of soot, and the floor was much like the ground outside, only not nearly so clean. In a corner stood the usual " bunk,"* a mass of mingled rags and buffalo

---

* American writers derive this word from the Anglo-Saxon *benc,* whence the modern English " bench." It means a wooden case used in country taverns and in offices, and serving alike for a seat during the day and a bed at night. In towns it is applied to the tiers of standing bed peculiar to the lowest class of lodging-houses. In the West it is a frame-work, in size and shape like a berth on board ship, sometimes single, sometimes double or treble.

robes; the centre of the room was occupied by a ricketty table,
and boxes, turned-up on their long sides, acted as chairs. The
unescapable stove was there, filling the interior with the aroma
of meat. As usual, the materials for ablution, a " dipper " or
cup, a dingy tin skillet of scanty size, a bit of coarse gritty
soap, and a public towel, like a rag of gunny bag, were deposited
upon a ricketty settle outside.

There being no " lady " at the station on Lodge-pole Creek,
milk was unprocurable. Here, however, began a course of
antelope venison, which soon told upon us with damaging effect.
I well knew the consequences of this heating and bilious diet in
Asia and Africa; but thinking it safe to do at Rome as the
Romans do, I followed in the wake of my companions, and
suffered with them. Like other wild meats, bear, deer, elk, and
even buffalo, antelope will disagree with a stranger ; it is, however, juicy, fat, and well-flavoured, especially when compared
with the hard, dry, stringy stuff which the East affords; and
the hunter and trapper, like the Indian, are loud in its praise.

The habitat of the prong-horn antelope (*Antelocapra Americana*, called " le cabris " by the Canadian, and " the goat "
by the unpoetic mountain man) extends from the plains west of
the Missouri to the Pacific Ocean — it is also abundant on Minnesota and on the banks of the Red River; its southern limit
is Northern Mexico, whence it ranges to 53° north lat. on the
Saskatchewan. It is about the size of a small deer, the male
weighing 65 lbs. in good condition. The coat is coarse and wiry,
yellow dun on the back, with dull white under the belly, and
the tanned skin is worth three dollars. It is at once the fleetest
and the wariest animal on the prairies, and its sense of hearing as
acute as its power of smell. The best time for " still hunting "
(*i.e.* stalking) is at early dawn, when the little herds of four or
five are busy grazing. They disappear during the midday heats
of summer, and in the evening, as in India and Arabia, they are
wild and wary. They assemble in larger bodies near the Rocky
Mountains, where pasturage — not sage, which taints the meat
— abounds, and the Indian savages kill them by surrounds,
especially in winter, when the flesh is fattest. White men
usually stalk them. During the migration season few are
seen near the road ; at other times they are often sighted. They
are gifted, like the hippopotamus, with a truly feminine curiosity;

they will stand for minutes to stare at a red wagon-bed, and despite their extreme wariness, they will often approach, within shot, a scarlet kerchief tied to a stick, or any similar decoy. In manner they much resemble the Eastern gazelle. When the herd is disturbed, the most timid moves off first, followed by the rest; the walk gradually increases from a slow trot to a bounding gallop. At times they halt, one by one, and turn to gaze, but they presently resume flight, till they reach some prominent place where their keen vision can command the surrounding country. When well roused, they are thoroughly on the alert; the hunter will often find that, though he has moved towards them silently, up the wind and under cover, they have suspected sinister intentions and have shifted ground.

Besides the antelope, there are three species of deer in the regions east of the Rocky Mountains. Perhaps the most common is the red deer of the Eastern States (*Cervus Virginianus; le chevreuil*): it extends almost throughout the length of the continent, and is seemingly independent of altitude as of latitude. The venison is not considered equal to that of the antelope; travellers, however, kill off the deer to save butchers' bills, so that it is now seldom " glimpsed " from the line of route. The black-tailed or long-eared deer (*Cervus macrotis*) is confined to the higher ground; it has similar habits to the red variety, and is hunted in the same way. The long-tailed, or jumping deer (*Cervus leucrurus*, vulgarly called the roebuck), affects, like the black-tailed, the Rocky Mountains. The elk (*Cervus Canadensis*) is found in parts of Utah Territory and forty miles north of the mail-road, near the Wind River Mountains — a perfect paradise for sportsmen. It is noble shooting, but poor eating as the Indian sambar.* The moose (*Cervus Alces*), the giant of the deer kind, sometimes rising seventeen hands high, and weighing 1200 lbs., is an inhabitant of higher latitudes, — Nova Scotia, Canada, Maine, and other parts of New England.

At Lodge-pole Station, the mules, as might be expected from animals allowed to run wild every day in the week except

* The elk is being domesticated in the State of New York; it is still, however, doubtful whether the animals will fatten well or supply milk, or serve for other than ornamental purposes.

one, were like newly-caught mustangs.* The herdsman — each station boasts of this official — mounted a nag barebacked, and, jingling a bell, drove the cattle into the corral, a square of twenty yards, formed by a wall of loose stones, four to five feet high. He wasted three quarters of an hour in this operation, which a well-trained shepherd's dog would have performed in a few minutes. Then two men entering with lassos or lariats, thongs of flexible plaited or twisted hide, and provided with an iron ring at one end to form the noose — the best are made of hemp, Russian, not Manilla — proceeded, in a great " muss " on a small scale, to secure their victims. The lasso † in their hands was by no means the " unerring necklace " which the Mexican *vaquéro* has taught it to be : they often missed their aim, or caught the wrong animal. The effect, however, was magical : a single haul at the noose made the most stiffnecked mule tame as a coster-monger's ass. The team took, as usual, a good hour to trap and hitch up : the latter was a delicate operation, for the beasts were comically clever with their hoofs.

At 3 P. M., after a preliminary ringing, intended to soothe the fears of Madame, we set out *au grand galop*, with a team that had never worked together before. They dashed down the cahues with a violence that tossed us as in a blanket, and nothing could induce them, while fresh, to keep the path. The yawing of the vehicle was ominous : fortunately, however, the road, though self-made, was excellent ; the sides were smooth, and the whole country fit to be driven over. At first the view was sadly monotonous. It was a fair specimen of the rolling prairie, in nowise differing from any other land, except in the absence of trees. According to some travellers, there is in

* The mustang is the Spanish *mesteño*. The animal was introduced by the first colonists, and allowed to run at large. Its great variety of coat proves the mustang's degeneracy from the tame horse ; according to travellers, cream-colour, skewbald, and piebald, being not uncommon. " Sparing in diet, a stranger to grain, easily satisfied whether on growing or dead grass, inured to all weathers, and capable of great labour," the mustang-pony is a treasure to the prairie-man.

† According to Mr. Bartlett, the lasso (Span. " lazo") is synonymous with "lariat" (Span. " lariata"). In common use, however, the first word is confined to the rope with which buffalos, mustangs, or mules are caught ; the second, which in the West is popularly pronounced "lariet," or "lariette," more generally means the article with which animals are picketed. Many authors, however, have made "lariat" the equivalent of "lasso." The Texans use, instead of the hide lasso, a hair rope called " caberes," from the Spanish " cabestro," a halter.

several places an apparently progressive decay of the timber; showing that formerly it was more extensive than it is now. Others attribute the phenomenon to the destruction of forests in a former era by fires or by the aborigines. It is more satisfactory to account for it by a complication of causes, —a want of proper constituents, an insufficiency of rain, the depth of the water below the surface, the severity of the eight months of winter snow, the fierce winds — the hardiest growths that present their heads above the level of the prairies have dead tops, — the shortness of the summers, and last, but not least, the clouds of grasshoppers. According to Lieutenant Warren, whose graphic description is here borrowed, these insects are "nearly the same as the locusts of Egypt ; and no one who has not travelled on the prairie, and seen for himself, can appreciate the magnitude of the swarms. Often they fill the air for many miles of extent, so that an inexperienced eye can scarcely distinguish their appearance from that of a shower of rain or the smoke of a prairie fire. The height of their flight may be somewhat appreciated, as Mr. E. James saw them above his head, as far as their size would render them visible, while standing on the top of a peak of the Rocky Mountains, 8,500 feet above the plain, and an elevation of 14,500 above that of the sea, in the region where the snow lies all the year. To a person standing in one of these swarms as they pass over and around him, the air becomes sensibly darkened, and the sound produced by their wings resembles that of the passage of a train of cars on a railroad when standing two or three hundred yards from the track. The Mormon settlements have suffered more from the ravages of these insects than probably all other causes combined. They destroyed nearly all the vegetables cultivated last year at Fort Randall, and extended their ravages east as far as Iowa."

As we advanced, the horizon, everywhere within musket-shot — a wearying sight! — widened out, and the face of the country notably changed. A scrap of blue distance and high hills—the "Court-house" and others—appeared to the north-west. The long, curved lines, the gentle slopes and the broad hollows of the divide facing the South Fork changed into an abrupt and precipitous descent, "gullied" like the broken ground of subranges attached to a mountain chain. Deep ravines were parted by long narrow ridges, sharp-crested and water-washed, exposing ribs and backbones of sandstone and silicious lime, like the vertebræ of some huge saurian: scatters of kunker, with a detritus of quartz and granite, clothed the ground, and, after passing Lodge-pole Creek, which bears away to the west, the rocky steps required the perpetual application of the break. Presently we saw a dwarf cliff enclosing in an elliptical sweep a green amphitheatre, the valley of our old friend the Platte. On the far bank of its northern fork lay a forty-mile-stretch of sandy, barren, glaring, heat-recking ground, not unlike that which the overland traveller looking southwards from Suez sees.* We left far to the right a noted spot, Ash Hollow, situated at the mouth of the creek of the same prenomen. It is described as a pretty bit in a barren land, about twenty acres, surrounded by high bluffs, well timbered with ash and cedar, and rich in clematis and other wild flowers. Here, in 1855, the doughty General Harney, with 700 to 800 men, " gave Jessie " to a large war-party of Brulé Sioux under their chief Little Thunder, of whom more anon, killing 150, and capturing 60 squaws and children, with but seven or eight casualties in his own force.

Descending into the bed of a broad "arroyo,"† at this season bone dry, we reached, at 5.45 P.M., Mud Spring Station, which takes its name from a little run of clear water in a black miry hollow. A kind of cress grows in it abundantly, and the banks are bright with the "morning glory" or convolvulus. The station-house was not unlike an Egyptian Fellah's hut. The material was sod, half peat with vegetable matter; it is taken up in large flakes after being furrowed with the plough, and is cut to proper lengths with a short-handled spade. Cedar timber ‡, brought from the neighbouring hills, formed the roof. The only accommodation was an open shed, with a sort of doorless dormitory by its side. We dined in the shed, and amused ourselves with feeding the little brown-speckled swamp-

* According to Lieut. Warren, the tract called the Sandhills occupies an area, north of the Platte, not less than 20,000 square miles; from between the Niobrara and White Rivers to the north, probably beyond the Arkansas in the south.

† The Arabo-Spanish "arroyo," a word almost naturalised by the Anglo-Americans, exactly corresponds with the Italian "fiumara," and the Indian nullah.

‡ The word "cedar," in the United States, is applied to various genera of the pine family. The red cedar (*J. Virginiana*) is a juniper. The "white cedar" of the southern swamps is a cypress.

blackbirds that hopped about us tame and " peert " as wrens, and when night drew near we sought shelter from the furious southern gale, and heard tales of Mormon suffering which made us think lightly of our little hardships.* Dreading the dormitory — if it be true that the sultan of fleas inhabits Jaffa and his wazir Grand Cairo, it is certain that his vermin officials have settled *pro tem.* on Emigration Road — I cast about for a quieter retreat. Fortune favoured me by pointing out the body of a dismantled wagon, an article — like the Tyrian keels which suggested the magalia — often used as a habitation in the Far West, and not unfrequently honoured by being converted into a bridal-chamber after the short and sharp courtship of the " Perraries." The host, who was a kind, intelligent, and civil man, lent me a " buffalo " by way of bedding ; the waterproof completed my outfit, provided with which I bade adieu for a while to this weary world. The thermometer sank before dawn to 62° (F.). After five nights more or less in the cramping wagon it might be supposed that we should have enjoyed the unusual rest; on the contrary, we had become inured to the exercise, we could have kept it up for a month, and we now grumbled only at the loss of time.

Past the Court House and Scott's Bluffs.   August 13th.

At 8 A.M., after breaking our fast upon a tough antelope-steak, and dawdling whilst the herdsman was riding wildly about in search of his runaway mules -- an operation now to become of daily occurrence — we dashed over the Sandy Creek

* The Mormon emigrants usually start from Council Bluffs, on the left bank of the Missouri River, in north lat. 41° 18′ 50″, opposite Kanesville, otherwise called Winter Quarters. According to the "Overland Guide," Council Bluffs is the natural crossing of the Missouri River, on the route destined by nature for the great thoroughfare to the Pacific, This was the road selected by " nature's civil engineers," the buffalo and the elk, for their western travel. The Indians followed them in the same trail ; then the travellers ; next the settlers came. After ninety-four miles' marching, the Mormons are ferried across Loup Fork, a stream thirteen rods wide, full of bars, with banks and a bottom all quicksand. Another 150 miles takes them to the Platte River, where they find good camping-places with plenty of water, buffalo-chips, and grass. Eighty-two miles beyond that point (a total of 306), they arrive at " Last Timber," a station so called because, for the next 200 miles on the north side of the Platte, the only sign of vegetation is "Lone Tree." Many emigrants avoid this dreary "spell" by crossing the Platte opposite Ash Hollow. Others pass it at Platte River Ferry, a short distance below the mouth of Laramie River, whilst others keep the old road to the north.

with an *élan* calculated to make timid passengers look "skeery," and began to finish the rolling divide between the two Forks. We crossed several arroyos and "criks" heading in the line of clay highlands to our left, a dwarf sierra which stretches from the northern to the southern branch of the Platte.   The principal are Omaha Creek, more generally known as "Little Punkin,"* and Lawrence Fork.† The latter is a pretty bubbling stream, running over sand and stones washed down from the Courthouse Ridge; it bifurcates above the ford, runs to the northeast through a prairie four to five miles broad, and swells the waters of old Father Platte: it derives its name from a Frenchman slaughtered by the Indians, murder being here, as in Central Africa, ever the principal source of nomenclature. The heads of both streams afford quantities of currants, red, black, and yellow, and cherry-sticks which are used for spears and pipe-stems.

After twelve miles' drive we fronted the Court-house, the remarkable portal of a new region, and this new region teeming with wonders will now extend about 100 miles.   It is the *mauvaises terres,* or Bad lands, a tract about 60 miles wide and 150 long, stretching in a direction from the north-east to the south-west, or from the Mankizitah (White Earth) River, over the Niobrara (*Eau qui court*) and Loup Fork to the south banks of the Platte: its eastern limit is the mouth of the Keya Paha.   The term is generally applied by the trader to any section of the prairie country where the roads are difficult, and by dint of an ill name the Bad lands have come to be spoken of as a Golgotha, white with the bones of man and beast. American travellers, on the contrary, declare that near parts of the White River "some as beautiful valleys are to be found as anywhere in the far West," and that many places "abound in the most lovely and varied forms in endless variety, giving the most striking and pleasing effects of light and shade."   The formation is the pliocene and miocene tertiary, uncommonly rich in vertebrate remains : the *mauvaises terres* are composed

---

* Punkin (*i. e.* pumpkin) and corn (*i. e.* zea maize) are, and were from time immemorial, the great staples of native American agriculture.

† According to Webster, "forks" (in the plural) — the point where a river divides, or rather where two rivers meet and unite in one stream.   Each branch is called a "fork."   The word might be useful to English travellers.

of nearly horizontal strata, and "though diversified by the effects of denuding agencies, and presenting in different portions striking characteristics, yet they are, as a whole, a great uniform surface, gradually rising towards the mountains, at the base of which they attain an elevation varying between 3000 and 5500 feet above the level of the sea."

The Court-house, which had lately suffered from heavy rain, resembled anything more than a court-house; that it did so in former days we may gather from the tales of many travellers, old Canadian voyageurs, who unanimously accounted it a fit place for Indian spooks, ghosts, and hobgoblins to meet in pow-wow, and to "count their coups" delivered in the flesh. The Court-house lies about eight miles from the river, and three from the road; in circumference it may be half a mile, and in height 300 feet; it is, however, gradually degrading, and the rains and snows of not many years will lay it level with the ground. The material is a rough conglomerate of hard marl; the mass is apparently the flank or shoulder of a range forming the southern buttress of the Platte, and which, being composed of softer stuff, has gradually melted away, leaving this remnant to rise in solitary grandeur above the plain. In books it is described as resembling a gigantic ruin, with a huge rotunda in front, windows in the sides, and remains of roofs and stages in its flanks: verily potent is the eye of imagination! To me it appeared in the shape of an irregular pyramid, whose courses were inclined at an ascendable angle of 35°, with a detached outwork composed of a perpendicular mass based upon a slope of 45°; in fact, it resembled the rugged earthworks of Sakkara, only it was far more rugged. According to the driver the summit is a plane upon which a wagon can turn. My military companion remarked that it would make a fine natural fortress against Indians, and perhaps, in the old days of romance and Colonel Bonneville, it has served as a refuge for the harried fur-hunter. I saw it when set off by weather to advantage. A blazing sun rained fire upon its cream-coloured surface — at 11 A.M. the glass showed 95° in the wagon; — and it stood boldly out against a purple-black nimbus which overspread the southern skies, growling distant thunders, and flashing red threads of " chained lightning."

I had finished a hasty sketch, when suddenly appeared to us

a most interesting sight,—a neat ambulance*, followed by a fourgon and mounted soldiers, from which issued an officer in uniform, who advanced to greet Lieutenant Dana. The traveller was Captain, or rather Major, Marcy, who was proceeding westward on leave of absence. After introduction, he remembered that his vehicle contained a compatriot of mine. The compatriot, whose length of facial hair at once told his race,—for

" The larger the whisker the greater the Tory,"—

was a Mr. A——, British vice-consul at * * *'s, Minnesota. Having lately tried his maiden hand upon buffalo, he naturally concluded that I could have no other but the same object. Pleasant estimate, forsooth, of a man's brain, that it can find nothing in America worthy of its notice but bison-shooting! However, the supposition had a *couleur locale.* Every week the New York papers convey to the New World the interesting information that some distinguished Britisher has crossed the Atlantic and half crossed the States to enjoy the society of the " monarch of our prairies." Americans consequently have learned to look upon this Albionic eccentricity as " the thing." That unruly member the tongue was upon the point of putting in a something about the earnest, settled purpose of shooting a prairie-dog, when the reflection that it was hardly fair so far from home to " chaff " a compatriot evidently big with the paternity of a great exploit, with bit and bridle curbed it fast.

Shortly after "liquoring up" and shaking hands, we found ourselves once more in the valley of the Platte, where a lively green relieved eyes which still retained retina-pictures of the barren, Sindh-like divide. The road, as usual, along the river-side was rough and broken, and puffs of Simum raised the sand and dust

---

* The price of the strong light travelling-waggon called an ambulance, in the West is about $250; in the East it is much cheaper. With four mules it will vary from $750 to $900; when resold, however, it rarely fetches half that sum. A journey between St. Joseph and Gt. S. L. City can easily be accomplished in an ambulance within forty days. Officers and sportsmen prefer it, because they have their time to themselves, and they can carry stores and necessaries. On the other hand, " strikers,"—soldier-helps,—or Canadian *engagés*, are necessary; and the pleasure of travelling is by no means enhanced by the nightly fear that the stock will "bolt," not to be recovered for a week, if then.

in ponderous clouds. At 12.30 p.m. we nooned for an hour at a little hovel called a ranch, with the normal corral; and I took occasion to sketch the far-famed Chimney Rock. The name is not, as is that of the Court-house, a misnomer: one might almost expect to see smoke or steam jetting from the summit. Like most of these queer malformations, it was once the knuckle-end of the main chain which bounded the Platte Valley; the

CHIMNEY ROCK.

softer adjacent strata of marl and earthy limestone were dis-integrated by wind and weather, and the harder material, better resisting the action of air and water, has gradually assumed its present form. Chimney Rock lies two and a half miles from the south bank of the Platte. It is composed of a friable yellowish marl, yielding readily to the knife. The shape is a thin shaft, perpendicular and quasi conical. Viewed from the south-east it is not unlike a giant jackboot based upon a high py-ramidal mound, which, disposed in the natural slope, rests upon the plain. The neck of sandstone connecting it with the adjacent hills has been distributed by the floods around the base, leaving an ever-widening gap between. This " Pha-ros of the prairie-sea" towered in former days 150 to 200 feet above the apex of its foundation*, and was a land-

* According to M. Preuss, who accompanied Colonel Frémont's expedition, " tra-vellers who visited it some years since placed its height at upwards of 500 feet," though in his day (1842) it had diminished to 200 feet above the river.

mark visible for 40 to 50 miles: it is now barely 35 feet in height. It has often been struck by lightning; *imber edax* has gnawed much away, and the beginning of the end is already at hand. It is easy to ascend the pyramid; but whilst Pompey's Pillar, Peter Botte, and Ararat have all felt the Anglo-Scandinavian foot, no venturous scion of the race has yet trampled upon the top of Chimney Rock. Around the waist of the base runs a white band which sets off its height and relieves the uniform tint. The old sketches of this curious needle now necessarily appear exaggerated; moreover those best known represent it as a column rising from a confused heap of boulders, thus conveying a completely false idea. Again the weather served us: nothing could be more picturesque than this lone pillar of pale rock lying against a huge black cloud, with the forked lightning playing over its devoted head.

After a frugal dinner of biscuit and cheese we remounted and pursued our way through airy fire, which presently changed from our usual pest — a light dust-laden breeze—into a Punjaubian dust-storm, up the valley of the Platte. We passed a ranch called "Robidoux' Fort," from the well-known Indian trader of that name*; it is now occupied by a Canadian or a French creole,

* From the *St. Joseph* (Mo.) *Gazette:*—"Obituary.—Departed this life, at his residence in this city, on Wednesday, the 29th day of August, 1860, after a long illness, Antoine Robidoux, in the sixty-sixth year of his age. Mr. Robidoux was born in the city of St. Louis, in the year 1794. He was one of the brothers of Mr. Joseph Robidoux, founder of the city of St. Joseph. He was possessed of a sprightly intellect and a spirit of adventure. When not more than twenty-two years of age he accompanied Gen. Atkinson to the then very wild and distant region of the Yellow Stone. At the age of twenty-eight he went to Mexico, and lived there fifteen years. He then married a very interesting Mexican lady, who returned with him to the States. For many years he traded extensively with the Navajoes and Apaches. In 1840 he came to this city with his family, and has resided here ever since. In 1845 he went out to the mountains on a trading expedition, and was caught by the most terrible storms, which caused the death of one or two hundred of his horses, and stopped his progress. His brother Joseph, the respectable founder of this city, sent to his relief and had him brought in, or he would have perished. He was found in a most deplorable condition, and saved. In 1846 he accompanied Gen. Kearny, as interpreter and guide, to Mexico. In a battle with the Mexicans he was lanced severely in three places, but he survived his wounds, and returned to St. Joseph in 1849. Soon after that he went to California, and remained until 1854. In 1855 he removed to New Mexico with his family, and in 1856 he went to Washington, and remained there a year, arranging some business with the government. He then returned to St.

who, as usual with his race in these regions, has taken to himself a wife in the shape of a Sioux squaw, and has garnished his quiver with a multitude of whitey-reds. The driver pointed out the grave of a New-Yorker who had vainly visited the prairies in search of a cure for consumption. As we advanced the storm increased to a tornado of north wind, blinding our cattle till it drove them off the road. The gale howled through the pass with all the violence of a Khamsin, and it was followed by lightning and a few heavy drops of rain. The threatening weather caused a large party of emigrants to " fort themselves " in a corral near the base of Scott's Bluffs.

The corral, a Spanish and Portuguese word, which, corrupted to " kraal," has found its way through Southern Africa, signifies primarily a square or circular pen for cattle, which may be made of tree-trunks, stones, or any other convenient material. The corral of wagons is thus formed. The two foremost are brought near and parallel to each other, and are followed by the rest, disposed aslant, so that the near fore wheel of the hinder touches the off hind wheel of that preceding it, and *vice versâ* on the other side. The "tongues," or poles, are turned outwards, for convenience of yoking, when an attack is not expected, otherwise they are made to point inwards, and the gaps are closed by ropes and yoke and spare chains. Thus a large oval is formed with a single opening fifteen to twenty yards across; some find it more convenient to leave an exit at both ends. In dangerous places the passages are secured at night either by cords or by wheeling round the near wagons; the

Joseph, and has remained here ever since. Mr. Robidoux was a very remarkable man. Tall, slender, athletic, and agile, he possessed the most graceful and pleasing manners, and an intellect of a superior order. In every company he was affable, graceful, and highly pleasing. His conversation was always interesting and instructive, and he possessed many of those qualities which, if he remained in the States, would have raised him to positions of distinction. He suffered for several years before his death with a terrible soreness of the eyes, which defied the curative skill of the doctors; and for the past ten years he has been afflicted with dropsy. A week or two ago he was taken with a violent hæmorrhage of the lungs, which completely prostrated him, and from the effects of which he never recovered. He was attended by the best medical skill, and his wife and many friends were with him to the hour of his dissolution, which occurred on Monday morning, at four o'clock, at his residence in this city. He will be long remembered as a courteous, cultivated, agreeable gentleman, whose life was one of great activity and public usefulness, and whose death will be long lamented."

cattle are driven in before sundown, especially when the area of
the oval is large enough to enable them to graze, and the
men sleep under their vehicles.   In safer travel the tents are
pitched outside the corral with their doors outwards, and in
front of these the camp-fires are lighted.   The favourite spots
with teamsters for corraling are the re-entering angles of deep
streams, especially where these have high and precipitous
banks, or the crests of abrupt hills and bluffs — the position for
nighting usually chosen by the Australian traveller —where one
or more sides of the encampment is safe from attack, and the
others can be protected by a cross fire.   As a rule Indians avoid
attacking strong places; this, however, must not always be
relied upon; in 1844 the Utah Indians attacked Uintah Fort,
a trading post belonging to M. A. Robidoux, then at St. Louis,
slaughtered the men, and carried off the women.   The corral is
especially useful for two purposes: it enables the wagoners to
yoke up with ease, and it secures them from the prairie traveller's
prime dread—the stampede.   The Western savages are perfectly
acquainted with the habits of animals, and in their marauding
expeditions they instinctively adopt the system of the Bedouins,
the Gallas, and the Somal.   Providing themselves with rattles
and other implements for making startling noises, they ride
stealthily up close to the cattle, and then rush by like the whirlwind with a volley of horrid whoops and screams.   When the
" cavallard " flies in panic fear, the plunderers divide their
party; some drive on the plunder, whilst the others form a
rear-guard to keep off pursuers.   The prairie-men provide for
the danger by keeping their fleetest horses saddled, bridled, and
ready to be mounted at a moment's notice.   When the animals
have stampeded, the owners follow them, scatter the Indians,
and drive, if possible, the madriña, or bell-mare, to the front of
the herd, gradually turning her towards the camp, and slacking
speed as the familiar objects come in sight.   Horses and mules
appear peculiarly timorous upon the prairies.   A band of buffalo, a wolf, or even a deer, will sometimes stampede them;
they run to great distances, and not unfrequently their owners
fail to recover them.

" Scott's Bluffs," situated 285 miles from Fort Kearny and
51 from Fort Laramie, was the last of the great marl formations which we saw on this line, and was of all by far the

most curious.   In the dull uniformity of the prairies it is a
striking and attractive object, far excelling the castled crag of
Drachenfels or any of the beauties of romantic Rhine.   From a
distance of a day's march it appears in the shape of a large blue
mound, distinguished only by its dimensions from the detached
fragments of hill around.   As you approach within four or five
miles, a massive medieval city gradually defines itself, clustering, with a wonderful fulness of detail, round a colossal fortress,
and crowned with a royal castle.   Buttress and barbican, bastion,
demilune and guardhouse, tower, turret, and donjon-keep, all

SCOTT'S BLUFFS.

are there: in one place parapets and battlements still stand
upon the crumbling wall of a fortalice like the giant ruins of
Château Gaillard, the "Beautiful Castle on the Rock;" and, that
nothing may be wanting to the resemblance, the dashing rains
and angry winds have cut the old line of road at its base into a
regular moat with a semicircular sweep, which the mirage fills
with a mimic river.   Quaint figures develop themselves;
guards and sentinels in dark armour keep watch and ward upon
the slopes, the lion of Bastia crouches unmistakably overlooking the road; and as the shades of an artificial evening,
caused by the dust-storm, close in, so weird is its aspect that
one might almost expect to see some spectral horseman

with lance and pennant go his rounds about the deserted streets, ruined buildings, and broken walls. At a nearer aspect again, the quaint illusion vanishes: the lines of masonry become yellow layers of boulder and pebble imbedded in a mass of stiff, tamped, bald marly clay; the curtains and angles change to the gashings of the rains of ages, and the warriors are metamorphosed into dwarf cedars and dense shrubs, scattered singly over the surface. Travellers have compared this glory of the *mauvaises terres* to Gibraltar, to the Capitol at Washington, to Stirling Castle. I could think of nothing in its presence but the Arabs' "City of Brass," that mysterious abode of bewitched infidels, which often appears at a distance to the wayfarer toiling under the burning sun, but ever eludes his nearer search.

Scott's Bluffs derive their name from an unfortunate fur-trader there put on shore in the olden time by his boat's crew, who had a grudge against him: the wretch in mortal sickness crawled up the mound to die. The politer guide-books call them "Capitol Hills :" methinks the first name, with its dark associations, must be better pleasing to the *genius loci*. They are divided into three distinct masses. The largest, which may be 800 feet high, is on the right, or nearest the river. To its left lies an outwork, a huge detached cylinder whose capping changes aspect from every direction; and still further to the left, is a second castle, now divided from, but once connected with, the others. The whole affair is a spur springing from the main range, and closing upon the Platte so as to leave no room for a road.

After gratifying our curiosity we resumed our way. The route lay between the right-hand fortress and the outwork, through a degraded bed of softer marl, once doubtless part of the range. The sharp, sudden torrents which pour from the heights on both sides, and the draughty winds — Scott's Bluffs are the permanent head-quarters of hurricanes — have cut up the ground into a labyrinth of jagged gulches steeply walled in. We dashed down the drains and pitchholes with a violence which shook the nave-bands from our sturdy wheels.*

---

* The dry heat of the prairies in summer causes the wood to warp by the percolation of water which the driver restores by placing the wheels for a night to stand in some stream. Paint or varnish is of little use. Moisture may be drawn out, even through a nail hole, and exhaust the whole interior of the woodwork.

Ascending, the driver showed a place where the skeleton of
an " elephant " had been lately discovered.   On the summit, he
pointed out, far over many a treeless hill and barren plain, the
famous Black Hills and Laramie Peak, which has been compared to Ben Lomond, towering at a distance of eighty miles.
The descent was abrupt, with sudden turns round the head of
earth-cracks deepened to ravines by snow and rain ; and one
place showed the remains of a wagon and team which had
lately come to grief.   After galloping down a long slope of
twelve miles, with ridgelets of sand and gravel somewha; raised
above the bottom, which they cross on their way to the river,
we found ourselves at 5.30 P.M. once more in the valley of the
Platte.   I had intended to sketch the Bluffs more carefully from
the station, but the western view proved to be disappointingly
inferior to the eastern.   After the usual hour's delay we resumed
our drive through alternate puffs of hot and cold wind, the
contrast of which was not easy to explain.   The sensation was
as if Indians had been firing the prairies — an impossibility at
this season, when whatever herbage there is, is still green.   It
may here be mentioned that although the meteorology of the
earlier savans, namely, that the peculiar condition of the atmosphere, known as the Indian summer *, might be produced by
the burning of the plain-vegetation, was not thought worthy
of comment, their hypothesis is no longer considered trivial.
The smoky canopy must produce a sensible effect upon the
temperature of the season.   " During a still night, when
a cloud of this kind is overhead, no dew is produced ; the

---

* These remarks are borrowed from a paper by Professor Joseph Henry, Secretary of the Smithsonian Institution, entitled " Meteorology in its connection with
Agriculture."

The Indian summer is synonymous with our St. Martin's or Allhallows summer,
so called from the festival held on the 11th November.   " The Indians avail
themselves of this delightful time for harvesting their corn ; and the tradition is
that they were accustomed to say they always had a second summer of nine days
before the winter set in.   It is a bland and genial time, in which the birds,
insects, and plants feel a new creation, and enjoy a short-lived summer ere they
shrink finally from the rigour of the winter's blast.   The sky, in the meantime, is
generally filled with a haze of orange and gold, intercepting the direct rays of the
sun, yet possessing enough of light and heat to prevent sensations of gloom or
chill, while the nights grow sharp and frosty, and the necessary fires give cheer-
ful forecast of the social winter evenings near at hand."—The *National Intelli-
gencer*, Nov. 26th, 1857, quoted by Mr. Bartlett.

heat which is radiated from the earth is reflected or absorbed, and radiated back again by the particles of soot, and the coating of the earth necessary to prevent the deposition of water in the form of dew or hoar frost is prevented." According to Professor Henry of Washington, "it is highly probable that a portion of the smoke or fog-cloud, produced by the burning of one of the Western Prairies, is carried entirely across the eastern portion of the continent to the ocean."

Presently we dashed over the Little Kiowa Creek, forded the Horse Creek, and, enveloped in a cloud of villainous mosquitoes, entered at 8.30 P.M. the station in which we were to pass the night. It was tenanted by one Reynal, a French creole — the son of an old soldier of the Grand Armée, who had settled at St. Louis — a companionable man, but an extortionate; he charged us a florin for every " drink " of his well-watered whiskey. The house boasted of the usual squaw, a wrinkled old dame, who at once began to prepare supper, when we discreetly left the room. These hard-working, but surely ill-favoured beings, are accused of various horrors in cookery, such as grinding their pinole, or parched corn, in the impurest manner, kneading dough upon the floor, using their knives for any purpose whatever, and employing the same pot, unwashed, for boiling tea and tripe. In fact, they are about as clean as those Eastern Pariah servants who make the knowing Anglo-Indian hold it an abomination to sit at meat with a new arrival or with an officer of a " home regiment." The daughter was an usually fascinating half-breed, with a pale face and Franco-American features. How comes it that here, as in Hindostan, the French half-caste is pretty, graceful, amiable, coquette, whilst the Anglo-Saxon is plain, coarse, gauche, and ill-tempered? The beauty was married to a long, lean Down-Easter, who appeared most jealously attentive to her, occasionally hinting at a return to the curtained bed, where she could escape the admiring glances of strangers. Like her mother, she was able to speak English, but she could not be persuaded to open her mouth. This is a truly Indian prejudice, probably arising from the savage, childish sensitiveness which dreads to excite a laugh; even a squaw married to a white man, after uttering a few words in a moment of *épanchement,* will hide her face under the blanket.

The half-breed has a bad name in the land.   Like the negro, the Indian belongs to a species, sub-species, or variety — whichever the reader pleases — that has diverged widely enough from the Indo-European type to cause degeneracy, physical as well as moral, and often, too, sterility in the offspring.   These half-breeds are, therefore, like the mulatto, quasi-mules. The men combine the features of both races; the skin soon becomes coarse and wrinkled, and the eye is black, snaky, and glittering like the Indian's.   The mongrels are short-lived, peculiarly subject to infectious diseases, untrustworthy, and disposed to every villainy.   The half-bred women, in early youth, are sometimes attractive enough, uniting the figure of the mother to the more delicate American face; a few years, however, deprive them of all litheness, grace, and agility.   They are often married by whites, who hold them to be more modest and humble, less capricious and less exacting, than those of the higher type: they make good wives and affectionate mothers, and, like the quadroons, they are more " ambitious " — that is to say, of warmer temperaments—than either of the races from which they are derived.   The so-called red is a higher ethnic type than the black man; so in the United States, where all admixture of African blood is deemed impure, the aboriginal American entails no disgrace — some of the noblest of the land are descended from " Indian princesses."   The half-breed girls resemble their mothers in point of industry, and they barter their embroidered robes and moccasins, and mats and baskets, made of bark and bulrush, in exchange for blankets, calicoes, glass beads, — an indispensable article of dress, — mirrors, needles, rings, vermilion, and other luxuries.   The children, with their large black eyes, wide mouths, and glittering teeth, flattened heads and remarkable agility of motion, suggest the idea of little serpents.

The day had been fatiguing, and our eyes ached with the wind and dust.   We lost no time in spreading on the floor the buffalo robes borrowed from the house, and in defying the smaller tenants of the Ranch.   Our host, M. Reynal, was a study, but we deferred the lesson till the next morning.

To Fort Laramie, 14th August.

M. Reynal had been an Indian trader in his youth.   Of this race there were in his day two varieties: the regular trader and

the *coureur des bois,* or unlicensed pedlar, who was subject to
certain pains and penalties. The former had some regard for
his future; he had a permanent interest in the Indians, and
looked to the horses, arms, and accoutrements of his *protégés,* so
that hunting might not flag. The *bois brûlé* pedlar, having—
like an English advertising firm—no hope of dealing twice with
the same person, got all he could for what he could. These
men soon sapped the foundation of the Indian's discipline. One
of them, for instance, would take protection with the chief, pay
presents, and by increasing the wealth, enhance the importance
of his protector. Another would place himself under the charge
of some ambitious aspirant to power, who was thus raised to a
position of direct rivalry. A split would ensue, the weaker
would secede with his family and friends, and declare independence; a murder or two would be the result, and a blood-
feud would be bequeathed from generation to generation. The
licensed traders have ever strenuously opposed the introduction
of alcohol; a keg of which will purchase from the Indian everything that is his, his arms, lodge, horses, children, and wives.
In olden times, however, the Maine Liquor Law was not, as now,
in force through the territories. The *coureur des bois,* therefore, entered the country through various avenues, from the
United States and from Mexico, without other stock in trade
but some kegs of whiskey, which he retailed at the modest price
of $36 per gallon. He usually mixed one part of fire with five of
pure water, and then sold a pint-canful for a buffalo robe.
" Indian liquor " became a proverbial term. According to some
travellers, a barrel of " pure Cincinnati," even after running the
gauntlet of railroad and lake travel, has afforded a hundred
barrels of " good Indian liquor." A small bucketful is poured
into a washtub of water; a large quantity of " dog-leg "
tobacco and red pepper is then added, next a bitter root
common in the country is cut up into it, and finally it is
coloured with burnt sugar;—a nice recipe for a morning's
headache! The only drawback to this traffic is its danger.
The Indian when intoxicated is ready for any outrageous act of
violence or cruelty; vinosity brings out the destructiveness and
the utter barbarity of his character; it makes him thirst tiger-
like for blood. The *coureur des bois,* therefore, who in those
days was highly respected, was placed in the Trader's Lodge, a

kind of public house, like the Iwanza of Central Africa, and the village chief took care to station at the door a guard of sober youths, sometimes habited like Europeans, ready to check the unauthorised attempts of ambitious clansmen upon the whiskey-vendor's scalp.   The western men, who will frequently be alluded to in these pages, may be divided like the traders into two classes.   The first is the true mountaineer, whom the platitude and tame monotony of civilised republican life has in early youth driven, often from an honoured and wealthy family, to the wilds and wolds, to become the forlorn hope in the march of civilisation.   The second is the offscouring and refuse of the eastern cities, compelled by want, fatuity, or crime to exile himself from all he most loves.   The former, after passing through the preliminary stage greenhorn, is a man in every sense of the term : to more than Indian bravery and fortitude, he unites the softness of woman, and a child-like simplicity, which is the very essence of a chivalrous character ; you can read his nature in his clear blue eyes, his sun-tanned countenance, his merry smile, and his frank fearless manner. The latter is a knave or a fool ; it would " make bad blood," as the Frenchman says, to describe him.

M. Reynal's history had to be received with many grains of salt.   The western man has been worked by climate and its consequences, by the huge magnificence of nature and the violent contrasts of scenery, into a remarkable resemblance to the wild Indian.   He hates labour—which poet and divine combine to deify in the settled States — as the dire effect of a primæval curse ; " loaf " he must and will ; to him one hour out of the twenty-four spent in honest industry is *satis superque.* His imagination is inflamed by scenery and climate, difficulty and danger; he is as superstitious as an old man-o'-war's man of the olden school ; and he is a transcendental liar, like his prototype the aborigin, who in this point yields nothing to the African negro.   I have heard of a man riding eighty miles— forty into camp and forty out — in order to enjoy the sweet delights of a lie.   His yarns and stories about the land he lives in have become a proverbial ridicule ; he will tell you that the sun rises north of what it did *se puero ;* he has seen mountains of diamonds and gold nuggets scattered like rocks over the surface of our general mother.   I have been gravely told of a herd of bison which arrested the course of the Platte River, causing its waters, like those of the Red Sea, to stand up, wall fashion, whilst the animals were crossing. Of this western order is the well-known account of a ride on a buffalo's horns, delivered for the benefit of a gaping world by a popular author of the yellow-binding category. In this age, however, the western man has become sensitive to the operation of " smoking." A popular Joe Miller anent him is this:—A traveller, informed of what he might educe by "querying," asked an old mountaineer, who shall be nameless, what difference he observed in the country since he had first settled in it.

" Wal, stranger, not much ! " was the reply; " only when I fust come here, that 'ere mountain," pointing to the tall Uintah range, " was a hole ! "

Disembarrassing M. Reynal's recital of its masque of im-probabilities and impossibilities, remained obvious the naked fact, that he had led the life of a confirmed *coureur des bois*. The French Canadian and Creole both, like the true Français de France, is loth to stir beyond the devil-dispelling sound of his chapel-bell; once torn from his *chez lui,* he apparently cares little to return, and like the Englishman, to die at home in his own land. The adventurous Canadians—in whom extremes meet— have wandered through the length and breadth of the continent; they have left their mark even upon the rocks in Utah territory. M. Reynal had quitted St. Louis at an early age as trader, trapper, everything in short, pro-vided with a little outfit of powder, ball, and whiskey. At first he was unfortunate. In a war between the Sioux and the Pawnees, he was taken prisoner by the latter, and with much ado preserved, by the good aid of his squaw, that useful article his scalp. Then fickle fortune turned in his favour. He married several wives, identified himself with the braves, and became a little brother of the tribe, whilst his whiskey brought him in an abundance of furs and peltries. After many years, waxing weary of a wandering life, he settled down into the somewhat prosaic position in which we had the pleasure of finding him. He was garrulous as a veteran soldier upon the subject of his old friends the trappers, that gallant advance guard who, sixty years ago, unconsciously fought the fight of civilisation for the pure love of fighting ; who battled with the Indian in his own way, surpassing him in tracking, surprising, ambuscading and shooting, and never failing to raise the enemy's hair. They are well nigh extinct, those old pioneers, wild, reckless, and brave as the British tar of a century past; they live but in story; their place knows them no longer, it is now filled by the "prospector." Civilisation and the silk hat have exterminated them. How many deeds of stern fight and heroic endurance have been ignored by this world, which knows nothing of its greatest men, *carent quia vate sacro!* We talk of Thermopylæ and ignore Texas; we have all thrilled at the account of the Mameluke Bey's leap; but how many of us have heard of Major Macculloch's spring from the cliff?

Our breakfast was prepared in the usual prairie style. First the coffee—three parts burnt beans—which had been duly ground to a fine powder and exposed to the air, lest the aroma should prove too strong for us, was placed on the stove to simmer till every noxious principle was duly extracted from it. Then the rusty bacon, cut into thick slices, was thrown into the fry-pan; here the gridiron is unknown, and if known would be little appreciated, because it wastes the "drippings," which form with the staff of life a luxurious sop. Thirdly, antelope steak, cut off a corpse suspended for the benefit of flies outside, was placed to stew within influence of the bacon's aroma. Lastly came the bread, which of course should have been "cooked" first. The meal is kneaded with water and a pinch of salt; the raising is done by means of a little sour milk, or more generally by the deleterious yeast-powders of the trade. The carbonic acid gas evolved by the addition of water must be corrected and the dough must be expanded by saleratus or prepared carbonate of soda or alkali, and other vile stuff, which communicates to the food the green-yellow tinge, and suggests many of the properties of poison. A hundredfold better, the unpretending chapati, flap-jack, scone, or, as the Mexicans prettily called it, "tortilla"! The dough after being sufficiently manipulated upon a long, narrow smooth board is divided into "biscuits" and "dough nuts,"* and finally it is

* The western "biscuit" is English roll: "cracker" is English biscuit. The "dough-nut" is, properly speaking, a "small roundish cake, made of flour, eggs, and sugar, moistened with milk and boiled in lard" (Webster). On the prairies, where so many different materials are unprocurable, it is simply a diminutive loaf, like the hot roll of the English passenger steamer.

placed to be half cooked under the immediate influence of the rusty bacon and graveolent antelope. "Uncle Sam's stove," be it said with every reverence for the honoured name it bears, is a triumph of convenience, cheapness, unwholesomeness and nastiness—excuse the word, nice reader. This travellers' bane has exterminated the spit and gridiron, and makes everything taste like its neighbour : by virtue of it, mutton borrows the flavour of salmon-trout, tomatos resolve themselves into greens.— I shall lose my temper if the subject is not dropped.

We set out at 6 A.M. over a sandy bottom, from which the mosquitoes rose in swarms. After a twelve mile stretch the driver pointed out on the right of the road, which here runs between high earth banks, a spot still infamous in local story. At this place, in 1854, five Indians, concealing themselves in the bed of a dwarf arroyo, fired upon the mail wagon, killing two drivers and one passenger, and then plundered it of 20,000 dollars. "Long-chin," the leader, and the other murderers when given up by the tribe, were carried to Washington, D.C., where—with the ultra-philanthropy which has of modern days distinguished the "Great Father's" government of his "Poor Children of the Plains"—the villains were liberally rewarded and restored to their homes.* To cut off a bend of the Platte we once more left the valley, ascended sundry slopes of sand and clay deeply cut by dry creeks, and from the summit enjoyed a pretty view. A little to the left rose the aerial blue cone of that noble land-mark, Laramie Peak, based like a mass of solidified air upon a dark wall, the Black Hills, and lit up with the roseate hues of the morning. The distance was about sixty miles ; you would have guessed twenty. On the right lay a broad valley, bounded by brown rocks and a plain-coloured distance, with the stream winding through it like a thread of quicksilver ; in places it was hidden from sight by thickets of red willow, cypress clumps, and dense cool cottonwoods. All

* An United States official, fresh from Columbia, informed me that the Indians there think twice before they murder a King George's man (Briton), whilst they hardly hesitate to kill a Boston man or American citizen. He attributed this peculiarity principally to the over lenity of his own Government, and its want of persistency in ferretting out and punishing the criminal. Under these circumstances, it is hardly to be wondered at if the trader and traveller in Indian countries take the law in their own hands. This excessive clemency has acted evilly in "either Ind." We may hope that its day is now gone by.

was not still life; close below us rose the white lodges of the Ogalala tribe.

These Indian villages are very picturesque from afar when dimly seen dotting the verdure of the valleys, and when their tall white cones, half hidden by willow clumps, lie against a blue background. The river side is the savages' favourite site; next to it the hill foot, where little groups of three or four tents are often seen from the road, clustering mysteriously near a spring. Almost every prairie-band has its own way of constructing lodges, encamping and building fires, and the experienced mountaineer easily distinguishes them.

The Osages make their lodges in the shape of a wagon-tilt, somewhat like our gipsies' tents, with a framework of bent willow rods planted in the ground, and supporting their blankets, skins, or tree-basts.

The Kikapoos build dwarf hay-stack huts, like some tribes of Africans, setting poles in the earth, binding them over and lashing them together at the top; they are generally covered with clothes or bark.

The Wichetas, Wakos, Towakamis, and Tonkowas are described by the "Prairie Traveller" as erecting their hunting lodges of sticks put up in the form of the frustrum of a cone, and bushed over like "boweries."

All these tribes leave the framework of their lodges standing when they shift ground, and thus the particular band is readily recognised.

The Sacs, Foxes, Winnebagos and Menomenes build lodges in the form of an ellipsis, some of them 30 — 40 feet long, by 14 — 15 wide, and large enough to shelter twenty people permanently, and sixty temporarily.* The covering is of plaited rush-mats, bound to the poles, and a small aperture in the lodge acts as chimney.

The Delawares and Shawnees, Cherokees and Choktaws prefer the Indian pal, a canvass covering thrown like a *tente d'abri*, over a stick supported by two forked poles.

The Sioux, Arapahos, Cheyennes, Utahs, Snakes, Blackfeet, and Kiowas use the Comanche lodge covered with bison skins,

---

* The wigwams, huts, or cabins of the eastern American tribes were like these, large, solid, and well roofed with skins. The word "lodge" is usually applied to the smaller and less comfortable habitations of the Prairie Indians.

which by dressing become flexible as canvass. They are usually of a shining white, save where smoke-stained near the top ; the lodges of great chiefs are sometimes decorated with horizontal stripes of alternate black and white, and ornamented with figures human and bestial, crosses, circles, and arabesques. The lodge is made of eight to twenty-four straight peeled poles or saplings of ash, pine, cedar, or other wood, hard and elastic if possible, about 20 feet long; the largest marquees are 30 feet in diameter by 35 feet high, and are comprised of 26 — 30 buffalo skins; and they are sometimes planted round a " basement " or circular excavation two or three feet deep. When pitching, three poles lashed to one another with a long line, somewhat below the thinner points, are raised perpendicularly, and the thicker ends are spread out in a tripod to the perimeter of the circle which is to form the lodge floor ; the rest of the poles are then propped against the three first and disposed regularly and equi-distantly to make a steady and secure conical framework. The long line attached to the tripod is then wound several times round the point where the poles touch, and the lower end is made fast to the base of the lodge, thus securing the props in position. The covering of dressed, hairless, and waterproof cow-buffalo hide,— traders prefer Osnaburg,— cut and sewn to fit the frame like an envelope, and sometimes pinned together with skewers, is either raised at first with the tripod, or afterwards hoisted with a perch and spread round the complete structure. It is pinned to the ground with wooden pegs, and a narrow space forms a doorway, which may be closed with a blanket suspended from above and spread out with two small sticks. The apex is left open with a triangular wing or flap, like a lateen sail, and is prevented from closing by a pole inserted into a pocket at the end. The aperture points to windward when ventilation is required, and, drawing like a wind sail, it keeps the interior cool and comfortable ; when smoke is to be carried off, it is turned to leeward, thus giving draught to the fire and making the abode warm in the severest weather, whilst in lodges of other forms, you must lie down on the ground to prevent being asphyxiated. By raising the lower part so as freely to admit the breeze, it is kept perfectly free from mosquitoes, which are unable to resist the strong draught. The squaws are always the tent-pitchers, and they equal orientals in dexterity and judgment. Before the lodge of each warrior stands his light spear, planted Bedouin-fashion in the ground, near or upon a tripod of thin, cleanly-scraped wands, seven to eight feet long, which support his spotless white buffalo-skin targe, sometimes decorated with his "totem"—we translate the word "crest"— and guarded by the usual prophylactic, a buckskin sack containing medicine. Readers of "Ivanhoe"—they are now more numerous in the New than in the Old Country—ever feel "a passing impulse to touch one of these spotless shields with the muzzle of the gun, expecting a grim warrior to start from the lodge and resent the challenge." The fire, as in the old Hebridean huts, is built in the centre of the hard dirt floor, a strong stick planted at the requisite angle supports the kettle, and around the walls, are berths divided by matted screens; the extremest uncleanliness, however, is a feature never absent. In a quiet country these villages have a simple and patriarchal appearance. The tents, which number from fifteen to fifty, are disposed round a circular central space, where animals can be tethered. Some have attached to them corrals of wattled canes, and a few boast of fields where corn and pumpkins are raised.

The Comanche lodge is the favourite tenement of the Canadian and Creole voyageurs, on account of its coolness or warmth when wanted, its security against violent winds, and its freedom from mosquitoes. Whilst travelling in an Indian country they will use no other. It has been simplified by Major H. H. Sibley, of the U. S. army, who has changed the pole framework for a single central upright, resting upon an iron tripod, with hooks for suspending cooking utensils over the fire; when folded up, the tripod admits the upright between its legs, thereby reducing the length to one half—a portable size. The "Sibley tent" was the only shelter of the U. S. army at Fort Scott, in Utah Territory during the hard winter of 1857-8, and gave universal satisfaction. The officers still keep to the old wall-tent. This will, however, eventually be superseded by the new form, which can accommodate comfortably twelve, but not seventeen, the usual number allotted to it. Captain Marcy is of opinion that of the tents used in the different armies of Europe, "none in point of convenience, comfort, and economy, will compare with the 'Sibley tent,' for campaigning in cold weather." In summer, however, it has, like all conical tents, many disadvantages: there is always a loss of room; and for comfortably disposing kit — chair, table and camp couch — there is nothing equal to the wall-tent. The price of a " Sibley," when made of good material, is from $40 to $50 (£8 — £10), and it can be procured from Baltimore, Philadelphia, and New York.

At 10.20 A.M. we halted to change mules at Badeau's Ranch, or as it is more grandiloquently called, " Laramie City." The " city," like many a western " town," still appertains to the category of things about to be : it is at present represented by a single large " store," with outhouses full of small half-breeds. The principal articles of traffic are liquors and groceries for the whites, and ornaments for the Indians, which are bartered for stock (*i. e.* animals) and peltries. The prices asked for the skins were from $1 — $1.30 for a fox or a coyote, $3 for wolf, bear, or deer, $6 — $7 for an elk, $5 for a common buffalo, and from $8 to $35 for the same painted, pictograph'd, and em-broidered. Some of the party purchased moccasins, for which they paid $1 — $2 ; the best articles are made by the Snakes, and when embroidered by white women rise as high as $25. I bought, for an old friend who is insane upon the subject of pipes, one of the fine marble-like sandstone bowls brought from the celebrated Côteau (slope) des Prairies, at the head of Sioux River —

> " On the mountains of the Prairie,
> On the Great Red Pipestone Quarry."

This instrument is originally the gift of Gitche Manitou, who, standing on the precipice of the Red Pipe-stone Rock, broke off a fragment and moulded it into a pipe, which finished with a reed he smoked over his children to the north, south, east, and west. It is of queer shape, not unlike the clay and steatite articles used by the Abyssinians and the Turi or Sinaitic Bedouins. The length of the stick is 23 inches, of the stem 9·50, and of the bowl 5 inches; the latter stands at a right angle upon the former, both are circular, but the 2·75 inches of stem, which project beyond the bowl, are bevelled off so as to form an edge at the end. The peculiarity of the form is in the part where the tobacco is inserted ; the hole is not more than half an inch broad, and descends straight without a bulge, whilst the aperture in the stem is exactly similar. The red colour soon mottles and the bowl clogs, if smoked with tobacco: in fact, it is fit for nothing but the "kinnikinik" of the Indians. To prepare this hard material with the rude tools of a savage, must be a work of time and difficulty; also the bowls are expensive and highly valued : for mine I paid $5, and further west I could have exchanged it for an Indian pony.

Having finished our *emplettes* at M. Badeau's, we set out at 11.30 P.M. over a barren and reeking bit of sandy soil. Close to the station, and a little to the right of the road, we passed the barrow which contains the remains of Lieut. Grattan and his thirty men. A young second-lieutenant of Irish origin and fiery temper, he was marching westward with an interpreter, a small body of men, and two howitzers, when a dispute arose, it is said, about a cow, between his party and the Brûlés or Burnt-thigh Indians. The latter were encamped in a village of 450 to 500 lodges, which, reckoning five to each, gives a total of 2200 to 2500 souls. A fight took place, the whites imprudently discharged both their cannons, over-shooting the tents of the enemy : their muskets, however, did more execution, killing Matriya " the Scattering Bear," who had been made chief of all the Sioux by Colonel Mitchell of the Indian bureau. The savages, seeing the fall of Ursa Major, set to in real earnest : about 1200 charged the soldiers before they could reload, the little detachment broke, and not a man survived to tell the tale. The whites in the neighbourhood narrowly preserved their scalps,— M. Badeau owned that he owed his to his Sioux squaw,— and amongst other acts of violence, was the murder and highway robbery, which has already been recounted. Both these events occurred in 1854. As has been said, in 1855, Gen. W. S. Harney, who, whatever may be his faults as a diplomatist, is the most dreaded "Minahaska"* in the Indian country, punished the Brûlés severely at Ash Hollow. They were led by their chosen chief Little Thunder, who, not liking the prospect, wanted to palaver : the general replied by a charge, which, as usual, scattered the " chivalry of the prairies " to the four winds. " Little Thunder " was solemnly deposed, and Mato Chigukesa, " Bear's

---

* "Longknife." The whites have enjoyed this title since 1758, when Captain Gibson cut off with his sabre the head of Little Eagle, the great Mingo or Chief, and won the title of Big Knife Warrior. Savages in America as well as Africa who ignore the sword always look upon that weapon with horror. The Sioux call the Americans Wasichi, or bad men.

Rib," was ordered to reign in his stead: moreover, in 1856, a treaty was concluded, giving to whites, amongst other things, the privilege of making roads along the Platte and White Earth Rivers (Mankisita Wakpa— Smoking-earth Water) to Forts Pierre and Laramie, and to pass up and down the Missouri in boats. Since that time, with the exception of plundering an English sportsman, Sir G—— G——, opposing Lieut. Warren's expedition to the Black Hills, and slaughtering a few traders and obscure travellers, the Brûlés have behaved tolerably to their pale-face rivals.

As we advanced, the land became more barren; it sadly wanted rain : it suffers from drought almost every year, and what vegetable matter the soil will produce the grasshopper will devour. Dead cattle cumbered the way side, the flesh had disappeared, the bones were scattered over the ground, but the skins, mummified, as it were, by the dry heat, lay life-like and shapeless, as in the Libyan Desert, upon the ground. This phenomenon will last till we enter the humid regions between the Sierra Nevada and the Pacific Ocean, and men tell wonderful tales of the time during which meat can be kept. The road was a succession of steep ascents and jumps down sandy ground. A Sioux "buck," mounted upon a neat nag, and wrapped up, despite sun and glare, as if it had been the depth of winter, passed us, sedulously averting his eyes. The driver declared that he recognised the horse, and grumbled certain western facetiæ concerning " hearty-chokes and caper sauce."

In these lands, the horse thief is the great enemy of mankind, for him there is no pity, no mercy; Lynch-law is held almost too good for him ; to shoot him *in flagrante delicto* is like slaying a man-eating Bengal royal tiger, — it entitles you to the respect and gratitude of your species. I asked our conductor whether dandiness was at the bottom of the " buck's " heavy dress. " 'Guess," was the reply, " what keeps cold out, keeps heat out tew ! "

At 12.15 P.M. Crossing Laramie's Fork, a fine clear stream about forty yards broad, we reached Fort Laramie,— another " fort" by courtesy, or rather by order,— where we hoped to recruit our exhausted stores.

The straggling cantonment requires no description : it has

the usual big flag, barracks, store-houses, officers' quarters, guard-houses, sutlers' stores, and groceries, which doubtless make a good thing by selling deleterious " strychnine " to passing trains who can afford to pay $6 per gallon.

Fort Laramie, called Fort John in the days of the American Fur Company, was used by them as a store-house for the bear and buffalo skins, which they collected in thousands. The old adobe *enceinte,* sketched and described by Frémont and Stansbury, soon disappeared after the place was sold to the U. S. Government. Its former rival was Fort Platte, belonging in 1842 — when the pale-face first opened this road — to Messrs. Sybille, Adams, and Co., and situated immediately on the point of land at the junction of Laramie Fort with the Platte. The climate here is arid and parching in summer, but in winter tolerably mild, considering the altitude,—·4470 feet, — and the proximity of the Black Hills : yet it has seen hard frost in September. It is also well defended from the warm, moist, and light winds, which, coming from the Mexican Gulf, cause " calentures " on the lower course of the river. The soil around the settlement is gravelly and sterile, the rocks are sand, lime, and clay, and there is a solitary, desolate look upon everything but the bright little stream that bubbles from the dark heights. The course is from S. W. to N. E. : about half way it bifurcates, with a right fork to the west and main fork east, and near Laramie it receives its main influent, the Chugwater.

My companion kindly introduced me to the officer commanding the fort, Colonel B. Alexander, 10th infantry, and we were at once made at home. The amiable mistress of the house must find charitable work enough to do in providing for the wants of way-worn friends who pass through Laramie from east to west. We rested and dined in the cool comfortable quarters, with only one qualm at heart — we were so soon to leave them. On these occasions the driver seems to know by instinct that you are enjoying yourself, whilst he, as an outsider, is not. He becomes therefore unusually impatient to start ; perhaps, also, time runs more rapidly than it is wont. At any rate, after a short two hours, we were compelled to shake hands with our kind and considerate hosts, and to return to limbo—the mail wagon.

From Fort Laramie westward the geological formation

changes: the great limestone deposits disappear, and are succeeded by a great variety of sandstones, some red, argillaceous,
and compact; others grey or yellow, ferruginous, and coarse.
Pudding stones or conglomerates also abound, and the main
chain of the Laramie Mountains is supposed to be chiefly composed of this rock.

Beyond the fort there are two roads. The longer leads
to the right, near the Platte River. It was formerly, and
perhaps is still, a favourite with emigrants. We preferred the
left, which, crossing the edges of the Black Hills, is rough and
uneven, but is "some shorter," as the guide-book says, than
the other. The weather began to be unusually disagreeable
with heat and rain drops from a heavy nimbus, that forced us
to curtain up the rattling vehicle; perhaps, too, we were a little
cross, contrasting the present with the past,—civilised society,
a shady bungalow, and wonderfully good butter. At 4 P.M.,
following the Platte Valley, after two hours' drive, we halted to
change mules at Ward's Station, *alias* the "Central Star," where
several whites were killed by the Sioux in 1855, amongst them
M. Montalan, a Parisian.

Again we started for another twenty-five miles at 4 P.M. The
road was rough, and the driver had a curious proclivity for
losing the way. I have often found this to be the case after
passing through a station. There was little to remark, except
that the country was poor and bad, that there was clear water
in a ravine to the right, and that we were very tired and surly.
But as sorrow comes to an end as well as joy, so at 9.30 P.M. we
drove in somewhat consoled to Horse-shoe Station,—the old
Fer à Cheval,—where one of the road agents, Mr. Slade,
lived, and where we anticipated superior comfort.

We were *entichés* by the aspect of the buildings, which were
on an extensive scale—in fact, got up regardless of expense.
An ominous silence, however, reigned around. At last, by hard
knocking, we were admitted into a house with the Floridan
style of verandah previously described, and by the pretensions
of the room we at once divined our misfortune—we were
threatened with a "lady." The "lady" will, alas! follow us to
the Pacific: even in hymns we read,—

> " Now let the Prophet's heart rejoice,
> His noble lady's too."

Our mishap was really worse than we expected — we were exposed to two "ladies," and of these one was a Bloomer. It is only fair to state that it was the only hermaphrodite of the kind that ever met my eyes in the United States : the great founder of the order has long since subsided into her original obscurity, and her acolytes have relapsed into the weakness of petticoats. The Bloomer was an uncouth being, her hair, cut level with her eyes, depended with the graceful curl of a drake's tail around a flat Turanian countenance, whose only expression was sullen insolence. The body-dress, glazed brown calico, fitted her somewhat like a soldier's tunic, developing haunches which would be admired only in venison ; and — curious *inconséquence* of woman's nature ! — all this sacrifice of appearance upon the shrine of comfort did not prevent her wearing that kind of crinoline depicted by Mr. *Punch* upon " our Mary Hanne." The pantalettes of glazed brown calico, like the vest, tunic, blouse, shirt, or whatever they may call it, were in peg-top style, admirably setting off a pair of thin-soled Frenchified patent-leather bottines, with elastic sides, which contained feet large, broad, and flat as a negro's in Unyamwezi. The dear creature had a husband : it was hardly safe to look at her, and as for sketching her, I avoided it, as men are bidden by the poet to avoid the way of Slick of Tennessee. The other " lady," though more decently attired, was like women in this wild part of the world generally — cold and disagreeable in manner, full of " proper pride," with a touch-me-not air, which reminded me of a certain

> " Miss Baxter,
> Who refused a man before he axed her."

Her husband was the renowned Slade : —

> " Of gougers fierce, the eyes that pierce, the fiercest gouger he."

His was a noted name for " deadly strife ; " he had the reputation of having killed his three men ; and a few days afterwards the grave that concealed one of his murders was pointed out to me. This pleasant individual " for an evening party" wore the revolver and bowie-knife here, there, and everywhere. He had lately indeed had a strong hint not to forget his weapon. One M. Jules, a French trader, after a quarrel which took place at dinner, walked up to him and fired a pistol, wounding him in the breast. As he rose to run away Jules discharged a second,

which took effect upon his back, and then without giving him
time to arm, fetched a gun and favoured him with a dose of
slugs somewhat larger than revolver bullets.   The fiery Frenchman had two narrow escapes from Lynch-lawyers: twice he
was hung between wagons, and as often he was cut down.   At
last he disappeared in the farther West, and took to lodge and
squaw.   The avenger of blood threatens to follow him up, but
as yet he has taken no steps.

It at once became evident that the station was conducted
upon the principle of the western hotel-keeper of the last generation, and of continental Europe about A.D. 1500—the inn-
keeper of "Anne of Geierstein"—that is to say, for his own convenience ; the public there was the last thing thought of.   One
of our party who had ventured into the kitchen was fiercely
ejected by the "ladies."   In asking about dormitories we were
informed that "lady travellers" were admitted into the house,
but that the ruder sex must sleep where it could—or not sleep
at all if it preferred.   We found a barn outside; it was hardly
fit for a decently brought-up pig; the floor was damp and
knotty ; there was not even a door to keep out the night breeze,
now becoming raw, and several drunken fellows lay in different
parts of it.   Two were in one bunk, embracing maudlingly, and
freely calling for drinks of water.   Into this disreputable hole
we were all thrust for the night · amongst us, it must be remembered, was a federal judge, who had officiated for years as
minister at a European court.   His position, poor man ! procured him nothing but a broken-down pallet.   It was his first
trip to the Far West, and yet, so easily are Americans satisfied,
and so accustomed are they to obey the ridiculous jack-in-office
who claims to be one of the powers that be, he scarcely uttered
a complaint.   I for one grumbled myself to sleep.   May gracious Heaven keep us safe from all "ladies" in future !—better
a hundred times the squaw with her uncleanliness and civility.

We are now about to leave the land of that great and dangerous people, the Sioux, and before bidding adieu to them it will
be advisable to devote a few pages to their ethnology.

CHAP. II.

THE SIOUX OR DAKOTAS.

THE Sioux belong essentially to the savage, in opposition to the Aztecan peoples of the New World. In the days of Major Pike (1805–1807), they were the dread of all the neighbouring tribes, from the confluence of the Mississippi and the Missouri to the Raven River on the latter. According to Lieut. Warren, they are still scattered over an immense territory extending from the Mississippi on the east, to the Black Hills on the west, and from the forks of the Platte on the south, to Minsi Wakan or the Devil's Lake on the north. Early in the winter of 1837, they ceded to the United States all their lands lying east of the Mississippi which became the territory of Minnesota. They are to the North American tribes what the great Anizeh race is amongst the Bedouins of Arabia. Their vernacular name, Dakota, which some pronounce Lakota, and others Nakota, is translated " leagued " or, " allied," and they sometimes speak of themselves as Osheti Shakowin, or the " Seven Council Fires." The French call them " les Coupes-gorges," from their sign or symbol, and the whites generally know them as the Sues or Sioux, from the plural form of Nadonaisi, which in Ojibwe means an enemy. The race is divided into seven principal bands, viz. :

1. Mdewakantonwan (Minowa Kantongs* or Gens du Lac) meaning " village of the Mdewakan,"—Mille Lacs or Spirit Lake. They formerly extended from Prairie du Chien to Prairie des Français, thirty-five miles up the St. Peter's River. They have now moved further west. This tribe, which includes seven bands, is considered the bravest of the Sioux, and has even

* The first is the correct, the second is the old and incorrect form of writing the name.

The Western Swell.   The Sioux.   The old Shoshone.   The Arapaho.   Jake the Shoshone.   The Crow.

INDIANS.

waged an internecine war with the Folles Avoines* or Menomenes, who are reputed the most gallant of the Ojibwes
(Chippeways), and who, inhabiting a country intersected by
lakes, swamps, water-courses, and impenetrable morasses, long
bade defiance to all their neighbours. They have received an-
nuities since 1838, and their number enrolled in 1850 was
2000 souls.

2. Wahpekute (Washpeconte, translated Gens de Feuilles-
tirées, and by others, the "Leaf Shooters"). Their habitation lies westward of the Des Moines, Cannon, and Blue Earth
Rivers. According to Major Pike, they were like the Bedouin
Ghuzw, a band of vagabonds formed of refugees, who for
some bad deed had been expelled their tribes. The meaning
of their name is unknown; in 1850 they numbered 500 or
600 souls.

3. Sisitonwan (Sussitongs, or the Village of the Marsh).
This band used to hunt over the vast prairies lying eastward of
the Mississippi, and up that stream as high as Raven River.
They now plant their corn about Lake Traverse (Lac Travers)
and on the Côteau des Prairies, and numbered in 1850 about
2,500 souls.

4. Wahpetonwans (Washpetongs, Gens des Feuilles, because they lived in woods), the "Village in the Leaves." They
have moved from their old home about the little rapids of the
Minnesota River, to Lac qui Parle, and Big Stone Lake. In

---

* The Folles Avoines are a small tribe esteemed by the whites and respected
by their own race; their hunting grounds are the same as those of the Winnebagos.
They speak a peculiar dialect. But all understand the copious and sonorous
but difficult and complicated Algonquin or Ojibwe—the language of some of the
old New England races, Pequots, Delawares, Mohicans, Abenaki, Narragansetts,
Penobscots, and the tribes about the Lake regions, and the head waters of the
Mississippi, viz. Ottowa, Pottowotomis, Menomene, Kenistenoo or Cree, Sak,
Kikapoo, Maskigo, Shawnee, Miami, Kaskasia, &c. The other great north-
eastern language is that of the Mohawk, spoken by the Oneida, Onondaga, Seneca,
Cayuga, Tuscarora, Wyandot, and Cherokee.

"Folles Avoines" is the Canadian French for the wild rice (*Zizania aquatica*),
a tall tubular reedy water-plant, plentiful on the marshy margins of the northern
lakes, and in the plashy waters of the Upper Mississippi. Its leaves and spikes,
though much larger, resemble those of oats. Millions of migrating water-fowl
fatten on it, before their autumnal flights to the south; while in autumn it furnishes
the northern savages and the Canadian traders and hunters with their annual supply
of grain. It is used for bread by most of the tribes to the north-west.

1850 they numbered 1000 to 1200 souls. They plant corn, have substituted the plough for the hoe, and, according to the missionaries, have made some progress in reading and writing their own language.

The above four constitute the Mississippi and Minnesota Sioux, and are called by those on the Missouri, " Isánti," from Isanati or Isanyati, because they once lived near Isantamde, one of the Mille Lacs. They number, according to Major Pike, 5775 souls, according to Lieut. Warren, about 6200, and many of those on the Mississippi have long since become semi-civilised by contact with the white settlements, and have learned to cultivate the soil.   Others again follow the buffalo in their primitive wildness, and have of late years given much trouble to the settlers of Northern Iowa.

5. Ihanktonwans (Yanctongs, meaning " Village at the End "), also sometimes called Wichiyela, or First Nation. They are found at the mouth of the Big Sioux, between it and the Missouri River, as high up as Fort Lookout, and on the opposite bank of the Missouri.   In 1851, they were set down at 240 lodges = 2400 souls ; they have since increased to 360 lodges and 2880 souls, of whom 576 are warriors.   Distance from the buffalo country has rendered them poor ; the proximity of the pale face has degenerated them, and the United States have purchased most of their lands.

6. Ihanktonwannas (Yanctannas), one of the " end village " bands.   They range between the James and the Missouri Rivers, as far north as Devil's Lake.   The Dakota Mission numbered them at 400 lodges = 4000 souls; subsequent observers at 800 lodges = 6400 souls, and 1280 warriors ; and being spirited and warlike, they give much trouble to settlers in the Dakota territory.   A small portion live in dirt lodges during the summer.   This band suffered severely from small-pox in the winter of 1856–1857.   They are divided into the Hunkpatidans (of unknown signification), Pabakse or Cut-heads, and Kiyuksa, deriders or breakers of law.   From their subtribe the Wazikute, or Pine Shooters, sprang, it is said, the Assiniboin tribe of the Dakotas.   Major Pike divides the " Yanctongs " into two grand divisions, the Yanctongs of the north and the Yanctongs of the south.

7. Titonwan (Teton, " Village of the Prairies "), inhabit-

ing the trans-Missourian prairies, and extending westward to the dividing ridge between the Little Missouri and Powder River, and thence south on a line near the 106° meridian. They constitute more than one half of the whole Dakota nation. In 1850 they were numbered at 1250 lodges = 12,500 souls, but that number was supposed to be over-estimated. They are allied by marriage with the Cheyennes and Arikari, but are enemies of the Pawnees and Crows. The ₌Titonwan, according to Major Pike, are, like the Yanctongs, the most erratic and independent not only of the Sioux, but "of all the Indians in the world." They follow the buffalo as chance directs, clothing themselves with the robes, and making their lodges, saddles, and bridles, of the same material; the flesh of the animal furnishing their food. None but the few families connected with the whites have planted corn. Possessing an innumerable stock of horses, they are here this day and five hundreds of miles off in a week, moving with a rapidity scarcely to be imagined by the inhabitants of the civilised world: they find themselves equally at home in all places. The Titonwan are divided into seven principal bands, viz.:

The Hunkpapa, "they who camp by themselves" (?). They roam from the Big Cheyenne up to the Yellowstone, and west to the Black Hills, and number 365 lodges, 2920 souls, and 584 warriors.

The Sisahapa or Blackfeet live with Hunkpapa, and like them have little reverence for the whites; they number 165 lodges, 1321 souls, and 264 warriors.

The Itazipko, Sans Arc, or "No Bows;" a curious name, —like the Sans Arc Pawnees, they are good archers, — perhaps given to them in olden times, when, like certain tribes of negroes, they used the spear to the exclusion of other weapons: others however translate the word "Bow-pith." They roam over nearly the same lands as the Hunkpapa, number about 170 lodges, 1360 souls, and 272 warriors.

The Minnikanye-wozhipu, "those who plant by the water," dwell between the Black Hills and the Platte. They number about 200 lodges, 1600 inmates, and 320 warriors: they are favourably disposed towards the whites.

The Ogalala or Okandanda are generally to be found on or about the Platte, near Fort Laramie, and are the most friendly of all the Titonwan towards the whites. They number about 460 lodges, 3680 souls, and 736 warriors.

The Sichangu, Brûlés or Burnt Thighs, living on the Niobrara and White-earth Rivers, and ranging from the Platte to the Cheyenne, number about 380 lodges, containing 3680 inmates.

The Oohenonpa "Two Boilings" or " Two Kettle-band," are much scattered amongst other tribes, but are generally to be found in the vicinity of Fort Pierre. They number about 100 lodges, 800 inmates, and 160 warriors.

The author of the above estimate, allotting eight to ten inmates to a lodge, of whom between one-fifth and one-sixth are warriors, makes an ample allowance. It is usual to reckon in a population between one-fourth, one-fifth and one-sixth — according to the work — as capable of bearing arms, but the civilised rule will not apply to the N. A. Indian. The grand total of the number of the Sioux nations, including the Isánti, would amount to 30,200 souls. Half a century ago, it was estimated by Major Pike at 21,675, and in 1850, the Dakota Mission set them down at 25,000. It is the opinion of many that, notwithstanding the ravages of cholera and smallpox, the Dakota nation, except when mingled with the frontier settlements, rather increases than diminishes. It has been observed by missionaries, that whenever an account of births and deaths has been kept in a village the former usually exceed the latter. The original numbers of the Prairie Indians have been greatly over-estimated both by them-selves and by strangers ; the only practicable form of census is the rude proceeding of counting their " Tipi " or skin tents. It is still a moot question how far the Prairie Indians have dimi-nished in numbers, which cannot be decided for some years.*

The Dakotas are mostly a purely hunting tribe in the lowest condition of human society : they have yet to take the first step, and to become a pastoral people. The most civilised are the Mdewakantonwans who, even at the beginning of the present century, built log huts and " stocked" land with corn, beans, and pumpkins. The majority of the bands hunt the buffalo

---

* At the time of the first settlement of the country by the English no certain estimate was made ; at the birth of the thirteen original States, the Indians, according to Dr. Trumbull, did not exceed 150,000. In 1860, the number of Indians within the limits of the United States, was estimated by the Commissioner of Indian Affairs at 350,000.

within their own limits throughout the summer, and in the winter pitch their lodges in the clumps or fringes of tree and underwood along the banks of the lakes and streams. The bark of the cottonwood furnishes fodder for their horses during the snowy season, and to obtain it the creeks and branches have been thinned or entirely denuded of their beautiful groves. They buy many animals from the southern Indians, who have stolen them from New Mexico, or trapped them on the plains below the Rocky Mountains. Considerable numbers are also bred by themselves. The Dakota nation is one of the most warlike and numerous in the U. S. territory. In single combat on horseback they are described as having no superiors; a skill acquired by constant practice, enables them to spear their game at full speed, and the rapidity with which they discharge their arrows, and the accuracy of their aim, rival the shooting which may be made with a revolver. They are not, however, formidable warriors; want of discipline and of confidence in one another render them below their mark. Like the Moroccans in their last war with Spain, they never attack when they should, and they never fail to attack when they should not.

The Dakotas, when first visited by the whites, lived around the head waters of the Mississippi and the Red River of the north. They have gradually migrated towards the west and south-west, guarded by their allies the Cheyennes, who have given names successively to the Cheyenne of Red River, to the Big Cheyenne of the Missouri, and to the section of the country between the Platte and the Arkansas which they now occupy. The Dakota first moved to the land now occupied by the Ojibwe, (anciently known as Chippeways, Orechipewa, or Sauteurs*), which tribe inhabited the land between Sault † St. Marie and Lake Winnepeg, whilst their allies the Crees occupied the country from Lake Winnepeg to the Kisiskadjiwan and Assinniboin Rivers. The plains lying southward of the

---

* The Rev. Peter Jones (Kahkewagquódy) in his history of the Ojibwe Indians makes "Chippeway" a corrupted word, signifying the "Puckered Moccasin People;" the Abbé Domenech ("Seven Years Residence in the Great Deserts of North America"— a mere compilation) draws an unauthorised distinction between Chippeways and Ojibbeways, but cannot say what it is. He explains Ojibwe, the form of Ojidwa, to mean "a singularity in the voice or pronunciation."

† Pronounced "Soo :" the word is old French, still commonly used in Canada and the North, and means rapids.

latter river were the fields of many a fierce and bloody fight between the Dakotas and the other allied two tribes, until a feud caused by jealousy of the women arose amongst the former, and made a division which ended in their becoming irreconcileable enemies, as they are indeed to the present day. The defeated party fled to the craggy precipices of the Lake of the Woods, and received from the Ojibwe the name of Assinniboin or Dakota of the Rocks, by which they are now universally known to the whites. They retain, however, amongst themselves the term Dakota, although their kinsmen universally when speaking of them, called them "hohe" or enemies, and they still speak the Sioux language. After this feud the Assinniboins strengthened themselves by alliance with the Ojibwe and Cree tribes, and drove the Dakota from all the country north of the Cheyenne River, which is now regarded as the boundary line. The three races are still friendly and so hostile to the Dakota that no lasting peace can be made between them; in case of troubles with either party, the Government of the U. S. might economically and effectually employ one against the other. The common war-ground is the region about Lake Minsiwakan, where they all meet when hunting buffalo. The Assinniboin tribe now extends from the Red River westward along the Missouri as far as the mouth of Milk River: a large portion of their lands, like those of the Cree, is British territory. They suffered severely from smallpox in 1856–1857, losing about 1500 of their tribe, and now number about 450 lodges, or 3600 souls. Having comparatively few horses, they rely mainly upon the dog for transportation, and they use its flesh as food.

The Dakota, according to Lieut. Warren, are still numerous, independent, warlike, and powerful, and have the means of prolonging an able resistance to the advance of the western settlers. Under the present policy of the United States Government—this is written by an American—which there is no reason to believe likely to be changed, encroachments will continue, and battle and murder will be the result. There are many inevitable causes at work to produce war with the Dakota before many years.* The conflict will end in the

---

* Lieut. Warren considered the greatest point of his explorations to be the knowledge of the proper routes by which to invade their country and to conquer them. The project may be found in the Report of the Secretary of War. I quote Mr.

discomfiture of the natives, who will then fast fall away. Those dispossessed of their lands cannot, as many suppose, retire further west; the regions lying beyond one tribe are generally occupied by another, with whom deadly animosity exists. Even when the white settlers advance their frontier, the natives linger about till their own poverty and vice consign them to oblivion, and the present policy adopted by the Government is the best that could be devised for their extermination. It is needless to say that many of the Sioux look forward to the destruction of their race with all the feelings of despair with which the civilised man would contemplate the extinction of his nationality. How indeed, poor devils, are they to live when the paleface comes with his pestilent firewater and small-pox, followed up with paper and pen work, to be interpreted under the gentle auspices of fire and steel?

The advance of the settlements is universally acknowledged by the people of the United States to be a political necessity in the national development, and on that ground only is the displacement of the rightful owners of the soil justifiable. But the Government, instead of preparing the way for settlements by wise and just purchases from those in possession, and proper support and protection for the indigent and improvident race thus dispossessed, is sometimes behind its obligations. There are instances of Congress refusing or delaying to ratify the treaties made by its duly authorised agents. The settler and pioneer are thus precipitated into the Indian country, without the savage having received the promised consideration, and he often, in a manner that enlists the sympathies of mankind, takes up the tomahawk and perishes in the attempt. It frequently happens that the western settlers are charged with bringing about these wars; they are now, however, fighting the battles of civilisation exactly as they were fought three centuries ago upon the Atlantic shore, under circumstances that command equal admiration and approval. Whilst, therefore, we sympathise with the savage, we cannot but feel for the unhappy squatter, whose life is sacrificed to the Indian's vengeance by the errors or dilatoriness of those whose duty it is to protect him.

Warren's opinion concerning the future of the Dakotas as a contrast to that of the Dakota Mission. My own view will conclude the case in p. 124.

The people of the United States, of course, know themselves to be invincible by the hands of these half-naked savages. But the Indians, who on their own ground still outnumber the whites, are by no means so convinced of the fact. Until the army of Utah moved westward, many of them had never seen a soldier. At a grand council of the Dakota, in the summer of 1857, on the North Fork of the Platte River, they solemnly pledged themselves to resist the encroachments of the whites, and if necessary to " whip " them out of the country. The appearance of the troops has undoubtedly produced a highly beneficial effect; still, something more is wanted. Similarly in Hindustan, though the natives knew that the British army numbered hundreds of thousands, every petty independent prince thought himself fit to take the field against the intruder, till the failure of the attempt suggested to him some respect for *les gros bataillons.*

The Sioux differ greatly in their habits from the Atlantic tribes of times gone by. The latter lived in wigwams or villages of more stable construction than the lodge, they cultivated the soil, never wandered far from home, made their expeditions on foot, having no horses, and rarely came into action unless they could " tree " themselves. They inflicted horrid tortures on their prisoners, as every English child has read; but, Arab-like, they respected the honour of their female captives. The Prairie tribes are untamed and untamable savages, superior only to the "Arab" hordes of great cities, who appear destined to play in the history of future ages, the part of Goth and Vandal, Scythian, Bedouin, and Turk. Hitherto the *rôle* which these hunters have sustained in the economy of nature has been to prepare, by thinning off its wild animals, a noble portion of the world for the higher race about to succeed them. Captain Mayne Reid somewhere derides the idea of the Indian's progress towards extinction. A cloud of authorities bear witness against him. East of the Mississippi the savage has virtually died out, and few men allow him two prospective centuries of existence in the West, unless he be left, which he will not be, to himself.

" Wolves of women born," the Prairie Indians despise agriculture as the Bedouin does. Merciless free-booters, they delight in roaming; like all equestrian and uncivilised people, they are perfect horsemen, but poor fighters when dismounted, and they are nothing without their weapons. As a rule they rarely torture their prisoners, except when an old man or woman is handed over to the squaws and papooses " pour les amuser," as a Canadian expressed it. Near and west of the Rocky Mountains, however, the Shoshones and the Yutas (Utahs) are as cruel as their limited intellects allow them to be. Moreover, all the prairie tribes never fail to subject women to an ordeal worse than death. The best character given of late years to the Sioux was by a traveller in 1845, who writes that " their freedom and power have imparted to their warriors some gentlemanly qualities; they are cleanly, dignified and graceful in manners, brave, proud, and independent in bearing and deed."

The qualities of the Sioux, and of the Prairie Tribes generally, are little prized by those who have seen much of them. They ignore the very existence of gratitude; the benefits of years cannot win their affections. After boarding and lodging with a white for any length of time, they will steal his clothes; and, after receiving any number of gifts, they will haggle for the value of the merest trifle. They are inveterate thieves and beggars; the Western settlers often pretend not to understand their tongue for fear of exposing themselves to perpetual pilfering and persecution; and even the squaws, who live with the pale faces, annoy their husbands by daily applications for beads and other coveted objects; they are cruel to one another as children. The obstinate revengefulness of their vendetta is proverbial; they hate with the " hate of Hell;" and, like the Highlanders of old, if the author of an injury escape them, they vent their rage upon the innocent, because he is of the same clan or colour. If struck by a white man, they must either kill him or receive damages in the shape of a horse; and after the most trivial injury they can never be trusted. Their punishments are Draconic; for all things death, either by shooting or burning. Their religion is a low form of Fetissism. They place their women in the most degraded position. The squaw is a mere slave, living a life of utter drudgery; and when the poor creature wishes, according to the fashion of her sex, to relieve her feelings by a domestic " scene," followed by a " good cry," or to use her knife upon a sister squaw, as the Trasteverina mother uses her bodkin, the husband, after squatting muffled up, in hope that the breeze will blow over, enforces silence with a cudgel. The warrior, considering the chase an ample share of the labour-curse, is so lazy that he will not rise to saddle or unsaddle his pony: he will sit down and ask a white man to fetch him water, and only laugh if reproved. Like a wild beast he cannot be broken to work: he would rather die than employ himself in honest industry—a mighty contrast to the Negro, whose only happiness is in serving. He invariably attributes an act of kindness, charity, or for-bearance, to fear. Ungenerous, he extols, like the Bedouin, generosity to the skies. He never makes a present, except for the purpose of receiving more than its equivalent; and an "Indian gift" has come to be a proverb, meaning anything reclaimed after being given away. Impulsive as the African, his mind is blown about by storms of unaccountable contradic-tions. Many a white has suddenly seen the scalping-knife restored to its sheath instead of being buried in his flesh; whilst others have been as unexpectedly assaulted and slain by those from whom they expected kindness and hospitality. The women are mostly cold and chaste. The men have vices which cannot be named: their redeeming points are fortitude, and endurance of hardship; moreover, though they care little for their wives, they are inordinately fond of their children. Of their bravery, Indian fighters do not speak highly: they are notoriously deficient in the civilised quality called moral cour-age, and though a brave will fight single-handed stoutly enough, they rarely stand up long in action. They are great at sur-prises, ambuscades, and night attacks: as with the Arabs and Africans, their favourite hour for onslaught is that before dawn, when the enemy is most easily terrified,—they know that there is nothing which tries man's nerve so much as an unexpected night attack,—and when the cattle can be driven off to ad-vantage. In some points their characters have been, it is now granted, greatly misunderstood. Their forced gravity and calm-ness—purely "company manners"—were not suspected to cloak merriment, sociability, and a general fondness of feasts and fun. Their apathy and sternness, which were meant for reserve and dignity among strangers, gave them an air of un-geniality which does not belong to their mental constitutions. Their fortitude and endurance of pain is the result, as in the prize-fighter, of undeveloped brain.

The Sioux are tall men, straight, and well-made: they are never deformed, and are rarely crippled, simply because none but the able-bodied can live. The shoulders are high and somewhat straight; the figure, is the reverse of the sailor's, that is to say, whilst the arms are smooth, feeble, and etiolated, the legs are tolerably muscular; the bones are often crooked or bowed in the equestrian tribes; they walk as if they wanted the ligamentum teres; there is a general looseness of limb, which promises, however, lightness, endurance, and agility, and which, contrasted with the Caucasian race, suggests the gait of a wild compared with that of a tame animal. Like all savages, they are deficient in corporeal strength: a civilised man finds no difficulty in handling them: on this road there is only one Indian (a Shoshone) who can whip a white in a "rough and tumble." The temperament is usually bilious-nervous; the sanguine is rare, the lymphatic rarer, and I never knew or heard of an albino. The hands, especially in the higher tribes, are decidedly delicate, but this is more observable in the male than in the female; the type is rather that of the Hindu than of the African or the European. The feet being more used than the other extremities, and unconfined by boot or shoe, are somewhat splay, spreading out immediately behind the toes, whilst the heel is remarkably narrow. In consequence of being carried straight to the fore,— the only easy position for walking through grass, — they tread, like the anteater, more heavily on the outer than on the inner edge. The sign of the Indian is readily recognised by the least experienced tracker.

It is erroneously said that he who has seen a single Indian has seen them all. Of course there is a great similarity amongst savages and barbarians of the same race and climate. The same pursuits, habits, and customs naturally produce an identity of expression which, as in the case of husband and wife, parent and child, moulds the features into more or less of likeness. On the other hand, a practised eye will distinguish the Indian individually or by bands as easily as the shepherd, by marks invisible to others, can swear to his sheep. I have little doubt that to the savages all white men look alike.

The prairie Indian's hair and complexion have already been described. According to some savages the build of the former differs materially from that of the European and the Asiatic.

The animal development varies in the several races : the Pawnee's and Yuta's scalp-lock rarely exceeds eighteen inches in
length ; while that of the Crow, like the East Indian Jatawala's,
often sweeps the ground.   There are salient characteristics in
the cranium which bear testimony to many phrenological
theories.   The transverse diameter of the rounded skull between
the parietal bones, where Destructiveness and Secretiveness are
placed, is enormous, sometimes exceeding the longitudinal line
from sinciput to occiput, the direct opposite of the African
Negro's organisation.   The region of the cerebellum is deficient
and shrunken, as with the European in his second childhood :
it sensibly denotes that the subject wants " vim."   The coronal
region, where the sentiments are supposed to lie, is rather flat
than arched ; in extreme cases the face seems to occupy two
thirds instead of half the space between poll and chin.   The
low conical forehead recedes, as in Robespierre's head, from
the region of benevolence, and rises high at the apex where
firmness and self-esteem reside : a common formation amongst
wild tribes, as every traveller in Asia and Africa has remarked.   The facial angle of Camper varies, according to phre-
nologists, between 70° and 80°.   The projecting lower brow,
is strong, broad, and massive, showing that development of the
perceptions, which is produced by the constant and minute
observation of a limited number of objects.   The well-known
Indian art of following the trail is one result of this property.
The nose is at once salient and dilated, in fact, partaking of
the Caucasian and African types.   The nostrils are broad and
deeply whorled ; the nasal orifice is wide, and, according to
osteologists, the bones that protect it are arched and expanded ;
the eyebrows are removed, like the beard and moustache, by
vellication, giving a dull and bald look to the face ; the lashes,
however, grow so thickly that they often show a sooty black
line, suggesting the presence of the Oriental Kohl or Surma.
The orbits are large and square : largeness and squareness are,
in fact, the general character of the features : it doubtless produces that peculiar besotted look which belongs to the Indian
as to the Mongolian family.   The conjunctival membrane has
the whiteness and clearness of the European and the Asiatic ;
it is not, as in the African, brown, yellow, or red.   The
pupil, like the hair, is of different shades between black and

brown: when the organ is blue — an accident which leads to a suspicion of mixed blood — the owner generally receives a name from the peculiarity. Travellers, for the most part, describe the organ as " black and piercing, snaky and venomous; " others as " dull and sleepy ;" whilst some detect in its colour a min-gling of black and grey. The only peculiarity which I observed in the pupil was its similarity to that of the gipsy. The Indian first fixes upon you a piercing glance, which seems to look below the surface. After a few seconds, however, the eye glazes as though a film passed over it, and gazes, as it were, on vacancy. The look would at once convict him of Jattatura and Malocchio in Italy, and of El Ayn, or the Evil Eye, in the East. The mouth is at once full and compressed ; it opens widely ; the lips are generally *bordés* or everted, — decidedly the most unpleasant fault which that feature can have,— the corners are drawn down as if by ill temper, and the two seams which spring from the alæ of the nostrils are deeply traced. This formation of the oral, combined with the fullness of the circumoral regions, and the length and fleshiness of the naked upper lip, communicates a peculiar animality to the countenance. The cheek bones are high and bony ; they are not, however, expanded or spread backwards, nor do they, as in the Chinese, alter the appearance of the eyes by making them oblique. The cheeks are rather lank and falling in than full or oval. The whole maxillary organ is projecting and ponderous. The wide condyles of the lower jaw give a remarkable massiveness to the jowl, whilst the chin — perhaps the most characteristic fea-ture — is long, bony, large, and often parted in the centre. The teeth are faultless, full-sized and white, even and regular, strong and lasting ; and they are vertical, not sloping forward like the African's. To sum up, the evanishing of the forehead, the compression of the lips, the breadth and squareness of the jaw and the massiveness of the chin, combine to produce a normal expression of harshness and cruelty, which, heightened by red and black war-paint, locks like horsehair, plumes, and other savage decorations, form a " rouge dragon " whose *tout-ensemble* is truly revolting.

The women when in their teens have often that *beauté du diable,* which may be found even amongst the African negresses ; nothing, however, can be more evanescent. When full grown the figure becomes dumpy and *trapu ;* and the face though sometimes not without a certain comeliness, has a Turanian breadth and flatness.   The best portrait of a sightly Indian woman is that of Pocahontas, the Princess, published by M. Schoolcraft. The drudgery of the tent and field renders the squaw cold and unimpassioned ; and, like the coarsest-minded women in civilised races, her eye and her heart mean one and the same thing. She will administer " squaw medicine," a love philter, to her husband, but rather for the purpose of retaining his protection than his love.   She has all the modesty of a savage, and is not deficient in sense of honour.   She has no objection to a white man, but, Affghan-like, she usually changes her name to " John " or some other alias.   Her demerits are a habit of dunning for presents, and a dislike to the virtue that ranks next to godliness, which nothing but the fear of the rod will subdue. She has literally no belief, not even in the rude Fetissism of her husband, and consequently she has no religious exercises. As she advances in years, she rapidly descends in *physique* and *morale :* there is nothing on earth more fiend-like than the vengeance of a cretin-like old squaw.

The ancient Persians taught their progeny archery, riding, and truth-telling ; the Prairie Indian's curriculum is much the same, only the last of the trio is carefully omitted.   The Indian, like other savages, never tells the truth ; verity is indeed rather an intellectual than an instinctive virtue, which, as children prove, must be taught and made intelligible ; except when "counting his coups," in other words, recounting his triumphs, his life is therefore one system of deceit, the strength of the weak.   Another essential part of education is to close the mouth during sleep : the Indian has a superstition that all disease is produced by inhalation.   The children "born like the wild ass's colts " are systematically spoiled with the view of fostering their audacity ; the celebrated apophthegm of the Wise King — to judge from his notable failure at home, he probably did not practice what he preached — which has caused such an expenditure of birch and cane in higher races, would be treated with contempt by the Indians.   The fond mother when chastening her child never goes beyond dashing a little cold water in its face, — for which reason to besprinkle a man is a mortal insult, — a system which, perhaps, might be naturalised with advantage in some parts of Europe. The son is taught to make his mother toil for him, and openly to disobey his sire; at seven years of age he has thrown off all parental restraint; nothing keeps him in order but the fear of the young warriors. At ten or twelve, he openly rebels against all domestic rule, and does not hesitate to strike his father : the parent then goes off rubbing his hurt, and boasting to his neighbours of the brave boy whom he has begotten.

The religion of the North American Indians has long been a subject of debate. Some see in it traces of Judaism, others of Sabæanism ; M. Schoolcraft detects a degradation of Guebrism. His faith has, it is true, a suspicion of duality; Hormuzd and Ahriman are recognisable in Gitche Manitou and Mujhe Manitou, and the latter, the Bad-god, is naturally more worshipped, because more feared, than the Good-god. Moreover, some tribes show respect for and swear by the sun, and others for fire: there is a north-god and a south-god, a wood-god, a prairie-god, an air-god and a water-god : but — they have not risen to monotheism — there is not one God. None however appear to have that reverence for the elements which is the first article of the Zoroastrian creed; the points of difference are many, whilst those of resemblance are few and feeble, and it is hard to doubt that the instincts of mankind have been pressed by controversialists into the service of argument as traditional tenets.

To judge from books and the conversation of those who best know the Indians, he is distinctly a Fetissist like the African negro, and indeed like all the child-like races of mankind.* The medicine-man is his Mganga, Angekok, sorcerer, prophet, physician, exorciser, priest and rain-doctor; only, as he is rarely a cultivator of the soil, instead of heavy showers and copious crops, he is promised scalps, salmon-trout, and buffalo-beef in plenty. He has the true Fetissist's belief—invariably found in tribes who live dependent upon the powers of Nature — in the younger brothers of the human family, the bestial creation : he holds to a metamorphosis like that of

---

* The reader who cares to consult my studies upon the subject of Fetissism in Africa, where it is and ever has been the national creed, is referred to "The Lake Regions of Central Africa," chap. xix. The modes of belief, and the manners and customs of savage and barbarous races are so similar that a knowledge of the African is an excellent introduction to that of the American.

Abyssinia, and to speaking animals. Every warrior chooses a totem, some quadruped, bird or fish, to which he prays, and which he will on no account kill or eat. Dr. Livingstone shows (chap. i.) that the same custom prevails in its entirety amongst the Kafir Bachwana, and opines that it shows traces of addiction to animal-worship, like the ancient Egyptians; — in the prophecies of Israel the tribes are compared with animals, a true Totemic practice. The word totem also signifies a subclan or subtribe; and some nations, like the African Somal, will not allow marriage in the same totem. The medicine-men give away young children as an atonement, when calamities impend: they go clothed, not in sackcloth and ashes, but in coats of mire, and their macerations and self-inflicted tortures rival those of the Hindus: a fanatic has been known to drag about a buffalo skull with a string cut from his own skin till it is torn away. In spring time the braves and even the boys repairing to lonely places and hill-tops, their faces and bodies being masked, as if in mourning, with mud, fast and pray, and sing rude chants to propitiate the ghosts for days consecutively. The Fetissist is ever grossly superstitious; and the Indians, as might be expected, abound in local rites. Some tribes, as the Cheyennes, will not go to war without a medicine-man, others without sacred war-gourds * containing the tooth of the drum-head fish. Children born with teeth are looked upon as portents, and when grey at birth the phenomenon is attributed to evil ghosts.

I cannot but think that the two main articles of belief which have been set down to the credit of the Indian — namely, the Great Spirit or Creator, and the Happy Hunting-Grounds in a future world — are the results of missionary teaching, the work of Fathers Hennepin, Marquette, and their noble army of martyred Jesuit followers. In later days they served chiefly to inspire the Anglo-American muse, e.g. —

> " By midnight moons o'er moistening dews,
> In vestments for the chase arrayed,
> The hunter still the deer pursues —
> The hunter and the deer, a shade !

---

* This gourd or calabash is the produce of the *Cucurbita lagenaria* or calabash vine. In Spanish, Central and Southern America, Cuba and the West Indies, they use the large round fruit of the *Crescentia cujete*.

And long shall timorous fancy see
  The painted chief and pointed spear,
And Reason's self shall bow the knee
  To shadows and delusions here."

My conviction is, that the English and American's popular ideas
upon the subject are unreliable, and that their embodiment,
beautiful poetry, "Lo the poor Indian," down to "his faith-
ful dog shall bear him company," are but a splendid myth.
The North American aborigine believed, it is true, in an unseen
power, the Manitou, or, as we are obliged to translate it,
"Spirit," residing in every heavenly body, animal, plant, or
other natural object. This is the very essence of that form of
Fetissism which leads to Pantheism and Polytheism. There
was a Manitou, as he conceived, which gave the spark from
the flint, lived in every blade of grass, flowed in the streams,
shone in the stars, and thundered in the waterfall; but in each
example — a notable instance of the want of abstractive and
generalising power — the idea of the Deity was particular and
concrete. When the Jesuit Fathers suggested the unity of the
Great Spirit pervading all beings, it was very readily recognised; but the generalisation was not worked out by the Indian mind. He was, therefore, like all savages, atheistic in
the literal sense of the word. He had not arrived at the first
step, Pantheism, which is so far an improvement that it opens
out a grand idea, the omnipresence, and consequently the
omnipotence, of the Deity. In most North American languages
the Theos is known, not as the "Great Spirit," but as the
"Great Father," a title also applied to the President of the
United States, who is, I believe, though sometimes a step-father,
rather the more reverenced of the twain. With respect to the
happy hunting-grounds, it is a mere corollary of the monotheistic
theorem above proved. It is doubtful whether these savages
ever grasped the idea of a human soul. The Chicury of New
England, indeed, and other native words so anglicised, appear
distinctly to mean the African Pepo — ghost or larva.

Certain missionaries have left us grotesque accounts of the
simple good sense with which the Indians of old received the
Glad Tidings. The strangers were courteously received, the
calumet was passed round, and they were invited to make
known their wants in a "big talk." They did so by producing

a synopsis of their faith, beginning at Adam's apple and ending at the Saviour's cross. The patience of the Indian in enduring long speeches, sermons, and harangues, has ever been exemplary and peculiar as his fortitude in suffering lingering physical tortures. The audience listened with a solemn demeanour, not once interrupting what must have appeared to them a very wild and curious story. Called upon to make some remark these antipomologists simply ejaculated—

" Apples are not wholesome, and those who crucified Christ were bad men ! "

In their turn, some display of oratory was required. They avoided the tedious long drawn style of argument, and spoke, as was their wont, briefly to the point. " It is good of you," said they, " to cross the big water, and to follow the Indian's trail, that ye may relate to us what ye have related. Now listen to what our mothers told us. Our first father, after killing a beast, was roasting a rib before the fire, when a spirit, descending from the skies, sat upon a neighbouring bluff. She was asked to eat. She ate fat meat. Then she arose and silently went her way. From the place where she rested her two hands grew corn and pumpkin; and from the place where she sat sprang tobacco ! "

The missionaries listened to the savage tradition with an excusable disrespect, and, not unnaturally, often interrupted it. This want of patience and dignity, however, drew upon them severe remarks. " Pooh ! " observed the Indians. " When you told us what your mothers told you we gave ear in silence like men. When we tell you what our mothers told us ye give tongue like squaws. Go to ! Ye are no medicine-men, but silly fellows ! "

Besides their superstitious belief in ghosts, spirits, or familiars, and the practice of spells and charms, love-philters, dreams and visions, war-medicine, hunting-medicine, self-torture, and incantations, the Indians had, it appears to me, but three religious observances, viz. dancing, smoking, and scalping.

The war-dances, the corn-dances, the buffalo-dances, the scalp-dances, and the other multiform and solemn saltations of these savages, have been minutely depicted and described by many competent observers. The theme also is beyond the limits of an essay like this.

Smoking is a boon which the Old owes to the New World. It is a heavy call upon our gratitude, for which we have naturally been very ungrateful.

> " Non epulis tantum, non Bacchi pascimur usu,
> Pascimur et fumis, ingeniosa gula est.

We began by calling our new gift, the "holy herb;" it is now, like the Balm of Gilead, entitled, I believe, a weed. Amongst the North American Indians even the spirits smoke; the "Indian Summer" is supposed to arise from the puffs that proceed from the pipe of Nanabozhoo, the Ojibwe Noah. The pipe may have been used in the East before the days of tobacco, but if so it was probably applied to the inhalation of cannabis and other intoxicants.* On the other hand the Indian had no stimulants. He never invented the beer of Osiris, though maize grew abundantly around him†; the Koumiss of the Tartar was beyond his mental reach, and though "Jimsen weed"‡ overruns the land, he neglected its valuable intoxicating properties. His is almost the only race that has ever existed wholly without a stimulant; the fact is a strong proof of its autochthonic origin. It is indeed incredible that man having once learned should ever forget the means of getting drunk. Instead of the social cup the Indian smoked. As tobacco does not grow throughout the continent he invented kinnikinik. This Indian word has many meanings. By

---

* The word tobacco (West Indian, tobago or tobacco, a peculiar pipe) which has spread through Europe, Asia, and Africa, seems to prove the origin of the nicotiana and the non-mention of smoking in the "Arabian Nights" disproves the habit of inhaling any other succedaneum.

† It has long been disputed whether maize was indigenous to America or to Asia; learned names are found on both sides of the question. In Central Africa the cereal is now called as in English, "Indian corn," proving that in that Continent it first was introduced from Hindostan. The Italians have named it Gran' Turco, showing whence it was imported by them. The word maiz, mays, maize or mahiz, is a Carib word introduced by the Spaniards into Europe; in the United States, where "corn" is universally used, maize is intelligible only to the educated.

‡ Properly Jamestown weed, the *Datura stramonium*, the English thorn-apple, unprettily called in the northern States of America "stinkweed." It found its way into the higher latitudes from Jamestown (Virginia), where it was first observed springing on heaps of ballast and other rubbish discharged from vessels. According to Beverly ("Hist. of Virginia;" book ii., quoted by Mr. Bartlett), it is "one of the greatest coolers in the world;" and in some young soldiers who ate plentifully of it as a salad, to pacify the troubles of bacon, the effect was "a very pleasant remedy, for they turned natural fools upon it for several days."

the hunters and settlers it is applied to a mixture of half and half, or two-thirds tobacco and one of red willow bark; others use it for a mixture of tobacco, sumach leaves, and willow rind; others, like Ruxton ("Life in the Far West," p. 116), for the cortex of the willow only. This tree grows abundantly in copses near the streams and water-courses. For smoking, the twigs are cut when the leaves begin to redden. Some tribes, like the Sioux, remove the outer and use only the highly coloured inner bark; others again, like the Shoshones, employ the external as well as the internal cuticle. It is scraped down the twig in curling ringlets, without, however, stripping it off; the stick is then planted in the ground before the fire, and when sufficiently parched, the material is bruised, comminuted, and made ready for use. The taste is pleasant and aromatic, but the effect is that of the puerile rattan, rather than the manly tobacco. The Indian, be it observed, smokes like all savages, by inhaling the fumes into the lungs, and returning them through the nostrils; he finds pure tobacco, therefore, too strong and pungent. As has been said, he is catholic in his habits of smoking; he employs indifferently rose-bark (*Rosa blanda*?)* and the cuticle of a cornus, the lobelia†, the larb, a vaccinium, a Daphne-like plant, and many others. The Indian smokes incessantly, and the "calumet‡" is an important part of his household goods. He has many superstitions about the practice. It is a sacred instrument, and its red colour typifies the smoker's flesh. The Western travellers mention offerings of tobacco to, and smoking of pipes in honour of, the Great Spirit. Some men will vow never to use the pipe in public, others to abstain on particular days. Some will not smoke with their mocassins on, others

* The wild rose is everywhere met with growing in bouquets on the prairies.

† The *lobelia inflata* or Indian tobacco is corrupted by the ignorant Western man to low belia in contradistinction to high belia, better varieties of the plant.

‡ The calumet, a word introduced by the old French, is the red sand-stone pipe, described in a previous page, with a long tube, generally a reed, adorned with feathers. It is the Indian symbol of hatred or amity; there is a calumet of war, as well as a calumet of peace. To accept the calumet is to come to terms; to refuse it is to reject them. The same is expressed by burying and digging up the tomahawk or hatchet. The tomahawk and calumet are sometimes made of one piece of stone; specimens, however, have become very rare since the introduction of the iron axe. The "Song of Hiawatha" (Canto I. The Peace Pipe) and the interesting "Letters and Notes on the Manners, Customs and Conditions of the North American Indians" (vol. ii. p. 160), have made the Red Pipe Stone Quarry familiar to the Englishman.

with steel about their persons; some are pledged to abstain inside, others outside, the wigwam, and many scatter buffalo chip over their tobacco. When beginning to smoke there are certain observances; some, *exempli gratiâ*, direct, after the fashion of Gitche Manitou, the first puff upwards or heaven-wards, the second earthwards, and the third and fourth over the right and left shoulders, probably in propitiation of the ghosts, who are being smoked for in proxy; others, before the process of inhaling, touch the ground with the heel of the pipe-bowl, and turn the stem upwards and averted.

According to those who, like Pennant, derive the North American from the Scythians, scalping is a practice that origi-nated in High and North-Eastern Asia. The words of the Father of History are as follows: — "Of the first enemy a Scythian sends down, he quaffs the blood; he carries the heads of all that he has slain in battle to the king; for when he has brought a head, he is entitled to a share of the booty that may be taken — not otherwise; to skin the head, he makes a circular incision from ear to ear, and then, laying hold of the crown shakes out the skull; after scraping off the flesh with an ox's rib, he rumples it between his hands, and having thus softened the skin makes use of it as a napkin; he appends it to the bridle of the horse he rides, and prides himself on this, for the Scythian that has most of these skin napkins is adjudged the best man, &c. &c. They also use the entire skins as horse-cloths, also the skulls for drinking cups." ("Melpomene," iv. 64, Laurent's Trans.) The underlying idea is doubtless the natural wish to preserve a memorial of a foeman done to death; and at the same time to dishonour his hateful corpse by mutilation. Fashion and tradition regulate the portions of the human frame preferred.

Scalping is generally but falsely supposed to be a peculiarly American practice. The Abbé Em. Domenech ("Seven Years' Residence in the Great Deserts of North America," chap. xxxix.) quotes the *decalvare* of the ancient Germans, the *capillos et cutem detrahere* of the code of the Visigoths, and the annals of Flude, which prove that the "Anglo-Saxons" and the Franks still scalped about A.D. 879. And as the modern Ame-rican practice is traceable to Europe and Asia, so it may be found in Africa, where aught of ferocity is rarely wanting.

" In a short time after our return," says Mr. Duncan (" Travels in Western Africa in 1845 and 1846") " the Apadomey Regiment passed, on their return, in single file, each leading in a string a young male or female slave, carrying also the dried scalp of one man supposed to have been killed in the attack. On all such occasions when a person is killed in battle, the skin is taken from the head and kept as a trophy of valour. It must not be supposed that these female warriors kill according to the number of scalps presented; the scalps are the accumulation of many years. If six or seven men are killed during one year's war it is deemed a great thing; one party always run away in these slave-hunts; but where armies meet the slaughter is great. I counted 700 scalps pass in this manner." But mutilation, like cannibalism, tattooing, and burying in barrows, is so natural under certain circumstances to man's mind that we distinctly require no traditional derivation.

Scalp-taking is a solemn rite. In the good old times braves scrupulously awaited the wounded man's death before they " raised his hair;" in the laxity of modern days, however, this humane custom is too often disregarded. Properly speaking the trophy should be taken after fair fight with a hostile warrior; this also is now neglected. When the Indian sees his enemy fall he draws his scalp-knife — the modern is of iron, formerly it was of flint, obsidian, or other hard stone — and twisting the scalp-lock, which is left long for that purpose, and boastfully braided or decorated with some gaudy ribbon or with the war-eagle's plume, round his left hand, makes with the right two semicircular incisions, with and against the sun, about the part to be removed. The skin is next loosened with the knife point, if there be time to spare and if there be much scalp to be taken. The operator then sits on the ground, places his feet against the subject's shoulders by way of leverage, and holding the scalp-lock with both hands he applies a strain which soon brings off the spoils with a sound which, I am told, is not unlike " flop." Without the long lock it would be difficult to remove the scalp; prudent white travellers, therefore, are careful before setting out through an Indian country to " shingle off" their hair as closely as possible; the Indian moreover hardly cares for a half-fledged scalp. To judge from the long love-locks affected by the hunter and mountaineer, he seems to think lightly of this precaution, to hold it, in fact, a point of honour that the savage should have a fair chance. A few cunning men have surprised their adversaries with wigs. The operation of scalping must be exceedingly painful; the sufferer turns, wriggles, and "squirms" upon the ground like a scotched snake. It is supposed to induce brain fever; many instances, however, are known of men and even women recovering from it, as the former do from a more dreadful infliction in Abyssinia and Galla-land; cases are of course rare, as a disabling wound is generally inflicted before the bloodier work is done.

After taking the scalp, the Indian warrior—proud as if he had won a *médaille de sauvetage*—prepares for return to his village. He lingers outside for a few days, and then, after painting his hands and face lamp-black, appears slowly and silently before his lodge. There he squats for awhile; his relatives and friends, accompanied by the elders of the tribe, sit with him dumb as himself. Presently the question is put; it is answered with truth, although these warriors at other times will lie like Cretans. The "coup" is recounted, however, with abundant glorification; the Indians, like the Greek and Arab of their classical ages, are allowed to vent their self-esteem on such occasions without blame, and to enjoy a treat for which the civilised modern hero longs ardently, but in vain. Finally the "green scalp," after being dried and mounted, is consecrated by the solemn dance, and becomes then fit for public exhibition. Some tribes attach it to a long pole used as a standard, and others their horses' bridles, others to their targes, whilst others ornament with its fringes the outer seams of their leggings: in fact, its uses are many. The more scalps the more honour; the young man who cannot boast of a single murder or show the coveted trophy is held in such scant esteem as the English gentleman who contents himself with being passing rich on a hundred pounds a year. Some great war chiefs have collected a heap of these honourable spoils. It must be remembered by "curio" hunters that only one scalp can come off one head: namely, the centre lock or long tuft growing upon the coronal apex, with about three inches in diameter of skin. This knowledge is the more needful as the western men are in the habit of manufacturing half a dozen cut from different parts of the same head; they sell readily for $50 each, but the transaction is not considered reputable. The connoisseur, however, readily distinguishes the real article from "false scalping" by the unusual thickness of the cutis, which is more like that of a donkey than of a man. Set in a plain gold circlet it makes a very pretty brooch. Moreover each tribe has its own fashion of scalping derived from its forefathers. The Sioux, for instance, when they have leisure to perform the operation, remove the whole head-skin, including a portion of the ears; they then sit down and dispose the ears upon the horns of a buffalo skull, and a bit of the flesh upon little heaps of earth or clay, disposed in quincunx, apparently as an offering to the manes of their ancestors, and they smoke ceremoniously, begging the Manitou to send them plenty more. The trophy is then stretched upon a willow twig bent into an oval shape, and lined with two semi-ovals of black or blue and scarlet cloth. The Yutas and the Prairie tribes generally, when pressed for time, merely take off the poll skin that grows the long tuft of hair, while the Chyuagara or Nez Percés prefer a long strip about two inches wide, extending from the nape to the commissure of the hair and forehead. The fingers of the slain are often reserved for sévignés and necklaces. Indians are aware of the aversion with which the pale faces regard this barbarity. Near Alkali Lake, where there was a large Dakota "Tipi" or encampment of Sioux, I tried to induce a tribesman to go through the imitative process before me; he refused with a gesture indignantly repudiating the practice. A glass of whiskey would doubtless have changed his mind, but I was unwilling to break through the wholesome law that prohibits it.

It is not wonderful that the modern missionary should be unable to influence such a brain as the Prairie Indian's. The old propagandists, Jesuits and Franciscans, became medicinemen: like the great fraternity in India, they succeeded by the points of resemblance which the savages remarked in their observances, such as their images and rosaries, which would be regarded as totems, and their fastings and prayers, which were of course supposed to be spells and charms. Their successors have succeeded about as well with the Indian as with the African; the settled tribes have given ear to them, the Prairie wanderers have not; and the Europeanisation of the Indian generally is hopeless as the Christianisation of the Hindu. The missionaries usually live under the shadow of the different agencies, and even they own that nothing can be done with the children unless removed from the parental influence. I do not believe that an Indian of the plains ever became a Christian. He must first be humanised, then civilised, and lastly Christianised; and, as has been said before, I doubt his surviving the operation.

As might be expected of the Indian's creed, it has few rites and ceremonies; circumcision is unknown, and it ignores the complicated observances which, in the case of the Hindu Pantheist, and in many African tribes, wait upon gestation, parturition and allactation. The child is seldom named.* There are but five words given in regular order to distinguish one from another. There are no family names. The men, after notable exploits, are entitled by their tribes to assume the titles of the distinguished dead, and each fresh deed brings a new distinction. Some of the names are poetical enough, the "Black Night," for instance, the "Breaker of Arrows," or the "War Eagle's Wing;" others are coarse and ridiculous, such as "Squash-head," "Bull's-tail," "Dirty-saddle," and "Steam from a Cow's Belly;" not a few bear a whimsical likeness to those of the African negroes, as "His Great Fire," "The Water Goes in the Path," and "Buffalo Chips"—the "Mavi yá Guombe" of Unyamwezi. The son of a chief succeeding his father usually assumes his name, so that the little dynasty, like that of the Pharaohs, the Romuli, or the Numas, is perpetuated. The women are not unfrequently called after the parts and properties of some admired or valued animal, as the White Martin, the Young Mink †, or the Muskrat's Paw. In the north there have been men with as many as seven wives, all "Martins." The Prairie Indians form the names of the women like those of men, adding the feminine suffix, as Cloud-woman, Red-earth-woman, Black-day-woman. The white stranger is ever offending Indian

---

* The Ojibwe and other races have the ceremony of a burnt offering when the name is given.

† Putorius vison, a pretty dark-chesnut-coloured animal of the weasel kind, which burrows in the banks of streams near mills and farmhouses, where it preys upon the poultry like the rest of the family. It swims well and can dive for a long time. Its food is small fish, mussels, and insects, but it will also devour rats and mice.

etiquette by asking the savage "What's your name?"—the person asked looks aside for a friend to assist him; he has learned in boyhood that some misfortune will happen to him if he discloses his name. Even husbands and wives never mention each other's names. The same practice prevails in many parts of Asia.

Marriage is a simple affair with them. In some tribes the bride, as amongst the Australians, is carried off by force. In others the man who wants a wife courts her with a little present, and pickets near the father's lodge the number of horses which he supposes to be her equivalent. As amongst all savage tribes the daughter is a chattel, an item of her father's goods, and he will not part with her except for a consideration. The men are of course polygamists; they prefer to marry sisters, because the tent is more quiet, and much upon the principle with which marriage with a deceased wife's sister is advocated in England. The women, like the Africans, are not a little addicted to suicide. Before espousal the conduct of the weaker sex in many tribes is far from irreproachable. The "bundling" of Wales and of New England in a former day* is not unknown to them, and many think little of that *prægustatio matrimonii* which, in the eastern parts of the New World, goes by the name of Fanny Wrightism and Free-loveism. Several tribes make trial, like the Highlanders before the reign of James the Fifth, of their wives for a certain time—a kind of "hand-fasting," which is to Morality what Fetissism is to Faith. There are few nations in the world amongst whom this practice, originating in a natural desire not to "make a leap in the dark," cannot be traced. Yet after marriage they will live like

---

* Traces of this ancient practice may be found in the four quarters of the globe. Mr. Bartlett in his instructive volume quotes the Rev. Samuel Pike ("General History of Connecticut," London, 1781), who quaintly remarks: "Notwithstanding the great modesty of the females is such that it would be accounted the greatest rudeness for a gentleman to speak before a lady of a garter or a leg, yet it is thought but a piece of civility to ask her to *bundle*." The learned and pious historian endeavoured to prove that bundling was not only a Christian, but a very polite and prudent practice. So the Rev. Andrew Barnaby, who travelled in New England in 1759-60, thinks that though bundling may "at first appear the effect of grossness of character, it will, upon deeper research, be found to proceed from simplicity and innocence."

the Spartan matrons a life of austerity in relation to the other sex. In cases of divorce, the children, being property, are divided, and in most tribes the wife claims the odd one. If the mother takes any care to preserve her daughter's virtue it is only out of regard to its market value. In some tribes the injured husband displays all the philosophy of Cato and Socrates. In others the wife is punished, like the native of Hindostan, by cutting, or more generally by biting off, the nose-tip. Some slay the wife's lover; others accept a pecuniary compensation for their dishonour, and take as damages skins or horses. Elopement, as amongst the Arabs, prevails in places. The difference of conduct on the part of the women of course depends upon the bearing of the men. "There is no adulteress without an adulterer"—meaning that the husband is ever the first to be unfaithful—is a saying as old as the days of Mohammed. Amongst the Arapahos, for instance, there is great looseness; the Cheyennes on the contrary are notably correct. Truth demands one unpleasant confession, viz. on the whole chastity is little esteemed amongst those Indians who have been corrupted by intercourse with whites.

The dignity of chief denotes in the Indian language a royal title. It is hereditary as a rule, but men of low birth sometimes attain it by winning a name as warriors or medicine-men. When there are many sons it often happens that each takes command of a small clan. Personal prowess is a necessity in Sagamore and Sachem : an old man therefore often abdicates in favour of his more vigorous son, to whom he acts as guide and counsellor. There is one chief to every band, with several sub-chiefs. The power possessed by the ruler depends upon his individual character, and the greater or lesser capacity for discipline in his subjects. Some are obeyed grudgingly, as the Shaykh of a Bedouin tribe. Others are absolute monarchs, who dispose of the lives and properties of their followers without exciting a murmur. The counteracting element to despotism resides in the sub-chief and in the council of warriors, who obstinately insist upon having a voice in making laws, raising subsidies, declaring wars and ratifying peace.

Their life is of course simple : they have no regular hours for meals or sleep. Before eating they sometimes make a heave-

offering of a bit of food towards the heavens, where their forefathers are, and a second towards Earth, the mother of all
things: the pieces are then burned.   They are not cannibals,
except when a warrior after slaying a foe, eats, porcupine-like,
the heart or liver, with the idea of increasing his own courage.
The women rarely sit at meals with the men.   In savage and
semi-barbarous societies the separation of the sexes is the
general rule, because, as they have no ideas in common, each
prefers the society of its own.   They are fond of adoption and
of making brotherhoods, like the Africans, and so strong is the
tie that marriage with the sister of an adopted brother, is
within the prohibited degrees.   Gambling is a passion with
them: they play at cards, an art probably learnt from the
Canadians, and the game is that called in the States "match-
ing" on the principle of dominoes or beggar-my-neighbour.
When excited they ejaculate: Will! Will!—sharp and staccato—
it is possibly a conception of the English well!   But it often
comes out in the place of bad, as the Sepoy orderly in India,
reports to his captain " Ramnak Jamnak dead, Joti Prasad
very sick — all vell!"   The savages win and lose with the stoic-
ism habitual to them, rarely drawing the " navajon," like the
Mexican " lepero," over a disputed point; and when a man has
lost his last rag, he rises in nude dignity and goes home.   Their
language ignores the violent and offensive abuse of parents and
female relatives, which distinguishes the Asiatic and the African
from the European Billingsgate: the worst epithets that can be
applied to a man, are miser, coward, dog, woman.   With them
good temper is good breeding — a mark of gentle blood.   A
brave will stand up and harangue his enemies, exulting how he
scalped their sires and squaws and sons, without calling forth a
grunt of irritation.   Ceremony and manners, in our sense of the
word, they have none, and they lack the profusion of saluta-
tions which usually distinguishes barbarians.   An Indian ap-
pearing at your door, rarely has the civility to wait till
beckoned in: he enters the house, with his quiet catlike gait and
his imperturbable countenance, saying, if a Sioux: " How!" or
"How! How!" meaning Well? shakes hands, to which he expects
the same reply, if he has learned " paddling with the palms "
from the whites,— this however, is only expected by the chiefs
and braves,—and squats upon his hams in the Eastern way, I

had almost said the natural way, but to man, unlike all other animals, every way is equally natural, the chair or the seat upon the ground. He accepts a pipe, if offered to him, devours what you set before him — those best acquainted with the savage, however, avoid all unnecessary civility or generosity: Milesian-like he considers a benefit his due, and if withheld, he looks upon his benefactor as a "mean man,"— talks or smokes as long as he pleases, and then rising stalks off without a word. His ideas of time are primitive. The hour is denoted by pointing out the position of the sun; the days, or rather the nights, are reckoned by sleeps; there are no weeks; the moons, which are literally new, the old being nibbled away by mice, form the months, and suns do duty for years. He has, like the Bedouin and the Esquimaux, sufficient knowledge of the heavenly bodies, to steer his course over the pathless Sage-sea. Night-work, however, is no favourite with him except in cases of absolute necessity. Counting is done upon man's first abacus, the fingers, and it rarely extends beyond ten. The value of an article was formerly determined by beads and buffaloes: dollars however, are now beginning to be generally known.

The only arts of the Indians are medicine and the use of arms. They are great in the knowledge of simples and tisanes. The leaves of the white willow are the favourite emetic; wounds are dressed with astringent herbs, and inflammations are reduced by scarification and the actual cautery. Amongst some tribes, the Hammam or Turkish bath is invariably the appendage to a village. It is an oven sunk in the earth, with room for about a score of persons, and a domed roof of tamped and timber-propped earth,—often mistaken for a bulge in the ground,—pierced with a little square window for ventilation when not in use. A fire is kindled in the centre, and the patient, after excluding the air, sits quietly in this rude calidarium till half roasted and stifled by the heat and smoke. Finally, like the Russian peasant, he plunges into the burn that runs hard by and feels his ailments dropping off him with the dead cuticle. The Indians associating with the horse have learned a rude farriery which often succeeds where politer practice would fail. I heard of one who cured the bites of rattlesnakes and copperheads by scarifying the wounded beast's face, plastering the place with damped gunpowder paste and setting it on fire.

Amongst the prairie tribes are now to be found individuals
provided not only with the old muskets formerly supplied to
them, but with Yäges*, Sharp's breechloaders, alias "Beechers'
Bibles," Colt's revolvers, and other really good fire-arms.   Their
shooting has improved with their tools: many of them are now
able to " draw a bead " with coolness and certainty.   Those who
cannot afford shooting-irons, content themselves with their
ancient weapons, the lance and bow.   The former is a poor
affair, a mere iron spike from two to three inches long, inserted
into the end of a staff about as thick as a Hindostani's bamboo
lance; it is whipped round with sinew for strength, decorated
with a few bunches of gaudy feathers, and defended with the
usual medicine bag.   The bow varies in dimensions with the
different tribes.   On the prairies, for convenient use on horseback, it seldom exceeds three feet in length : amongst the
Southern Indians its size doubles, and in parts of South America
it is like that of the Andamans, a gigantic weapon with an
arrow six feet long, and drawn by bringing the aid of the feet
to the hands.   The best bows amongst the Sioux and Yutas are
of horn, hickory being unprocurable; an inferior sort is
made of a reddish wood, in hue and grain not unlike that called
" mountain mahogany."   A strip of raw hide is fitted to the
back for increase of elasticity, and the string is a line of twisted
sinew.   When not wanted for use the weapon is carried in a skin
case slung over the shoulder.   It is drawn with the two forefingers
— not with the forefinger and thumb, as in the East — and generally the third or ring finger is extended along the string to
give additional purchase.   Savage tribes do little in the way of
handicraft, but that little they do patiently, slowly, and therefore well.   The bow and arrow are admirably adapted to their
purpose.   The latter is either a reed or a bit of arrow-wood
(*Viburnum dentatum*) whose long, straight, and tough stems are
used by the fletcher from the Mississippi to the Pacific.   The
piles are triangles of iron, agate, flint, chalcedony, opal, or other
hard stone : for war purposes they are barbed, and bird-bolts
tipped with hard wood are used for killing small game.   Some
tribes poison their shafts : the material is the juice of a buffalo's,
or an antelope's liver when it has become green and decomposed

---

* An antiquated sort of German rifle, formerly used by the Federal troops.

after the bite of a rattlesnake: at least this is the account which all the hunters and mountaineers give of it. They have also, I believe, vegetable poisons. The feathers are three in number; those preferred are the hawk's and the raven's; and some tribes glue, whilst others whip, them on with tendon-thread. The stele is invariably indented from the feathers to the tip with a shallow spiral furrow: this vermiculation is intended, according to the traders, to hasten death by letting air into or letting blood out of the wound. It is probably the remnant of some superstition now obsolete, for every man does it, whilst no man explain why or wherefore. If the Indian works well, he does not work quickly; he will expend upon half a dozen arrows as many months. Each tribe has its own mark; the Pawnees, for instance, make a bulge below the notch. Individuals also have private signs which enable them to claim a disputed scalp or buffalo-robe. In battle or chase the arrows are held in the left hand and are served out to the right with such rapidity that one long string of them seems to be cleaving the air. A good Sioux archer will, it is said, discharge nine arrows upwards before the first has fallen to the ground. He will transfix a bison and find his shaft upon the earth on the other side; and he shows his dexterity by discharging the arrow up to its middle in the quarry and by withdrawing it before the animal falls. Tales are told of a single warrior killing several soldiers, and as a rule, at short distances, the bow is considered by the whites a more effectual weapon than the gun. It is related that when the Sioux first felt the effects of Colt's revolver, the weapon, after two shots, happened to slip from the owner's grasp; when he recovered it and fired a third time all fled, declaring that a white was shooting them with buffalo chips. Wonderful tales are told of the Indians' accuracy with the bow: they hold it no great feat to put the arrow into a key-hole at the distance of forty paces. It is true that I never saw anything surprising in their performances, but the savage will not take the trouble to waste his skill without an object.

The Sioux tongue, like the Pawnee, is easily learnt: government officials and settlers acquire it as the Anglo-Indian does Hindostani. They are assisted by the excellent grammar and dictionary of the Dakota language, collated by the members of the Dakota Mission, edited by the Rev. S. R. Riggs, M.A., and accepted for publication by the Smithsonian Institution, December 1851.   The Dakota-English part contains about 16,000 words, and the bibliography (spelling-books, tracts and translations) numbered ten years ago eighteen small volumes.   The work is compiled in a scholar-like manner.   The orthography, though rather complicated, is intelligible, and is a great improvement upon the old and unartistic way of writing the polysynthetic Indian tongues, syllable by syllable, as though they were monosyllabic Chinese ; the superfluous h (as Dakota$h$ for Dakota), by which the broad sound of the terminal a is denoted, has been justly cast out.   The peculiar letters ch, p, and t, are denoted by a dot beneath the simple sound; similarly the k (or Arabic kaf), the gh (the Semitic $ghain$) and the kh ($khá$), which, as has happened in Franco-Arabic grammars, was usually expressed by an R.   An apostrophe ($s'a$) denotes the hiatus, which is similar to the Arab's hamzah.

Vater long ago remarked that the only languages which had a character, if not similar, at any rate analogous to the American, are the Basque and the Congo, that is the South African or Kafir family.   This is the case in many points : in Dakota, for instance, as in Kisawahili, almost every word ends in a pure or a nasalised vowel.   But the striking novelty of the African tongues, the inflexion of words by an initial, not, as with us, by a terminal change and the complex system of euphony, does not appear in the American, which in its turn possesses a dual unknown to the African.   The Dakota, like the Kafir, has no gender, it uses the personal and impersonal, which is an older distinction in language.   It follows the primitive and natural arrangement of speech : it says, for instance, " aguyapi maku ye," bread to me give; as in Hindostani, to quote no other, "roti hamko do."   So in logical argument it begins with the conclusion and proceeds to the premisses, which renders it difficult for a European to think in Dakota.   Like other American tongues, it is polysynthetic, which appears to be the effect of arrested development.   Human speech begins with inorganic sounds, which represent symbolism by means of arrows pointed in a certain direction, bent trees, crossed rods and other similar contrivances.   Its first step is monosyllabic, which corresponds with the pictograph, the earliest attempt at writing amongst the uncivilised.* The next advance is polysynthesis, which is apparently built upon monosyllabism, as the idiograph of the Chinese upon a picture or glyph. The last step is the syllabic and inflected, corresponding with the Phœnico-Arabian alphabet, which gave rise to the Greek, the Latin, and their descendants. The complexity of Dakota grammar is another illustration of the phenomenon that man in most things, in language especially, begins with the most difficult and works on towards the facile. Savages, who have no mental exercise but the cultivation of speech, and semi-barbarous people, who still retain the habit, employ complicated and highly elaborate tongues, e.g. Arabic, Sanskrit, Latin, Greek, Kafir, and Anglo-Saxon. With time these become more simple; the *modus operandi* appears to be admixture of race.

The Dakotas have a sacred language, used by medicine-men, and rendered unintelligible to the vulgar, by words borrowed from other Indian dialects, and by synonyms, e.g. biped for man, quadruped for wolf. A chief, asking for an ox or cow, calls it a dog, and a horse, moccasins: possibly, like Orientals, he superstitiously avoids direct mention and speaks of the object wanted by a humbler name. Poetry is hardly required in a language so highly figurative: a hi-hi-hi-hi-hi occasionally interrupted by a few words composes their songs. The Rev. Mr. Pond gives the following specimen of " Blackboy's " Mourning Song for his Grandson, addressed to those of Ghostland:

> Friend, pause, and look this way;
> Friend, pause, and look this way;
> Friend, pause, and look this way;
> Say ye:
> A grandson of Blackboy is coming.

Their speech is sometimes metaphorical to an extent which conveys an opposite meaning: " Friend, thou art a fool: thou hast let the Ojibwe strike thee," is the highest form of eulogy to a brave who has killed and scalped a foe; possibly a Malocchio-like fear, the dread of praise, which, according to Pliny, kills in India, underlies the habit.

The funerals differ in every tribe: the Sioux expose their

---

* A Kafir girl wishing to give a hint to a friend of mine drew a setting sun, a tree, and two figures standing under it; intelligible enough, yet the Kafirs ignore a syllabarium.

dead, wrapped in blankets or buffalo robes upon tall poles —
a custom that reminds us of the Parsee's " Tower of Silence."
The Yutas make their graves high up the kanyons, usually in
clefts of rock.   Some bury the dead at full length ; others
sitting or doubled up ; others on horseback, with a barrow or tumulus of earth heaped up over their remains.   The
absence of graveyards in an Indian country is remarkable as in
the African interior; thinness of population and the savage's
instinctive dislike to any *memento mori* are the causes.   After
deaths the " keening " is long, loud, and lasting : the women and
often the men, cut their hair close, not allowing it to fall below
the shoulders, and not unfrequently gash themselves and ampu-
tate one or more fingers. The dead man, especially a chief, is in
almost all tribes provided with a viaticum, dead or alive, of squaws
and boys — generally those taken from another tribe — horses
and dogs ; his lodge is burned, his arms, cooking utensils, saddles
and other accoutrements are buried with him, and a goodly store
of buffalo meat or other provision is placed by his side, that his
ghost may want nothing which it enjoyed in the flesh.   Like all
savages, the Indian is unable to separate the idea of man's im-
material spirit from man's material wants : an impalpable and invisible form of matter,—called " spirit " because it is not cognis-
able to the senses, which are the only avenues of all knowledge,—
is as unintelligible to them as to a Latter Day Saint, or, indeed,
as to the mind of man generally.   Hence the Indian's smoking
and offerings over the graves of friends.   Some tribes mourn on
the same day of each moon till grief is satisfied ; others for a
week after the death.

A remarkable characteristic of the Prairie Indian is his habit
of speaking, like the deaf and dumb, with his fingers.   The pantomime is a system of signs, some conventional, others instinctive or imitative, which enables tribes who have no acquaintance with each other's customs and tongues to hold limited but
sufficient communication.   An interpreter who knows all the
signs, which, however, are so numerous and complicated, that to
acquire them is the labour of years, is preferred by the whites
even to a good speaker.   Some writers, as Captain H. Stansbury,
consider the system purely arbitrary ; others, Captain Marcy, for
instance, hold it to be a natural language similar to the gestures
which surd-mutes use spontaneously.   Both views are true, but

not wholly true : as the following pages will, I believe, prove, the pantomimic vocabulary is neither quite conventional nor the reverse.

The sign-system doubtless arose from the necessity of a communicating medium between races speaking many different dialects, and debarred by circumstances from social intercourse. Its area is extensive : it prevails amongst many of the Prairie tribes, as the Hapsaroke, or Crows, the Dakota, the Cheyenne and the Shoshone, the Pawnees, Yutas, and Shoshoko or Diggers, being vagrants and outcasts, have lost or never had the habit. Those natives who, like the Arapahos, possess a very scanty vocabulary, pronounced in a quasi-unintelligible way, can hardly converse with one another in the dark : to make a stranger understand them they must always repair to the camp fire for " pow-wow." A story is told of a man, who, being sent amongst the Cheyennes to qualify himself for interpreting, returned in a week, and proved his competence : all that he did, however, was to go through the usual pantomime with a running accompaniment of grunts. I have attempted to describe a few of the simpler signs : the reader, however, will readily perceive that without diagrams the explanation is very imperfect, and that in half an hour, with an Indian or an interpreter, he would learn more than by a hundred pages of print.

The first lesson is to distinguish the signs of the different tribes, and it will be observed that the French voyageurs and traders have often named the Indian nations from their totemic or masonic gestures.

The Pawnees (Les Loups) imitate a wolf's ears with the two forefingers — the right hand is always understood unless otherwise specified * — extended together, upright, on the left side of the head.

The Arapahos, or Dirty Noses, rub the right side of that organ with the forefinger : some call this bad tribe the Smellers, and make their sign to consist of seizing the nose with the thumb and forefinger.

The Comanches (Les Serpents) imitate by the waving of the hand or forefinger the fo. ward crawling motion of a snake.

The Cheyennes, Paikanavos, or Cut Wrists, draw the lower

---

* The left, as a rule, denotes inversion or contradiction.

edge of the hand across the left arm as if gashing it with a knife.

The Sioux (Les Coupe-gorges), by drawing the lower edge of the hand across the throat: it is a gesture not unknown to us, but forms a truly ominous salutation considering those by whom it is practised ; hence the Sioux are called by the Yutas, Pámpe Chyimina, or Hand-cutters.

The Hapsaroke (Les Corbeaux), by imitating the flapping of the birds' wings with the two hands — palms downwards — brought close to the shoulders.

The Kiowas or Prairie-men, make the signs of the prairie, and of drinking water. These will presently be described.

The Yutas, "they who live on mountains," have a compli- cated sign which denotes "living in mountains ;" these will be explained under " sit " and " mountains."

The Blackfeet, called by the Yutas, Paike or Goers, pass the right hand, bent spoon fashion, from the heel to the little toe of the right foot.

The following are a few preliminaries, indispensable to the prairie traveller :—

Halt ! — Raise the hand, with the palm in front, and push it backward and forwards several times — a gesture well known in the East.

I don't know you !— Move the raised hand, with the palm in front, slowly to the right and left.

I am angry !— Close the fist, place it against the forehead, and turn it to and fro in that position.

Are you friendly ?— Raise both hands, grasped, as if in the act of shaking hands, or lock the two forefingers together while the hands are raised.

These signs will be found useful upon the prairie in case of meeting a suspected band. The Indians, like the Bedouin and N. African Moslem, do honour to strangers and guests by putting their horses to speed, couching their lances and other pecu- liarities which would readily be dispensed with by gentlemen of peaceful pursuits and shaky nerves. If friendly, the band will halt when the hint is given and return the salute : if surly, they will disregard the command to stop, and probably will make the sign of anger. Then — ware scalp !

Come !—Beckon with the forefinger, as in Europe, not as is done in the East.

Come back !—Beckon in the European way, and draw the forefinger towards yourself.

Go !—Move both hands edgeways (the palms fronting the breast) towards the left with a rocking-horse motion.

Sit !—Make a motion towards the ground, as if to pound it with the ferient of the closed hand.

Lie down!—Point to the ground and make a motion as if of lying down.

Sleep !—Ditto, closing the eyes.

Look !—Touch the right eye with the index and point it outwards.

Hear ! Tap the right ear with the index tip.

Colours are expressed by a comparison with some object in sight. Many things, as the blowing of wind, the cries of beasts and birds, and the roaring of the sea are imitated by sound.

See !—Strike out the two forefingers forward from the eyes.

Smell !—Touch the nose tip. A bad smell is expressed by the same sign, ejaculating at the same time " pooh !" and making the sign of bad.

Taste !—Touch the tongue tip.

Eat ! Imitate the action of conveying food with the fingers to the mouth.

Drink ! – Scoop up with the hand imaginary water into the mouth.

Smoke !—With the crooked index describe a pipe in the air, beginning at the lips ; then wave the open hand from the mouth to imitate curls of smoke.

Speak !—Extend the open hand from the chin.

Fight !—Make a motion with both fists to and fro, like a pugilist of the eighteenth century who preferred a high guard.

Kill !—Smite the sinister palm earthwards with the dexter fist sharply, in sign of " going down ;" or strike out with the dexter fist towards the ground, meaning to " shut down ;" or pass the dexter index under the left forefinger, meaning to " go under."

To show that fighting is actually taking place, make the gestures as above described : tap the lips with the palm like an Oriental woman when " keening," screaming the while O-a! O-a! to imitate the war song.

Wash !—Rub the hand as with invisible soap in imperceptible water.

Think !—Pass the forefinger sharply across the breast from right to left.

Hide !—Place the hand inside the clothing of the left breast. This means also to put away or to keep secret. To express "I won't say," make the signs of "I" and "no" (which see) and hide the hand as above directed.

Love !—Fold the hands crosswise over the breast, as if embracing the object, assuming at the same time a look expressing the desire to carry out the operation. This gesture will be understood by the dullest squaw.

Tell truth !—Extend the forefinger from the mouth ("one word").

Tell lie !—Extend the two first fingers from the mouth ("double tongue," a significant gesture).

Steal !—Seize an imaginary object with the right hand from under the left fist. To express horse-stealing they saw with the right hand down upon the extended fingers of the left, thereby denoting rope-cutting.

Trade or exchange !—Cross the forefingers of both hands before the breast—"diamond cut diamond."

This sign also denotes the Americans, and indeed any white men, who are generically called by the Indians west of the Rocky Mountains "Shwop," from our swap or swop, an English Romany word for barter or exchange.

The pronouns are expressed by pointing to the person designated. For "I," touch the nose-tip, or otherwise indicate self with the index. The second and third persons are similarly made known.

Every animal has its precise sign, and the choice of gesture is sometimes very ingenious. If the symbol be not known, the form may be drawn on the ground, and the strong perceptive faculties of the savage enable him easily to recognise even rough draughts. A cow or a sheep denotes white men, as if they were their totems. The Indian's high development of locality also enables him to map the features of a country readily and correctly upon the sand. Moreover, almost every grand feature has a highly significant name, Flintwater, for instance, and nothing is easier than to combine the signs.

The *bear* is expressed by passing the hand before the face to mean ugliness, at the same time grinning and extending the fingers like claws.

The *buffalo* is known by raising the forefingers crooked inwards, in the semblance of horns on both sides of the head.

The *elk* is signified by simultaneously raising both hands with the fingers extended on both sides of the head to imitate palmated horns.

For the *deer*, extend the thumbs and the two forefingers of each hand on each side of the head.

For the *antelope*, extend the thumbs and forefingers along the sides of the head to simulate ears and horns.

Mountain sheep are denoted by placing the hands on a level with the ears, the palms facing backwards and the fingers slightly reversed to imitate the ammonite-shaped horns.

For the *beaver*, describe a parenthesis, *e. g.* ( ) with the thumb and index of both hands, and then with the dexter index imitate the wagging of the tail.

The *dog* is shown by drawing the two forefingers slightly opened horizontally across the breast, from right to left. This is a highly appropriate and traditional gesture: before the introduction of horses, the dog was taught to carry the tent poles, and the motion expressed the lodge-trail.

To denote the *mule* or *ass*, the long ears are imitated by the indices on both sides and above the head.

For the *crow*, and indeed any bird, the hands are flapped near the shoulders. If specification be required, the cry is imitated or some peculiarity is introduced. The following will show the ingenuity with which the Indian can convey his meaning under difficulties. A Yuta wishing to explain that the torpedo or gymnotus eel is found in Cottonwood Kanyon Lake, took to it thus: he made the body by extending his sinister index to the fore, touched it with the dexter index at two points on both sides to show legs, and finally sharply withdrew his right forefinger to convey the idea of an electric shock.

Some of the symbols of relationship are highly appropriate, and not ungraceful or unpicturesque. Man is denoted by a sign which will not admit of description; woman, by passing the hand down both sides of the head as if smoothing or stroking the long hair. A son or daughter is expressed by making with the hand a movement denoting issue from the loins: if the child be small, a bit of the index held between the antagonised thumb and medius is shown. The same sign of issue expresses both parents, with additional explanations:—To say, for instance, "*my mother*," you would first pantomime "*I*," or, which is the same thing, "*my;*" then "*woman;*" and, finally, the symbol of parentage. "*My grandmother*" would be conveyed in the same way, adding to the end clasped hands, closed eyes, and like an old woman's bent back. The sign for brother and sister is perhaps the prettiest:—the two first finger tips are put into the mouth, denoting that they fed from the same breast. For the wife—squaw is now becoming a word of reproach amongst the Indians—the dexter forefinger is passed between the extended thumb and index of the left.

Of course there is a sign for every weapon. The *knife*—scalp or other—is shown by cutting the sinister palm with the dexter ferient downward and towards oneself: if the cuts be made upward with the palm downwards, meat is understood. The *tomahawk*, hatchet, or axe is denoted by chopping the left hand with the right; the *sword* by the motion of drawing it; the *bow* by the movement of bending it; and a *spear* or *lance* by an imitation of darting it. For the *gun*, the dexter thumb and fingers are flashed or scattered, *i. e.* thrown outwards and upwards to denote fire. The same movement made lower down expresses a *pistol*. The *arrow* is expressed by nocking it upon an imaginary bow, and by "snapping" with the index and medius. The *shield* is shown by pointing with the index over the left shoulder, where it is slung ready to be brought over the breast when required.

The following are the most useful words:—

Yes.—Wave the hands straight forwards from the face.

No.—Wave the hand from right to left, as if motioning away. This sign also means, "I'll have nothing to do with you." Done slowly and insinuatingly it informs a woman that she is *charmante*—"not to be touched" being the idea.

Good.—Wave the hand from the mouth, extending the thumb from the index and closing the other three fingers. This sign means also "I know." "I don't know" is expressed by waving the right hand with the palm outwards before the right breast; or by moving about the two forefingers before the breast, meaning "two hearts."

Bad.—Scatter the dexter fingers outwards, as if spirting away water from them.

Now (at once).—Clap both palms together sharply and repeatedly; or make the sign of "to-day."

Day.—Make a circle with the thumb and forefinger of both, in sign of the sun. The *hour* is pointed out by showing the luminary's place in the heavens. The *moon* is expressed by a crescent with the thumb and forefinger: this also denotes a month. For a *year* give the sign of rain or snow.

Many Indians ignore the quadripartite division of the seasons, which seems to be an invention of European latitudes ;—the Persians, for instance, know it, but the Hindus do not. They have, however, distinct terms for the month, all of which are pretty and descriptive, appropriate and poetical ; *e. g.* the moon of light nights, the moon of leaves, the moon of strawberries, for April, May, and June. The Ojibwe have a queer quaternal division, called Of sap, Of abundance, Of fading, and Of freezing. The Dakota reckon five moons to winter and five to summer, leaving one to spring and one to autumn ; the year is lunar, and as the change of season is denoted by the appearance of sore eyes and of raccoons, any irregularity throws the people out.

Night.—Make a closing movement as if of the darkness by bringing together both hands with the dorsa upwards and the fingers to the fore : the motion is from right to left, and at the end the two indices are alongside and close to each other. This movement must be accompanied by bending forward with bowed head, otherwise it may be misunderstood for the freezing over of a lake or river.

To-day.—Touch the nose with the index tip, and motion with the fist towards the ground.

Yesterday.—Make with the left hand the circle which the sun describes from sunrise to sunset, or invert the direction from sunset to sunrise with the right hand.

To-morrow.—Describe the motion of the sun from east to west. Any number of days may be counted upon the fingers. The latter, I need hardly say, are the only numerals in the pantomimic vocabulary.

Among the Dakotas, when they have gone over the fingers and thumbs of both hands, one is temporarily turned down for one ten ; at the end of another ten a second finger is turned down, and so on, as amongst children who are learning to count. " Opawinge," one hundred, is derived from " pawinga," to go round in circles, as the fingers have all been gone over again for their respective tens ; " Kektopawinge " is from " ake," and " opawinge,"—" hundred again,"— being about to recommence the circle of their fingers already completed in hundreds. For numerals above a thousand there is no method of computing.

There is a sign and word for one half of a thing, but none to denote any smaller aliquot part.

Peace.—Intertwine the fingers of both hands.

Friendship.—Clasp the left with the right hand.

Glad (pleased).—Wave the open hand outwards from the breast, to express "good heart."

A Cup.—Imitate its form with both hands, and make the sign of drinking from it. In this way any utensil can be intelligibly described —of course provided that the interlocutor has seen it.

Paint.—Daub both the cheeks downwards with the index.

Looking-glass.—Place both palms before the face, and admire your countenance in them.

Bead.—Point to a bead, or make the sign of a necklace.

Wire.—Show it, or where it ought to be, in the ear-lobe.

Whiskey.—Make the sign of "bad" and "drink" for "bad water."

Blanket or Clothes.—Put them on in pantomime.

A Lodge.—Place the fingers of both hands ridge-fashion before the breast.

Fire.—Blow it, and warm the hands before it. To express the boiling of a kettle, the sign of fire is made low down, and an imaginary pot is eaten from.

It is cold.—Wrap up, shudder, and look disagreeable.

Rain.—Scatter the fingers downwards. The same sign denotes snow.

Wind.—Stretch the fingers of both hands outward, puffing violently the while.

A Storm.—Make the rain sign; then, if thunder and lightning are to be expressed, move, as if in anger, the body to and fro, to show the wrath of the elements.

A Stone.—If light, act as if picking it up: if heavy, as if dropping it.

A Hill.—Close the finger-tips over the head: if a mountain is to be expressed, raise them high. To denote an ascent on rising ground, pass the right palm over the left hand, half doubling up the latter, so that it looks like a ridge.

A Plain.—Wave both the palms outwards and low down.

A River.—Make the sign of drinking, and then wave both the palms outwards. A rivulet, creek, or stream is shown by the drinking sign, and by holding the index tip between the thumb and medius; an arroyo (dry water-course), by covering up the tip with the thumb and middle finger.

A Lake.—Make the sign of drinking, and form a basin with both hands. If a large body of water is in question, wave both palms outwards as in denoting a plain. The prairie savages have never seen the sea, so it would be vain to attempt explanation.

A Book.—Place the right palm on the left palm, and then open both before the face.

A Letter.—Write with the thumb and dexter index on the sinister palm.

A Waggon.—Roll hand over hand, imitating a wheel.

A Waggon-road.—Make the waggon sign, and then wave the hand along the ground.

Grass.—Point to the ground with the index, and then turn the fingers upwards to denote growth. If the grass be long, raise the hand high; and if yellow, point out that colour.

The pantomime, as may be seen, is capable of expressing detailed narratives. For instance, supposing an Indian would tell the following tale:—" Early this morning, I mounted my horse, rode off at a gallop, traversed a kanyon or ravine, then over a mountain to a plain where there was no water, sighted bison, followed them, killed three of them, skinned them, packed the flesh upon my pony, remounted and returned home"—he would symbolise it thus:—

Touches nose—" *I.*"

Opens out the palms of his hand—" *this morning.*"

Points to east—" *early.*"

Places two dexter forefingers astraddle over sinister index—" *mounted my horse.*"

Moves both hands upwards and rocking-horse fashion towards the left—"*galloped.*"

Passes the dexter hand right through thumb and forefinger of the sinister, which are widely extended—" *traversed a kanyon.*"

Closes the finger-tips high over the head, and waves both palms outwards—" *over a mountain to a plain.*"

Scoops up with the hand imaginary water into the mouth, and then waves the hand from the face to denote "no"—" *where there was no water.*"

Touches eye—" *sighted.*"

Raises the forefingers crooked inwards on both sides of the head—" *bison.*"

Smites the sinister palm downwards with the dexter fist—" *killed.*"

Shows three fingers—" *three of them.*"

Scrapes the left palm with the edge of the right hand—"*skinned them.*"

Places the dexter on the sinister palm, and then the dexter palm on the sinister dorsum—"*packed the flesh upon my pony.*"

Straddles the two forefingers on the index of the left—" *remounted ;*" and finally,

Beckons towards self—" *returned home.*"

To conclude, I can hardly flatter myself that these descriptions have been made quite intelligible to the reader. They may, however, serve to prepare his mind for a *vivâ voce* lesson upon the prairies, should fate have such thing in store for him.

After this digression, I return to my prosaic Diary.

CHAP. III.

CONCLUDING THE ROUTE TO THE GREAT SALT LAKE CITY.

" Along the Black Hills to Box Elder, 15th August.

I AROSE "between two days," a little before 4 A.M., and watched the dawn, and found in its beauties a soothing influence which acted upon stiff limbs and discontented spirit as if it had been a spell.

The stars of the Great Bear — the prairie night-clock — first began to pale without any seeming cause, till presently a faint streak of pale light — *dum i gurg,* or the wolf's tail, as it is called by the Persian — began to shimmer upon the eastern verge of heaven. It grew and grew through the dark-blue air: one unaccustomed to the study of the " grey-eyed morn " would have expected it to usher in the day, when, gradually as it had struggled into existence, it faded, and a deeper darkness than before once more invaded the infinitude above. But now the unrisen sun is more rapidly climbing the gloomy walls of Koh i Kaf — the mountain rim which encircles the world, and through whose lower gap the False Dawn had found its way — preceded by a warm flush of light, which chases the shades till, though loth to depart, they find neither on earth nor in the firmament a place where they can linger. Warmer and warmer waxes the heavenly radiance, gliding up to the keystone of the vault above; fainter and fainter grows the darkness, till the last stain disappears behind the Black Hills to the west, and the stars one by one, like glow-worms, " pale their ineffectual fires " — the " Pointers " are the longest to resist — retreat backwards, as it were, and fade away into endless space. Slowly, almost imperceptibly, the marvellous hues of " glorious morn," here truly a fresh " birth of heaven and earth," all gold and

sapphire, acquire depth and distinctness, till at last a fiery flush
ushers from beneath the horizon the source of all these
splendours,

> " Robed in flames and amber light; "

and another day, with its little life of joys and sorrows, of
hopes and fears, is born to the world.

Though we all rose up early, packed, and were ready to proceed, there was an unusual *vis inertiæ* on the part of the driver :
Indians were about; the mules of course had bolted; but that
did not suffice as explanation. Presently the " wonder leaked
out;" our companions were transferred from their comfortable
vehicle to a real " shandridan," a Rocky-Mountain bone-setter.
They were civil enough to the exceedingly drunken youth —
a runaway new Yorker — who did us the honour of driving us :
for *quand on a besoin du diable on lui dit, " Monsieur."* One
cannot expect, however, the *diable* to be equally civil : when
we asked him to tidy our vehicle a little, he simply replied, that
he'd be darned if he did. Long may be the darning needle and
sharp to him ! But tempers seriously soured must blow up or
burst, and a very pretty little quarrel was the result : it was
settled bloodlessly, because one gentleman, who to do him
justice showed every disposition to convert himself into a target,
displayed such perfect unacquaintance with the weapons — revolvers — usually used on similar occasions, that it would have
been mere murder to have taken pistol in hand against him.

As we sat very disconsolate in the open verandah, five Indians stalked in, and the biggest and burliest of the party, a
middle-aged man, with the long straight Indian hair, high harsh
features, and face bald of eyebrows and beard, after offering
his paw to Mrs. Dana and the rest of the party, sat down with
a manner of natural dignity, somewhat trenching upon the im-
pertinent. Presently, diving his hand into his breast, the old
rat pulled out a thick fold of leather, and after much manipu-
lation, disclosed a dirty-brown, ragged-edged sheet of paper,
certifying him to be " Little Thunder," and signed by " General
Harney." This, then, was the chief who showed the white-
feather at Ash Hollow, and of whom some military poet sang :

> " We didn't make a blunder,
> We rubbed out Little Thunder,
> And we sent him to the other side of Jordan."

Little Thunder did not look quite rubbed out; but for poesy
fiction is, of course, an element far more appropriate than fact.
I remember a similar effusion of the Anglo-Indian muse, which
consigned "Akbar Khan the Yaghi" to the tune and fate of the
King of the Cannibal Isles, with a contempt of actualities
quite as refreshing. The Western Indians are as fond of these
testimonials as the East Indians : they preserve them with care
as guarantees of their good conduct, and sometimes, as may be
expected, carry about certificates in the style of Bellerophons'
letters. Little Thunder was *en route* to Fort Laramie, where
he intended to lay a complaint against the Indian agent, who
embezzled, he said, half the rations and presents intended for his
tribe. Even the whites owned that the " Maje's " bear got
more sugar than all the Indians put together.

Nothing can be worse, if the *vox populi occidentalis* be taken
as the *vox Dei*, than the modern management of the Indian
Bureau at Washington. In former times, the agencies were in
the hands of the military authorities, and the officer commanding the department was responsible for malversation of office.
This was found to work well; the papers signed were signed
on honour. But in the United States, the federal army, though
well paid, is never allowed to keep any appointment that can
safely be taken away from it. The Indian department is now
divided into six superintendencies, viz. Northern, Central,
Southern, Utah, New Mexico, Washington, and Oregon Territory, who report to the Indian Office or Bureau of the Com-
missioners of Indian affairs at Washington, under the charge of
the department of the Interior. The bond varies from $50,000
to $75,000, and the salary from $2000 to $2500 per annum.
The northern superintendency contains four agencies, the central
fourteen, the southern five, the Utah three, New Mexico six, and
the miscellaneous, including Washington, eight. The grand total
of agents, including two specials for Indians in Texas, is forty-
two. Their bond is between $5000 and $75,000, and the salary
between $1000 and $1550. There are also various sub-agencies,
with pay of $1000 each, and giving in bonds $2000. There
ought to be no perquisites; an unscrupulous man, however,
finds many opportunities of making free with the presents; and
the reflection that his office tenure shall expire after the fourth

year must make him but the more reckless. As fifty or sixty appointments = 50 or 60 votes, × 20 in President election-eering, fitness for the task often becomes quite a subordinate consideration; the result is, necessarily, peculation producing discontent among the Indians, and the finale, death to the whites. To become a good Indian agent a man requires the variety of qualifications which would fit him for the guardianship of children, experience and ability, benevolence and philanthropy: it would be difficult to secure such phœnix for $200 per annum, and it is found easier not to look for it. The remedy of these evils is not far from the surface—the restoration of the office into the hands of the responsible military servant of the state, who would keep it *quamdiu se benè gesserit*, and become better capable of serving his masters, the American people, by the importance which the office would give him in the eyes of his *protégés*. This is the system of the French Bureau Arabe, which, with its faults, I love still. But the political mind would doubtless determine the cure to be worse than the disease. After venting his grievances, Little Thunder arose, and, accom-panied by his braves, remounted and rode off towards the east.

Whilst delayed by the mules and their masters, we may amuse ourselves and divert our thoughts from the battle, and, perhaps, murder and sudden death, which may happen this evening, by studying the geography of the Black Hills. The range forms nearly a right angle, the larger limb— ninety miles — running east to west with a little southing along the Platte, the shorter leg—sixty miles—trending from north to south with a few degrees of easting and westing. Forming the easternmost part of the great Trans-Mississippian mountain-region, in the 44th parallel and between the 103rd and 105th meridians, these masses cover an area of 6000 square miles. They are supposed to have received their last violent upheaval at the close of the cretaceous period; their bases are elevated from 2500 to 3500 feet—the highest peaks attaining 6700 feet—above river level, whilst their eastern is from 2000 to 3000 feet below the western foundation. Their materials, as determined by Lieut. Warren's exploration, are successively metamorphosed azoic rock, includ-ing granite, lower Silurian (Potsdam sandstone), Devonian (?), carboniferous, Permian, Jurassic, and cretaceous. Like Ida,

they are " abundant in springs and flowing streams," which
shed mainly to the north-east and the south-east, supplying
the Indians with trout and salmon-trout, catfish (*Prinelodus*),
and pickerel. They abound in small rich valleys, well grown
with grass, and wild fruits, choke-cherries (*P. Virginiana*),
currants, sand-buttes fruit (*C. pumila?*) and buffalo-berries
(*Shepherdia argentea*, or grains de bœuf). When irrigated, the
bottoms are capable of high cultivation. They excel in fine
timber for fuel and lumber, covering an area of 1500 square
miles; in carboniferous rock of the true coal measures; and in
other good building material. As in most of the hill ranges
which are offsets from the Rocky Mountains, they contain gold
in valuable quantities, and doubtless a minute examination will
lead to the discovery of many other useful minerals. The Black
Hills are appropriately named: a cloak of gloomy forest, pine
and juniper, apparently springing from a rock denuded of less
hardy vegetation, seems to invest them from head to foot. The
Laramie Hills are subranges of the higher ridge, and the well-
known Peak, the pharos of the prairie mariner, rises about 1° due
west of Fort Laramie to the height of 6500 feet above sea level.
Beyond the meridian of Laramie the country totally changes.
The broad prairie lands, unencumbered by timber, and covered with a rich pasturage, which highly adapts them for grazing,
are now left behind. We are about to enter a dry, sandy, and
sterile waste of sage, and presently of salt, where rare spots are
fitted for rearing stock, and this formation will continue till we
reach the shadow of the Rocky Mountains.

At length, the mules coming about 10·45, A.M. we hitched up,
and nothing loth, bade adieu to Horseshoe Creek and the
" ladies." The driver sentimentally informed us that we were to
see no more specimens of ladyhood for many days — gladdest
tidings to one of the party at least. The road, which ran out of
sight of the river, was broken and jagged ; a little labour would
have made it tolerable, but what could the good pastor of Ober-
lin do with a folk whose only thought in life is dram-drinking,
tobacco-chewing, trading, and swopping ? * The country was

---

* The civilised Anglo-Americans are far more severe upon their half-barbarous
brethren than any stranger ; to witness, the following.

A Hoosier (native of Indiana) was called upon the stand, away out west, to
testify to the character of a brother Hoosier. It was as follows :—

cut with creeks and arroyos, which separated the several bulges of
ground, and the earth's surface was of a dull brick-dust red, thinly
scrubbed over with coarse grass, ragged sage, and shrublets fit
only for the fire.   After a desolate drive, we sighted below us
the creek La Bonté,—so called from a French *voyageur*,—green
and bisected by a clear mountain stream whose banks were
thick with self-planted trees.   In the labyrinth of paths we
chose the wrong one: presently we came to a sheer descent of
four or five feet, and after deliberation as to whether the vehicle
would "take it" or not, we came to the conclusion that we had
better turn the restive mules to the right about.   Then cheered
by the sight of our consort, the other waggon, which stood
temptingly shaded by the grove of cotton-wood, willows, box
elder (*Negundo aceroides*) and wild cherry, at the distance
of about half a mile, we sought manfully the right track;
and the way in which the driver charged the minor obstacles
was "a caution to mules."   We ought to have arrived at
2·45 P.M.; we were about an hour later.   The station had yet
to be built; the whole road was in a transition state at the
time of our travel; there was, however, a new corral for
"forting" against Indians, and a kind of leafy arbour, which the
officials had converted into a "cottage near a wood."

A little after 4 P.M. we forded the creek painfully, with our
new cattle,—three rats and a slug.   The latter was pronounced
by our driver, when he condescended to use other language than
anathemata, "the meanest cuss he ever seed."   We were careful,
however, to supply him at the shortest intervals, with whiskey-
drams, which stimulated him, after breaking his whip, to perform
a tattoo with clods and stones, kicks and stamps, upon the
recreant animals' haunches, and by virtue of these we accom-

" How long have you known Bill Bushwhack?"
" Ever since he war born."
" What is his general character?"
" Letter A. No. 1.—'bove par a very great way."
" Would you believe him on oath?"
" Yes, Sir-ee, on or off, or any other way!"
" What is your opinion on his qualifications to good conduct?"
" He's the best shot on the prairies, or in the woods; he can shave the eye-bristles
off a wolf as far as a shootin'-iron 'll carry a ball; he can drink a quart of grog
any day, and he chaws tobacker like a horse."
So Bill Bushwhack passed muster.—*N. Y. Spirit of the Times*.

plished our twenty-five miles in tolerable time. For want of
other pleasantries to contemplate, we busied ourselves in
admiring the regularity and accuracy with which our consort
waggon secured for herself all the best teams. The land was
a red waste, such as travellers find in Eastern Africa, which
after rains sheds streams like blood. The soil was a decomposition
of ferruginous rock, here broken with rugged hills, precipices of
ruddy sandstone 200 feet high, shaded or dotted with black-
green cedars, there cumbered by huge boulders; the ravine-like
water-courses which cut the road showed that after heavy rains
a net-work of torrents must add to the pleasures of travelling,
and the vegetation was reduced to the dull green artemisia, the
azalia, and the jaundiced potentilla. After six miles we saw on
the left of the path a huge natural pile or burrow of primitive
boulders, about 200 feet high and called " Brigham's Peak,"
because, according to Jehu's whiskeyfied story, the prophet,
revelator, and seer of the Latter Day Saints had there, in
1857 (!), pronounced a 4th of July oration in the presence of
200 or 300 fair devotees.

Presently we emerged from the Red Region into the normal
brown clay, garnished with sage as moors are with heather, over
a road which might have suggested the nursery rhyme : —

> " Here we go up, up, up,
> There we go down, down, down."

At last it improved, and once more, as if we never were to
leave it, we fell into the valley of the Platte. About eight miles
from our destination we crossed the sandy bed of the La
Prêle River, an arroyo of twenty feet wide, which, like its
brethren, brims in spring with its freight of melted snow. In
the clear shade of evening we traversed the " timber " or well
wooded lands lying upon Box Elder Creek, — a beautiful little
stream, some eight feet broad ; and at 9 P.M., arrived at the
station. The master, Mr. Wheeler, was exceptionally civil and
communicative, he lent us buffalo robes for the night, and sent
us to bed after the best supper the house could afford. We
were not however to be baulked of our proper pleasure, a
" good grumble," so we hooked it on to another peg. One of
the road-agents had just arrived from Gt. S. L. City in a neat
private ambulance after a journey of three days, whilst we

could hardly expect to make it under treble that time.   It was
agreed on all sides that such conduct was outrageous; that
Messrs. Russell and Co. amply deserved to have their contract
taken from them, and—on these occasions your citizen looks
portentous, and deals darkly in threatenings, as if his single vote
could shake the spheres—we came to a mutual understanding
that *that* firm should never enjoy our countenance or support.
We were unanimous; all, even the mortal quarrel, was " made
up" in the presence of the general foe, the Mail Company.
Briefly we retired to rest, a miserable Public, and soothed by
the rough lullaby of the coyote, whose shrieks and screams
perfectly reproduced the Indian jackal, we passed into the
world of dreams.

To Platte Bridge, August 16th.

At 8·30 A.M., we were once more under way along the valley
of Father Platte, whose physiognomy had now notably changed
for the better.   Instead of the dull, dark, silent stream of the
lower course, whose muddy monotonous aspect made it a
grievance to behold, we descried with astonishment a bright
little river, hardly a hundred yards wide — one's ideas of pota-
mology are enlarged with a witness by American travel! a
mirrory surface, and waters clear and limpid as the ether above
them.   The limestones and marls which destroy the beauty of
the Lower Platte, do not extend to the upper course.   The
climate now became truly delicious.   The height above sea-
level—5000 feet—subjects the land to the wholesome action of
gentle winds, which, about 10—11 A. M., when the earth has
had time to air, set in regularly as the sea-breezes of tropical
climes, and temper the keen shine of day.   These higher grounds,
where the soil is barren rather for want of water than from
the character of its constituents, are undoubtedly the healthiest
part of the plains: no noxious malaria is evolved from the
sparse growth of tree and shrub upon the banks of the river; and
beyond them the plague of brulés (sand flies), and mosquitoes is
unknown; the narrowness of the bed also prevents the shrinking
of the stream in autumn, at which season the lower Platte ex-
poses two broad margins of black infected mire.   The three
great elements of unhealthiness, heavy and clammy dews,

moisture exhaled from the earth's surface, and the overcrowding of population — which appears to generate as many artificial diseases as artificial wants — are here unknown : the soil is never turned up, and even if it were, it probably would not have the deleterious effect which climatologists have remarked in the damp hot regions near the equator. The formation of the land begins to change from the tertiary and cretaceous to the primary, — granites and porphyries,—warning us that we are approaching the Rocky Mountains.

On the road, we saw for the first time, a train of Mormon waggons, twenty-four in number, slowly wending their way towards the Promised Land. The "Captain" — those who fill the dignified office of guides are so designated, and once a captain always a captain is the far western rule — was young Brigham Young, a nephew of the prophet ; a *blondin*, with yellow hair and beard, an intelligent countenance, a six-shooter by his right, and a bowie-knife by his left side. It was impossible to mistake, even through the veil of freckles and sunburn with which a two months' journey had invested them, the nationality of the emigrants ; " British-English" was written in capital letters upon the white eyelashes and tow-coloured curls of the children, and upon the sandy brown hair and staring eyes, heavy bodies, and ample extremities of the adults. One young person concealed her facial attractions under a manner of mask. I thought that perhaps she might be a Sultana, ro served for the establishment of some very magnificent Mormon bashaw; but the driver, when appealed to, responded with contempt, " 'Guess old Briggy wont stampede many o' that 'ere lot !" Though thus homely in appearance, few showed any symptoms of sickness or starvation ; in fact, their condition first impressed us most favourably with the excellence of the Perpetual Emigration Funds' travelling arrangements.

The Mormons who can afford such luxury generally purchase for the transit of the plains an emigrant's waggon, which in the West seldom costs more than $185. They take a full week before well *en route*, and endeavour to leave the Mississippi in early May, when "long forage" is plentiful upon the prairies. Those prospecting parties who are bound for California, set out in March or April, feeding their animals with grain till the new grass appears; after November the road over the Sierra Nevada being almost impassable to way-worn oxen. The ground in the low parts of the Mississippi Valley becomes heavy and muddy after the first spring-rains, and by starting in good time the worst parts of the country will be passed before the travel becomes very laborious. Moreover, grass soon disappears from the higher and less productive tracts; between Scott's Bluffs and Gt. S. L. City, we were seldom out of sight of starved cattle, and on one spot I counted fifteen skeletons. Travellers, however, should not push forward early, unless their animals are in good condition and are well supplied with grain; the last year's grass is not quite useless, but cattle cannot thrive upon it as.they will upon the grammas, festucas, and buffalo clover (*Trifolium reflexum*) of Utah and New Mexico. The journey between St. Jo and the Mormon capital usually occupies from two to three months. The Latter Day Saints march with a quasi-military organisation. Other emigrants form companies of fifty to seventy armed men, — a single waggon would be in imminent danger from rascals like the Pawnees, who, though fonder of bullying than of fighting, are ever ready to cut off a straggler, — elect their " Cap.," who holds the office only during good conduct, sign and seal themselves to certain obligations, and bind themselves to stated penalties in case of disobedience or defection. The " Prairie Traveller" strongly recommends this systematic organisation, without which indeed no expedition, whether emigrant, commercial, or exploratory, ought ever or in any part of the world to begin its labours: justly observing that, without it, discords and dissensions sooner or later arise which invariably result in breaking up the company.

In this train I looked to no purpose for the hand-carts with which the poorer Saints add to the toils of earthly travel, a semi-devotional work of supererogation expected to win a proportionate reward in heaven.*

* The following estimate of outfit was given to me by a Mormon elder, who has frequently travelled over the Utah route. He was accompanied by his wife and family and help—six persons in total; and having money to spare, he invested it in a speculation which could hardly fail at least to quadruple his outlay at the end of the march: the stove, for instance, bought at $28, would sell for $80 to $120. The experienced emigrant, it may be observed, carries with him a little of everything that may or might be wanted; such as provisions, clothing, furniture,

After ten miles of the usual number of creeks, "Deep," "Small," "Snow," " Muddy," &c., and heavy descents, we reached at 10 A.M. Deer Creek, a stream about thirty feet wide, said to abound in fish. The station boasts of an Indian agent, Major Twiss, a post-office, a store, and of course a grog-shop. M. Bissonette, the owner of the two latter and an old Indian trader, was the usual creole, speaking a French not unlike that of the Channel Islands, and wide awake to the advantages derivable from travellers; the large straggling establishment seemed to pro-duce in abundance large squaws and little half-breeds. For-tunately stimulants are not much required on the plains: I wish my enemy no more terrible fate than to drink excessively with M. Bissonette of M. B.'s liquor. The good creole, when asked to join us, naïvely refused: he reminded me of certain wine merchants in more civilised lands, who, when dining with their pratique, sensibly prefer small-beer to their own concoc-tions.

A delay of fifteen minutes and then we were hurried for-wards. The ravines deepened; we were about entering the region of kanyons.* Already we began to descry bunch-grass

---

drugs, lint, stationery, spices, ammunition, and so forth: above all things he looks to his weapons as likely to be at a pinch his best friends:—

2 yokes oxen .	at $180 to $200	100 lbs. ham and bacon .	. $14
1 cow (milch) . . .	25	150 lbs. crackers (sea biscuits),	13·13
1 waggon	87·30	100 lbs. sugar . . .	9·50
1 double cover . . .	8·50	25 lbs. crystallised ditto .	3
2 ox-yokes	8	24 lbs. raisins . . .	4
1 ox chain	1·50	20 lbs. currants . . .	3
1 tar-bucket	1	25 lbs. rice	2·25
1 large tent ($9 for smaller sizes)	15	1 bushel dried apples . .	6
Camp equipment, axes, spades, shovels, triangles for fires, &c. }	10	1 " " peaches. .	4·30
		1 " beans . . .	2
600 lbs. flour . . .	25·50	1 stove	28
		Grand total . .	$490·98

* The Spanish cañon—Americanised to kanyon—signifies, primarily, a cannon or gun barrel, secondarily, a tube, shaft of a mine or a ravine of peculiar form, common in this part of America. .The word is loosely applied by the Western men, but properly, it means those gorges through a line of mountains, whose walls are high and steep, even to a tunnel-like overhanging, whilst their soles which afford pas-sages to streams are almost flat. In northern Mexico the kanyon becomes of stupendous dimensions; it is sometimes a crack in the plains 2000 feet deep, ex-

clothing the hills. This invaluable and anomalous provision
of nature is first found, I believe, about fifty miles westward of the meridian of Fort Laramie, and it extends to
the eastern slope of the Sierra Nevada.   On the Pacific watershed it gives way to the wild oats (*Avena fatua*), which are
supposed to have been introduced into California by the
Spaniards. The festuca is a real boon to the land, which,
without it, could hardly be traversed by cattle. It grows by
clumps, as its name denotes, upon the most unlikely ground,
the thirsty sand and the stony hills : in fact, it thrives best
upon the poorest soil. In autumn, about September, when
all other grasses turn to hay, and their nutriment is washed out
by the autumnal rains ; the bunch-grass, after shedding its seed,
begins to put forth a green shoot within the apparently
withered sheath. It remains juicy and nutritious, like winter
wheat in April, under the snows, and, contrary to the rule of
the *gramineæ*, it pays the debt of nature, drying and dying
about May ; yet, even when in its corpse-like state, a light
yellow straw, it contains abundant and highly flavoured nutriment ; it lasts through the summer, retiring up the mountains,
again becomes grass in January, thus feeding cattle all the
year round.   The small dark pyriform seed, about half the
size of an oat, is greedily devoured by stock, and has been found
to give an excellent flavour to beef and mutton.   It is curious
how little food will fatten animals upon the elevated portions of
the prairies, and in the valleys of the Rocky Mountains.   I remarked the same thing in Somali-land, where, while far as the
eye could see the country wore the semblance of one vast
limestone ledge, white with desolation, the sheep and bullocks
were round and plump as stall-fed animals.   The idea forces
itself upon one's mind that the exceeding purity and limpidity
of the air, by perfecting the processes of digestion and assimi-
lation must stand in lieu of quantity.   I brought back with me
a small packet of the bunch-grass seed, in the hope that it
may be acclimatised : the sandy lands about Aldershott, for
instance, would be admirably fitted for the growth.

  We arrived at a station, called the " Little Muddy Creek,"
after a hot drive of twenty miles. It was a wretched place,

posing all the layers that clothe earth's core, with a stream at the bottom, in sight,
but impossible for the traveller dying of thirst to drink at.

built of " dry stones," viz. slabs without mortar, and the interior was garnished with certain efforts of pictorial art, which were rather *lestes* than otherwise. The furniture was composed of a box and a trunk, and the negative catalogue of its supplies was extensive,—whiskey forming the only positive item.

We were not sorry to resume our journey at 1·15 P.M. After eight miles we crossed the vile bridge which spans "Snow Creek," a deep water, and hardly six feet wide. According to the station men, water here was once perennial, though now reduced to an occasional freshet after rain: this phenomenon, they say, is common in the country, and they attribute it to the sinking of the stream in the upper parts of the bed, which have become porous, or have given way. It is certain that in the Sinaitic regions many springs, which within a comparatively few years supplied whole families of Bedouins, have unaccountably dried up; perhaps the same thing happens in the Rocky Mountains.

After about two hours of hot sun, we debouched upon the bank of the Platte, at a spot where once was the Lower Ferry.* The river bed is here so full of holes and quicksands, and the stream is so cold and swift, that many have been drowned when bathing, more when attempting to save time by fording it. A wooden bridge was built at this point some years ago, at an expense of $26,000, by one Regshaw, who, if report does not belie him, has gained and lost more fortunes than a Wall Street professional "lame-duck." We halted for a few minutes at the indispensable store,—the *tête de pont*,— and drank our whiskey with ice, which, after so long a disuse, felt unenjoyably cold. Remounting, we passed a deserted camp, where in times gone by two companies of infantry had been stationed: a few stumps of crumbling wall, broken floorings, and depressions in the ground, were the only remnants which the winds and rains had left. The banks of the Platte were stained with coal: it has been known to exist for some years, but has only lately been worked. Should the supply prove sufficient for the wants of

---

* The first ferry, according to the old guide books, was at Deer Creek: the second was at this place, thirty-one miles above the former; and the third was four miles still further on.

the settlers, it will do more towards the civilisation of these regions than the discovery of gold.

The lignite tertiary of Nebraska extends north and west to the British line : the beds are found throughout this formation sometimes six and seven feet thick, and the article would make good fuel.   The true coal measures have been discovered in the south-eastern portion of the Nebraska prairies, and several small seams at different points of the Platte Valley.   Dr. F. V. Hayden, who accompanied Lieut. Warren as geologist, appears to think that the limestones which contain the supplies, though belonging to the true coal measures, hold a position above the workable beds of coal, and deems it improbable that mines of any importance will be found north of the southern line of Nebraska.   But as his examination of the ground was some- what hurried, there is room to hope that this unfavourable verdict will be cancelled.   The coal as yet discovered is all, I believe, bituminous.   That dug out of the Platte bank runs in a vein about six feet thick, and is as hard as cannel coal : the texture of the rock is a white limestone.   The banks of the Deer and other neighbouring creeks are said also to contain the requisites for fuel.

Our station lay near the upper crossing or second bridge, a short distance from the town.   It was also built of timber at an expense of $40,000, about a year ago, by Louis Guenot, a Quebecquois, who has passed the last twelve years upon the plains.   He appeared very downcast about his temporal prospects, and handed us over, with the *insouciance* of his race, to the tender mercies of his venerable squaw.   The usual toll is $0.50, but from trains, especially of Mormons, the owner will claim $5 ; in fact, as much as he can get without driving them to the opposition lower bridge, or to the ferry boat.   It was impossible to touch the squaw's supper; the tin cans that contained the coffee were slippery with grease, and the bacon looked as if it had been dressed side by side with " boyaux." I lighted my pipe, and air-cane in hand, sallied forth to look at the country.

The heights behind the station were our old friends the Black Hills, which, according to the Canadian, extend with few breaks, as far as Denver city.   They are covered with dark green pine ; at a distance it looks black, and the woods shelter a variety of wild beasts, the grizzly bear amongst the number. In the more grassy spaces mustangs, sure-footed as mountain goats, roam uncaught; and at the foot of the hills the slopes are well stocked with antelope, deer, and hares, here called rabbits. The principal birds are the sage-hen (*Tetrao uropha-sianus*) and the prairie-hen *(T. pratensis)*. The former, also called the cock of the plains, is a fine strong-flying grouse, about the size of a full-grown barn-door fowl, or when younger of a European pheasant, which indeed the form of the tail, as the name denotes, greatly resembles, and the neck is smooth like the partridge of the Old World.* Birds of the year are considered good eating: after their first winter the flesh is so impregnated with the intolerable odour of wild sage, that none but a starving man can touch it. The prairie-hen, also called the "heath-hen," and the "pinnated grouse," affects the plains of Illinois and Missouri, and is rarely found so far west as the Black Hills: it is not a migratory bird. The pinnæ from which it derives its name are little wing-like tufts on both sides of the neck, small in the female, large in the male. The cock, moreover, has a stripe of skin running down the neck, which changes its natural colour towards pairing time, and becomes of a reddish yellow: it swells like a turkey cock's wattles, till the head seems buried between two monstrous protuberances, the owner spreading out its tail, sweeping the ground with its wings, and booming somewhat like a bittern. Both of these birds, which are strong on the wing, and give good sport, might probably be naturalised in Europe, and the "Société d'Acclimatisation" would do well to think of it.

Returning to the station I found that a war-party of Arapahos had just alighted in a thin copse hard by. They looked less like warriors than like a band of horsestealers; and though they had set out with the determination of bringing back some Yutah scalps and fingers†, they had not succeeded. On these

---

* The trivial names for organic nature are as confused and confusing in America as in India, in consequence of the old country terms applied, *per fas et nefas,* to new country growths: for instance, the spruce grouse is the Canadian partridge; the ruffled grouse is the partridge of New England and New York, and the pheasant of New Jersey and the Southern States; whilst in the latter the common quail (*O. Virginiana*) is called "partridge."

† The enemy's fore or other finger, crooked and tied with two bits of the skin which are attached to the wrist or the forehead, is a favourite and picturesque

occasions, the young braves are generally very sulky,— a fact which they take care to show by short speech and rude gestures, throwing about and roughly handling, like spoiled children, whatever comes in their way. At such times one must always be prepared for a word and a blow; and, indeed, most Indian fighters justify themselves in taking the initiative, as, of course, it is a great thing to secure first chance. However we may yearn towards our "poor black brother," it is hard not to sympathise with the white in many aggressions against the ferocious and capricious so-called red man. The war party consisted of about a dozen warriors, with a few limber lither-looking lads. They had sundry lean sore-backed nags, which were presently turned out to graze. Dirty rags formed the dress of the band; their arms were the usual light lances, garnished with leather at the handles, with two cropped tufts and a long loose feather dangling from them. They had bows shaped like the Grecian Cupid's, strengthened with sinews and tipped with wire, and arrows of light wood, with three feathers, — Captain Marcy says, two intersecting at right angles; but I have never seen this arrangement,— and small triangular iron piles. Their shields were plain targes,— double folds of raw buffalo hide, apparently unstuffed, and quite unadorned. They carried mangy buffalo robes; and scattered upon the ground was a variety of belts, baldricks, and pouches, with split porcupine quills dyed a saffron yellow.

The Arapahos, generally pronounced 'Rapahos, — called by their Shoshone neighbours Sháretikeh, or dog-eaters, and by the French Gros Ventres,— are a tribe of thieves living between the South Fort of the Platte and the Arkansas Rivers. They are bounded north by the Sioux, and hunt in the same grounds with the Cheyennes. This breed is considered fierce, treacherous, and unfriendly to the whites, who have debauched and diseased them, whilst the Cheyennes are comparatively chaste and uninfected. The Arapaho is distinguished from the Dakota by the superior gauntness of his person, and the boldness of his look; there are also minor points of difference in the moccasins, arrowmarks, and weapons. His language, like that of the Cheyennes, has never, I am told, been thoroughly learned by a stranger:

ornament. That failing, the bear's (especially the grizzly's) talons, bored at the base, and strung upon their sinews, are considered highly honourable.

It is said to contain but a few hundred words, and these being almost all explosive growls, or guttural grunts, are with difficulty acquired by the civilised ear. Like the Cheyennes, the Arapahos have been somewhat tamed of late by the transit of the United States army in 1857.

Amongst the Prairie Indians, when a war chief has matured the plans for an expedition, he habits himself in the garb of battle. Then, mounting his steed, and carrying a lance adorned with a flag and eagle's feathers, he rides about the camp chaunting his war-song. Those disposed to volunteer join the parade also on horseback, and, after sufficiently exhibiting themselves to the admiration of the village, return home. This ceremony continues till the requisite number is collected. The war-dance, and the rites of the medicine-man, together with perhaps private penances and propitiations, are the next step. There are also copious pow-wows, in which, as in the African parlance, the chiefs, elders, and warriors sit for hours in grim debate, solemn as if the fate of empires hung upon their words, to decide the momentous question whether Jack shall have half a pound more meat than Jim. Neither the chief nor the warriors are finally committed by the procession to the expedition; they are all volunteers, at liberty to retire; and jealousy, disappointment, and superstition often interpose between themselves and glory.

The war-party when gone is thoroughly gone; once absent they love to work in mystery, and look forward mainly to the pleasure of surprising their friends. After an absence which may extend for months, a loud, piercing, peculiar cry suddenly announces the vanguard courier of the returning braves. The camp is thrown at once from the depths of apathy to the height of excitement, which is also the acmé of enjoyment for those whose lives must be spent in forced inaction. The warriors enter with their faces painted black, and their steeds decorated in the most fantastic style; the women scream and howl their exultation, and feasting and merriment follow with the ceremonious scalp-dance. The braves are received with various degrees of honour according to their deeds. The highest merit is to ride single-handed into the enemy's camp, and to smite a lodge with lance or bow. The second is to take a

warrior prisoner.   The third is to strike a dead or fallen man
—an idea somewhat contrary to the Englishman's fancies of fair
play, but intelligible enough where it is the custom, as in
Hindostan, to lie upon the ground " playing 'possum," and
waiting the opportunity to hamstring or otherwise disable the
opponent.   The least of great achievements is to slay an enemy
in hand-to-hand fight.   A Pyrrhic victory, won even at an incon-
siderable loss is treated as a defeat; the object of the Indian
guerilla chief is to destroy the foe with as little risk to himself
and his men as possible; this is his highest boast, and in this
are all his hopes of fame.   Should any of the party fall in
battle, the relatives mourn by cutting off their hair and the
manes and tails of their horses, and the lugubrious lamentations
of the women introduce an ugly element into the triumphal
procession.

In the evening, as Mrs. Dana, her husband, and I, were sitting
outside the station, two of the warriors came and placed themselves without ceremony upon the nearest stones.   They were exceedingly unprepossessing with their small gipsy eyes, high rugged
cheek bones, broad flat faces, coarse sensual mouths everted as to
the lips, and long heavy chins ; they had removed every sign of
manhood from their faces, and their complexions were a dull
oily red, the result of vermilion, ochre, or some such pigment,
of which they are as fond as Hindus, grimed-in for years.
They watched every gesture, and at times communicated their
opinions to each other in undistinguishable gruntings with
curious attempts at cachinnation.   It is said that the wild dog is
unable to bark and that the tame variety has acquired the faculty by attempting to imitate the human voice; it is certain that,
as a rule, only the civilised man can laugh loudly and heartily.
I happened to mention to my fellow-travellers the universal
dislike of savages to anything like a sketch of their physiogno-
mies; they expressed a doubt that the Indians were subject to
the rule.   Pencil and paper were at hand, so we proceeded to
proof.   The savage at first seemed uneasy under the operation,
as the Asiatic or African will do, averting his face at times, and
shifting position to defeat my purpose.   When I passed the
caricature round it excited some merriment; the subject forthwith rising from his seat made a sign that he also wished to see it.
At the sight, however, he screwed up his features with an expres-

sion of intense disgust, and managing to "smudge" over the
sketch with his dirty thumb, he left us with a "pooh!" that
told all his outraged feelings.

Presently the warriors entered the station to smoke and
tacitly beg for broken victuals. They squatted in a circle, and
passed round the red sandstone calumet with great gravity,
puffing like steam tugs, inhaling slowly and lingeringly, swal-
lowing the fumes, and with upturned faces exhaling them
through the nostrils. They made no objections to being joined
by us, and always before handing the pipe to a neighbour,
they wiped the reed mouth-piece with the cushion of the
thumb. The contents of their calumet were kinnikinik, and
though they accepted tobacco, they preferred replenishing
with their own mixture. They received a small present of
provisions, and when the station people went to supper they
were shut out.

We are now slipping into Mormon land; one of the station
keepers belonged to the new religion. The "madam" on entering the room had requested him to depose a cigar which
tainted the air with a perfume like that of greens-water; he
took the matter so coolly that I determined he was not an
American, and, true enough, he proved to be a cabinet-maker
from Birmingham. I spent the evening reading poor Albert
Smith's "Story of Mont Blanc"— Mont Blanc in sight of the
Rocky Mountains!—and admiring how the prince of enter-
tainers led up the reader to what he called the crowning glory
of his life, the unperilous ascent of that monarch of the Alps,
much in the same spirit with which one would have addressed
the free and independent voters of some well-bribed English
borough.

We are now about to quit the region which nature has prepared, by ready-made roads and embankments, for a railway;
all beyond this point difficulties are so heaped upon difficulties
—as the sequel will prove—that we must hope against hope
to see the "iron-horse" (I believe he is so called) holding his
way over the mountains.

"*17th August.—To the Valley of the Sweetwater.*"

The morning was bright and clear, cool and pleasant. The

last night's abstinence had told upon our squeamishness : we managed to secure a fowl, and with its aid we overcame our repugnance to the massive slices of egg-less bacon. At 6·30 A. M. we hitched up, crossed the ricketty bridge at a slow pace, and proceeded for the first time to ascend the left bank of the Platte. The valley was grassy, the eternal sage, how-ever, haunted us; the grouse ran before us, and the prairie dogs squatted upon their house-tops, enjoying the genial morning rays. After ten miles of severe ups and downs, which, by-the-bye, nearly brought our consort, the official's waggon, to grief, we halted for a few minutes at an old-established trading-post, called "Red Buttes."* The feature from which it derives its name lies on the right bank of, and about five miles distant from, the river, which here cuts its way through a ridge. These bluffs are a fine bold formation, escarpments of ruddy argillaceous sandstones, and shells, which dip towards the west : they are the eastern wall of the mass that hems in the stream, and rear high above it their conical heads and fantastic figures. The ranch was on the margin of a cold clear spring, of which we vainly attempted to drink. The banks were white, as though by hoar-frost, with nitrate and carbonate of soda efflorescing from the dark mould. Near Red Buttes the water is said to have a chalybeate flavour, but of that we were unable to judge.

Having allowed the squaws and half-breeds a few minutes to gaze, we resumed our way, taking off our caps in token of adieu to old father Platte, our companion for many a weary mile. We had traced his course upwards, through its various phases and vicissitudes, from the dignity and portliness of his later career as a full-grown river to his small and humble youth as a mountain rivulet, and—interest, either in man or stream, often results from the trouble we take about them—I looked upon him

---

* This French word is extensively used in the Rocky Mountains and Oregon, "where," says Colonel Frémont ("Expedition to the Rocky Mountains," p. 145), "it is naturalised, and which, if desirable to render into English, there is no word which would be its precise equivalent. It is applied to the detached hills and ridges which rise abruptly and reach too high to be called hills or ridges, and are not high enough"—he might have added, are not massive enough—"to be called mountains. *Knob*, as applied in the Western States, is their most descriptive term in English ; but no translation or periphrasis would preserve the identity of these picturesque landmarks."

for the last time with a feeling akin to regret. Moreover, we had been warned that from the crossing of the north Platte to the Sweetwater, all is a dry, and dreary, and desolate waste.

On the way we met a mounted Indian, armed with a rifle, and habited in the most grotesque costume. "Jack"—he was recognised by the driver—wore a suit of buckskin, and a fool's cap made out of an old blanket, with a pair of ass-ear appendages that hung backwards viciously like a mule's; his mouth grinned from ear to ear, and his eyes were protected by glass and wire goggles, which gave them the appearance of being mounted on stalks like a crustacean's. He followed us for some distance, honouring us by riding close to the carriage, in hopes of a little black-mail; but we were not generous, and we afterwards heard something which made us glad that we had not been tempted to liberality. He was followed by an ill-favoured squaw, dressed in a kind of cotton gown, remarkable only for the shoulders being considerably narrower than the waist. She sat her bare nag cavalierly, and eyed us as we passed with that peculiarly unpleasant glance which plain women are so fond of bestowing.

After eighteen miles' drive, we descended a steep hill, and were shown the Devil's Backbone. It is a jagged, broken ridge of huge sandstone boulders, tilted up edgeways, and running in a line over the crest of a long roll of land: the *tout-ensemble* looks like the vertebræ of some great sea-serpent or other long crawling animal; and on a nearer view the several pieces resolve themselves into Sphinxes, Veiled Nuns, Lot's pillars, and other freakish objects. I may here remark that the *aut Cæsar aut diabolus* of the mediæval European antiquary, when accounting for the architecture of strange places, is in the Far West consigned without partnership to the genius loci, the Fiend who, here as in Europe, has monopolised all the finest features of scenery. We shall pass successively the Devil's Gate, the Devil's Post-office, and the Devil's Hole,—in fact, we shall not be thoroughly rid of his Satanic Majesty's appurtenances till Monte Diablo, the highest of the Californian coast-range, dips slowly and unwillingly behind the Pacific's tepid wave.

We nooned at Willow Springs, a little doggery boasting of a

shed and a bunk, but no corral; and we soothed, with a drink of our whiskey, the excited feelings of the Rancheros. The poor fellows had been plundered of their bread and dried meat by some petty thief, who had burrowed under the wall, and they sorely suspected our goggled friend, Jack the Arapaho. Master Jack's hair might have found itself suspended near the fire-plàce if he had then been within rifle shot: as it was, the two victims could only indulge in consolatory threats about wreaking their vengeance upon the first " doggond red-bellied crittur " whom good fortune might send in their way. The water was unusually good at Willow Springs: unfortunately, however, there was nothing else.

At 2·30 P.M. we resumed our way through the yellow-flowered rabbit-bush—it not a little resembled wild mustard—and a thick sage-heath, which was here and there spangled with the bright blossoms of the wilderness. After about twenty miles we passed, to the west of the road, a curious feature, to which the Mormon exodists first, *on dit*, gave the name of Saleratus Lake.* It lies to the west of the road, and is only one of a chain of alka-line waters and springs whose fetor, without exaggeration, taints the land. Cattle drinking of the fluid are nearly sure to die; even those that eat of the *herbe salée* or salt grass growing upon its borders, and known by its reddish-yellow and some-times bluish tinge, will suffer from a disease called the "Alkali," which not unfrequently kills them. The appearance of the Saleratus Lake startles the traveller who, in the full blaze of mid-day upon this arid waste, where mirage mocks him at every turn, suddenly sees outstretched before his eyes a kind of Wen-ham Lake solidly overfrozen. The illusion is so perfect that I was completely deceived, nor could the loud guffaws of the driver bring me at once to the conclusion that seeing in this case is not believing. On a near inspection the icy surface

---

* According to Dr. L. D. Gale (Appendix F. to Captain Stansbury's " Expedition to the Great Salt Lake "), who tested specimens of this saleratus, " it is composed of the sesqui-carbonate of soda, mixed with the sulphate of soda and chloride of soda, and is one of the native salts called *Trona*, found in the Northern Lakes, in Hungary, Africa, and other countries."

" Three grammes of this salt in dry powder, cleared of its earthy impurities, gave carbonic acid 0·9030 of a gramme, which would indicate 1·73239 grammes of the sesqui-carbonate. The other salts were found to be the muriate and sulphate of soda: the proportions were not determined."

turns out to be a dust of carbonate of soda, concealing beneath it masses of the same material, washed out of the adjacent soil, and solidified by evaporation. The Latter Day Saints were charmed with their *trouvaille,* and laid in stores of the fetid alkaline matter, as though it had been manna, for their bread and pastry. It is still transported westward, and declared to be purer than the saleratus of the shops. Near the lake is a deserted ranch, which once enjoyed the title of "Sweetwater Station."

Four miles beyond this "Waterless Lake" — Bahr bila Ma as the Bedouin would call it — we arrived at Rock Independence, and felt ourselves in a new region, totally distinct from the clay formation of the Mauvaises Terres, over which we have travelled for the last five days. Again I was startled by its surprising likeness to the scenery of Eastern Africa : a sketch of Jiwe la Mkoa, the Round Rock in eastern Unyamwezi*, would be mistaken, even by those who had seen both, for this grand *échantillon* of the Rocky Mountains. It crops out of an open plain, not far from the river bed, in dome shape wholly isolated, about 1000 feet in length, by 400—500 in breadth ; it is 60 to 100 in height†, and in circumference 1·50 to 2 miles. Except upon the summit, where it has been weathered into a feldspathic soil; it is bare and bald : a scanty growth of shrubs protrudes however from its poll. The material of the stern looking dome is granite, in enormous slabs and boulders, cracked, flaked, seared and cloven, as if by igneous pressure from below. The prevailing tradition in the West is, that the mass derived its name from the fact that Colonel Frémont there delivered an Independence Day Oration : but read a little further. It is easily ascended at the northern side and the south-eastern corner, and many climb its rugged flanks for a peculiarly Anglo-American purpose ; — Smith and Brown have held high jinks here. In Colonel Frémont's time (1842), everywhere within six or eight feet of the ground, where the surface is sufficiently smooth, and in some places sixty or eighty feet above, the rock was

---

* I crave the reader's pardon for referring him to my own publications; but the only account of this Round Rock which has hitherto been published is to be found in the "Lake Regions of Central Africa," chap. viii.

† Colonel Frémont gives its dimensions as 650 yards long and 40 feet high.

inscribed with the names of travellers. Hence the Indians have named it Timpe Nabor, or the Painted Rock, corresponding with the Sinaitic " Wady Mukattab." In the present day, though much of the writing has been washed away by rain, 40,000—50,000 souls are calculated to have left their dates and marks from the coping of the wall to the loose stones below this huge sign-post. There is, however, some reason in the proceeding : it does not in these lands begin and end with the silly purpose, as amongst climbers of the Pyramids, and *fouilleurs* of the sarcophagi of Apis, to bequeath one's few poor letters to a little athanasia.   Prairie travellers and emigrants expect to be followed by their friends, and leave, in their vermilion outfit, or their white house-paint or their brownish-black tar—a useful article for waggons — a homely but hearty word of love or direction upon any conspicuous object.   Even a bull or a buffalo's skull which lying upon the road will attract attention, is made to do duty at this *Poste Restante.*

I will here take the liberty of digressing a little ; with the charitable purpose of admiring the serious turn with which the United States explorers perform their explorations.

Colonel Frémont* thus calls to mind the earnest deeds of a bygone day.   " One George Weymouth was sent out to Maine by the Earl of Southampton, Lord Arundel, and others ; and in the narrative of their discoveries he says : 'the next day we ascended in our pinnace that part of the river which lies more to the westward, carrying with us a cross—a thing never omitted by any Christian traveller—which we erected at the ultimate end of our route.'   This was in the year 1605, and in 1842 I obeyed the feeling of early travellers, and left the impressions of the cross deeply engraved on the vast rock, one thousand miles beyond the Mississippi, to which discoverers have given the national name of Rock Independence."

Captain Stansbury † is not less scrupulous upon the subject of travelling proprieties.   One of his entries is couched as follows : " Sunday, June 10, barometer 28·82, themometer 70°.   The camp rested : it had been determined, from the commencement of the expedition, to devote this day whenever practicable to its legitimate purpose, as an interval of rest

---

* Report of the Exploring Expedition to the Rocky Mountains, p. 72.
† Stansbury's Expedition, ch. i. p. 22.

for man and beast. I here beg to record, as the result of my experience, derived not only from the present journey, but from the observations of many years spent in the performance of similar duties, that, as a mere matter of pecuniary consideration, apart from all higher obligations, it is wise to keep the Sabbath."

Lieutenant W. F. Lynch, United States Navy, who in 1857 commanded the United States expedition to the river Jordan and the Dead Sea*, and published a narrative not deficient in interest, thus describes his proceedings at El Meshra, the bathing place of the Christian pilgrims :—

" This ground is consecrated by tradition as the place where the Israelites passed over with the ark of the covenant; and where the blessed Saviour was baptized by John. Feeling that it would be desecration to moor the boats at a place so sacred, we passed it, and with some difficulty found a landing below.

" My first act was to bathe in the consecrated stream, thanking God, first, for the precious favour of being permitted to visit such a spot ; and secondly, for his protecting care throughout our perilous passage. For a long time after, I sat upon the bank, my mind oppressed with awe, as I mused upon the great and wondrous events which had here occurred." In strange contrast with these passages stands the characteristic prophecy— " The time is coming—the beginning is come now—when the whole worthless list of kings with all their myrmidons, will be swept from their places and made to bear a part in the toils and sufferings of the great human family," &c. &c.

I would not willingly make light in others of certain finer sentiments —veneration, for instance, and conscientiousness— which Nature has perhaps debarred me from over enjoying; nor is it in my mind to console myself for the privation by debasing the gift in those gifted with it. But—the but, I fear, will, unlike " if," be anything rather than a great peacemaker in this case — there are feelings which, when strongly felt, when they well from the bottom of the heart, man conceals in the privacy of his own bosom ; and which if published to the world, are apt to remind the world that it has heard of a form

* Chap. iii. Authorised Edition. Sampson Low, Son, and Co. 47, Ludgate Hill, 1859.

of speech, as well as of argument, ranking under the category
of *ad captandum vulgus.*

About a mile beyond Independence Rock we forded the
Sweetwater. We had crossed the divide between this stream
and the Platte, and were now to ascend our fourth river
valley, the three others being the Missouri, the Big Blue, and
the Nebraska. The Canadian voyageurs have translated the
name Sweetwater from the Indian Pina Pa; but the term
is here more applicable in a metaphorical than in a literal
point of view. The water of the lower bed is rather hard than
otherwise, and some travellers have detected brackishness in it,
yet the banks are free from the saline hoar, which deters the
thirstiest from touching many streams on this line. The Sweetwater, in its calmer course, is a perfect Naiad of the mountains;
presently it will be an Undine hurried by that terrible Anagké, to
which Jove himself must bend his omniscient head, into the
grisly marital embrace of the gloomy old Platte. Passing pleasant after the surly ungenial silence of the Shallow River, is
the merry prattle with which she answers the whisperings of
those fickle flatterers, the winds, before that wedding day when
silence shall become her doom. There is a something in
the Sweetwater which appeals to the feelings of rugged men:
even the drivers and the station keepers speak of " her" with a
bearish affection.

After fording the swift Pina Pa, at that point about seventy
feet wide and deep to the axles, we ran along its valley about
six miles, and reached at 9·15 P.M. the muddy station kept by
M. Planté, the usual Canadian. En route we had passed by
the Devil's Gate, one of the great curiosities of this line of
travel. It is the beau ideal of a kanyon, our portal opening
upon the threshold of the Rocky Mountains: I can compare its
form from afar only with the Brêche de Roland in the Pyrenees.
The main pass of Aden magnified twenty fold is something of
the same kind, but the simile is too unsavoury. The height
of the gorge is from 300 to 400 feet: perpendicular, and on the
south side threatening to fall, it has already done so in parts, as
the masses which cumber the stream-bed show. The breadth
varies from a minimum of 40 to a maximum of 105 feet,
where the fissure yawns out, and the total length of the cleft
is about 250 yards. The material of the walls is a grey granite,

traversed by dykes of traps : and the rock in which the
deep narrow crevasse has been made, runs right through the
extreme southern shoulder of a ridge, which bears appropriately
enough the name of " Rattlesnake Hills." Through this wild
gorge the bright stream frets and forces her way, singing, unlike
Liris, with a feminine untaciturnity, that awakes the echoes of
the pent-up channel,— tumbling and gurgling, dashing and
foaming over the snags, blocks, and boulders which, fallen
from the cliffs above, obstruct the way, and bedewing the cedars
and bright shrubs which fringe the ragged staples of the gate.
Why she should have not promenaded gently and quietly round,
instead of through, this grizzly barrier of rock, goodness only
knows : however, wilfull and womanlike, she has set her heart
upon an apparent impossibility, and, as usual with her sex
under the circumstances, she has had her way. Sermons in
stones — I would humbly suggest to my gender.

Procrastination once more stole my chance : I had reserved
myself for sketching the Devil's Gate from the S.-W., but the
station proved too distant to convey a just idea of it. For the
truest representation of the gate, the curious reader will refer
to the artistic work of Mr. Fred. Piercy*; that published in
Captain Marcy's " List of Itineraries " is like anything but the
Devil's Gate; even the rough lithograph in Colonel Frémont's
report is more truthful.

We supped badly as mankind well could at the cabaret, where
a very plain young person, and no neat handed Phyllis withal,
supplied us with a cock whose toughness claimed for it the
honours of grandpaternity. Chickens and eggs there were
none ; butcher's meat, of course, was unknown, and our hosts
ignored the name of tea; their salt was a kind of saleratus, and
their sugar at least half Indian meal. When asked about fish,
they said that the Sweetwater contained nothing but suckers†,
and that these, though good eating, cannot be caught with a
hook. They are a queer lot these French Canadians who have
" located" themselves in the Far West. Travellers who have
hunted with them speak highly of them as a patient, sub-

---

* Route from Liverpool to Great Salt Lake City.

† A common fish of the genus Labio, of which there are many species,— chub,
mullet, barbel, horned dace, &c.: they are found in almost all the lakes and rivers
of North America.

missive, and obedient race, inured to privations, and gifted
with the reckless *abandon* — no despicable quality in prairie
travelling — of the old Gascon adventurer, armed and ever
vigilant, hardy, handy, and hearty children of nature, combining
with the sagacity and the instinctive qualities all the superstitions of the Indians; enduring as mountain-goats; satisfied
with a diet of wild meat, happiest when it could be followed
by a cup of strong milkless coffee, a "chasse café" and a "brule-
gueule;" invariably and contagiously merry; generous as cou-
rageous; handsome, active, and athletic; sashed, knived, and
dressed in buckskin, to the envy of every Indian "brave,"
and the admiration of every Indian belle, upon whom, if the
adventurer's heart had not fallen into the snares of the more
attractive half-breed, he would spend what remained of his $10
a-month, after coffee, alcohol, and tobacco had been extrava-
gantly paid for, in presents of the gaudiest trash. Such
is the voyageur of books : I can only speak of him as I found
him, a lazy dog, somewhat shy and proud, much addicted to
loafing, and to keeping cabarets, because, as the old phrase is,
the cabarets keep him — in idleness too. Probably his good
qualities lie below the surface : — those who hide a farthing
rushlight under a bushel can hardly expect us, in this railway
age, to take the trouble of finding it. I will answer, however, for the fact, that the bad points are painfully prominent.
By virtue of speaking French and knowing something of
Canada, I obtained some buffalo robes, and after a look at
the supper, which had all the effect of a copious feed, I
found a kind of outhouse, and smoked till sleep weighed down
my eyelids.

Up the Sweetwater.—19th August.

We arose at 6 A.M., before the rest of the household, who,
when aroused "hifered" and sauntered about all *desœuvrés*
till their wool-gathering wits had returned. The breakfast
was a little picture of the supper; for watered milk, half baked
bread, and unrecognisable butter, we paid the somewhat "steep"
sum of $0·75, we privily had our grumble and we set out at
7 A.M. to ascend the valley of the Sweetwater. The river plain is
bounded by two parallel lines of hills, or rather rocks, running
nearly due east and west. Those to the north are about a

hundred miles in extreme length, and rising from a great plateau lie perpendicular to the direction of the real Rocky Mountains towards which they lead: half the course of the Pina Pa
subtends their southern base.   The Western men know them
as the Rattlesnake Hills, whilst the southern are called after
the river.   The former, a continuation of the ridge in which
the Sweetwater has burst a gap — is one of those long lines of
lumpy, misshapen, barren rock, that suggested to the Canadians
for the whole region the name of Les Montagnes Rocheuses.   In
parts they are primary, principally syenite and granite, with a
little gneiss, but they have often so regular a line of cleavage,
perpendicular as well as horizontal, that they may readily be
mistaken for stratifications.   The stratified are slaty, micaceous
hale and red sandstone, dipping northwards and cut by
quartz veins and trap dykes.   The remarkable feature in both
formations is the rounding of the ridges or blocks of smooth
naked granite: hardly any angles appeared; the general effect
was, that they had been water-washed immediately after birth.
The upper portions of this range shelter the Bighorn, or
American moufflon, and the cougar * the grizzly bear and the
wolf.   The southern or Sweetwater range is vulgarly known as
the Green River Mountains: seen from the road their naked,
barren and sandy flanks appear within cannon shot, but they
are distant seven miles.

After a four miles drive up the pleasant valley of the little
river-nymph, to whom the grisly hills formed an effective foil,
we saw on the south of the road " Alkali Lake," another of the
Trona formations with which we were about to become familiar; in the full glare of burning day it was undistingishable
as to the surface from the round pond in Hyde Park.   Presently
ascending a little rise, we were shown for the first time a real
bit of the far-famed Rocky Mountains, which was hardly to be
distinguished from, except by a shade of solidity, the fleecy
sunlit clouds resting upon the horizon: it was Frémont's
Peak, the sharp snow-clad apex of the Wind River range.   Behind
us and afar rose the distant heads of black hills.   The valley was

---

* Locally called the Mountain Lion.   This animal (*F. unicolor*) is the largest
and fiercest feline of the New World: it is a beast of many names — puma, cougar,
American lion, panther or painter, &c.   Its habit of springing upon its prey from
trees makes it feared by hunters.   It was once in the Kaatskills.

charming with its bright glad green, a tapestry of flowery grass,
willow copses where the grouse ran in and out, and long lines
of aspen, beech and cottonwood, while pine and cedar, cypress
and scattered evergreens crept up the cranks and crannies of
the rocks.   In the midst of this Firdaus — so it appeared
to us after the horrid unwithering artemisia Jehannum of last
week — flowed the lovely little stream, transparent as crystal,
and coquettishly changing from side to side in her bed of golden
sand.   To see her tamely submit to being confined within
those dwarf earthen cliffs you would not have known her to be
the same that had made that terrible breach in the rock-wall
below.   "Varium et mutabile semper," &c.: I will not conclude
the quotation, but simply remark that the voyageurs have
called her "She."   And everywhere, in contrast with the deep
verdure and the bright flowers of the valley, rose the stern
forms of the frowning rocks, some apparently hanging as
though threatening a fall, others balanced upon the slenderest
foundations, all split and broken, as though earthquake-riven,
loosely piled into strange figures, the Lion Couchant, Sugar-
loaf, Tortoise and Armadillo, — not a mile in fact was without
its totem.

The road was good, especially when hardened by frost.   We
are now in altitudes where, as in Tibet, parts of the country for
long centuries never thaw.   After passing a singular stone
bluff, on the left of the road, we met a party of discharged
soldiers, who were travelling eastward comfortably enough
in government waggons drawn by six mules.   Not a man saluted
Lieutenant Dana, though he was in uniform, and all looked
surly as Indians after a scalpless raid.   Speeding merrily
along, we were shown on the right of the road a ranch belonging to a Canadian, a "mighty mean man," said the driver,
"who onst gin me ole mare's meat for b'ar."   We were much
shocked by this instance of the awful depravity of the unre-
generate human heart, but our melancholy musings were presently interrupted by the same youth, who pointed out on the
other side of the path, a mass of clay (conglomerate, I presume),
called the Devil's Post-office.   It has been lately washed with
rains so copious, that half the edifice lies at the base of that
which is standing.   The structure is not large: it is highly
satisfactory — especially to a man who in this life has suffered

severely as the Anglo-Indian ever must from endless official
and semi-official correspondence — to remark that the London
Post-office is about double its size.

Beyond the post-office was another ranch belonging to a
Portuguese named Luis Silva, married to an Englishwoman who
had deserted the Salt Lake Saints. We " stayed a piece " there,
but found few inducements to waste our time. Moreover, we
had heard from afar of an " ole 'ooman," an Englishwoman, a
Miss Moore — Miss is still used for Mrs. by Western men and
negroes — celebrated for cleanliness, tidiness, civility, and
housewifery in general, and we were anxious to get rid of the
evil flavour of Canadians, squaws, and " ladies."

At 11 A.M. we reached "three crossings," when we found the
" miss " a stout, active, middle-aged matron, deserving of all
the praises that had so liberally been bestowed upon her. The
little ranch was neatly swept and garnished, papered and ornamented. The skull of a full-grown Bighorn hanging over the
doorway represented the spoils of a stag of twelve. The table
cloth was clean, so was the cooking, so were the children ; and I
was reminded of Europe by the way in which she insisted upon
washing my shirt, an operation which, after leaving the Missouri,
ça va sans dire, had fallen to my own lot. In fact, this day
introduced me to the third novel sensation experienced on the
western side of the Atlantic. The first is to feel (practically)
that all men are equal ; that you are no man's superior, and
that no man is yours. The second — this is spoken as an
African wanderer — to see one's quondam acquaintance, the
Kafir, laying by his grass kilt and coat of grease, invest himself
in broadcloth, part his wool on one side, shave what pile nature
has scattered upon his upper lip, chin, and cheeks below a line
drawn from the ear to the mouth-corner after the fashion of the
times when George the Third was king, and call himself, not
Sambo, but Mr. Scott. The third was my meeting in the
Rocky Mountains with this refreshing specimen of that far old
world, where, on the whole, society still lies in strata, as originally deposited, distinct, sharply defined and rarely displaced,
except by some violent upheaval from below, which, however,
never succeeds long in producing total inversion. Miss Moore's
husband, a decent appendage, had transferred his belief from
the Church of England to the Church of Utah, and the good

wife, as in duty bound, had followed in his wake whom she was bound to love, honour, and obey. But when the serpent came and whispered in Miss Moore's modest, respectable, one-idea'd ear that the Abrahams of Great Salt Lake City are mere " Shamabrams," that not content with Sarahs they add to them an unlimited supply of Hagars, then did our stout English-woman's power of endurance break down never to rise again. " Not an inch would she budge ; " not a step towards U. T. would she take. She fought pluckily against the impending misfortune, and — *à quelque chose malheur est bon !* — she succeeded in re-ducing her husband to that state which is typified by the wife using certain portions of the opposite sex's wardrobe, and in making him make a good livelihood as station master on the waggon-line.

After a copious breakfast, which broke the fast of the four days that had dragged on since our civilised refection at Fort Laramie, we spread our buffalos and water-proofs under the ample eaves of the ranch, and spent the day in taking time with the sextant,— every watch being wrong—in snoozing, dozing, chatting, smoking, and contemplating the novel view. Straight before us rose the Rattlesnake Hills, a nude and grim horizon, frowning over the soft and placid scene below, whilst at their feet flowed the little river,— *splendidior vitro,*— purling over its pebbly bed with graceful meanderings through clover prairil-lons and garden spots full of wild currants, strawberries, goose-berries, and rattlesnakes ; whilst contrasting with the green River Valley, and the scorched and tawny rock-wall, patches of sand-hill raised by the winds, here and there cumbered the ground. The variety of the scene was much enhanced by the changeful skies. The fine breeze which had set in at 8 A.M. had died in the attempt to thread these heat-refracting ridges, and vapoury clouds, sublimated by the burning sun, floated lazily in the empyrean, casting fitful shadows that now inter-cepted, then admitted, a blinding glare upon the mazy stream and its rough cradle.

In the evening we bathed in the shallow bed of the Sweet-water. It is vain to caution travellers against this imprudence. *Video meliora proboque :*—it is doubtless unwise—but it is also *mera stultitia* to say to men who have not enjoyed ablutions

for a week or ten days, "If you do take that delicious dip you
may possibly catch fear." *Deteriora sequor*,— bathed. Miss
Moore warned us strongly against the rattlesnakes, and during
our walk we carefully observed the Indian rule, to tread upon
the log and not to overstep it.   The crotalus, I need hardly say,
like other snakes, is fond of lurking under the shade of fallen
or felled trunks, and when a heel or a leg is temptingly set
before it, it is not the beast to refuse a bite.   Accidents are
very common, despite all precautions, upon this line, but they
seldom, I believe, prove fatal. The remedies are almost endless :
e. g. hartshorn, used externally and drunk in dilution ; scarification and irrumation of the part, preceded, of course, by a
ligature between the limb and the heart ; application of the
incised breast of a live fowl or frog to the wound ; the dried
and powdered blood of turtle, of this two pinches to be
swallowed and a little dropped upon the place bitten ; a plaster
of chewed or washed plantain-leaves—it is cooling enough, but
can do little more   bound upon the puncture, peppered with a
a little finely powdered tobacco ; pulverised indigo made into a
poultice with water ; cauterisation by gunpowder, hot iron, or
lunar caustic ; cedron, a nut growing on the Isthmus of Panama
—of this remedy I heard, *in loco*, the most wonderful accounts,
dying men being restored, as if by magic, after a bit about
the size of a bean had been placed in their mouths.   As will
be seen below, the land is rich in snake-roots, but the superstitious snake-stone of Hindostan — which acts, if it does act, as
an absorbent of the virus by capillary attraction—is apparently
unknown.   The favourite remedy now in the United States is the
"whiskey cure," which, under the form of arrack, combined in
the case of a scorpion-sting with a poultice of chewed tobacco,
was known for the last fifty years to the British soldier in India
It has the advantage of being a palatable medicine ; it must also
be taken in large quantities, a couple of bottles sometimes producing little effect.   With the lighted end of a cigar applied
as moxa to the wound, a *quantum sufficit* of ardent spirits,
a couple of men to make me walk about when drowsy by the
application of a stick, and above all, with the serious resolu-
tion not to do anything so mean as to "leap the twig," I
should not be afraid of any snake yet created.   The only pro-

viso is that our old enemy must not touch an artery, and that the remedies must be at hand. Fifteen minutes lost, you are "down among the dead men." The history of fatal cases always shows some delay.*

We supped in the evening merrily. It was the best coffee we had tasted since leaving New Orleans; the cream was excellent, so was the cheese. But an antelope had unfortunately been brought in; we had insisted upon a fry of newly killed flesh, which was repeated in the morning, and we had bitterly to regret it. Whilst I was amusing myself by attempting to observe an immersion of Jupiter's satellites, with a notable failure in the shape of that snare and delusion a portable telescope, suddenly there arose a terrible hubbub. For a moment it was believed that the crotalus horridus had been taking liberties with one of Miss Moore's progeny. The seat of pain, however, soon removed the alarming suspicion, and — the rattle-snake seldom does damage at night — we soon came to the conclusion that the dear little fellow who boo-hoo'd for forty had been bitten by a mosquito somewhat bigger than its fellows. The poor mother soon was restored to her habits of happiness and hard labour. Not contented with supporting her own family, she was doing supererogation by feeding a little rat-eyed, snub-nosed, shark-mouthed, half-breed girl, who was, I believe, in the market as a "chattel." Mrs. Dana pointed out to me one sign of demoralisation on the part of Miss Moore. It was so microscopic that only a woman's acute eye could detect it. Miss Moore was teaching her children to say " Yes surr ! " to every driver.

To the Foot of South Pass, 19th August.

With renewed spirit, despite a somewhat hard struggle with the mosquitoes, we set out at the respectable hour of 5·45 A.M. We had breakfasted comfortably, and an interesting country lay before us. The mules seemed to share in our gaiety. Despite a long ringing, the amiable animals kicked and bit, bucked and

---

* The author of " The Quadroon " (chap. xxxii., &c.) adduces a happy instance of a " hero " who, after a delay and an amount of exertion which certainly would have cost him his life, was relieved by tobacco and cured by the snake-root (*Polygala Senega*). The popular snake-roots quoted by Mr. Bartlett, are the Seneca snake-root, above alluded to, the black snake-root (*Cimicifuga racemosa*), and the Virginia snake-root (*Aristolochia serpentaria*).

backed, till their recalcitrancies had almost deposited us in the
first ford of the Sweetwater. For this, however, we were amply
consoled by the greater misfortunes of our consort, the official
wagon. After long luxuriating in the pick of the teams,
they were to-day so thoroughly badly "muled" that they were
compelled to apply for our assistance.

We forded the river twice within fifty yards, and we recognised with sensible pleasure a homely-looking magpie (*Pica
Hudsonica*), and a rattle-snake, not inappropriately, considering where we were, crossed the road. Our path lay between
two rocky ridges, which gradually closed inwards, forming a
regular kanyon, quite shutting out the view. On both sides white
and micaceous granite towered to the height of 300 or 400 feet,
terminating in jagged and pointed peaks, whose partial disruption covered the angle at their base. Arrived at Ford No. 5,
we began an ascent, and reaching the summit, halted to enjoy
the fine back view of the split and crevassed mountains.

A waterless and grassless tract of fifteen to sixteen miles led
us to a well-known place,— the Ice Springs,— of which, somewhat unnecessarily, a marvel is made. The ground, which lies
on the right of the road, is a long and swampy trough between
two waves of land which permit the humidity to drain down,
and the grass is discoloured, suggesting the presence of alkali.
After digging about two feet, ice is found in small fragments.
Its presence, even in the hottest seasons, may be readily
accounted for by the fact that hereabouts water will freeze
in a tent during July, and by the depth to which the
wintry frost extends. Upon the same principle, snow gathering
in mountain ravines and hollows long outlasts the shallower
deposits. A little beyond Ice Springs, on the opposite side of
and about a quarter of a mile distant from the road, lie the
Warm Springs : one of the many alkaline pans which lie scattered over the face of the country. From the road nothing is to
be seen but a deep cunette full of percolated water.

Beyond the Warm Springs lay a hopeless-looking land, a vast
slope, barren and desolate as Nature could well make it. The
loose sands and the granite masses of the valley had disappeared ; the surface was a thin coat of hard gravelly soil. Some
mosses, a scanty yellow grass, and the dark grey artemisia, now

stunted and shrunk, were sparsely scattered about. It had already begun to give way before an even hardier creation, the rabbit-bush and the grease-wood. The former, which seems to thrive under the wintry snow, is a favourite food with hares which abound in this region; the latter (*Obione*, or *Atriplex canescens*, the chamizo of the Mexicans) derives its name from the oleaginous matter abundant in its wood, and is always a sign of a poor and sterile soil. Avoiding a steep descent by a shorter road, called "Landers' Cut-off," we again came upon the Sweetwater, which was here somewhat broader than below, and lighted upon good grass and underbrush, willow copses, and a fair halting place. At Ford No. 6 — three followed one another in rapid succession — we found the cattle of a travelling trader scattered over the pasture grounds. He proved to be an Italian driven from the low country by a band of Sioux, who had slain his Shoshone wife, and at one time had thought of adding his scalp to his squaw's. After Ford No. 8, we came upon a camping ground, usually called in guide-books "River Bank and Stream." The Sweetwater is here twenty-five feet wide. About three miles beyond it lay the "Foot of Ridge Station," near a willowy creek, called from its principal inhabitants the Muskrat.* The ridge from which it derives its name is a band of stone that will cross the road during to-morrow's ascent. Being a frontier place, it is a favourite camping ground with Indians. To-day a war party of Sioux rode in, *en route* to provide themselves with a few Shoshone scalps.

We made a decided rise to-day, and stood at least 6000 feet above the level of the sea. The altitude of St. Louis being in round numbers 500 feet, and reckoning the diminution of temperature at 1° F. = 100 yards, we are already 19° to 20° F. colder than before. The severity of the atmosphere and the rapid evaporation from the earth cause an increase of frigidity, to which the salts and nitrates upon the surface of the soil, by absorbing the hydrogen of the atmosphere,—as is shown by the dampness of the ground and the absence of dust around the Saleratus Lakes,— greatly add. Another remark made by every

---

* *Fiber Zibeticus*, a beaver-like animal that inhabits the banks of ponds and streams: it has a strong musky odour in summer only, and is greedily eaten by the Indians.

traveller in these regions, is the marked influence upon the temperature caused by the presence and the absence of the sun. The day will be sultry and oppressive, and a fire will be required at night.   In the morning about 11 A.M., the thermometer showed 80° Fahrenheit; at 4 P.M., the sky being clouded over, it fell 25°: before dawn, affected by the cold north wind from the snows about the pass, it stood at 40°.

The lowering firmament threatened rain, of which, however, the thirsty land was disappointed. Moreover, all were agreed that snow was to be expected in another fortnight, if not sooner. Glacial storms occasionally occur in July and August, so that in some years the land may be said to have no summer.   In winter the sharpness of the cold is such that it can be kept out only by clothes of the closest texture; the mountain-men, like the Esquimaux, prefer to clothe themselves cap-a-piè in the prepared skins of animals. We were all animated with a nervous desire for travel, but there was the rub.   The station-master declared that he had no driver, no authority to forward two wagons-full, and no cattle; consequently, that the last comers must be last served, and wait patiently at Rocky Ridge till they could be sent on. They would find antelopes in plenty, perhaps a grizzly, and plenty of plover, crows, and delicate little ground squirrels* by the burrowfull, to "keep their hands in." We being the first comers, a title to preference rarely disputed in this law-and-rule-abiding land, prudently held ourselves aloof.   The judiciary, however, was sorely "exercised."   Being a "professor," that is, a serious person, he could not relieve his mind by certain little *moyens* which naturally occurred to the rest of the party. Many and protracted were the pow-wows that took place on this momentous occasion.   Sometimes our quondam companions —we now looked upon them as friends lost to us—would mysteriously disappear as though the earth had opened and swallowed them, and presently they would return with woe-begone step and the wrinkled brow of care, simulating an ease which they were far from feeling.

---

* I had no opportunity of observing this clean, pretty, and vivacious little animal, whose chirruping resembles that of a bird; but it appeared to be quite a different species from the common striped and spotted prairie squirrel (*Spermophilus tredecimlineatus*), or the Chipmonk or Chipmuk (*S. striatus*).

The station rather added to than took from our discomfort : it was a terrible unclean hole; milk was not procurable within thirty-five miles; one of the officials was suffering sorely from a stomach ache; there was no sugar, and the cooking was atrocious.   With a stray title-pageless volume of some natural history of America, and another of agricultural reports — in those days, before reform came, these scientific and highly elaborate compositions, neatly printed and expensively got up at the public expense, were apparently distributed to every ranch and station in the line of road — I worked through the long and tedious afternoon.   We were not sorry when the night came, but then the floor was knobby, the mosquitoes seemed rather to enjoy the cold, and the banks swarmed with " chinches." *   The coyotes and wolves made night vocal with their choruses, and had nearly caused an accident.   One of the station-men arose, and having a bone to pick with the animals for having robbed his beef barrel, cocked his revolver, and was upon the point of firing, when the object aimed at started up and cried out in the nick of time that he was a Federal marshal, not a wolf.

To the South Pass, August 20th.

We rose with the daybreak; we did not start till nearly 8 A.M., the interim having been consumed by the tenants of our late consort in a vain palaver.   We bade adieu to them and mounted at last, loudly pitying their miseries as they disappeared from our ken.   But the driver bade us reserve our sympathy and humane expressions for a more fitting occasion, and declared — it was probably a little effort of his own imagination — that those faithless friends had spent all their spare time in persuading him to take them on and to leave us behind.   I, for one, will never believe that anything of the kind had been attempted; a man must be created with a total absence of the bowels of compassion, who would leave a woman and a young child for days together at the Foot of Ridge Station.

---

* The chinch or chints is the Spanish *chinche* — the popular word for the *cimex lectularius* in the Southern States.   In other parts of the United States the English bug is called a bed-bug: without the prefix it is applied to beetles and a variety of coleopters, as the May-bug, June-bug, golden-bug, &c.

The road at once struck away from the Sweetwater, winding up and down rugged hills and broken hollows.   From Fort Laramie the land is all a sandy and hilly desert where one can easily starve, but here it shows its worst features.   During a steep descent a mule fell and was not made to regain its footing without difficulty.   Signs of wolves, coyotes, and badgers were abundant, and the *coqs de prairie* (sage-chickens) still young and toothsome at this season, were at no pains to get out of shot.   After about five miles we passed by " Three Lakes," dirty little ponds north of the road, two near it and one distant, all about a quarter of a mile apart, and said by those fond of tasting strange things to have somewhat the flavour, as they certainly have the semblance, of soapsuds.   Beyond this point we crossed a number of influents of the pretty Sweetwater, some dry, others full : the most interesting was Strawberry Creek : it supplies plenty of the fragrant wild fruit, and white and red willows fringe the bed as long as it retains its individuality.   To the north a mass of purple nimbus obscured the mountains — on Frémont's Peak it is said always to rain or snow — and left no visible line between earth and sky.   Quaking Asp Creek was bone dry.   At MacAchran's Branch of the Sweetwater we found, pitched upon a sward near a willow copse, a Provençal Frenchman — by what " hasard que les sceptiques appellent l'homme d'affaires du bon Dieu," did he come here ? — who begged us to stop and give him the news, especially about the Indians : we could say little that was reassuring.   Another spell of rough steep ground placed us at Willow Creek, a pretty little prairillon, with verdure, water, and an abundance of the larger vegetation, upon which our eyes, long accustomed to artemisia and rabbit-bush, dwelt with a compound sense of surprise and pleasure.   In a well-built ranch at this place of plenty were two Canadian traders, apparently settled for life ; they supplied us, as we found it necessary to " liquor up," with a whiskey which did not poison us, and that is about all that I can say for it.   At Ford No. 9, we bade adieu to the Sweetwater with that natural regret which one feels when losing sight of the only pretty face and pleasant person in the neighbourhood ; and we heard with a melancholy satisfaction the driver's tribute to departing worth, viz. that its upper course is the " healthiest water in the world."   Near this spot, since my departure, has been founded " South Pass City," one of the many mushroom growths which the presence of gold in the Rocky Mountains has caused to spring up.

Ten miles beyond Ford No. 9, hilly miles, ending in a long champaign having some of the characteristics of a rolling prairie, with scatters of white, rose, and smoky quartz, granite, hornblende, porphyry, marble-like lime, sandstone and mica slate,— the two latter cropping out of the ground and forming rocky ridges,— led us to the South Pass, the great *Wasserscheide* between the Atlantic and the Pacific ; and the frontier points between the territory of Nebraska and the State of Oregon. From the mouth of the Sweetwater, about 120 miles, we have been rising so gradually, almost imperceptibly, that now we unexpectedly find ourselves upon the summit.   The distance from Fort Laramie is 320 miles, from St. Louis 1580, and from the mouth of the Oregon about 1400 : it is therefore nearly midway between the Mississippi and the Pacific.   The dimensions of this memorial spot are 7490 feet above sea-level, and 20 miles in breadth.   The last part of the ascent is so gentle that it is difficult to distinguish the exact point where the versant lies : a stony band crossing the road on the ridge of the table-land is pointed out as the place, and the position has been fixed at north latitude 48° 19′, and west longitude 108° 40′.*
The northern limit is the noble chain of Les Montagnes Rocheuses, which goes by the name of the Wind River; the southern is called Table Mountain, an insignificant mass of low hills.

A pass it is not : it has some of the features of Thermopylæ or the Gorge of Killicrankie; of the European St. Bernard or Simplon; of the Alleghany Passes or of the Mexican *Barrancas*. It is not, as it sounds, a ghaut between lofty mountains, or, as the traveller may expect, a giant gateway, opening through cyclopean walls of beetling rocks that rise in forbidding grandeur as he passes onwards to the Western continent.   And yet the

---

* Some guide-books place the watershed between two small hills, the " Twin Peaks," about fifty or sixty feet high ; the road, however, no longer passes between them.

word " Pass " has its significancy. In that New World, where nature has worked upon the largest scale, where every feature of scenery, river and lake, swamp and forest, prairie and mountain, dwarf their congeners in the old hemisphere, this majestic level-topped bluff, the highest steppe of the continent, upon whose iron surface there is space enough for the armies of the globe to march over, is the grandest and the most appropriate of avenues.

A watershed is always exciting to the traveller. What shall I say of this, where, on the topmost point of American travel, you drink within a hundred yards of the waters of the Atlantic and the Pacific Oceans?—that divides the "doorways of the west wind" from the "portals of the sunrise." On the other side of yon throne of storms, within sight, did not the Sierra interpose, lie separated by a trivial space the fountain-heads that give birth to the noblest rivers of the continent, the Columbia, the Colorado, and the Yellowstone, which is to the Missouri what the Missouri is to the Mississippi; — whence the waters trend to four opposite directions; the Wind River to the north-east; to the south-east the Sweetwater and the Platte; the various branches of the Snake River to the north-east; and to the south-west the Green River, that finds its way into the Californian Gulf.* It is a suggestive spot this "divortia aquarum:" it compels Memory to revive past scenes before plunging into the mysterious "Lands of the Hereafter," which lie before and beneath the feet. The Great Ferry, which steam has now bridged, the palisaded banks of the Hudson, the

---

* As early as A.D. 1772 (Description of the Province of Carolana, &c. &c., by Daniel Cox) it was suggested that there was a line of water communication by means of the "Northern branch of the Great Yellow River, by the natives called the River of the Massorites" (Missouri River), and a branch of the Columbia River, which, however, was erroneously supposed to disembogue through the Great Salt Lake into the Pacific. The idea has been revived in the present day. Some assert that the upper waters of the Yellowstone, which approach within three hundred miles of Gt. S. L. City, are three feet deep, and therefore navigable for flat-bottomed boats during the annual inundation. Others believe that, as in the case of the Platte, shallowness would be an insuperable obstacle, except for one or two months. This point will doubtless be settled by Captain W. F. Raynolds, of the United States Topographical Engineers, who, accompanied by Colonel J. Bridger was, at the time of my visit to Gt. S. L. City, exploring the Valley of the Yellowstone.

soft and sunny scenery of the Ohio, and the kingly course of the Upper Mississippi, the terrible beauty of Niagara, and the marvels of that chain of inland seas which winds its watery way from Ontario to Superior; the rich pasture lands of the North, the plantations of the semitropical South, and the broad cornfields of the West: finally the vast meadow-land and the gloomy desert-waste of sage and saleratus, of clay and *mauvaise terre*, of red *butte* and tawny rock: all pass before the mind in rapid array ere they are thrust into oblivion by the excitement of a new departure.

But we have not yet reached our destination, which is two miles below the South Pass. Pacific Springs is our station; it lies a little down the hill, and we can sight it from the road. The springs are a pond of pure, hard, and very cold water surrounded by a strip of shaking bog, which must be boarded over before it will bear a man. The hut would be a right melancholy abode, were it not for the wooded ground on one hand and the glorious snow peaks on the other side of the "Pass." We reached Pacific Springs at 3 P.M. and dined without delay; the material being bouilli and potatoes — unusual luxuries. About an hour afterwards the west wind, here almost invariable, brought up a shower of rain, and swept a vast veil over the forms of the Wind River Mountains. Towards sunset it cleared away, the departing luminary poured a flood of gold upon the majestic pile — I have seldom seen a view more beautiful.

From the South, the barren rolling table-land that forms the Pass trends northwards, till it sinks apparently below a ridge of offsets from the main body, black with timber,—cedar, cypress, fir, and balsam pine. The hand of nature has marked, as though by line and level, the place where vegetation shall go and no farther. Below the waist the mountains are robed in evergreens; above it, to the shoulders, they would be entirely bare, but for the atmosphere, which has thrown a thin veil of light blue over their tawny grey, whilst their majestic heads are covered with ice and snow, or are hidden from sight by thundercloud or the morning mist. From the south on clear days the cold and glittering radiance may be seen at a distance of a hundred miles. The monarch of these mountains is "Frémont's Peak;" its height is laid down at 13,570 feet above sea level; and second to it is a hoary cone called by the station-people Snowy Peak.

That evening the Wind River Mountains appeared in marvellous majesty. The huge purple hangings of rain-cloud in the northern sky set off their huge proportions, and gave prominence, as in a stereoscope, to their gigantic forms, and their upper heights, hoar with the frosts of ages. The mellow radiance of the setting sun diffused a charming softness over their more rugged features, defining the folds and ravines with a distinctness which deceived every idea of distance. And as the light sank behind the far western horizon, it travelled slowly up the mountain side, till, reaching the summit, it mingled its splendours with the snow — flashing and flickering for a few brief moments, then wasting them in the dark depths of the upper air. Nor was the scene less lovely in the morning hour, as the first effulgence of day fell upon the masses of dew-cloud, —at this time mist always settles upon their brows,—lit up the peaks, which gleamed like silver, and poured its streams of light and warmth over the broad skirts reposing upon the plain.

This unknown region was explored in August 1842, by Colonel, then Brevet-Captain, J. C. Frémont, of the United States Topographical Engineers; and his eloquent descriptions of the magnificent scenery that rewarded his energy and enterprise prove how easily men write well when they have a great subject to write upon. The concourse of small green tarns, rushing waters, and lofty cascades, with the gigantic disorder of enormous masses, the savage sublimity of the naked rock, broken, jagged cones, slender minarets, needles, and columns, and serrated walls, 2000 to 3000 feet high, all naked and destitute of vegetable earth; the vertical precipices, chasms, and fissures, insecure icy passages, long moraines, and sloping glaciers — which had nearly proved fatal to some of the party ;—the stern recesses, shutting out from the world dells and ravines of exquisite beauty, smoothly carpeted with soft grass, kept green and fresh by the moisture of the atmosphere, and sown with gay groups of brilliant flowers, of which yellow was the predominant colour: all this glory and grandeur seems to be placed like a picture before our eyes. The reader enjoys, like the explorer, the fragrant odour of the pines, and the pleasure of breathing, in the bright, clear morning, that "mountain air which makes a constant theme of the hunter's praise," and which causes man to feel as if he had been inhaling some exhilarating gas. We sympathise with his joy in having hit upon " such a beautiful entrance to the mountains," in his sorrow, caused by accidents to barometer and thermometer, and in the honest pride with which, fixing a ramrod in the crevice of " an unstable and precarious slab, which it seemed a breath would hurl into the abyss below," he unfurled the Stars and the Stripes, to wave in the breeze where flag never waved before — over the topmost crest of the Rocky Mountains. And every driver upon the road now can tell how, in the profound silence and terrible stillness and solitude that affect the mind as the great features of the scene, while sitting on a rock at the very summit, where the silence was absolute, unbroken by any sound, and the stillness and solitude were completest, a solitary "humble-bee," * winging through the black-blue air his flight from the eastern valley, alit upon the knee of one of the men, and, helas! " found a grave in the leaves of the large book, among the flowers collected on the way."

The Wind River range has other qualities than mere formal beauty to recommend it. At Horse-shoe Creek I was shown a quill full of large gold-grains from a new digging. Probably all the primitive masses of the Rocky Mountains will be found to contain the precious metal. The wooded heights are said to be a very paradise of sport, full of elk and every kind of deer; pumas; bears, brown† as well as grizzly; the wolverine‡; in parts the mountain-buffalo — briefly, all the noble game of the Continent. The Indian tribes, Shoshones and Blackfeet, are not deadly to whites. Washiki, the chief of the former, had, during the time of our visit, retired to hilly ground, about

---

* A species of *bromus* or *bombus*. In the United States, as in England, the word is often pronounced bumble-bee. Johnson says we call a bee an humble bee that wants a sting ; so the States call black cattle without horns " humble cows." It is the general belief of the mountaineers that the bee, the partridge, the plantain, and the "Jamestown weed" follow the footsteps of the white pioneers westward.

† Some authorities doubt that the European brown bear is found in America.

‡ The wolverine (*gulo luscus*), carcajou, or glutton, extends throughout Utah Territory : its carnivorous propensities render it an object of peculiar hatred to fur-hunters. The first name is loosely used in the States : the people of Michigan are called wolverines, from the large number of *mischievous prairie wolves* found there (Bartlett).

forty miles north of the Foot of Ridge Station. This chief — a fine, manly fellow, equal in point of physical strength to the higher race — had been a firm friend, from the beginning, to emigrant and settler; but he was complaining, according to the road officials, that the small amount of inducement prevented his affording good conduct any longer, that he must rob, like the rest of the tribe. Game, indeed, is not unfrequently found near the Pacific Springs; they are visited, later in the year, by swans, geese, and flights of ducks. At this season they seem principally to attract coyotes, — five mules have lately been worried by the little villains, — huge cranes, chicken-hawks, a large species of trochilus, and clouds of mosquitoes, which neither the altitude, the cold, nor the eternal wind-storm that howls through the Pass, can drive from their favourite breeding-bed. Near nightfall a flock of wild geese passed over us, audibly threatening an early winter. We were obliged, before resting, to insist upon a smudge*, without which fumigation, sleep would have been impossible.

The shanty was perhaps a trifle more uncomfortable than the average; our only seat was a kind of trestled plank, which suggested a certain obsolete military punishment, called riding on a rail. The station-master was a *bon enfant*; but his help, a Mormon lad, still in his teens, had been trained to go in a "sorter" jibbing and somewhat uncomfortable "argufying," "highfalutin'" way. He had the furor for fire-arms that characterises the ingenuous youth of Gt. S. L. City, and his old rattletrap of a revolver, which always reposed by his side at night, was as dangerous to his friends as to himself. His vernacular was peculiar; like Mr. Boatswain Chucks (Mr. D——s), he could begin a sentence with polished and elaborate diction, but it always ended, like the wicked, badly. He described himself, for instance, as having lately been "slightly inebriated;" but the euphuistic periphrasis concluded with an asseveration that he would be "Gord domned," if he did it again.

The night was, like the day, loud and windy, the log hut being somewhat crannied and creviced, and the door had a porcelain handle, and a shocking bad fit — a characteristic com-

---

* This old North of England word is used in the West for a heap of green bush or other damp combustibles, placed inside or to windward of a house or tent, and partially lighted, so as to produce a thick, pungent steam.

bination. We had some trouble to keep ourselves warm. At sunrise the thermometer showed 35° Fahrenheit.

We rose early, despite the cold, to enjoy once more the lovely aspect of the Wind River Mountains, upon whose walls of snow the rays of the unrisen sun broke with a splendid effect; breakfasted, and found ourselves *en route* at 8 A.M. The day did not begin well: Mrs. Dana was suffering severely from fatigue, and the rapid transitions from heat to cold; Miss May, poor child! was but little better, and the team was reinforced by an extra mule returning to its proper station; this fourfooted Xantippe caused us, without speaking of the dust from her hoofs, an immensity of trouble.

At the Pacific Creek, two miles below the springs, we began the descent of the Western watershed, and the increase of temperature soon suggested a lower level. We were at once convinced that those who expect any change for the better on the counterslope of the mountains labour under a vulgar error. The land was desolate, a red waste, dotted with sage and grease-bush, and in places pitted with large rain-drops. But looking backwards we could admire the Sweetwater's Gap heading far away, and the glorious pile of mountains which, disposed in crescent shape, curtained the horizon; their southern and western bases wanted however one of the principal charms of the upper view, the snow had well nigh been melted off. Yet, according to the explorer, they supply within the space of a few miles the Green River with a number of tributaries, which are all called the New Forks. We kept them in sight till they mingled with the upper air like immense masses of thunder cloud gathering for a storm.

From Pacific Creek the road is not bad, but at this season the emigrant parties are sorely tried by drought, and when water is found it is often fetid or brackish. After seventeen miles we passed the junction of the Gt. S. L. and Fort Hall roads. Near Little Sandy Creek — a feeder of its larger namesake — which after rains is about 2·5 feet deep, we found nothing but sand, caked clay, sage, thistles, and the scattered fragments of camp fires, with large ravens picking at the bleaching skeletons, and other indications of a halting-ground,

an eddy in the great current of mankind, which, ceaseless as
the Gulf Stream, ever courses from east to west. After a long
stage of twenty-nine miles, we made Big Sandy Creek, an important influent of the Green River; the stream, then shrunken,
was in breadth not less than five rods, each = 16·5 feet, run
ning with a clear swift current through a pretty little prairillon, bright with the blue lupine, the delicate pink malvacea, the
golden helianthus, purple aster acting daisy, the white mountain heath, and the green Asclepias tuberosa*, a weed common
throughout U. T. The Indians, in their picturesque way, term
this stream Wágáhongopá, or the Glistening Gravel Water.†
We halted for an hour to rest and dine; the people of the station, man and wife, the latter very young, were both English,
and of course Mormons; they had but lately become tenants of
the ranch, but already they were thinking, as the Old Country
people will, of making their surroundings "nice and tidy."

Beyond the Glistening Gravel Water lies a *mauvaise terre*,
sometimes called the First Desert, and upon the old road water
is not found in the dry season within forty-nine miles--a terrible *jornada* ‡ for laden waggons with tired cattle. We prepared for drought by replenishing all our canteens—one of
them especially, a tin flask, covered outside with thick cloth,
kept the fluid deliciously cold—and we amused ourselves by the
pleasant prospect of seeing wild mules taught to bear harness.
The tricks of equine viciousness and asinine obstinacy played
by the mongrels were so distinct, that we had no pains in determining what was inherited from the father and what from the
other side of the house. Before they could be hitched up
they were severally hustled into something like a parallel line
with the pole, and were then forced into their places by a rope

* Locally called milk-weed. The whites use the silky cotton of the pods, as in
Arabia, for bed stuffings, and the Sioux Indians of the Upper Platte boil and eat
the young pods with their buffalo flesh. Col. Frémont asserts that he never saw
this plant without remarking "on the flower a large butterfly, so nearly resembling
it in colour as to be distinguishable at a little distance only by the motion of its
wings."

† Similarly the Snake River, an eastern influent of the Colorado, is called Yampa
pa or Sweet Root (*Anethum graveolens*) Water.

‡ The Spanish-Mexican term for a day's march. It is generally applied to a
waterless march, *e.g.* "Jornada del Muerto" in New Mexico, which, like some
in the Sahara, measures ninety miles across.

attached to the forewheel and hauled at the other end by two or three men. Each of these pleasant animals had a bell; it is sure, unless corralled, to run away, and at night sound is necessary to guide the pursuer. At last, being "all aboord," we made a start, dashed over the Big Sandy, charged the high stiff bank with an impetus that might have carried us up an otter-slide or a Montagne Russe, and took the right side of the valley, leaving the stream at some distance.

Rain-clouds appeared from the direction of the hills; apparently they had many centres, as the distant sheet was rent into a succession of distinct streamers. A few drops fell upon us as we advanced. Then the fiery sun "ate up" the clouds, or raised them so high that they became playthings in the hands of the strong and steady western gale. The thermometer showed 95° in the carriage, and 111° exposed to the reflected heat upon the black leather cushions. It was observable, however, that the sensation was not what might have been expected from the height of the mercury, and perspiration was unknown except during severe exercise; this proves the purity and salubrity of the air. In St. Jo. and New Orleans the effect would have been that of India or of a Turkish steam-bath. The heat, however, brought with it one evil — a green-headed horsefly, that stung like a wasp, and from which cattle must be protected with a coating of grease and tar. Whenever wind blew, tourbillons of dust coursed over the different parts of the plain, showing a highly electrical state of the atmosphere. When the air was unmoved the mirage was perfect as the sarab in Sindh or Southern Persia; earth and air were both so dry that the refraction of the sunbeams elevated the objects acted upon more than I had ever seen before. A sea lay constantly before our eyes, receding of course as we advanced, but in all other points a complete *lusus naturæ*. The colour of the water was a dull cool sky-blue, not white, as the "looming" generally is; the broad expanse had none of that tremulous upward motion which is its general concomitant; it lay placid, still, and perfectly reflecting in its azure depths — here and there broken by projecting capes and bluff headlands — the forms of the higher grounds bordering the horizon.

After twelve miles' driving we passed through a depression called Simpson's Hollow, and somewhat celebrated in local

story. Two semicircles of black still charred the ground; on
a cursory view they might have been mistaken for burnt-out
lignite. Here, in 1857, the Mormons fell upon a coralled
train of twenty-three wagons, laden with provisions and other
necessaries for the Federal troops, then halted at Camp Scott
awaiting orders to advance. The wagoners, suddenly attacked,
and, as usual, unarmed,— their weapons being fastened inside
their awnings,— could offer no resistance, and the whole convoy
was set on fire except two conveyances, which were left to carry
back supplies for the drivers till they could reach their homes.
On this occasion the *dux facti* was Lot Smith, a man of reputation for hard riding and general gallantry. The old saint is
always spoken of as a good man who lives by "Mormon rule
of wisdom." As at Fort Sumter, no blood was spilt. So far
the Mormons behaved with temper and prudence; but this
their first open act of rebellion against, or secession from, the
Federal authority, nearly proved fatal to them; had the
helm of government been held by a firmer hand than poor
Mr. Buchanan's the scenes of Nauvoo would have been acted
again at Gt. S. L. City. As it was, all turned out *à merveille*
for the saints militant. They still boast loudly of the achieve-
ment, and on the marked spot where it was performed, the
juvenile emigrants of the creed erect dwarf graves and nameless
" wooden " tomb-" stones " in derision of their enemies.

As sunset drew near we approached the banks of the Big Sandy
River. The bottom through which it flowed was several yards
in breadth, bright green with grass, and thickly feathered with
willows and cottonwood. It showed no sign of cultivation; the
absence of cereals may be accounted for by its extreme cold;
it freezes there every night, and none but the hardiest grains,
oats and rye, which here are little appreciated, could be made
to grow. We are now approaching the valley of the Green
River, which, like many of the rivers in the eastern States, appears formerly to have filled a far larger channel. Flat tables
and elevated terraces of horizontal strata, — showing that the
deposit was made in still waters — with layers varying from a few
lines to a foot in thickness, composed of hard clay, green and
other sandstones, and agglutinated conglomerates, rise like
islands from barren plains, or form escarpments that buttress
alternately either bank of the winding stream. Such, according

to Captain Stansbury, is the general formation of the land between the South Pass and the "Rim" of the Utah Basin.

Advancing over a soil alternately sandy and rocky—an iron flat that could not boast of a spear of grass—we sighted a number of coyotes, fittest inhabitants of such a waste, and a long distant line of dust, like the smoke of a locomotive, raised by a herd of mules which were being driven to the corral. We were presently met by the Pony-Express rider; he reined in to exchange news, which *de part et d'autre* were simply *nil*. As he pricked onwards over the plain, the driver informed us, with a portentous rolling of the head, that Ichabod was an a'mighty fine "shyoot." Within five or six miles of Green River we passed the boundary stone which bears Oregon on one side and Utah on the other. We had now traversed the south-eastern corner of the country of Long-eared men*, and were entering Deserét, the Land of the Honey Bee.

At 6·30 P.M. we debouched upon the bank of the Green River. The station was the home of Mr. Macarthy, our driver. The son of a Scotchman who had settled in the U. S. he retained many signs of his origin, especially freckles, and hair which one might almost venture to describe as sandy; perhaps also at times he was rather o'er fond of draining "a cup o' kindness yet." He had lately taken to himself an English wife, the daughter of a Birmingham mechanic, who, before the end of her pilgrimage to "Zion on the tops of the mountains," had fallen considerably away from grace, and had incurred the risk of being buffeted by Satan for a thousand years—a common form of commination in the New Faith—by marrying a Gentile husband.† The station had the indescribable scent of a Hindoo village, which appears to result from the burning of *bois de vache*

---

* Oregon is supposed by Mr. Eward to have been named by the Spaniards from the immensely lengthened ears (*orejones*) of the Indians who inhabited it.

† Mr. Brigham Young, one of the most tolerant of a people whose motto is toleration, would not, I believe, offer any but an official objection to a Mormon member marrying a worthy Gentile : but even he—and it could hardly be expected that he should—cannot overlook the sin of apostacy. The order of the faith runs thus : "We believe that it is not right to prohibit members of the Church from marrying out of the Church, if it be their determination so to do, but such persons will be considered weak in the faith of our Lord and Saviour Jesus Christ." The same view of the subject is taken, I need hardly say, by the more rigid kind of Roman Catholic.

and the presence of cattle: there were sheep, horses, mules, and a few cows, the latter so lively that it was impossible to milk them. The ground about had the effect of an oasis in the sterile waste, with grass and shrubs, willows, and flowers, wild geraniums, asters, and various *cruciferæ*. A few trees, chiefly quaking asp, lingered near the station, but dead stumps were far more numerous than live trunks. In any other country their rare and precious shade would have endeared them to the whole settlement: here they were never safe when a log was wanted. The Western man is bred and perhaps born — I believe devoutly in transmitted and hereditary qualities — with an instinctive dislike to timber in general. He fells a tree naturally as a bull-terrier worries a cat, and the admirable woodsman's axe which he has invented only serves to whet his desire to try conclusions with every more venerable patriarch of the forest.* Civilised Americans, of course, lament the destructive mania, and the Latter Day Saints have learned by hard experience the inveterate evils that may arise in such a country from disforesting the ground. We supped comfortably at Green River Station, the stream supplying excellent salmon-trout. The Kichimichi, or buffalo-berry †, makes tolerable jelly, and alongside of the station is a store where Mr. Burton (of Maine) sells "Valley Tan" whiskey.‡

The Green River is the Rio Verde of the Spaniards, who named it from its timbered shores and grassy islets ; it is called by the Yuta Indians Piya Ogwe, or the Great Water, by the other tribes Sitskidiágí, or " Prarie-grouse river." It was nearly at its lowest when we saw it : the breadth was not more than 330 feet. In the flood time it widens to 800 feet, and the depth increases from three to six. During the inundation season a ferry is necessary, and when transit is certain the owner sometimes nets $500 a week, which is not unfrequently squandered in a day. The banks are, in places, thirty feet high, and the

* Many of the blades being made by convicts at the State prisons are sold cheap. The extent of the timber regions necessitated this excellent implement, and the saving of labour on the European article is enormous.

† A shrub 10—15 feet high, with a fruit about the size of a pea, red like a wild rose hip, and with a pleasant sub-acid flavour : the Indians eat it with avidity and it is cultivated in the gardens at Gt. S. L. City.

‡ Tannery was the first technological process introduced into the Mormon Valley : hence, all home industry has obtained the sobriquet of " Valley Tan."

bottom may average three miles from side to side. It is a swift flowing stream, running as if it had no time to lose, and truly it has a long way to go.   Its length, volume, and direction entitle it to the honour of being called the head water of the Great Rio Colorado, or Coloured River, a larger and more important stream than even the Columbia.   There is some grand exploration still to be done upon the line of the Upper Colorado, especially the divides which lie between it and its various influents, the Grand River and the Yaquisilla, of which the wild trapper brings home many a marvellous tale of beauty and grandeur. Capt. T. A. Gove, of the 10th Reg. of Infantry, then stationed at Camp Floyd, told me that an expedition had often been projected : a party of twenty-five to thirty men, well armed and provided with inflatable boats, might pass without unwarrantable risk through the sparsely populated Indian country: a true report concerning regions of which there are so many false reports, all wearing more or less the garb of fable—beautiful valleys inclosed in inaccessible rocks, Indian cities and golden treasures—would be equally interesting and important.   I cannot recommend the undertaking to the European adventurer: the U. S. have long since organised and perfected what was proposed in England during the Crimean war, and which fell, as other projects then did, to the ground, namely a corps of Topographical Engineers, a body of well-trained and scientific explorers, to whose hands the task may safely be committed.*

---

* The principal explorers under the U. S. Government of the regions lying W. of the Mississippi, and who have published works upon the subject, are the following :—

1. Messrs. Lewis and Clarke, in 1804–6, first explored the Rocky Mountains to the Columbia River.

2. Major Z. M. Pike, in 1805–7, visited the upper waters of the Mississippi and the western regions of Louisiana.

3. Major, afterwards Colonel S. H. Long of the U. S. Top. Eng., made two expeditions, one in 1819–20 to the Rocky Mountains, another in 1823 to the Sources of the St. Peter and the Lake of the Woods—whereby 4 vols. octavo were filled.

4. Governor Cass and Mr. Schoolcraft in 1820 explored the Sources of the Mississippi and the regions west and south of Lake Superior.

5. Colonel H. Dodge, U. S. army, in 1835 travelled 1600 miles from Fort Leavenworth and visited the regions between the Arkansas and the Platte Rivers.

6. Captain Canfield, U.S. Top. Eng., in 1838 explored the country between Forts Leavenworth and Snelling.

We passed a social evening at Green River Station. It boasted of no less than three Englishwomen, two married, and one, the help, still single. Not having the Mormonite *retenue*, the dames were by no means sorry to talk about Birmingham and Yorkshire, their birth-places. At 9 P.M. arrived one of the road agents, Mr. Cloete, from whom I gathered that the mail wagon which once ran from Gt. S. L. city had lately been taken off the road. The intelligence was by no means consolatory, but a course of meditation upon the saying of the sage, "in for a penny, in for a pound," followed by another visit to my namesake's grog-shop, induced a highly philosophical turn, which enabled me — with the aid of a buffalo — to pass a comfortable night in the store.

22nd August. To Hams Fork and Millersville.

We were not under weigh before 8 A.M. Macarthy was again to take the lines, and a *Giovinetto* returning after a temporary absence to a young wife, is not usually rejoiced to run his course. Indeed he felt the inconveniences of a semi-bachelor life so severely, that he often threatened in my private ear, *chemin faisant*, to throw up the whole concern.

7. Mr. M'Clew of Missouri surveyed the boundaries of the Indian reservations: his work was in part revised by the late Capt. Hood, U.S. Top. Eng.

8. Mr. Nicollet (French) in 1833–38 mapped the country west of the Upper Mississippi: he was employed in 1838–9 to make a similar scientific reconnoissance between the Mississippi and the Missouri, on which occasion he was accompanied by Mr. Frémont. He died in 1842.

The explorations of Colonel Frémont, Captain Howard Stansbury, Lieutenant Gunnison and Lieutenant Warren have been frequently alluded to in these pages.

9. Lieutenant, afterwards Captain Charles Wilkes, U.S. navy, set out in 1838, and after a long voyage of discovery in S. America, Oceanica and the Antarctic continent, made San Francisco on August 11, 1841. It is remarkable that this officer's party were actually pitched upon the spot (New Helvetia, afterwards called Sacramento City) where Californian gold was dug by the Mormons.

10. Captain R. B. Marcy, U.S. army, "discovered and explored, located and marked out the wagon road from Fort Smith, Arkansas, to Santa Fé, New Mexico." The road explorers, however, are too numerous to specify.

11. Governor I. I. Stevens, of Washington Territory, surveyed in 1853 the northern land proposed for a Pacific railway near the 47°—49° parallels, from St. Paul to Puget Sound. No portion of that line had been visited since the days of Lewis and Clarke, except a small portion towards the Pacific Ocean.

12. Captain Reynolds, U. S. Top. Eng., accompanied by Colonel Bridger as guide and interpreter, is still (1860) exploring the head waters of the Yellow Stone River.

After the preliminary squabble with the mules, we forded the pebbly and gravelly bed of the river — in parts it looks like a lake exhausted by drainage — whose swift surging waters wetted the upper spokes of the wheels and gurgled pleasantly around the bags which contained the mail for Gt. S. L. City.* We then ran down the river valley, which was here about one mile in breadth, in a smooth flooring of clay, sprinkled with water-rolled pebbles, overgrown in parts with willow, wild cherry, buffalo berries, and quaking asp. Macarthy pointed out in the road-side a rough grave, furnished with the normal tombstone, two pieces of wagon-board: it was occupied by one Farren, who had fallen by the revolver of the redoubtable Slade. Presently we came to the store of Michael Martin, an honest Creole, who vended the staple of prairie goods, champagne, bot-

---

* Sticklers for strict democracy in the U.S. maintain, on the principle that the least possible power should be delegated to the Federal Government, that the transmission of correspondence is no more a national concern than the construction of railways and telegraphs or the transit of passengers and goods. The present system was borrowed from the monopolies of Europe, and was introduced into America at a time when individual enterprise was inadequate to the task ; in the year one of the Republic it became, under the direction of Benjamin Franklin, a State department, and, though men argue in the abstract, few care to propose a private mail system, which would undertake the management of some 27,000 scattered offices, and 40,000 poorly paid clerks.

On this line we saw all the evils of the contract system. The requisite regularity and quickness was neglected, letters and papers were often lost, the mail bags were wetted or thrown carelessly upon the ground, and those entrusted to the conductors were perhaps destroyed. Both parties complain — the postmaster that the contractors seek to drive too hard a bargain with the department, and the contractors that they are carrying the mails at a loss. Since the restoration (in 1858) of the postal communication with the U.S. which was interrupted in 1857, the Mormons attempt to secure good service by advertising their grievances, and with tolerable success. Postmaster Morrill — a Gentile — complained energetically of the mail service during the last year, that letters were wetted and jumbled together, two of one month perhaps and one of another; that magazines often arrived four months after date, and that thirty sacks left at Rocky Ridge were lost. The consequence was that during my stay at Gt. S. L. City the contractors did their duty.

When salaries are small and families large post-office robberies must at times be expected. The postal department have long adopted the system of registered letters : upon payment of five cents. instead of three the letter is placed in a separate bag, entered separately in the office books, forwarded with certain precautions and delivered to the address only after a receipt from the recipient. But the department disclaims all responsibility in case of loss or theft, and the only value of the higher stamp is a somewhat superior facility of tracking the document that bears it.

tled cocktail, "eye-opener," and other liquors, dry goods,—linen-drapery,—a few fancy goods, ribbons, and finery; brandied fruits, jams and jellies, potted provisions, buckskins, moccasins, and so forth. Hearing that Lieut. Dana was *en route* for Camp Floyd, he requested him to take charge of $500, to be paid to Mr. Livingston the sutler, and my companion, with the obligingness that marked his every action, agreed to deliver the dollars, *sauve* the judgment of God in the shape of Indians, or "White Indians."* At the store we noticed a paralytic man. This original lived under the delusion that it was impossible to pass the Devil's Gate: his sister had sent for him to St. Louis, and his friends tried to transport him eastward in chairs; the only result was that he ran away before reaching the Gate, and after some time was brought back by Indians.

Resuming our journey, we passed two places where trains of fifty-one wagons were burned in 1857 by the Mormon Rangers: the black stains had bitten into the ground like the blood marks in the palace of Holyrood — a neat foundation for a structure of superstition. Not far from it was a deep hole, in which the plunderers had " cached" the iron-work which they were unable to carry away. Emerging from the river plain we entered upon another *mauvaise terre*, with knobs and elevations of clay and green gault, striped and banded with lines of stone and pebbles: it was a barren desolate spot, the divide between the Green River and its western influent, the shallow and somewhat sluggish Black's Fork. The name is derived from an old trader: it is called by the Snakes Ongo Ogwe Pa, or " Pine-tree Stream;" it rises in the Bear River Mountains, drains the swamps and lakelets on the way, and bifurcates in its upper bed forming two principal branches, Hams Fork and Muddy Fork.

Near the Pine-tree Stream we met a horse thief driving four bullocks: he was known to Macarthy and did not look over comfortable. We had now fallen into the regular track of Mormon emigration, and saw the wayfarers in their worst plight, near the end of the journey. We passed several families and

---

* A cant term for white thieves disguised as savages, which has a terrible significancy a little further west.

parties of women and children trudging wearily along : most of
the children were in rags or half nude, and all showed gratitude
when we threw them provisions.   The greater part of the men
were armed, but their weapons were far more dangerous to
themselves and their fellows than to the enemy.   There is not
on earth a race of men more ignorant of arms as a rule than the
lower grades of English ; becoming an emigrant, the mechanic
hears that it may be necessary to beat off Indians, so he buys
the first old fire-arm he sees and probably does damage with it.
Only last night a father crossed Green River to beg for a piece
of cloth ; it was intended to shroud the body of his child, which
during the evening had been accidentally shot, and the station
people seemed to think nothing of the accident, as if it were of
daily recurrence.   I was told of three, more or less severe, that
happened in the course of a month.   The western Americans,
who are mostly accustomed to the use of weapons, look upon
these awkwardnesses with a profound contempt.   We were now
in a region of graves, and their presence in this wild was not a
little suggestive.

Presently we entered a valley in which green grass, low
and dense willows, and small but shady trees, an unusually
vigorous vegetation, refreshed, as though with living water,
our eyes parched and dazed by the burning glare.   Stock
strayed over the pasture, and a few Indian tents rose at the
further side ; the view was probably *pas grand' chose*, but we
thought it splendidly beautiful.   At mid-day we reached Hams
Fork, the north-western influent of Green River, and there we
found a station.   The pleasant little stream is called by the
Indians Turugempa, the " Blackfoot Water."

The station was kept by an Irishman and a Scotchman —
" Dawvid Lewis :" it was a disgrace ; the squalor and filth were
worse almost than the two — Cold Springs and Rock Creek —
which we called our horrors, and which had always seemed to
be the *ne plus ultra* of western discomfort.   The shanty was
made of dry-stone piled up against a dwarf cliff to save back-
wall, and ignored doors and windows.   The flies — unequivocal
sign of unclean living ! — darkened the table and covered everything put upon it : the furniture, which mainly consisted of
the different parts of wagons, was broken, and all in disorder ;
the walls were impure, the floor filthy.   The reason was at once

apparent. Two Irishwomen, sisters*, were married to Mr.
Dawvid, and the house was full of "childer," the noisiest and
most rampageous of their kind. I could hardly look upon the
scene without disgust. The fair ones had the porcine Irish
face — I need hardly tell the reader that there are three orders
of physiognomy in that branch of the Keltic family, viz.
porcine, equine, and simian: the pig-faced, the horse-faced, and
the monkey-faced. Describing one I describe both sisters; her
nose was "pugged," apparently by gnawing hard potatoes before
that member had acquired firmness and consistency; her face
was powdered with freckles; her hair, and indeed her general
costume looked, to quote Mr. Dow's sermon, as though she had
been rammed through a bush-fence into a world of wretchedness
and woe. Her dress was unwashed and in tatters, and her feet
were bare; she would not even take the trouble to make for
herself moccasins. Moreover I could not but notice, that
though the house contained two wives it boasted only of one
cubile, and had only one cubiculum. Such things would excite
no surprise in London or Naples, or even in many of the country
parts of Europe, but here, where ground is worthless, where
building material is abundant, and where a few hours of daily
labour would have made the house look at least respectable, I
could not but wonder at it. My first impulse was to attribute
the evil, uncharitably enough, to Mormonism, to renew, in
fact, the stock-complaint of nineteen centuries' standing —

> "Fœcunda culpæ secula nuptias
> Primùm inquinavere, et genus et domus."

A more extended acquaintance with the regions west of the
Wasach taught me that the dirt and discomfort were the growth
of the land. To give the poor devils their due, Dawvid was
civil and intelligent, though a noted dawdler, as that rare
phenomenon a Scotch idler generally is. Moreover his wives
were not deficient in charity; several Indians came to the door
and none went away without a "bit" and a "sup." During
the process of sketching one of these men, a Snake, distinguished
by his vermilion'd hair-parting, eyes blackened, as if by lines of

---

* A man (Mormon) may even marry a mother and her daughters: usually the
relationship with the former is Platonic; the tie, however, is irregular, and has
been contracted in ignorance of the prohibited degrees.

soot or surma, and delicate Hindu-like hands, my eye fell upon
the German-silver handle of a Colt's revolver, which had been
stowed away under the blankets, and a revolver in the Lamanite's
hands breeds evil suspicions.

Again we advanced. The air was like the breath of a
furnace; the sun was a blaze of fire — accounting by-the-bye
for the fact that the human nose in these parts seems invariably
to become cherry-red — all the nullahs were dried up and
the dust-pillars and mirage were the only moving objects on
the plain. Three times we forded Black's Fork, and then
debouched once more upon a long flat. The ground was
scattered over with pebbles of granite, obsidian, flint, and white,
yellow, and smoky quartz, all water-rolled. After twelve miles
we passed Church Butte, one of many curious formations lying
to the left hand or south of the road. This isolated mass of
stiff clay has been cut and ground by wind and rain into folds
and hollow channels which from a distance perfectly simulate
the pillars, groins, and massive buttresses of a ruinous Gothic
cathedral. The foundation is level, except where masses have
been swept down by the rain, and not a blade of grass grows
upon any part. An architect of genius might profitably study
this work of nature: upon that subject, however, I shall presently have more to say. The Butte is highly interesting in a
geological point of view; it shows the elevation of the adjoining
plains in past ages, before partial deluges and the rains of
centuries had effected the great work of degradation.

Again we sighted the pretty valley of Black's Fork, whose
cool clear stream flowed merrily over its pebbly bed. The road
was now populous with Morman emigrants; some had good
teams, others hand-carts, which looked like a cross between a
wheelbarrow and a tax-cart. There was nothing repugnant in
the demeanour of the party; they had been civilised by
travelling, and the younger women who walked together, and
apart from the men, were not too surly to exchange a greeting.
The excessive barrenness of the land presently diminished; gen-
tian and other odoriferous herbs appeared, and the grease-wood,
which somewhat reminded me of the Sindhian camel-thorn, was
of a lighter green than elsewhere, and presented a favourable
contrast with the dull glaucous hues of the eternal prairie sage.
We passed a dwarf copse so strewed with the bones of cattle as

to excite our astonishment: Macarthy told us that it was the place where the 2nd Dragoons encamped in 1857, and lost a number of their horses by cold and starvation. The wolves and coyotes seemed to have retained a predilection for the spot; we saw troops of them in their favourite "location,"— the crest of some little rise, whence they could keep a sharp look out upon any likely addition to their scanty larder.

After sundry steep inclines we forded another little stream, with a muddy bed, shallow, and about thirty feet wide; it is called Smith's Fork, rises in the "Bridger Range" of the Uinta Hills, and sheds into Black's Fork, the main drain of these parts. On the other side stood Millersville, a large ranch with a whole row of unused and condemned wagons drawn up on one side. We arrived at 5·15 P.M., having taken 3 hrs. 15′ to get over twenty miles. The tenement was made of the component parts of vehicles, the chairs had backs of yoke-bows, and the fences which surrounded the corral were of the same material. The station was kept by one Holmes, an American Mormon and an individual completely the reverse of genial; he dispensed his words as if shelling out coin, and he was never — by us at least — seen to smile. His wife was a pretty young Englishwoman, who had spent the best part of her life between London and Portsmouth; when alone with me she took the opportunity of asking some few questions about old places, but this most innocent *téte-à-téte* was presently interrupted by the protrusion through the open door of a *téte de mari au naturel*, with a truly *renfrogné* and vinegarish aspect, which made him look like a calamity. After supplying us with a supper which was clean and neatly served, the pair set out for an evening ride, and towards night we heard the scraping of a violin, which reminded me of Tommaso Scarafaggio :

> " Detto il sega del villagio
> Perché suona il violino."

The " fiddle " was a favourite instrument with Mr. Joseph Smith as the harp with David ; the Mormons, therefore, at the instance of their prophet, are not a little addicted to the use of the bow. We spent a comfortable night at Millersville ; after watching the young moon as she sailed through the depths of a firmament unstained by the least fleck of mist, we found some scattered volumes which rendered us independent of our unsocial Yankee host.

23rd August.—Fort Bridger.

We breakfasted early the next morning and gladly settled accounts with the surly Holmes who had infected — probably by following the example of Mr. Caudle in later life — his pretty wife with his own surliness. Shortly after starting — at 8.30 A.M. — we saw a little clump of seven Indian lodges, which our experience soon taught us were the property of a white; the proprietor met us on the road, and was introduced with due ceremony by Mr. Macarthy. " Uncle Jack " (Robinson, really) is a well known name between South Pass and Gt. S. L. City; he has spent thirty-four years in the mountains, and has saved some $75,000, which have been properly invested at St. Louis; as might be expected, he prefers the home of his adoption and his Indian spouse, who has made him the happy father of I know not how many children, to good society and bad air further east.

Our road lay along the valley of Black's Fork, which here flows from the S.-W. to the N.-E.; the bottom produced in plenty luxuriant grass, the dandelion, and the purple aster, thickets of a shrub like hawthorn (*cratœgus*), black and white currants, the willow and the cotton wood. When almost in sight of the military post we were addressed by two young officers, one of them an assistant-surgeon, who had been engaged in the healthful and exciting pursuit of a badger, whose markings, by-the-bye, greatly differ from the European; they recognised the uniform and accompanied us to the station.

Fort Bridger lies 124 miles from Gt. S. L. City; according to the drivers, however, the road might be considerably shortened. The position is a fertile basin cut into a number of bits by Black's Fork, which disperses itself into four channels about 1·5 mile above the station, and forms again a single bed about two miles below. The fort is situated upon the westernmost islet. It is, as usual, a mere cantonment without any attempt at fortification, and at the time of my visit was garrisoned by two companies of foot, under the command of Captain F. Gardner of the 10th Regiment. The material of the houses is pine and cedar brought from the Uinta Hills, whose black flanks supporting snowy cones rise at the distance of about thirty-five miles. They are a sanitarium, except in winter, when under their influence the mercury sinks to −20° F., not much less rigorous than Minnesota, and they are said to shelter grizzly bears and an abundance of smaller game.

The fort was built by Col. James Bridger, now the oldest trapper on the Rocky Mountains, of whom Messrs. Frémont and Stansbury have both spoken in the highest terms. He divides with Christopher Carson, the Kit Carson of the Wind River and the Sierra Nevada explorations, the honour of being the best guide and interpreter in the Indian country : the palm for prudence is generally given to the former ; for dash and hard fighting to the latter — although, it is said, the mildest mannered of men. Col. Bridger, when an Indian trader, placed this post upon a kind of neutral ground between the Snakes and Crows (Hapsaroke) on the north, the Ogalalas and other Sioux to the east, the Arapahos and Cheyennes on the south, and the various tribes of Yutas (Utahs) on the south-west. He had some difficulties with the Mormons, and Mrs. Mary Ettie Smith, in a volume concerning which something will be said at a future opportunity, veraciously reports his barbarous murder, some years ago, by the Danite band. He was at the time of my visit absent on an exploratory expedition with Captain Raynolds.

Arrived at Fort Bridger, our first thought was to replenish our whiskey-keg : its emptiness was probably due to "the rapid evaporation in such an elevated region imperfectly protected by timber;" but however that may be, I never saw liquor disappear at such a rate before. *Par parenthèse*, our late friends the officials had scarcely been more fortunate : they had watched their whiskey with the eyes of Argus, yet, as the driver facetiously remarked, though the quantity did not diminish too rapidly, the quality lost strength every day. We were conducted by Judge Carter to a building which combined the function of post-office and sutler's store, the judge being also sutler, and performing both parts, I believe, to the satisfaction of every one. After laying in an ample provision of biscuits for Miss May and korn-schnapps for ourselves, we called upon the C. O., who introduced us to his officers, and were led by Captain Cumming to his quarters, where, by means of chat, " solace-tobacco," and toddy, — which in these regions signifies "cold with,"—we soon worked our way through the short three-quarters of an hour allowed us. The officers complained very naturally of their isolation and unpleasant duty, which principally consists in keeping the roads open for, and the Indians from cutting off, parties of unmanageable emigrants, who look upon the Federal army as their humblest servants. At Camp Scott, near Bridger, the army of the Federal Government halted under canvas during the severe winter of 1857–1858, and the subject is still sore to military ears.

We left Bridger at 10 A.M. Macarthy explained away the disregard for the comfort of the public on the part of the contractors in not having a station at the fort, by declaring that they could obtain no land in a government reservation; moreover that forage there would be scarce and dear, whilst the continual influx of Indians would occasion heavy losses in cattle. At Bridger the road forks: the northern line leads to Soda or Beer Springs*, the southern to Gt. S. L. City. Following the latter, we crossed the rough timber bridges that spanned the network of streams, and entered upon another expanse of degraded ground, covered as usual with water-rolled pebbles of granite and porphyry, flint and greenstone. On the left was a butte with steep bluff sides called the Racecourse: the summit, a perfect *mesa*, is said to be quite level, and to measure exactly a mile round — the rule of the American hippodrome. Like these earth-formations generally, it points out the ancient level of the land before water had washed away the outer film of earth's crust. The climate in this part, as indeed everywhere between the South

---

* These springs of sadly prosaic name are the greatest curiosity to be seen on the earth. They lie but a short distance east of the junction of the Fort Hall and the California roads, and are scattered over, perhaps, 40 acres of volcanic ground. They do not, like most springs, run out of the sides of hills, but boil up directly from a level plain. The water contains a gas, and has quite an acid taste: when exposed to the sun or air, it passes but a short distance before it takes the formation of a crust or solid coat of scarlet hue, so that the continued boiling of any of these fountains will "create a stone to the height of its source (15 or 20 feet) some 10 to 20 feet in diameter at the bottom, and from 2 to 3 feet at the top." After arriving at a uniform height, the water has ceased to run from several of the "eyes" to burst out in some other place. The water spurts from some of these very beautifully. Horn's "Overland Guide to California," p. 38. They are also described by Colonel Frémont: "Expedition to Oregon and North California (1843–44)," p. 136.

Pass and the Gt. S. L. Valley, was an exaggeration of the Italian, with hot days, cool nights, and an incomparable purity and tenuity of atmosphere. · We passed on the way a party of emigrants, numbering 359 souls and driving 39 wagons. They were commanded by the patriarch of Mormondom, otherwise Captain John Smith, the eldest son of Hyrum Smith, a brother of Mr. Joseph Smith the prophet, and who, being a child at the time of the murderous affair at Carthage, escaped being coiffe'd with the crown of martyrdom. He rose to the patriarchate on the 18th Feb. 1855 : his predecessor was "old John Smith,"— uncle to Mr. Joseph and successor to Mr. Hyrum Smith,— who died 23rd May, 1854. He was a fair-complexioned man with light hair. His followers accepted gratefully some provisions with which we could afford to part.

After passing the Mormons we came upon a descent which appeared little removed from an angle of 35°, and suggested the propriety of walking down. There was an attempt at a zigzag, and for the benefit of wagons, a rough wall of stones had been run along the sharper corners. At the foot of the hill we remounted, and passing through a wooded bottom, reached at 12·15 P.M.— after fording the Big Muddy — Little Muddy Creek, upon whose banks stood the station. Both these streams are branches of the Hams Fork of Green River ; and, according to the well-known "rule of contrairy," their waters are clear as crystal, showing every pebble in their beds.

Little Muddy was kept by a Canadian, a chatty lively good-humoured fellow blessed with a sour English wife. Possibly the heat — the thermometer showed 95° F. in the shade — had turned her temper ; fortunately it had not similarly affected the milk and cream, which were both unusually good. Jean-Baptiste, having mistaken me for a *Français de France*, a being which he seemed to regard as little lower than the angels,— I was at no pains to disabuse him,— was profuse in his questionings concerning H. I. M. the Emperor, carefully confounding him with the first of the family, and so pleased was he with my responses, that for the first time on that route I found a man ready to spurn *cet animal féroce qu'on appelle la pièce de cinq francs:* in other words, the "almighty dollar."

We bade adieu to Little Muddy at noon, and entered a new country, a broken land of spurs and hollows, in parts absolutely bare, in others clothed with a thick vegetation. Curiously shaped hills, and bluffs of red earth capped with a clay which much resembled snow, bore a thick growth of tall firs and pines whose sombre uniform contrasted strangely with the brilliant leek-like excessive-green foliage, and the tall note-paper-coloured trunks of the ravine-loving quaking-asp (*Populus tremuloides*). The mixture of colours was bizarre in the extreme, and the lay of the land, an uncouth system of converging, diverging, and parallel ridges, with deep divisions — in one of these ravines which is unusually broad and grassy, rise the so-called Copperas Springs, was hardly less striking. We ran winding along a crest of rising ground, passing rapidly, by way of further comparison, two wretched Mormons, man and woman, who were driving, at a snail's pace, a permanently lamed ox, and after a long ascent stood upon the summit of Quaking Asp Hill.

Quaking Asp Hill, according to the drivers, is 1000 feet higher than the South Pass, which would exalt its station to 8400 feet; other authorities, however, reduce it to 7900. The descent was long and rapid, so rapid indeed, that oftentimes when the block of wood which formed our break dropped a bit of the old shoe-sole nailed upon it to prevent ignition, I felt, as man may be excused for feeling, that catching of the breath that precedes the first five-barred gate after a night of "heavy wet." The sides of the road were rich in vegetation, stunted oak, black-jack, and box-elder of the stateliest stature; above rose the wild cherry, and the service tree formed the bushes below. The descent, besides being decidedly sharp, was exceedingly devious, and our frequent "shaves,"— a train of Mormon wagons was crawling down at the same time,— made us feel somewhat thankful that we reached the bottom without broken bones.

The train was commanded by a Captain Murphy, who, as one might expect from the name, had hoisted the Stars and Stripes— it was the only instance of such loyalty seen by us on the plains. The emigrants had left Council Bluffs on the 20th June, an unusually late date, and though weather-beaten, all looked well. Inspirited by our success in surmounting the various difficulties of the way, we "poked fun" at an old Yorkshireman who was

assumed, by way of mirth, to be a Cœlebs in search of polygamy at an epoch of life when perhaps the blessing might
come too late ; and at an exceedingly plain middle-aged and
full-blooded negro-woman, who was fairly warned—the children of Ham are not admitted to the communion of the Saints,
and consequently to the forgiveness of sins and a free seat in
Paradise—that she was " carrying coals to Newcastle."

As the rays of the sun began to slant we made Sulphur Creek ;
it lies at the foot of a mountain called Rim Base, because it is
the Eastern wall of the Great Inland Basin ; westward of this
point the waters can no longer reach the Atlantic or the Pacific ;
each is destined to feed the lakes,

" Nec Oceani pervenit ad undas."

Beyond Sulphur Creek, too, the face of the country changes ;
the sedimentary deposits are no longer seen, the land is broken
and confused, upheaved into huge masses of rock and mountains broken by deep kanyons, ravines, and water-gaps, and
drained by innumerable streamlets.   The exceedingly irregular
lay of the land makes the road devious, and the want of level
ground, which is found only in dwarf parks and prairillons,
would greatly add to the expense of a railway.   We crossed the
Creek, a fetid stagnant water, about ten feet wide, lying in a bed
of black infected mud : during the spring rains, when flowing, it
is said to be wholesome enough.   On the southern side of the val
ley there are some fine fountains, and on the eastern are others
strongly redolent of sulphur ; broad seams of coal crop out from
the northern bluffs, and about a mile distant in the opposite
direction are the Tar Springs, useful for greasing wagon wheels
and curing galled-backed horses.

Following the valley, which was rough and broken as it well
could be, we crossed a small divide, and came upon the plain of
the Bear River, a translation of the Indian Kuiyápá.   It is one
of the most important tributaries of the Gt. S. Lake.   Heading in the Uinta Range to the east of Kamas Prairie*, it flows
with a tortuous course to the north-west, till reaching Beer

---

* So called from the *Camassia esculenta*, the Pomme des Prairies or Pomme
Blanche of the Canadians, and the prairie turnip and breadroot of the Western
hunters.   The Kamas Prairie is a pretty little bit of clear and level ground near
the head of the Timpanagos River.

Springs it turns sharply round with a horse-shoe bend, and sets to the south-west, falling into the general reservoir at a bight called Bear River Bay. According to the mountaineers, it springs not far from the sources of the Weber River and of the Timpanagos water. Coal was found some years ago upon the banks of the Bear River, and more lately near Weber River and Silver Creek. It is the easternmost point to which Mormonism can extend *main forte:* for fugitives from justice, "over Bear River" is like "over Jordan." The aspect of the valley, here half a mile broad, was prepossessing. Beyond a steep terrace, or step which compelled us all to dismount, the clear stream, about 400 feet in width, flowed through narrow lines of willows, cottonwood, and large trees, which waved in the cool refreshing western wind; grass carpeted the middle levels, and above all rose red cliffs and buttresses of frowning rock.

We reached the station at 5·30 P.M. The valley was dotted with the tents of the Mormon emigrants, and we received sundry visits of curiosity: the visitors, mostly of the sex conventionally termed the fair, contented themselves with entering, sitting down, looking hard, tittering to one another, and departing with Parthian glances that had little power to hurt. From the men we heard tidings of "a massacree" of emigrants in the north, and a defeat of Indians in the west. Mr. Myers, the Station-master, was an English Saint, who had lately taken to himself a fifth wife, after severally divorcing the others; his last choice was not without comeliness, but her reserve was extreme; she could hardly be coaxed out of a "Yes, sir." I found Mr. Myers diligently perusing a translation of "Volney's Ruins of Empire;" we had a chat about the Old and the New country, which led us to sleeping time. I had here a curious instance of the effect of the association of words, in hearing a bystander apply to the Founder of Christianity the "Mr." which is the '*Pyrios*' of the West, and is always prefixed to "Joseph Smith:" he stated that the mission of the latter was "far ahead of" that of the former Prophet—which, by the bye, is not the strict Mormon doctrine. My companion and his family preferred as usual the interior of the mail wagon, and it was well that they did so after a couple of hours, entered Mr. Macarthy, very drunk and "fighting-mad." He called for supper, but supper was past and gone. so he supped upon "fids" of raw meat. Excited by this

lively food he began a series of caprioles which ended, as might be
expected, in a rough-and-tumble with the other three youths who
occupied the hard floor of the ranch. To Mr. Macarthy's language on that occasion *horresco referens ;* every word was apparently English, but so perverted, mis-used, and mangled, that
the home reader would hardly have distinguished it from high
Dutch : *e. g.* " I'm intire mad as a meat axe ; now du don't, I tell
ye ; say, *you*, shut up in a winkin, or I'll be chawed up if I
don't run over *you;* 'can't come that 'ere tarnal carryin' on over
me," and — *O si sic omnia !* As no weapons, revolvers, or bowie
knives were to the fore, I thought the best thing was to lie still
and let the storm blow over, which it did in a quarter of an hour.
Then, all serene, Mr. Macarthy called for a pipe, excused himself ceremoniously to himself for taking the liberty with the
" Cap's." meerschaum, solely upon the grounds that it was the
only article of the kind to be found at so late an hour, and presently fell into a deep slumber upon a sleeping contrivance composed of a table for the upper, and a chair for the lower portion
of his person. I envied him the favours of Morpheus : the fire
soon died out, the cold wind whistled through the crannies, and
the floor was knotty and uneven.

Echo Kanyon, August 24th.

At 8·15 A.M. we were once more *en voyage.* Mr. Macarthy
was very red-eyed as he sat on the stool of penitence : what
seemed to vex him most was having lost certain newspapers
directed to a friend and committed to his private trust, a
mode of insuring their safe arrival concerning which he had
the day before expressed the highest opinion. After fording
Bear River — this part of the land was quite a graveyard— we
passed over rough ground and, descending into a bush, were
shown on a ridge to the right a huge Stonehenge, a crown of
broken and somewhat lanceolate perpendicular conglomerates
or cemented pudding stones called not inappropriately Needle
Rocks. At Egan's Creek, a tributary of the Yellow Creek, the
wild geraniums and the willows flourished despite the six feet of
snow which sometimes lies in these bottoms. We then crossed
Yellow Creek, a water trending north-eastwards, and feeding, like
those hitherto forded, Bear River: the bottom, a fine broad
meadow, was a favourite camping ground, as the many fire places

proved.   Beyond the stream we ascended Yellow Creek Hill,
a steep chain which divides the versant of the Bear River east-
wards from that of Weber River to the west.   The ascent might
be avoided, but the view from the summit is a fine panorama.
The horizon behind us is girt by a mob of hills, Bridger's
Range, silver veined upon a dark blue ground : nearer, mountains and rocks, cones and hogsbacks are scattered about in
admirable confusion, divided by shaggy rollers and dark ravines,
each with its own little water-course.   In front the eye runs
down the long bright red line of Echo Kanyon, and rests with
astonishment upon its novel and curious features, the sublimity
of its broken and jagged peaks, divided by dark abysses, and
based upon huge piles of disjointed and scattered rock.   On the
right, about half a mile north of the road, and near the head
of the kanyon is a place that adds human interest to the scene.
Cache Cave is a dark, deep, natural tunnel in the rock, which
has sheltered many a hunter and trader from wild weather and
wilder men : the wall is probably of marl and earthy limestone, whose whiteness is set off by the ochreish brick red of
the ravine below.

Echo Kanyon has a total length of twenty-five to thirty miles,
and runs in a south-easterly direction to the Weber River.
Near the head it is from half to three quarters of a mile wide,
but its irregularity is such that no average breadth can be
assigned to it.   The height of the buttresses on the right or
northern side varies from 300 to 500 feet ; they are denuded and
water-washed by the storms that break upon them under the
influence of southerly gales ; their strata here are almost horizontal ; there are inclined at an angle of 45°, and the strike
is north-east and south-west.   The opposite or southern flank,
being protected from the dashing and weathering of rain and
wind, is a mass of rounded soil-clad hills, or sloping slabs of
rock, earth-veiled, and growing tussocks of grass.   Between them
runs the clear swift bubbling stream in a pebbly bed now hugging one then the other side of the chasm : it has cut its
way deeply below the surface ; the banks or benches of stiff
alluvium are not unfrequently twenty feet high ; in places it is
partially dammed by the hand of nature, and every where the
watery margin is of the brightest green and overgrown with
grass, nettles, willow thickets, in which the hop is conspicuous,

quaking asp, and other taller trees. Echo Kanyon has but one fault: its sublimity will make all similar features look tame.

We entered the kanyon in somewhat a serious frame of mind; our team was headed by a pair of exceedingly restive mules; we had remonstrated against the experimental driving being done upon our vile bodies, but the reply was that the animals must be harnessed at some time. We could not, however, but remark the wonderful picturesqueness of a scene — of a nature which in parts seemed lately to have undergone some grand catastrophe. The gigantic red wall on our right was divided into distinct blocks or quarries by a multitude of minor lateral kanyons, which, after rains, add their tribute to the main artery, and each block was subdivided by the crumbling of the softer and the resistance of the harder material—a clay conglome-rate. The colour varied in places from white and green, to yellow, but for the most part it was a dull ochreish red, that brightened up almost to a straw tint where the sun beams fell slantingly upon it from the strip of blue above. All served to set off the curious architecture of the smaller masses. A whole Petra was there, a system of projecting prisms, pyramids, and pagoda towers, a variety of form that enabled you to see whatever your peculiar vanity might be; columns, porticoes, façades, and pedestals. Twin lines of bluffs, a succession of but-tresses all fretted and honey-combed, a double row of steeples slipped from perpendicularity, frowned at each other across the gorge. And the wondrous variety was yet more varied by the kaleidoscopic transformation caused by change of posi-tion: at every different point the same object bore a different aspect.

And now whilst we are dashing over the bouldered crossings, whilst our naughty mules, as they tear down the short steep pitches, swing the wheels of the mail-wagon within half a foot of the high bank's crumbling edge: whilst poor Mrs. Dana closes her eyes and clasps her husband's hand, and Miss May, happily unconscious of all peril, amuses herself by persever-ingly perching upon the last toe that I should have been in-clined to offer, the monotony of the risk may be relieved by diverting our thoughts to the lessons taught by the scenery around.

An American artist might extract from such scenery as Church Butte and Echo Kanyon, a system of architecture as original and national as Egypt ever borrowed from her sandstone ledges, or the North of Europe from the solemn depths of her fir-forests. But Art does not at present exist in America; as amongst their forefathers further east, of artists they have plenty, of Art nothing.   We can explain the presence of the phenomenon in England, where that grotesqueness and bizarrerie of taste which is observable in the uneducated, and which despite collections and art-missions hardly disappears in those who have studied the purest models, is the natural growth of man's senses and perceptions exposed for generation after generation to the unseen, unceasing, ever-active effect of homely objects, the desolate aspects of the long and dreary winters, and the humidity which shrouds the visible world with its dull grey colouring.   Should any one question the fact that Art is not yet English, let him but place himself in the centre of the noblest site in Europe, Trafalgar Square, and own that no city in the civilised world ever presented such a perfect sample of barbarous incongruity, from mast-headed Nelson with his coil behind him, the work of the Satirist's " one man and small boy," to the two contemptible squirting things that throw water upon the pavement at his feet.   Mildly has the " Thunderer " described it as the "chosen home of exquisite dulness and stilted mediocrity." The cause above assigned to the fact is at least reasonable.   Every traveller who, after passing through the fruitful but unpicturesque orchard grounds lying between La Manche and Paris and the dull flats with their melancholy poplar lines between Paris and Lyons, arrives at Avignon, and observes the picturesqueness which every object, natural or artificial begins to assume, the grace and beauty which appear even in the humblest details of scenery, must instinctively feel that he is entering the land of Art.   Not of that Art which depends for development upon the efforts of a few exceptional individuals, but the living Art which the constant contemplation of a glorious nature,

> "That holy Virgin of the sage's creed,"

makes part of a people's organisation and development.   Art, heavenly maid, is not easily seduced to wander far from her place of birth.   Born and cradled upon the all-lovely shores of that inland sea, so choicely formed by Nature's hand to become the source and centre of mankind's civilisation, she loses health and spirits in the frigid snowy north, whilst in the tropical regions — Nubia and India — her mind is vitiated by the rank and luxuriant scenery around her. A "pretty bit of home scenery," with dumpy church tower—battlemented as the house of worship ought *not* to be — on the humble hill, red brick cottages, with straight tiled roofs and parallelogramic casements, and dwelling-houses, all stiff-ruled lines and hard sharp angles, the straight road and the trimmed hedgerow: such scenery, I assert never can make an artistic people; it can only lead, in fact, to a nation's last phase of artistic bathos — a Trafalgar Square.

The Anglo-Americans have other excuses, but not this. Their broad lands teem with varied beauties of the highest order, which it would be tedious to enumerate. They have used, for instance, the Indian corn for the acanthus in their details of architecture — why cannot they try a higher flight? Man may not, we readily grant, expect to be a great poet because Niagara is a great cataract: yet the presence of such objects must quicken the imagination of the civilised as of the savage race that preceded him. It is true that in America the class that can devote itself exclusively to the cultivation and the study of refinement and art is still, comparatively speaking, small. That the care of politics, the culture of science, mechanical and theoretic, and the pursuit of cash have at present more hold upon the national mind than what it is disposed to consider the effeminating influences of the humanising studies. That, more-over, the efforts of youthful genius in the body corporate, as in the individual, are invariably imitative, leading through the progressive degrees of reflection and reproduction to originality. But valid as they are, these reasons will not long justify such freaks as the Americo-Grecian capitol at Richmond, a barn with the tritest of all exordiums, a portico which is original in one point only, viz. that it wants the portico's only justification — steps: or the various domes originally borrowed from that bulb which has been demolished at Washington, scattered over the country, and suggesting the idea that the shape has been borrowed from the butt end of a sliced cucumber. Better far the warehouses of Boston, with their monoliths and frontages of rough Quincy granite; they, at least, are unpretending, and of native growth, no bad test of the native mind.

After a total of eighteen miles we passed Echo Station, a half-built ranch, flanked by well piled haystacks for future mules. The ravine narrowed as we advanced to a mere gorge, and the meanderings of the stream contracted the road and raised the banks to a more perilous height. A thicker vegetation occupied the bottom, wild roses and dwarfish oaks contending for the mastery of the ground. About four miles from the station we were shown a defile where the Latter Day Saints, in 1857, headed by General D. H. Wells, now the third member of the Presidency, had prepared modern Caudine Forks for the attacking army of the United States. Little breastworks of loose stones, very like the " sangahs " of the Affghan Ghauts, had been thrown up where the precipices commanded the road, and there were four or five remains of dams intended to raise the water above the height of the soldiers' ammunition pouches. The situation did not appear to me well chosen. Although the fortified side of the bluff could not be crowned on account of deep chasms that separated the various blocks, the southern acclivities might have been occupied by sharp-shooters so effectually that the fire from the breastworks would soon have been silenced: moreover, the defenders would have risked being taken in rear by a party creeping through the chapparal * in the sole of the kanyon. Mr. Macarthy related a characteristic trait concerning two warriors of the Nauvoo Legion. Unaccustomed to perpendicular fire, one proposed that his comrade should stand upon the crest of the precipice and see if the bullet reached him or not; the comrade thinking the request highly reasonable, complied with it, and received a yäger-ball through his forehead.

Traces of beaver were frequent in the torrent-bed; the " broad-tailed animal " is now molested by the Indians rather than by the whites. On this stage magpies and ravens were unusually numerous; foxes slunk away from us, and on one of the

---

* The Spanish "chapparal" means a low oak copse. The word has been naturalised in Texas and New Mexico, and applied to the dense and bushy undergrowth, chiefly of briars and thorns, disposed in patches from a thicket of a hundred yards to the whole flank of a mountain range (especially in the Mexican Tierra Caliente), and so closely entwined that nothing larger than a wolf can force a way through it.

highest bluffs a coyote stood as on a pedestal; as near Baffin Sea, these craggy peaks are their favourite howling-places during the severe snowy winters. We longed for a thunder-storm : flashing lightnings, roaring thunders, stormy winds, and dashing rains — in fact a tornado — would be the fittest setting for such a picture so wild, so sublime as Echo Kanyon. But we longed in vain. The day was persistently beautiful, calm and mild, as a May forenoon in the Grecian Archipelago. We were also disappointed in our natural desire to hold some converse with the nymph who had lent her name to the ravine — the reverberation is said to be remarkably fine — but the temper of our animals would not have endured it, and the place was not one that admitted experiments. Rain had lately fallen, as we saw from the mud-puddles in the upper course of the Kanyon, and the road was in places pitted with drops which were not frequent enough to allay the choking dust. A fresh yet familiar feature now appeared. The dews, whose existence we had forgotten on the prairies, were cold and clammy in the early mornings ; the moist air, condensed by contact with the cooler substances on the surface of the ground, stood in large drops upon the leaves and grasses. As we advanced the bed of the ravine began to open out, the angle of descent became more obtuse ; a stretch of level ground appeared in front where for some hours the windings of the kanyon had walled us in, and at 2·30 P.M. we debouched upon the Weber River Station. It lies at the very mouth of the ravine almost under the shadow of lofty red bluffs, called " The Obelisks," and the green and sunny landscape contrasting with the sterile grandeur behind, is exceedingly pleasing.

After the emotions of the drive, a little rest was by no means unpleasant. The station was tolerably comfortable, and the welcome addition of potatoes and onions to our usual fare was not to be despised. The tenants of the ranch were Mormons, civil and communicative. They complained sadly of the furious rain-storms, which the funnel-like gorge brings down upon them, and the cold draughts from five feet deep of snow which pour down upon the milder valley.

At 4·30 we resumed our journey along the plain of the Weber or Webber River. It is second in importance only to the Bear River : it heads near the latter, and flowing in a devious course towards the north-west falls into the Great Salt Lake, a few miles south of its sister stream, and nearly opposite Frémont's Island. The valley resembles that described in yesterday's diary; it is, however, narrower, and the steep borders, which if water-washed would be red like the kanyon rocks, are well clothed with grass and herbages. In some places the land is defended by snake-fences in zigzags *, to oppose the depredations of emigrants' cattle upon the wheat, barley, and stunted straggling corn within. After fording the river and crossing the bottom, we ascended steep banks, passed over a spring of salt water five miles from the station, and halted for a few minutes to exchange news with the mail-wagon that had left Gt. S. L. City this (Friday) morning. Followed a rough and rugged tract of land apparently very trying to the way-worn cattle; many deaths had taken place at this point, and the dead lay well preserved as the monks of St. Bernard. After a succession of chuck-holes, rises, and falls, we fell into the Valley of Bauchmin's Creek. It is a picturesque hollow; at the head is a gateway of red clay, through which the stream passes; the sides also are red, and as the glow and glory of the departing day lingered upon the heights, even artemisia put on airs of bloom and beauty, blushing in contrast with the sharp metallic green of the quaking-asp and the duller verdure of the elder (*Alnus viridis*). As the evening closed in, the bottom land became more broken, the path less certain and the vegetation thicker : the light of the moon, already diminished by the narrowness of the valley, seemed almost to be absorbed by the dark masses of copse and bush. We were not sorry to make at 7·45 P.M., the " Carson House Station " at Bauchmin's Fork — the travelling had been fast, seven miles an hour — where we found a log hut, a roaring fire, two civil Mormon lads, and some few " fixins " in the way of food. We sat for a time talking about matters of local im-

---

* This is the simplest of all fences, and therefore much used in the West. Tree trunks are felled, and either used whole or split into rails ; they are then disposed in a long, serrated line, each resting upon another at both ends, like the fingers of a man's right hand extended and inserted between the corresponding fingers of the left, The zigzag is not a picturesque object: in absolute beauty it is inferior even to our English trimmed hedgerow ; but it is very economical, it saves space, it is easily and readily made, it can always serve for fuel, and, therefore, is to be respected, despite the homeliness of its appearance.

portance, the number of emigrants, and horsethieves, the prospects of the road and the lay of the land.   Bauchmin's Fork, we learned, is a branch of East Kanyon Creek, itself a tributary of the Weber River *; from the station an Indian trail leads over the mountains to Provo City.   I slept comfortably enough upon the boards of an inner room, not, however, without some apprehensions of accidentally offending a certain skunk (*Mephitis mephitica*), which was in the habit of making regular nocturnal visits.   I heard its puppy-like bark during the night, but escaped what otherwise might have happened.

And why, naturally asks the reader, did you not shut the door ?   Because there was none.

The End — Hurrah! August 25th.

To-day we are to pass over the Wásách†, the last and highest chain of the mountain mass between Fort Bridger and the Gt. S. L. Valley, and —by the aid of St. James of Compostella, who is, I believe, bound over to be the patron of pilgrims in general, — to arrive at our destination, New Hierosolyma, or Jerusalem, alias Zion on the tops of the mountains, the future city of Christ, where the Lord is to reign over the Saints, as a temporal king, in power and great glory.

So we girt our loins and started after a cup of tea and a biscuit at 7 A.M., under the good guidance of Mr. Macarthy, who after a whiskeyless night looked forward not less than ourselves to the run in.   Following the course of Bauchmin's Creek, we completed the total number of fordings to thirteen in eight miles.   The next two miles were along the bed of a watercourse, a complete fiumara, through a bush full of tribulus, which accompanied us to the end of the journey. Presently the ground became rougher and steeper : we alighted and set our breasts manfully against " Big Mountain," which lies about four miles from the station.   The road bordered upon the wide arroyo, a tumbled bed of block and boulder, with water in places oozing and trickling from the clay walls,

---

* In Captain Stansbury's map, Bauchmin's Fork is a direct influent, and one of the largest too, of the Weber River.

† The word is generally written *Wasatch* or *Wahsatch*. In the latter the *h* is, as usual, *de trop ;* and in both the *t*, though necessary in French, is totally uncalled for in English.

from the sandy soil, and from beneath the heaps of rock,—
living fountains these, most grateful to the parched traveller.
The synclinal slopes of the chasm were grandly wooded with
hemlocks, firs, balsam-pines, and other varieties of abies ;
some tapering up to the height of ninety feet, with an admirable regularity of form, colour, and foliage.   The varied
hues of the quaking asp were there ; the beech, the dwarf oak,
and a thicket of elders and wild roses ; whilst over all the warm
autumnal tints already mingled with the bright green of
summer.   The ascent became more and more rugged : this
steep pitch, at the end of a thousand miles of hard work and
semi-starvation, causes the death of many a wretched animal,
and we remarked that the bodies are not inodorous among the
mountains as on the prairies.   In the most fatiguing part, we
saw a handcart halted, whilst the owners, a man, a woman, and
a boy, took breath.   We exchanged a few consolatory words
with them and hurried on.   The only animal seen on the line,
except the grasshopper, whose creaking wings gave forth an
ominous note, was the pretty little chirping squirrel.   The
trees, however, in places bore the marks of huge talons, which
were easily distinguished as the sign of bears.   The grizzly
does not climb except when young : this was probably the
common brown variety.   At half-way the gorge opened out,
assuming more the appearance of a valley ; and in places, for a
few rods, were dwarf stretches of almost level ground.   Towards
the Pass-summit the rise is sharpest : here we again descended
from the wagon, which the four mules had work enough to
draw, and the total length of its eastern rise was five miles.   Big
Mountain lies eighteen miles from the city.   The top is a
narrow crest, suddenly forming an acute based upon an obtuse
angle.

From that eyrie, 8000 feet above sea level, the weary
pilgrim first sights his shrine, the object of his long wanderings,
hardships, and perils, the Happy Valley of the Great Salt Lake.
The western horizon, when visible, is bounded by a broken wall
of light blue mountain, the Oquirrh, whose northernmost bluff
buttresses the southern end of the lake, and whose eastern
flank sinks in steps and terraces into a river basin, yellow with
the sunlit golden corn, and somewhat pink with its car-
peting of heath-like moss.   In the foreground a semicircular

sweep of hill top, and an inverted arch of rocky wall, shuts out all but a few spans of the Valley. These heights are rough with a shaggy forest, in some places black-green, in others of brownish-red, in others of the lightest ash colour, based upon a ruddy soil; whilst a few silvery veins of snow still streak the bare grey rocky flanks of the loftiest peak.

After a few minutes' delay to stand and gaze, we resumed the footpath way, whilst the mail-wagon, with wheels rough-locked, descended what appeared to be an impracticable slope. The summit of the pass was well nigh cleared of timber; the wood-man's song informed us that the evil work was still going on, and that we are nearly approaching a large settlement. Thus stripped of their protecting fringes, the mountains are exposed to the heat of summer, that sends forth countless swarms of devastating crickets, grasshoppers, and blue-worms; and to the wintry cold, that piles up, four to six feet high,—the mountain men speak of thirty and forty,— the snows drifted by the unbroken force of the winds. The pass from November to February can be traversed by nothing heavier than "sleighs," and during the snow storms even these are stopped. Falling into the gorge of Big Kanyon Creek, after a total of twelve hard miles from Bauchmin's Fork, we reached at 11·30 the station that bears the name of the water near which it is built. We were received by the wife of the proprietor, who was absent at the time of our arrival; and half stifled by the thick dust and the sun which had raised the glass to 103°, we enjoyed copious draughts—*tant soit peu* qualified—of the cool but rather hard water, that trickled down the hill into a trough by the house side. Presently the station master, springing from his light "sulky," entered, and was formally introduced to us by Mr. Macarthy as Mr. Ephe Hanks. I had often heard of this individual, as one of the old triumvirate of Mormon desperadoes, the other two being Orrin Porter Rockwell and Bill Hickman— as the leader of the dreaded Danite band, and in short as a model ruffian. The ear often teaches the eye to form its pictures: I had eliminated a kind of mental sketch of those assassin faces which one sees on the Apennines and Pyrenees, and was struck by what met the eye of sense. The "vile villain," as he has been called by anti-Mormon writers, who verily do not try to *ménager* their epithets, was a middle-sized, light-haired, good looking man, with regular features, a pleasant and humorous countenance, and the manly manner of his early sailor life, touched with the rough cordiality of the mountaineer. " Frank as a bear hunter," is a proverb in these lands. He had, like the rest of the triumvirate, and like most men (Anglo-Americans) of desperate courage and fiery excitable temper, a clear pale blue eye, verging upon grey, and looking as if it wanted nothing better than to light up, together with a cool and quiet glance that seemed to shun neither friend nor foe.

The terrible Ephe began with a facetious allusion to all our new dangers under the roof of a Danite, to which in similar strain, I made answer that Danite or Damnite was pretty much the same to me. After dining, we proceeded to make trial of the air-cane, to which he took, as I could see by the way he handled it, and by the nod with which he acknowledged the observation, " almighty convenient sometimes not to make a noise, Mister," a great fancy. He asked me whether I had a mind to " have a slap" at his namesake*, an offer which was gratefully accepted, under the promise that " cuffy " should previously be marked down so as to save a long ride and a troublesome trudge over the mountains. His battery of " killb'ars " was heavy and in good order, so that on this score there would have been no trouble, and the only tool he bade me bring was a Colt's revolver, dragoon size. He told me that he was likely to be in England next year, when he had set the " ole woman " to her work. I suppose my look was somewhat puzzled, for Mrs. Dana graciously explained that every western wife, even when still, as Mrs. Ephe was, in her teens, commands that venerable title, venerable, though somehow not generally coveted.

From Big Kanyon Creek Station to the city, the driver " reckoned," was a distance of seventeen miles. We waited till the bright and glaring day had somewhat burned itself out; at noon heavy clouds came up from the south and south-west, casting a grateful shade and shedding a few drops of rain. After taking friendly leave of the " Danite " chief,—whose cordiality of manner had prepossessed me strongly in his favour— we entered the mail-wagon and prepared ourselves for the finale over the westernmost ridge of the stern Wasach.

---

* " Ole Ephraim " is the mountain-man's *sobriquet* for the grizzly bear.

After two miles of comparatively level ground we came to the foot of " Little Mountain," and descended from the wagon to relieve the poor devils of mules.   The near slope was much shorter, but also it was steeper far than " Big Mountain."   The counterslope was easier, though by no means pleasant to contemplate with the chance of an accident to the break, which in all inconvenient places would part with the protecting shoe-sole.   Beyond the eastern foot, which was ten miles distant from our destination, we were miserably bumped and jolted over the broken ground at the head of Big Kanyon.   Down this pass, whose name is a translation of the Yuta name Obitkokichi, a turbulent little mountain-stream tumbles over its boulder-bed, girt with the usual sunflower, vines of wild hops, red and white willows, cotton-wood, quaking-asp, and various bushes near its cool watery margin, and upon the easier slopes of the ravine, with the shin or dwarf oak (*Quercus nana*), mountain mahogany, balsam and other firs, pines, and cedars.   The road was a narrow shelf along the broader of the two spaces between the stream and the rock, and frequent fordings were rendered necessary by the capricious wanderings of the torrent.   I could not but think how horrid must have been its appearance when the stout-hearted Mormon pioneers first ventured to thread the defile, breaking their way through the dense bush, creeping and clinging like flies to the sides of the hills.   Even now accidents often occur ; here, as in Echo Kanyon, we saw in more than one place, unmistakable signs of upsets in the shape of broken spokes and yoke bows.   At one of the most ticklish turns Macarthy kindly pointed out a little precipice where four of the mail passengers fell and broke their necks, a pure invention on his part, I believe, which fortunately, at that moment, did not reach Mrs. Dana's ears.   He also entertained us with many a tale, of which the hero was the redoubtable Hanks ; how he had slain a buffalo-bull single-handed with a bowie knife, and how on one occasion, when refused hospitality by his Lamanite brethren, he had sworn to have the whole village to himself, and had redeemed his vow by reappearing *in cuerpo*, with gestures so maniacal that the sulky Indians all fled, declaring him to be " bad medicine."   The stories had at least local colouring.

In due time, emerging from the gates and portals and deep

serrations of the upper course, we descended into a lower level: here Big, now called Emigration, Kanyon gradually bulges out, and its steep slopes of grass and fern, shrubbery and stunted brush, fall imperceptibly into the plain. The valley presently lay full before our sight. At this place the pilgrim emigrants, like the Hajis of Mecca and Jerusalem, give vent to the emotions long pent up within their bosoms by sobs and tears, laughter and congratulations, psalms and hysterics. It is indeed no wonder that the children dance, that strong men cheer and shout, and that nervous women, broken with fatigue and hope deferred, scream and faint; that the ignorant should fondly believe that the " Spirit of God pervades the very atmosphere," and that Zion on the tops of the mountains is nearer heaven than other parts of earth. In good sooth, though uninfluenced by religious fervour — beyond the natural satisfaction of seeing a bran new Holy City — even I could not, after nineteen days in' a mail-wagon, gaze upon the scene without emotion.

The Sublime and the Beautiful were in present contrast. Switzerland and Italy lay side by side. The magnificent scenery of the past mountains and ravines still floated before the retina, as emerging from the gloomy depths of the Golden Pass — the mouth of Emigration Kanyon is more poetically so called — we came suddenly in view of the Holy Valley of the West.

The hour was about 6 P.M., the atmosphere was touched with a dreamy haze,— as it generally is in the vicinity of the Lake — a little bank of rose-coloured clouds, edged with flames of purple and gold, floated in the upper air, whilst the mellow radiance of an American autumn, that bright interlude between the extremes of heat and cold, diffused its mild soft lustre over the face of earth.

The sun, whose slanting rays shone full in our eyes, was setting in a flood of heavenly light behind the bold jagged outline of "Antelope Island," which, though distant twenty miles to the north-west, hardly appeared to be ten. At its feet, and then bounding the far horizon, lay, like a band of burnished silver, the Great Salt Lake, that still innocent Dead Sea. South-westwards, also, and equally deceptive as regards distance, rose the boundary of the valley plain, the Oquirrh

Range, sharply silhouetted by a sweep of sunshine over its summits, against the depths of an evening sky, in that direction, so pure, so clear, that vision, one might fancy, could penotrate behind the curtain into regions beyond the confines of man's ken. In the brilliant reflected light, which softened off into a glow of delicate pink, we could distinguish the lines of Brigham's, Coon's and other kanyons, which water has traced through the wooded flanks of the Oquirrh down to the shadows already purpling the misty benches at their base. Three distinct and several shades, light azure, blue, and brown blue, graduated the distances, which extended at least thirty miles.

The undulating valley-plain between us and the Oquirrh Range is 12·15 miles broad, and markedly concave, dipping in the centre like the section of a tunnel, and swelling at both edges into bench-lands, which mark the ancient bed of the Lake. In some parts the valley was green; in others, where the sun shot its oblique beams, it was of a tawny yellowish red, like the sands of the Arabian desert, with scatters of trees, where the Jordan of the West rolls its opalline wave through pasture lands of dried grass dotted with flocks and herds, and fields of ripening yellow corn. Everything bears the impress of handiwork, from the bleak benches behind to what was once a barren valley in front. Truly the Mormon prophecy had been fulfilled: already the howling wilderness — in which twelve years ago a few miserable savages, the half naked Digger Indians, gathered their grass-seed, grasshoppers, and black crickets to keep life and soul together, and awoke with their war cries the echo of the mountains, and the bear, the wolf, and the fox prowled over the site of a now populous city — "has blossomed like the rose."

This valley, this lovely panorama of green and azure and gold, this land, fresh as it were from the hands of God, is apparently girt on all sides by hills: the highest peaks, raised 7000 to 8000 feet above the plain of their bases, show by gulches veined with lines of snow that even in this season winter frowns upon the last smile of summer.

Advancing, we exchanged the rough cahues, and the frequent fords of the ravine, for a broad smooth highway, spanning the easternmost valley-bench: a terrace that drops like a Titanic step from the midst of the surrounding mountains to the level of the present valley-plain. From a distance—the mouth of Emigration Kanyon is about 4·30 miles from the city—Zion, which is not on a hill, but on the contrary lies almost in the lowest part of the river-plain, is completely hid from sight, as if no such thing existed. Mr. Macarthy, on application, pointed out the notabilia of the scene.

Northwards curls of vapour ascending from a gleaming sheet—the Lake of the Hot Springs—set in a bezel of emerald green, and bordered by another lake-bench upon which the glooms of evening were rapidly gathering, hung like a veil of gauze around the waist of the mountains. Southwards for twenty-five miles stretched the length of the valley with the little river winding its way like a silver thread in a brocade of green and gold. The view in this direction was closed by "Mountain Point," another formation of terraced range, which forms the water gate of Jordan, and which conceals and separates the fresh water that feeds the Salt Lake — the Sea of Tiberias from the Dead Sea.

As we descend the Wasach Mountains, we could look back and enjoy the view of the eastern wall of the Happy Valley. A little to the north of Emigration Kanyon, and about one mile nearer the settlement, is the Red Butte, a deep ravine, whose quarried sides show mottlings of the light ferruginous sandstone which was chosen for building the Temple wall.* A little beyond it lies the single City of the Dead, decently removed three miles from the habitations of the living, and further to the north is City-Creek Kanyon, which supplies the Saints with water for drinking and for irrigation. South-east of Emigration Kanyon are other ravines, Parley's, Mill Creek, Great Cottonwood, and Little Cottonwood, deep lines winding down the timbered flanks of the mountains, and thrown into relief by the darker and more misty shading of the farther flank-wall.

The "Twin Peaks," the highest points of the Wasach Mountains, are the first to be powdered over with the autumnal snow. When a black nimbus throws out these piles, with

---

* At first a canal was dug through the bench to bring this material : the grey granite now used for the Temple is transported in carts from the southern part of the valley.

their tilted up rock strata, jagged edges, black flanks, rugged
brows and bald heads, gilt by a gleam of sunset, the whole
stands boldly out with that phase of sublimity of which the sense
of immensity is the principal element. Even in the clearest
weather they are rarely free from a fleecy cloud, the condensa-
tion of cold and humid air rolling up the heights and vanishing
only to be renewed.

The bench-land then attracted our attention. The soil is
poor, sprinkled with thin grass, in places showing a suspicious
whiteness, with few flowers, and chiefly producing a salsolaceous
plant like the English samphire. In many places lay long
rows of bare circlets, like deserted tent-floors: they proved to
be ant-hills, on which light ginger-coloured swarms were working hard to throw up the sand and gravel that everywhere in
this valley underlie the surface. The eastern valley-bench,
upon whose western declivity the city lies, may be traced on a
clear day along the base of the mountains for a distance of
twenty miles: its average breadth is about eight miles.

After advancing about 1·50 mile over the bench ground, the
city by slow degrees broke upon our sight. It showed, one may
readily believe, to special advantage after the succession of Indian
lodges, Canadian ranchos, and log-hut mail-stations of the
prairies and the mountains. The site has been admirably
chosen for drainage and irrigation — so well indeed that a
"Deus ex machinâ" must be brought to account for it.*
About two miles north, and overlooking the settlements from a
height of 400 feet, a detached cone called Ensign Peak or
Ensign Mount rises at the end of a chain which, projected westward from the main range of the heights, overhangs and shelters
the north-eastern corner of the valley. Upon this " big toe of
the Wasach range," as it is called by a local writer, the spirit of
the martyred prophet, Mr. Joseph Smith, appeared to his suc-

---

* I have frequently heard this legend from Gentiles, never from Mormons; yet
even the Saints own that as early as 1842 visions of the mountains and kanyons,
the valley and the lake, were revealed to Mr. Joseph Smith, jun., who declared it
privily to the disciples whom he loved. Thus Messrs. O. Pratt and E. Snow,
apostles, were enabled to recognise the Promised Land, as, the first of the pioneers,
they issued from the ravines of the Wasach. Of course the Gentiles declare that the
exodists hit upon the valley by the purest chance. The spot is becoming classical :
here Judge and Apostle Phelps preached his " Sermon on the Mount," which, anti-
Mormons say, was a curious contrast to the first discourse so named.

cessor Mr. Brigham Young, and pointed out to him the position of the New Temple, which, after Zion had "got up into the high mountain," was to console the Saints for the loss of Nauvoo the Beautiful.   The city—it is about two miles broad—runs parallel with the right bank of the Jordan, which forms its western limit.   It is twelve to fifteen miles distant from the western range, ten from the debouchure of the river, and eight to nine from the nearest point of the lake — a respectful distance, which is not the least of the position's merits.   It occupies the rolling brow of a slight decline at the western base of the Wasach, in fact the lower, but not the lowest level of the eastern valley-bench; it has thus a compound slope from north to south, on the line of its water supplies, and from east to west, thus enabling it to drain off into the river.

The city revealed itself, as we approached, from behind its screen, the inclined terraces of the upper table-land, and at last it lay stretched before us as upon a map.   At a little distance the aspect was somewhat Oriental, and in some points it reminded me of modern Athens — without the Acropolis.   None of the buildings, except the Prophet's house, were whitewashed. The material — the thick, sun-dried adobe, common to all parts of the Eastern world * — was of a dull leaden blue, deepened by the atmosphere to a grey, like the shingles of the roofs.   The number of gardens and compounds — each tenement within the walls originally received 1·50 square acre, and those outside from five to ten acres, according to their distance — the dark clumps and lines of bitter cottonwood, locust or acacia, poplars and fruit trees, apples, peaches, and vines — how lovely they appeared, after the baldness of the prairies !—and, finally, the fields of long-eared maize and sweet sorghum strengthened the similarity to an Asiatic rather than to an American settlement. The differences presently became as salient.   The farm-houses, with their stacks and stock, strongly suggested the old country. Moreover domes and minarets — even churches and steeples — were wholly wanting—an omission that somewhat surprised me. The only building conspicuous from afar was the block occupied by the present head of the church.   The court-house, with its tinned Muscovian dome, at the west end of the city; the arsenal,

---

*The very word is Spanish, derived from the Arabic الطوب, meaning "the brick:" it is known throughout the West, and is written *adobies*, and pronounced *dobies*.

a barn-like structure, on a bench below the Jebel Nur of the valley—Ensign Peak ; and a saw-mill, built beyond the southern boundary, were the next in importance.

On our way we passed the vestiges of an old moat, from which was taken the earth for the bulwarks of Zion. A Romulian wall, of puddle, mud, clay, and pebbles, six miles — others, say, 2600 acres — in length, twelve feet high, six feet broad at the base, and two and three-quarters at the top, with embrasures five to six feet above the ground, and semi-bastions at half musket range, was decided, in 1853-54, to be necessary, as a defence against the Lamanites, whose name in the vulgar is Yuta Indians. Gentiles declare that the bulwarks were erected because the people wanting work were likely to "strike" faith, and that the amount of labour expended upon this folly would have irrigated as many thousand acres. Anti-Mormons have, of course, detected in the proceeding treacherous and treasonable intentions. Parenthetically, I must here warn the reader that in Gt. S. L. City there are three distinct opinions concerning, three several reasons for, and three diametrically different accounts of, everything that happens, viz. that of the Mormons, which is invariably one-sided; that of the Gentiles, which is sometimes fair and just; and that of the anti-Mormons, which is always prejudiced and violent. A glance will show that this much talked-of fortification is utterly harmless; it is commanded in half a dozen places; it could not keep out half a dozen sappers for a quarter of an hour; and now, as it has done its work, its foundations are allowed to become salt, and to crumble away.

The road ran through the Big Field, south-east of the city, six miles square, and laid off in five-acre lots. Presently, passing the precincts of habitation, we entered, at a slapping pace, the second ward, called Denmark, from its tenants, who mostly herd together. The disposition of the settlement is like that of the nineteenth century New World cities—from Washington to the future metropolis of the great Terra Australis—a system of right angles, the roads, streets, and lanes, if they can be called so, intersecting one another. The advantages or disadvantages of the rectangular plan have been exhausted in argument; the new style is best suited, I believe, for the New, as the old must, perforce, remain in the Old World. The

suburbs are thinly settled; the mass of habitations lie around
and south of Temple Block.   The streets of the suburbs are
mere roads, cut by deep ups and downs, and by gutters on both
sides, which, though full of pure water, have no bridge save a
plank at the *trottoirs*.   In summer the thoroughfares are dusty
— in wet weather deep with viscid mud.

The houses are almost all of one pattern—a barn shape, with
wings and lean-tos, generally facing, sometimes turned endways
to, the street, which gives a suburban look to the settlement;
and the diminutive casements show that window-glass is not
yet made in the Valley.   In the best abodes the adobe rests
upon a few courses of sandstone, which prevent undermining
by water or ground-damp, and it must always be protected by a
coping from the rain and snow.   The poorer are small, low, and
hut-like; others are long single-storied buildings, somewhat
like stables, with many entrances.   The best houses resemble
East Indian bungalows, with flat roofs, and low, shady verandahs, well trellised, and supported by posts or pillars.   All
are provided with chimneys, and substantial doors to keep out
the piercing cold.   The offices are always placed, for hygienic
reasons, outside; and some have a story and a half—the latter
intended for lumber and other stores.   I looked in vain for the
outhouse-harems, in which certain romancers concerning things
Mormon had informed me that wives are kept, like any other
stock.   I presently found this but one of a multitude of delusions.   Upon the whole the Mormon settlement was a vast
improvement upon its contemporaries in the valleys of the
Mississippi and the Missouri.

The road through the faubourg was marked by posts and
rails, which, as we advanced towards the heart of the city, were
replaced by neat palings.   The garden plots were small, as sweet
earth must be brought down from the mountains; and the
flowers were principally those of the old country — the red
French bean, the rose, the geranium, and the single pink;
the ground or winter cherry was common; so were nas-
turtiums, and we saw tansy, but not that plant for which our
souls, well nigh weary of hopes of juleps long deferred, chiefly
lusted — mint.   The fields were large and numerous, but the
Saints have too many and various occupations to keep them
Moravian-like neat and trim; weeds overspread the ground;

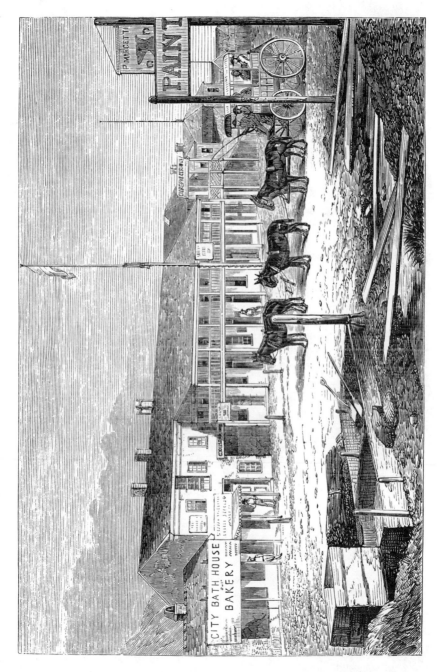

STORES IN MAIN STREET.

often the wild sunflower-tops outnumbered the heads of maize. The fruit had suffered from an unusually nipping frost in May; the peach trees were barren, the vines bore no produce, only a few good apples were in Mr. Brigham Young's garden, and the water-melons were poor, yellow, and tasteless, like the African. On the other hand, potatoes, onions, cabbages and cucumbers, were good and plentiful, the tomato was ripening everywhere, fat full-eared wheat rose in stacks, and crops of excellent hay were scattered about near the houses. The people came to their doors to see the mail-coach, as if it were the "Derby dilly," of old, go by. I could not but be struck by the modified English appearance of the colony, and by the prodigious numbers of the white-headed children.

Presently we debouched upon the main thoroughfare, the centre of population and business, where the houses of the principal Mormon dignitaries, and the stores of the Gentile merchants, combine to form the city's only street which can be properly so called. It is, indeed, both street and market, for, curious to say, New Zion has not yet built for herself a bazaar or market-place. Nearly opposite the Post-office, in a block on the eastern side, with a long verandah, supported by trimmed and painted posts, was a two-storied, pent-roofed building, whose sign-board, swinging to a tall, gibbet-like flagstaff, dressed for the occasion, announced it to be the Salt Lake House, the principal, if not the only establishment of the kind in New Zion. In the Far West, one learns not to expect much of the hostelry*; I had not seen aught so grand for many a day. Its depth is greater than its frontage, and behind it, secured by a *porte cochère*, is a large yard, for coralling cattle. A rough-looking crowd of drivers, drivers' friends, and idlers, almost every man openly armed with revolver and bowie-knife, gathered round the doorway, to greet Jim, and "prospect" the "new lot;" and the host came out to assist us in transporting our scattered effects. We looked vainly for a bar on the ground floor; a bureau for registering names was there, but (temperance, in public at least, being the order of the day) the usual tempting array of

---

* I subjoin one of the promising sort of advertisements:—

"Tom Mitchell!!! dispenses comfort to the weary (!) feeds the hungry (!!) and cheers the gloomy (!!!) at his old, well-known stand, thirteen miles east of Fort Des Moines. *Don't pass by me.*"

bottles and decanters was not forthcoming; upstairs we found a Gentile ball-room, a tolerably furnished sitting-room, and bed chambers, apparently made out of a single apartment by partitions too thin to be strictly agreeable. The household had its deficiencies; blacking, for instance, had run out, and servants could not be engaged till the expected arrival of the hand-cart train. However, the proprietor, Mr. Townsend, a Mormon, from the State of Maine — when expelled from Nauvoo, he had parted with land, house, and furniture for $50 — who had married an Englishwoman, was in the highest degree civil and obliging, and he attended personally to our wants, offered his wife's services to Mrs. Dana, and put us all in the best of humours, despite the closeness of the atmosphere, the sadness ever attending one's first entrance into a new place, the swarms of "emigration flies"—so called because they appear in September with the emigrants, and after living for a month die off with the first snow — and a certain populousness of bedstead, concerning which the less said the better. Such, gentle reader, are the results of my first glance at Zion on the tops of the mountains, in the Holy City of the Far West.

Our journey had occupied nineteen days, from the 7th to the 25th of August, both included; and in that time we had accomplished not less than 1136 statute miles.

CHAP. XI.

[*After a stay of a little more than three weeks, Burton had succeeded in collecting enough "facts, not theories" about Utah Territory and Mormonism to arrive at the following conclusions.—Editor's note.*]

It will, I think, be abundantly evident, that U. T. has been successful in its colonisation. Every where, indeed, in the New World, the stranger wonders that a poor man should tarry in Europe, or that a rich man should remain in America — nothing but the strongest chains of habit and *vis inertiæ* can reconcile both to their miserable lots. I cannot help thinking, that, morally and spiritually, as well as physically, the *protégés* of the Perpetual Emigration Fund gain by being transferred to the Far West. Mormonism is emphatically the faith of the poor, and those acquainted with the wretched condition of the English mechanic, collier, and agricultural labourer,— it is calculated that a million of them exist on 25*l.* per annum — who, after a life of ignoble drudgery, of toiling through the year from morning till night, are ever threatened with the workhouse, must be of the same opinion. Physically speaking there is no comparison between the conditions of the Saints and the class from which they are mostly taken. In point of mere morality, the Mormon community is perhaps purer than any other of equal numbers. I have no wish to commend their spiritual, or rather their materialistic vagaries — a materialism so levelling in its unauthorised deductions, that even the materialist must reject it: but with the mind as with the body, bad food is better than none. When wealth shall be less unequally distributed in England, thus doing away with the contrast of excessive splendour and utter destitution, and when Home Missions shall have done their duty in educating and evangelising the unhappy pariahs of town and country, the sons of the land which boasts herself to be the foremost among the nations, will blush no more to hear that the Mormons or Latter Day Saints are mostly English.

About the middle of September, the time of my departure drew nigh. Judge Flennikin found a change of *venue* to Carson Valley necessary; Thomas, his son, was to accompany him, and the Territorial Marshal, Mr. Grice, — a quondam volunteer in the Mexican War,—was part of the cortége. Escort and ambulance had been refused; it was imperative to find both. Several proposals were made and rejected. At last an eligible presented himself. Mr. Kennedy, an Irishman from the neighbourhood of Dublin, and an *incola* of California, where evil fate had made him a widower, had " swopped " stock, and was about to drive thirty-three horses and mules to the " El Dorado of the west." For the sum of $150 each he agreed to convey us, to provide an ambulance which cost him $300, and three wagons which varied in price from $25 to $75. We had reason to think well of his probity, concerning which we had taken counsel, and as he had lost'a horse or two, and had received a bullet through the right arm, in an encounter with the Yuta Indians near Deep Creek, on the 3rd July of the same year, we had little doubt of his behaving with due prudence. He promised also to collect a sufficient armed party, and as the road had lately seen troubles — three drivers had been shot and seventeen Indians had been reported slain in action, by the Federal troops — we were certain that he would keep his word. It was the beginning of the hungry season, when the Indians would be collecting their pine nuts and be plotting onslaughts upon the spring emigrants.

I prepared for difficulties by having my hair " shingled off," till my head somewhat resembled a pointer's dorsum, and deeply regretted having left all my wigs behind me. The marshal undertook to lay in our provisions: we bought flour, hard bread or biscuit, eggs and bacon, butter, a few potted luxuries, not forgetting a goodly allowance of whiskey and korn-schnapps, whose only demerit was that it gave a taste to the next morning. The travelling canteen consisted of a little china, tin cups and plates, a coffee pot, frying pan, and large ditto for bread baking, with spoons, knives, and forks.

The last preparations were soon made. I wrote to my friends, amongst others to Dr. Norton Shaw, who read out the missive *magno cum risu audientium*, bought a pair of leather leggings for $5, settled with M. Gebow, a Gamaliel at whose feet I had sat as a student of the Yuta dialect, and defrayed the expenses of living, which, though the bill was curiously worded, were exemplarily inexpensive.* Col. Stambaugh favoured me with a parting gift, the "Manual of Surveying Instructions," which I preserve as a reminiscence, and a cocktail whose aroma still lingers in my olfactories. My last evening was spent with Mr. S——, when Mr. John Taylor was present, and where, with the kindly aid of Madame, we drank a *café au lait* as good as the *Café de Paris* affords. I thanked the governor for his frank and generous hospitality, and made my acknowledgments to his amiable wife. All my adieux were upon an extensive scale, the immediate future being somewhat dark and menacing.

The start in these regions is coquettish as in Eastern Africa. We were to depart on Wednesday the 19th September, at 8 A.M. — then 10 A.M. then 12 A.M. then, after a deprecatory visit, on the morrow. On the morning of the eventful next day, after the usual amount of "smiling," and a repetition of adieux, I found myself "all aboord," wending southwards, and mentally ejaculating *Hierosolymam quando revisam?*

---

* The bill in question:—

Gt. S. L. City, Septeber 18th, 1860.

Captain Burten to James Townsend, Dr.

Aug. 27.	14 Bottle Beer	.	.	.	600
	Belt & Scabbord	.	.	.	500
	Cleaning Vest and Coat	.	.	.	250
	2 Bottles Branday	.	.	.	450
	Washing	.	.	.	525
	to Cash, five dollars	.	.	.	500
	to 3 weaks 3 days Bord	.	.	.	3425
					62·50
	Cash, five dollars	.	.	.	500
					67·50

MOUNT NEBO.

CHAP. XII.

TO RUBY VALLEY.

MOUNTED upon a fine mule, here worth $240, and "bound" to fetch in California $400, and accompanying a Gentile youth who answered to the name of Joe, I proceeded to take my first lesson in stock driving. We were convoying ten horses, which, not being wild, declined to herd together, and by their straggling made the task not a little difficult to a tyro. The road was that leading to Camp Floyd before described. At the Brewery near Mountain Point we found some attempts at a station, and were charged $1·50 for frijoles, potatoes, and bread: amongst other decorations on the wall was a sheet of prize fighters, in which appeared the portraiture of an old man, once the champion of the light weights in the English ring, now a Saint in Gt. S. L. City. The day was fine and wondrous clear, affording us a splendid back view of the Happy Valley before it was finally shut out from sight, and the Utah Lake looked a very gem of beauty, a diamond in its setting of steelly blue mountains. After fording the Jordan we were overtaken by Mr. Kennedy, who had been delayed by more last words, and at the dug-out we drank beer with Shropshire Joe the Mormon, who had been vainly attempting to dig water by a divining rod of peach tree. When moonlight began to appear Joe•the Gentile was ordered by the "boss" to camp out with the horses, where fodder could be found gratis, a commandment which he obeyed with no end of grumbling. It was deep in the night before we entered Frogtown, where a creaking little Osteria supplied us with supper, and I found a bed at the quarters of my friend Capt. Heth, who obligingly insisted upon my becoming his guest.

The five days between the 20th and the 26th September sped merrily at my new home, Camp Floyd; not pressed for time, I embraced with pleasure the opportunity of seeing the most of my American brothers in arms. My host was a son of that Old Dominion of Queen Elizabeth, where still linger traces of the glorious cavalier and the noble feudal spirit, which (alas!) have almost disappeared from the mother country, where the genealogical tree still hangs against the wall, where the principal families, the Nelsons, Harrisons, Pages, Seldens, and Allens, intermarry and bravely attempt to entail, and where the houses, built of brick brought out from England, still retain traces of the seventeenth century. A winter indeed might be passed most pleasantly on the banks of James River and in the West of Virginia,— a refreshing winter to those who love as I do, the traditions of our ancestors.

From Capt. Heth I gathered that in former times, in Western America, as in British India, a fair aborigine was not unfrequently the co-partner of an officer's hut or tent. The improved communication, however, and the frequency of marriage, have abolished the custom by rendering it unfashionable. The Indian squaw, like the Beebee, seldom looked upon her "mari" in any other light but her banker. An inveterate beggar, she would beg for all her relations, for all her friends, and all her tribe, rather than not beg at all, and the lavatory process required always to be prefaced with the bribe. Officers who were long thrown amongst the Prairie Indians, joined, as did the Anglo-Indian, in their nautches and other amusements, where, if whiskey was present, a cut or stab might momentarily be expected. The skin was painted white, black, and red, the hair was dressed and decorated, and the shirt was tied round the waist, whilst broad cloth and blanket, leggings and moccasins completed the costume. The "crack thing to do" when drinking with Indians, and listening to their monotonous songs and tales, was to imitate Indian customs, to become, under the influence of the jolly god, a Hatim Tai, exceedingly generous; to throw shirt to one man, blanket to another, leggings to a third, in fact to return home in breech-cloth. Such sprees would have been severely treated by a highly respectable government; they have now, however, like many a pleasant hour in British India, had their day, and are sunk, many a fathom deep, in the genuine Anglo-Scandinavian gloom.

I heard more of army grievances during my second stay at Camp Floyd. The term of a soldier's enlistment, five years, is too short, especially for the cavalry branch, and the facilities for desertion are enormous. Between the two, one-third of the army disappears every year. The company which should number 84 has often only 50 men. The soldier has no time to learn his work; he must drive wagons, clear bush, make roads, and build huts and stables. When thoroughly drilled, he can take his discharge, and having filled a purse out of his very liberal pay ($11 per mensem), he generally buys ground and becomes a landed proprietor. The officers are equally well salaried, but marching, counter-marching, and contingent expenses are heavy enough to make the profession little better than it is in France. The Secretary of War being a civilian, with naturally the highest theoretical idea of discipline and command combined with economy, is always a martinet; no one can exceed the minutest order, and leave is always obtained under difficulties. As the larger proportion of the officers are southern men, especially Virginians, and as the soldiers are almost entirely Germans and Irish—the Egyptians of modern times—the Federal army will take little part in the ensuing contest. It is more than probable that the force will disband, break in two like the nationalities from which it is drawn. As far as I could judge of American officers, they are about as republican in mind and tone of thought as those of the British army. They are aware of the fact that the bundle of sticks requires a tie, but they prefer, as we all do, King Stork to King Log, and King Log to King Mob.

I took sundry opportunities of attending company inspections, and found the men well dressed and tolerably set up, whilst the bands, being German, were of course excellent. Mr. Chandless

and others talk of the U. S. army discipline as something
Draconian ; severity is doubtless necessary in a force so constituted, but—a proof of their clemency—desertion is the only
crime punishable by flogging. The uniform is a study. The
States have attempted in the dress of their army, as in the
forms of their government, a moral impossibility. It is expected to be at once cheap and soldier-like, useful and ornamental, light and heavy, pleasantly hot in the arctic regions,
and agreeably cool under the tropics. The " military tailors "
of the English army similarly forget the number of changes required in civilian raiment, and looking to the lightness of the
soldier's kit, wholly neglect its efficiency, its capability of preserving the soldier's life. The Federal uniform consists of a brigand-
like and bizarre sombrero, with mephistophelian cock-plume, and
of a blue broad-cloth tunic, imitated from the old Kentuckian
hunter's surtout or wrapper, with terminations sometimes made
to match, at other times too dark and dingy to please the eye.
Its principal merit is a severe republican plainness, very consistent with the prepossessions of the people, highly inconsistent
with the customs of military nations. Soldiers love to dress up
Mars, not to clothe him like a butcher's boy.

The position of Camp Floyd is a mere brickyard, a basin surrounded by low hills, which an Indian pony would have little
difficulty in traversing ; sometimes, however, after the fashion of
the land, though apparently easy from afar, the summits assume
a mural shape, which would stop anything but a mountain
sheep. The rim shows anticlinal strata, evidencing upheavals,
disruption, and lastly, drainage through the kanyons which
break the wall. The principal vegetation is the dwarf cedar
above, the sage greenwood and rabbit bush below. The only
animals seen upon the plain are jackass-rabbits, which in places
afford excellent sport. There are but few Mormons in the
valley ; they supply the camp with hay and vegetables, and are
said to act as spies. The officers cannot but remark the coarse
features and the animal expression of their countenances. On
the outskirts of camp are a few women that have taken
sanctuary among the Gentiles, who here muster too strong for
the Saints. The principal amusement seemed to be that of
walking into and out of the sutlers' stores, the hospitable Messrs.
Gilbert's and Livingston's, — a *passe-temps* which I have seen at

"Sukkur Bukkur Rohri"—and in an evening ride, dull, monotonous, and melancholy, as if we were in the vicinity of
Hyderabad, Sindh.

I had often heard of a local lion, the Timpanogos Kanyon,
and my friends Captains Heth and Gove had obligingly offered
to show me its curiosities. After breakfast on the 23rd September—a bright warm day—we set out in a good ambulance,
well provided with the materials of a two days' picnic, behind a
fine team of four mules, on the road leading to the Utah Lake.
After passing Simple Joe's dug-out we sighted the water once
more; it was of a whitish blue, like the milky waves of Jordan,
embosomed in the embrace of tall and bald-headed hills and
mountains, whose monarch was Nebo of the jagged cone. Where
the wind current sets there are patches of white sand strewn
with broken shells and dried waterweed. Near Pelican Point, a
long projecting rocky spit, there is a fine feeding ground for
geese and ducks, and swimmers and divers may always be seen
dotting the surface. On the south rises a conspicuous buttress
of black rock, and thirty miles off we could see enormous dust
columns careering over the plain. The western part of the valley,
cut with sun cracks and nullahs, and dotted with boulders, shelves
gradually upwards from the selvage of the lake to small divides
and dwarf-hill ranges, black with cedar bush, and traversed only
by wood roads. On the east is the best wheat country in this part
of the Territory; it is said to produce 106 bushels per acre.

After seventeen miles we crossed Jordan Bridge, another
rickety affair, for which, being Mormon property, we paid
$0·50 ; had we been Saints the expense would have been one half.
Two more miles led us to Lehi, a rough miniature of Gt. S. L.
City, in which the only decent house was the bishop's: in
British India it would have been the collector and magistrate's.
My companions pointed out to me a hut in which an apostate
Mormon's throat had been cut by blackened faces. It is grati-
fying to observe that throughout the U.S., as in the Old
Country, all historical interest pales before a barbarous murder.
As we advanced a wall of rock lay before us; the strata were in
confusion as if a convulsion had lately shuddered through their
frame, and tumbled fragments cumbered the base, running up
by precipitous ascents to the middle heights. The colours were
as grotesque; the foreground was a mass of emerald cane, high

and bushy; beyond it, the near distance was pink with the beautiful bloom, most unpoetically termed "hogweed," and azure with a growth like the celebrated blue grass of Kentucky; whilst the wall itself was a blood stone, dark green with cedar,— which, 100 feet tall, was dwarfed to an inch,—and red stained with autumnal maple; whilst below and around the brightest yellow of the faded willow formed the bezel, a golden rim.

Two miles and a half from Lehi led us to American Fork, a soft sweet spring of snow water, with dark shells adhering to white stones, and a quantity of trout swimming the limpid wave. The bridge was rickety and loose planked; in fact, the worst I ever saw in the U. S., where as a rule the country bridges can never be crossed without fear and trembling; the moderate toll was $1 both ways. Three miles and a half more placed us at Battle Creek, where in 1853 the Yuta Indians fled precipitately from a Mormon charge. Six miles over a dusty beach conducted us to the mouth of the kanyon, a brown tract crossed by a dusty road and many a spring, and showing the base of the opposite wall encumbered with degraded masses, super-imposed upon which were miniature castles. The mouth of the ravine was a romantic spot: the staples were sister giants of brown rock—here sheer, there sloping—where pines and firs found a precarious root-hold, and ranged in long perspective lines, whilst between them, through its channel, verdant with willow, and over a clear, pebbly bed, under the screes and scaurs, coursed a mountain torrent more splendid than Ruknabad.

We forded the torrent and pursued the road, now hugging the right then the left side of the chasm. The latter was exceedingly beautiful, misty with the blue of heaven, and rising till its solidity was blent with the tenuity of ether. The rest of the scenery was that of the great Cottonwood Kanyon; painting might express the difference, language cannot. After six miles of a narrow winding road, we reached the place of Cataracts, the principal lion of the place, and found that the season had reduced them to two thin milky lines coursing down bitumen-coloured slopes of bare rock, bordered by shaggy forests of firs and cedars. The shrinking of the water's volume lay bare the forma-tion of the cascades, two steps and a slope, which at a happier time would have been veiled by a continuous sheet of foam.

After finding a suitable spot we outspanned, and, whilst

recruiting exhausted nature, allowed our mules to roll and rest.
After dining and collecting a few shells, we remounted and
drove back through a magnificent sunset to American Fork,
where the bishop, Mr. Lysander Dayton, of Ohio, had offered us
bed and board.   The good episkopos was of course a Mormon,
as we could see by his two pretty wives; he supplied us with
an excellent supper as a host, not as an inn-keeper.   The little
settlement was Gt. S. L. City on a small scale; full of the fair
sex; every one, by the bye, appeared to be or about to be a
mother.   Fair, but, alas! not fair to us, — it was verily

> "Water, water, every where,
> And not a drop to drink!"

Before setting out homewards on the next day we met O.
Porter Rockwell, and took him to the house with us.   This old
Mormon, in days gone by, suffered or did not suffer imprison-
ment for shooting or not shooting Governor Boggs, of Missouri:
he now herds cattle for Messrs. Russell and Co.   His tastes are
apparently rural; his enemies declare that his life would not be
safe in the City of the Saints.   An attempt had lately been made
to assassinate him in one of the kanyons, and the first report
that reached my ears when *en route* to California was the
murder of the old Danite by a certain Mr. Marony.   He is
one of the triumvirate, the First Presidency of "executives,"
the two others being Ephe Hanks and Bill Hickman — whose
names were loud in the land; they are now, however, going
down; middle age has rendered them comparatively inactive,
and the rising generation, Lot Huntington, Ike Clawson, and
other desperadoes, whose teeth and claws are full grown, are
able and willing to stand in their stead.   Porter Rockwell was a
man about fifty, tall and strong, with ample leather leggings
overhanging his huge spurs, and the saw-handles of two revolvers peeping from his blouse.   His forehead was already a
little bald, and he wore his long grizzly locks after the ancient
fashion of the U. S., plaited and gathered up at the nape of the
neck; his brow puckered with frowning wrinkles contrasted
curiously with his cool determined grey eye, jolly red face,
well touched up with "paint," and his laughing good-humoured
mouth.   He had the manner of a jovial, reckless, devil-may-
care English ruffian.   The officers called him Porter, and pre-

ferred him to the "slimy villains" who will drink with a man
and then murder him.   After a little preliminary business about
a stolen horse, all conducted on the amiable, he pulled out a
dollar, and sent to the neighbouring distillery for a bottle of
Valley Tan.   The *aguardiente* was smuggled in under a cloth, as
though we had been respectables in a Moslem country, and we
were asked to join him in a "squar' drink," which means spirits
without water.   The mode of drinking was peculiar.   Porter,
after the preliminary sputation raised the glass with cocked
little finger to his lips, with a twinkle of the eye ejaculated
" Wheat !" that is to say "good," and drained the tumbler to the
bottom : we acknowledged his civility with a " here's how," and
drank Kentucky-fashion, which   in English is midshipman's
grog.   Of these "squar' drinks" we had   at least four, which,
however, did not shake Mr. Rockwell's nerve, and then he sent
out for more.   Meanwhile he told us his last adventure, how
when ascending the kanyon he suddenly found himself covered
by two long rifles ; how he had thrown himself from his horse,
drawn his revolver and crept behind a bush, and how he had
dared the enemy to come out and fight like men.   He spoke
of one Obry, a Frenchman, lately killed in a street quarrel,
who rode on business from Santa Fé to Independence, about
600 miles in 110 hours.   Porter offered, for the fun of the
thing, to excel him by getting over 900 in 144.   When he
heard that I was preparing for California he gave me abundant
good advice — to carry a double-barrelled gun loaded with buck-
shot ; to "keep my eyes skinned," especially in kanyons and
ravines ; to make at times a dark camp — that is to say, un-
hitching for supper and then hitching up and turning a few
miles off the road — ever to be ready for attack when the
animals were being inspanned and outspanned, and never to
trust to appearances in an Indian country, where the red
varmint will follow a man for weeks, perhaps peering through a
wisp of grass on a hill top, till the time arrives for striking the
blow.   I observed that, when thus speaking, Porter's eyes
assumed the expression of an old mountaineer's, ever rolling as
if set in quicksilver.   For the purpose of avoiding " White
Indians," the worst of their kind, he advised me to shun the
direct route, which he represented to be about as fit for travelling as is h—ll for a powder magazine, and to journey *viâ*

Fillmore and the wonder-bearing White Mountains*; finally, he comforted me with an assurance that either the Indians would not attempt to attack us and our stock — ever a sore temptation to them — or that they would assault us in force and " wipe us out."

When the drinking was finished we exchanged a cordial *poignée de main* with Porter and our hospitable host, who appeared to be the *crême de la crême* of Utah county, and soon found ourselves again without the limits of Camp Floyd.

On the evening of the 25th September, the Judge, accompanied by his son and the Marshal of the Territory, entered the cantonment, and our departure was fixed for the next day. The morning of the start was spent in exchanging adieux and little gifts with men who had now become friends, and in stirrup-cups which succeeded one another at no longer intervals than quarter hours. Judge Crosbie, who had arrived by the last mail, kindly provided me with fishing tackle which could relieve a diet of eggs and bacon, and made me regret that I had not added to my outfit a Maynard. This, the best of breechloading guns, can also be loaded at the muzzle; a mere carbine in size, it kills at 1300 yards, and in the U. S. costs only $40 = 8*l*. The Judge, a remarkable contrast to the usual Elijah Pogram style that still affects birdseye or speckled white tie, black satin waistcoat, and swallow-tailed coat of rusty broadcloth, with terminations to match, had been employed for some time in Oregon and at St. Juan; he knew one of my expatriated friends — poor J. de C. whose exile we all lament — and he gave me introductions which I found most useful in Carson Valley. Like the best Americans he spoke of the English as brothers, and freely owned the deficiencies of his Government, especially in dealing with the frontier Indians.

We started from Lieut. Dudley's hospitable quarters, where a crowd had collected to bid us farewell. The ambulance, with four mules driven by Mr. Kennedy in person, stood at the door, and the parting stirrup-cup was exhibited with a will. I bade

---

* An emigrant company lately followed this road, and when obliged by the death of their cattle to abandon their kit they found on the tramp a lump of virgin silver, which was carried to California : an exploring party afterwards despatched failed, however, to make the lead. At the western extremity of the White Mountains there is a mammoth cave, of which one mile has been explored : it is said to end in a precipice, and the enterprising Major Egan is eager to trace its course.

farewell with a true regret to my kind and gallant hosts, whose brotherly attentions had made even wretched Camp Floyd a pleasant *séjour* to me. At the moment I write it is probably desolate : the " Secession " disturbances having necessitated the withdrawal of the unhappies from U. T.

About 4 P.M., as we mounted, a furious dust-storm broke over the plain; perhaps it may account for our night's *méprise*, which a censorious reader might attribute to our copious libations of whiskey. The road to the first mail station, " Meadow Creek," lay over a sage barren ; we lost no time in missing it by forging to the west. After hopelessly driving about the country till 10 P.M. in the fine cool night, we knocked at a hut and induced the owner to appear. He was a Dane who spoke but little English, and his son, " skeert" by our fierceness, began at once to boohoo. At last, however, we were guided by our " foreloper " to " Johnston's settlement," in Rock Valley, and we entered by the unceremonious process of pulling down the zigzag fences. After some trouble we persuaded a Mormon to quit the bed in which his wife and children lay, to shake down for us sleeping places among the cats and hens on the floor, and to provide our animals with oats and hay. Mr. Grice, the Marshal, one of the handiest of men, who during his volunteer service in Mexico had learned most things from carrying a musket to cooking a steak, was kind enough to prepare our supper, after which, still sorely laden with whiskey dying within us, we turned in.

To Meadow Creek, 27th September.

We rose with the dawn, the cats, and the hens, sleep being impossible after the first blush of light, and I proceeded to inspect the settlement. It is built upon the crest of an earth-wave rising from grassy hollows ; the haystacks told of stock, and the bunch-grass on the borders of the ravines and nullahs rendered the place particularly fit for pasturage. The land is too cold for cereals : in its bleak bottoms frost reigns throughout the year; and there is little bench-ground. The settlement consisted of half a dozen huts, which swarmed, however, with women and children. Mr. Kennedy introduced us to a Scotch widow of mature years, who gave us any amount of butter and butter-milk in exchange for a little tea. She was but a lukewarm Mormon, declaring polygamy to be an abomination, complaining that she had been inveigled to a mean place, and that the poor in Mormondom were exceedingly poor.   Yet the canny body was stout and fresh ; her house was clean and neat; and she washed her children and her potatoes.

We had wandered twenty-five miles out of the right road, and were still distant fifteen to sixteen from the first mail station. For the use of the floor, flies, and permission to boil water, we paid our taciturn Mormon $2, and at noon, a little before the bursting of the dusty storm-gusts, which reproduced the horrors of Sindh, we found ourselves once more in the saddle and the ambulance. We passed by a cattle track on rolling ground dotted with sage and greasewood, which sheltered hosts of jackass-rabbits, and the sego with its beautiful lily-like flowers.   After crossing sundry nullahs and pitch-holes, with deep and rugged sides, we made the mail station at the west end of Rush Valley, which is about twenty miles distant from Camp Floyd.   The little green bottom, with its rush-bordered sinking spring, is called by Capt. Simpson "Meadow Creek."   We passed a pleasant day in revolver practice, with Al. Huntington, the renowned brother of Lot, who had lately bolted to South California, in attempts at rabbit-shooting — the beasts became very wild in the evening — and in dining on an antelope, which a youth had ridden down and pistolled.   With the assistance of the station-master, Mr. Faust, a civil and communicative man, who added a knowledge of books and drugs to the local history, I compiled an account of the several lines of communication between Gt. S. L. City and California.

Three main roads connect the land of the Saints with the Eldorado of the West — the northern, the central, and the southern.

The northern road rounds the upper end of the Great Salt Lake, and falls into the valleys of the Humboldt and Carson Rivers.   It was explored in 1845 by Col. Frémont*, who, when

---

* Explored is used in a modified sense. Every foot of ground passed over by Colonel Frémont was perfectly well known to the old trappers and traders, as the interior of Africa to the Arab and Portuguese pombeiros. But this fact takes nothing away from the honours of the man who first surveyed and scientifically observed the country. Amongst those who preceded Colonel Frémont the most remarkable, perhaps, was Sylvester Pattie, a Virginian, who having lost his wife in his adopted home on the Missouri, resolved to trap upon and to trace out the head waters of the Yellow River. The little company of five persons, amongst

passing over the seventy waterless miles of the western, a continuation of the eastern desert, lost ten mules and several horses. The " first overland trip " was followed in 1846 by a party of emigrants under a Mr. Hastings, who gave his name to the " cut off " which has materially shortened the distance. The road has been carefully described in Kelly's California, in Horn's " Overland Guide," and by M. Remy. It is still, despite its length, preferred by travellers, on account of the abundance of grass and water : moreover, there are now but two short stretches of desert.

The southern road, *viâ* Fillmore and San Bernardino, to San Pedro, where the traveller can embark for San Francisco, is long and tedious ; water is found at thirty mile distances ; there are three deserts ; and bunch and other grasses are not plentiful. It has one great merit, namely, that of being rarely snowed up, except between the Rio Virgen and Gt. S. L. City : the best travelling is in spring, when the melting snows from the eastern hills fill the rivulets. This route has been travelled over by Messrs. Chandless and Remy, who have well described it in their picturesque pages. I add a few notes, collected from men who have ridden over the ground for several years, concerning the stations : the information, however, it will be observed, is merely hearsay.*

whom were Pattie and his son, set out on the 20th June 1824, and on the 2nd August arrived at the head waters of the Platte, where they found General Pratt proceeding towards Santa Fé. Pattie in command of 116 men crossed the dividing ridge, descended into the valley of the Rio Grand del Norto, entered Santa Fé and trapped on the Gila River. The party broke up on the 27th November 1826, when Pattie accompanied by his son and six others descended the Colorado, and after incredible hardships reached the Hispano-American Missions, where they were received with the customary inhumanity. The father died in durance vile, the son, after being released and vaccinated at San Diego, reached San Francisco, whence he returned home *viâ* Vera Cruz and New Orleans, after an absence of six years. The whole tale is well told in " Harper's Magazine."

* The distance from Gt. S. L. City to San Bernardino is, according to my informant, about 750 miles, and has been accomplished in fourteen days. The road runs through Provo to Salt Cruz formed by a desert of 50–60 miles, and making Sevier River the half-way point to the capital. At Corn Creek is an Indian farm, and Weaver is 64 miles from Fillmore. Cedar Spring is the entrance to Paravan Valley, where as early as 1806 there was a fort and a settlement. Then comes Fillmore, the territorial capital, and 96 miles afterwards it passes through Paravan City in Little Salt Lake Valley. At Cold Creek it forks, the central road being that mostly preferred. The next station is Mountain Meadows, the Southern Rim of the Basin, celebrated for its massacre ; ensues

The central route is called Egan's by the Mormons, Simpson's by the Gentiles. Mr. or Major Howard Egan is a Saint and well-known guide, an indefatigable mountaineer, who for some time drove stock to California in the employ of Messrs. Livingston, and who afterwards became mail agent under Messrs. Chorpenning and Russell. On one occasion he made the distance in twelve days, and he claims to have explored the present post-office route between 1850 and the winter of 1857–1858. Capt. J. H. Simpson, of the Federal army, whose itinerary is given in Appendix I., followed between May and June 1859. He travelled along Egan's path, with a few unimportant deviations, for 300 miles, and left it ten miles west of Ruby Valley, trending southwards to the suite of the Carson River. On his return he pursued a more southerly line, and fell into Egan's route about thirty miles west of Camp Floyd. The *employés* of the route prefer Egan's line, declaring that on Simpson's there is little grass, that the springs are mere fiumaras of melted snow, and that the wells are waterless. Bad, however, is the best, as the following pages will, I think, prove.

To Tophet, 28th September.

On a cool and cloudy morning, which at 10 A.M. changed into a clear sunny day, we set out, after paying $3 for three feeds, to make the second station. Our road lay over the seven miles of plain that ended Rush Valley: we saw few rabbits, and the sole vegetation was stunted sage. Ensued a rough divide, stony and dusty, with cahues and pitch-holes: it is known by the name of

---

the Santa Clara River, and thence a total of 70 miles, divided into several stages, lead to the Rio Virgen. After following the latter for 20–30 miles, the path crosses the divide of Muddy River and enters a desert 55–67 miles in breadth leading to Las Vegas. Thirty miles beyond that point lies a pretty water called " Mountain Springs," a preliminary to " Dry Lake," a second desert 40–45 miles broad, and ending at an alkaline water called Kingston Springs. The third desert, 40 miles broad, leads to a post established for the protection of emigrants, and called Bitter or Bidder's Springs, 115 miles from Las Vegas. The next stage of 35 is to the Indian River, a tributary of the Colorado, whence there is another military establishment : the land is now Californian. Thence following and crossing the course of the stream, the traveller sights the Sierra Nevada. After 50 miles down the Mohave kanyon is San Bernardino, once a thriving Mormon settlement, 90 miles from San Pedro and 120 from San Diego, where water conveyance is found to San Francisco.

General Johnson's Pass. The hills above it are grey and bald-headed, a few bristles of black cedar protruding from their breasts, and the land wears an uninhabitable look. After two miles of toil we halted near the ruins of an old station. On the right side of the road was a spring half way up the hill: three holes lay full of slightly alkaline water, and the surplus flowed off in a black bed of vegetable mud, which is often dry in spring and summer. At " Point Look Out," near the counterslope of divide, we left on the south Simpson's route, and learned by a sign-post that the distance to Carson is 533 miles. The pass led to Skull Valley, of ominous sound. According to some, the name is derived from the remains of Indians which are found scattered about a fine spring in the southern parts. Others declare that the mortal remains of bison here lie like pavement stones or cannon-balls in the Crimean Valley of Death. Skull Valley stretches nearly S. W. of the Great Salt Lake plain, with which it communicates, and its drainage, as in these parts generally, feeds the lake. Passing out of Skull Valley, we crossed the cahues and pitch-holes of a broad bench which rose above the edge of the desert, and after seventeen miles beyond the Pass reached the station which Mormons call Egan's Springs, anti-Mormons Simpson's Springs, and Gentiles Lost Springs.

Standing upon the edge of the bench, I could see the Tophet in prospect for us till Carson Valley; a road narrowing in perspective to a point, spanned its grisly length, awfully long, and the next mail station had shrunk to a little black knob. All was desert: the bottom could no longer be called basin or valley: it was a thin fine silt, thirsty dust in the dry season, and putty-like mud in the spring and autumnal rains. The hair of this unlovely skin was sage and greasewood: it was warted with sand-heaps; in places mottled with bald and horrid patches of salt soil, whilst in others minute crystals of salt, glistening like diamond-dust in the sunlight, covered tracts of moist and oozy mud. Before us, but a little to the right or north, and nearly due west of Camp Floyd, rose Granite Mountain, a rough and jagged spine or hogsback, inhabited only by wolves and antelopes, hares and squirrels, grasshoppers, and occasionally an Indian family. Small sweet springs are found near its northern and southern points. The tradition of the country declares it to be rich in gold, which, however, no one dares to dig. Our road is about to round the southern extremity, wheeling successively S. and S.-E., then W. and N.-W., then S.-W. and S.-E., and S.-W. and N.-W. — in fact, round three quarters of the compass; and for three mortal days we shall sight its ugly frowning form. A direct passage leads between it and the corresponding point of southern hill: we contemplate, through the gap, a blue ridge where lies Willow Spring Station, the destination of our after to-morrow; but the straight line which saves so much distance is closed by bogs for the greater part of the year, and the size of the wild sage would impede our wagon wheels.

The great desert of Utah Territory extends in length about 300 miles along the western side of the Great Salt Lake. Its breadth varies: a little further south it cannot be crossed; the water, even where not poisonous, being insufficient. The formation is of bottoms like that described above, bench-lands, with the usual parallel and perfectly horizontal water-lines, leaving regular steps, as the sea settled down, by the gradual upheaval of the land. They mark its former elevation upon the sides of the many detached ridges trending mostly N. and S. Like the rim of the Basin, these hills are not a single continuous mountain range which might be flanked, but a series of disconnected protrusions above the general level of the land. A paying railway through this country is as likely as a profitable canal through the Isthmus of Suez: the obstacles must be struck at right angles, with such assistance as the rough kanyons and the ravines of various levels afford.

We are now in a country dangerous to stock. It is a kind of central point, where Pávant, Gosh-Yuta (popularly called Gosh Ute), and Panak (Bannacks) meet. Watches, therefore, were told off for the night. Next morning, however, it was found that all had stood on guard with unloaded guns.

To Fish Springs, 29th September.

At Lost Springs the party was mustered. The following was found to be the material. The Ras Kafilah was one Kennedy, an Irishman, whose brogue, doubly-Dublin, sounded startlingly in the Great American Desert. On a late trip he had been victimised by Indians. The savages had driven off two of his horses, into a kanyon within sight of the Deep Creek Station. In the hurry of pursuit he spurred up the ravine, followed by a friend, when sighting jerked meat, his own property, upon the trees, he gave the word *sauve qui peut*. As they whirled their horses the Yutas rushed down the hill to intercept them at the mouth of the gorge, calling them in a loud voice dogs and squaws, and firing sundry shots, which killed Kennedy's horse and pierced his right arm. Most men, though they jest at scars before feeling a wound, are temporarily cowed by an infliction of the kind, and of that order was the good Kennedy.

The next was an excellent traveller, by name Howard. On the road between Gt. S. L. City and Camp Floyd I saw two men, who addressed me as Mr. Kennedy the boss, and finding out their mistake, followed us to the place of rendezvous. The party, with one eye grey and the other black, mounted upon a miserable pony, was an American. After a spell at the gold diggings of California he had re-visited the States, and he now wished to return to his adopted country without loss of time. He was a hardy, fine-tempered fellow, exceedingly skilled in driving stock. His companion was a Frenchman and ex-Zouave, who, for reasons best known to himself, declared that he came from Cuba, and that he had forgotten every word of Spanish. Like foreigners amongst Anglo-Scandinavians generally, the poor devil fared badly. He could not hold his own. With the most labour he had the worst of everything. He felt himself *mal placé*, and before the end of the journey he slunk away.

At Lost Springs we were joined by two Mormon fugitives, "pilgrims of love," who had, it was said, secretly left the city at night, fearing the consequences of having "loved not wisely, but too well." The first of the Lotharios was a Mr. R——, an English farrier-blacksmith, mounted upon an excellent horse and leading another. He soon took offence at our slow rate of progress, and afflicted by the thought that the avenger was behind him, left us at Deep Creek, and "made tracks" to Carson City in ten days, with two horses and a total travelling kit of two blankets. We traced him to California by the trail of falsehoods which he left on the road. His comrade, Mr. A——, a New Englander, was also an apostate Mormon, a youth of good family and liberal education, who, after ruining himself by city sites and copper mines on Lake Superior, had permanently compromised himself with society by becoming a Saint. Also a Lothario, he had made his escape, and he proved himself a good and useful mem-

ber of society.   I could not but admire the acuteness of both
these youths, who, flying from justice, had placed themselves
under the protection of a judge.   They reminded me of a debtor
friend who found himself secure from the bailiff only within the
walls of Spike Island or Belvidere Place, Southwark.

Another notable of the party was an apostate Jew and *soi-
disant* apostate Mormon, who answered to the name of Rose.
He had served as missionary in the Sandwich Islands, and he
spoke Kanaka like English.   His features were those which
Mr. Thackeray loves to delineate; his accents those which
Robson delights to imitate.   He denied his connection with the
Hebrews.   He proved it by eating more, by driving a better
bargain, by doing less work than any of the party.   It was truly
refreshing to meet this son of old Hounsditch in the land of
the Saints, under the shadow of New Zion, and the only drawback to our enjoyment was the general suspicion that the
honourable name of apostate covered the less respectable calling
of spy.   He contrasted strongly with Jim Gilston of Illinois, a
lath-like specimen of humanity, some six feet four in length—
a perfect specimen of the Indianised white, long hair, sun-
tanned, and hatchet-faced; running like an ostrich, yelping like
a savage, and ready to take scalp at the first provocation.   He
could not refrain, as the end of the journey drew nigh, from the
temptation of deserting without paying his passage.   Mr. Col-
ville, a most determined Yankee, far advanced in years, was
equally remarkable.   He had $90 in his pocket.   He shivered
for want of a blanket, and he lived on hard bread, bacon, and tea,
of which no man was ever seen to partake.   Such were the seven
"free men," the independent traders of the company.   There were
also six "broths of boys," who paid small sums up to $40 for the
benefit of our escort, and who were expected to drive and to do
general work.   Travelling soon makes friends.   No illusions of
amicitia, however, could blind my eyes to the danger of entering an Indian country with such an escort.   Untried men, for
the most part, they wou'd have discharged their weapons in the
air and fled at the whoop of an Indian, all of them, including
Jake the Shoshone, who had been permitted to accompany us as
guide, and excepting our staunch ones, Howard, "Billy" the
colt, and "Brandy" the dog.

The station was thrown somewhat into confusion by the pre-

sence of a petticoat, an article which in these regions never fails
to attract presents of revolvers and sides of bacon. " Gentle
Annie," attended by three followers, was passing in an ambulance from California to Denver City, where her "friend" was.
To most of my companions' inquiries about old acquaintances in
California, she replied, in western phrase, that the individual
subject of their solicitude had " got to git up and git," which
means that he had found change of air and scene advisable.
Most of her sentences ended with a " you *bet*," even under circumstances where such operation would have been quite uncalled
for. So it is related that when Dr. P—— of Camp Floyd was
attending Mrs. A. B. C. at a most critical time, he asked her
tenderly, " Do you suffer much, Mrs. C. ? " to which the new
matron replied, " You *bet !* "

We set out about noon, on a day hot as midsummer by contrast
with the preceding nights, for a long spell of nearly fifty miles.
Shortly after leaving the station the road forks. The left-hand
path leads to a grassy spring in a dwarf kanyon near the
southern or upper part of a river bottom, where emigrants are
fond of camping. The hills scattered around the basin were
of a dark metallic stone, sun-burnt to chocolate. The strata were
highly tilted up and the water-lines distinctly drawn. After eight
miles we descended into the yellow silty bed of a bald and barren
fiumara, which was not less than a mile broad. The good
Judge sighed when he contrasted it with Monongahela, the "river
of the falling banks." It flows northwards, and sinks near the
western edge of the Lake. At times it runs three feet of water.
The hills around are white-capped throughout the winter, but
snow seldom lies more than a week in the bottoms.

After twenty miles over the barren plain we reached, about
sunset, the station at the foot of the Dugway. It was a mere
" dug out"— a hole four feet deep, roofed over with split cedar
trunks, and provided with a rude adobe chimney. The tenants
were two rough young fellows — station master and express rider
—with their friend, an English bulldog. One of them had
amused himself by decorating the sides of the habitation with
niches and Egyptian heads. Rude art seems instinctively to
take that form which it wears on the banks of Nilus, and should
some Professor Rafinesque discover these traces of the aborigines,
after a sepulture of a century, they will furnish materials for a

rich chapter on anti-Columbian immigration. Water is brought
to the station in casks. The youths believe that some seven
miles north of the "Dugway" there is a spring, which the
Indians, after the fashion of that folk, sensibly conceal from the
whites. Three wells have been sunk near the station. Two
soon led to rock; the third has descended 120 feet, but is still
bone dry. It passes first through a layer of surface silt, then
through three or four feet of loose, friable, fossilless, chalky
lime, which, when slaked, softened, and mixed with sand, is used
as mortar. The lowest strata are of quartz gravel, forming in the
deeper parts a hard conglomerate. The workmen complained
greatly of the increasing heat as they descend. Gold now
becomes uppermost in man's mind. The youths seeing me
handle the rubbish at once asked me if I was prospecting for gold.

After roughly supping we set out, with a fine round moon
high in the skies, to ascend the "Dugway Pass" by a rough
dusty road winding round the shoulder of a hill, through which
a fiumara has burst its way. Like other Utah mountains,
the highest third rises suddenly from a comparatively gradual
incline, a sore formation for cattle, requiring draught to
be at least doubled. Arriving on the summit we sat down,
whilst our mules returned to help the baggage wagons, and
amused ourselves with the strange aspect of the scene. To the
north or before us and far below lay a long broad stretch, white
as snow — the Saleratus Desert, west of the Gt. S. Lake. It
wore a grisly aspect in the silvery light of the moon. Behind
us was the brown plain, sparsely dotted with shadows, and dewless
in the evening as in the morning. As the party ascended the
summit with much noisy shouting, they formed a picturesque
group — the well-bred horses wandering to graze, the white-
tilted wagons with their panting mules, and the men in felt
capotes and huge leather leggings. In honour of our good star
which had preserved every hoof from accident we "liquored
up" on that summit, and then began the descent.

Having reached the plain the road ran for eight miles over a
broken surface, with severe pitch-holes and wagon tracks
which have lasted many a month; it then forked. The left,
which is about six miles the longer of the two, must be taken
after rains, and leads to the Devil's Hole, a curious formation in
a bench under "High Mountain," about ninety miles from

Camp Floyd, and south, with a little westing, of the Gt. S. Lake. The Hole is described as shaped like the frustum of an inverted cone, forty feet in diameter above, twelve to fifteen below. As regards the depth, four lariats, of forty feet each and a line at the end, did not, it is said, reach the bottom. Capt. Simpson describes the water as brackish. The drivers declare it to be half salt. The Devil's Hole is popularly supposed to be an air-vent or shaft communicating with the waters of the Gt. S. Lake, in their subterraneous journey to the sea (Pacific Ocean). An object cast into it, they say, is sucked down and disappears; hence, if true, probably the theory.

We chose the shorter cut, and after eight miles rounded Mountain Point, the end of a dark brown butte falling into the plain. Opposite us and under the western hills, which were distant about two miles, lay the station, but we were compelled to double, for twelve miles, the intervening slough, which no horse can cross without being mired. The road hugged the foot of the hills at the edge of the saleratus basin, which looked like a furrowed field in which snow still lingers. In places warts of earth tufted with greasewood emerged from hard, flakey, curling silt cakes; in others, the salt frosted out of the damp black earth like the miniature sugar-plums upon chocolate bon-bons. We then fell into a saline, resembling freshly fallen snow. The whiteness changes to a slatey blue, like a frozen pond when the water still underlies it; and to make the delusion perfect, the black rutted path looked as if lately cut out after a snow storm. Weird forms appeared in the moonlight. A line of sand-heaps became a row of railroad cars; a raised bench was mistaken for a paling; and the bushes were anything between a cow and an Indian. This part of the road must be terrible in winter; even in the fine season men are often compelled to unpack half a dozen times.

After ascending some sand-hills we halted for the party to form up in case of accident, and Mr. Kennedy proceeded to inspect whilst we prepared for the worst part of the stage — the sloughs. These are three in number, one of twenty and the two others of 100 yards in length. The tule, the bayonet-grass, and the tall rushes enable animals to pass safely over the deep slushy mud, but when the vegetation is well trodden down, horses are in danger of being permanently mired. The principal inconvenience

to man is the infectious odour of the foul swamps. Our cattle were
mad with thirst; however, they crossed the three sloughs successfully, although some had nearly made Dixie's Land in the second.

Beyond the sloughs we ascended a bench, and travelled on an
improved road. We passed sundry circular ponds, garnished
with rush; the water is sulphury, and according to season is
warm, hot, or cold. Some of these debord, and send forth what
the Somal would call Biya Gora, "night-flowing streams."
About 3 A.M., cramped with cold, we sighted the station, and
gave the usual "Yep! Yep!" A roaring fire soon revived us;
the strong ate supper and the weak went to bed, thus ending
a somewhat fatiguing day.

To Willow Creek, 30th September.

On this line there are two kinds of stations; the mail station,
where there is an agent in charge of five or six "boys," and the
express station — every second — where there is only a master
and an express rider. The boss receives $50 — $75 per mensem,
the boy $35. It is a hard life, setting aside the chance of death
— no less than three murders have been committed by the
Indians during this year — the work is severe; the diet is sometimes reduced to wolf-mutton, or a little boiled wheat and rye,
and the drink to brackish water; a pound of tea comes occasionally, but the droughty souls are always "out" of whiskey
and tobacco. At "Fish Springs," where there is little danger
of savages, two men had charge of the ten horses and mules;
one of these was a German Swiss, from near Schaffhausen, who
had been digging for gold to little purpose in California.

A clear cool morning succeeding the cold night aroused us
betimes. Nature had provided an ample supply of warm water,
though slightly sulphury, in the neighbouring pot-holes, and at
a little distance from the station was one conveniently cool. The
fish from which the formation derives its name, is a perch-like
species, easily caught on a cloudy day. The men, like the citizens of Suez, accustom themselves to the "rotten water," as
strangers call it, and hardly relish the purer supplies of Simpson's Springs, or Willow Springs: they might have built the
station about one mile north, near a natural well of good cool
water, but apparently they prefer the warm bad.

The saleratus valley looked more curious in daylight than

in moonlight. The vegetation was in regular scale; smallest, the rich bunch-grass on the benches; then the greasewood and the artemisia, where the latter can grow; and largest of all the dwarf cedar. All was of lively hue, the herbage bright red, yellow, and sometimes green, the shrubs were grey and glaucous, the cedars almost black, and the rim of hills blue-brown and blue. We had ample time to contemplate these curiosities, for Kennedy, whose wits, like those of Hiranyaka, the mouse, were mightily sharpened by the possession of wealth, had sat up all night and wanted a longer sleep in the morning. After a breakfast which the water rendered truly detestable, we hitched up about 10 A.M. and set out *en route* for Willow Springs.

About an hour after our departure, we met the party commanded by Lieut. Weed, two subaltern officers, ninety dragoons, and ten wagons; they had been in the field since May, and had done good service against the Gosh-Yutas. We halted and "liquored up," and, after American fashion, talked politics in the wilderness. Half an hour then led us to what we christened " Kennedy's Hole," another circular bowl, girt with grass and rush, in the plain under a dark brown rock, with black bands and scatters of stone. A short distance beyond, and also on the right of the road, lay the " Poison Springs," in a rushy bed: the water was temptingly clear, but the bleached bones of many a quadruped skeleton bade us beware of it. After turning a point we saw in front a swamp, the counterpart of what met our eyes last night; it renewed also the necessity of rounding it by a long southerly sweep. The scenery was that of the Takhashshua near Zayla, or the delicious land behind Aden, the Arabian sea-board. Sand-heaps — the only dry spots after rain — fixed by tufts of metallic green salsolæ, and guarded from the desert wind by rusty cane-grass, emerged from the wet and oozy plain, in which the mules often sank to the fetlock. The unique and snowy floor of thin nitre, blueish where deliquescent, was here solid as a sheet of ice, there a net-work of little ridges, as if the salt had expanded by crystallisation, with regular furrows worked by rain. After heavy showers it becomes a soft, slippery, tenacious, and slushy mud, that renders travelling exceeding laborious; the glare is blinding by day, and at night, the refrigerating properties of the salt render the wind bitterly cold, even when the mercury stands at 50° F.

We halted to bait at the half-way house, the fork of the road leading to Pleasant Valley, an unpleasant place, so called because discovered on a pleasant evening. As we advanced the land improved, the salt disappeared, the grass was splendidly green, and approaching the station we passed Willow Creek, where gophar-holes and snipes, willows and wild roses, told of life and gladdened the eye. The station lay on a bench beyond the slope. The express rider was a handsome young Mormon, who wore in his felt hat the effigy of a sword ; his wife was an Englishwoman, who, as usual under the circumstances, had completely thrown off the Englishwoman. The station-keeper was an Irishman, one of the few met amongst the Saints. Nothing could be fouler than the log hut, the flies soon drove us out of doors ; hospitality, however, was not wanting, and we sat down to salt beef and bacon, for which we were not allowed to pay. The evening was spent in setting a wolf-trap, which consisted of a springy pole and a noose : we strolled about after sunset with a gun, but failed to bag snipe, wild-fowl or hare, and sighted only a few cunning old crows, and black swamp birds with yellow throats. As the hut contained but one room we slept outside ; the Gosh-Yuta are apparently not a venturesome people, still it is considered advisable at times to shift one's sleeping quarters, and to acquire the habit of easily awaking.

To Deep Creek and halt, 1st and 2nd October, 1860.

A " little war" had been waging near Willow Springs. In June the station was attacked by a small band of Gosh-Yuta, of whom three were shot and summarily scalped ; an energetic proceeding, which had prevented a repetition of the affair. The savages, who are gathering their pine-nut harvest, and are driven by destitution to beg at the stations, to which one meal a week will attach them, are now comparatively peaceful : when the emigration season re-commences they are expected to be troublesome, and their numbers — the Pa-Yutas can bring 12000 warriors into the field — render them formidable. " Jake," the Shoshone, who had followed us from Lost Springs, still considered his life in danger ; he was as unwilling to wend his way alone as an Arab Bedouin or an African negro in their respective interiors. With regard to ourselves, Lieut. Weed had declared that there was no danger ; the station people thought, on the contrary, that the snake, which had been scotched not killed, would recover after the departure of the soldiers, and that the work of destruction had not been carried on with sufficient vigour.

At 6 A.M. the thermometer showed 45° F.; we waited two hours, till the world had time to warm. After six miles we reached " Mountain Springs," a water-sink below the bench land, tufted round with cotton-wood, willow, rose, cane, and grass. On our right, or eastward, lay Granite Rock, which we had well nigh rounded, and through a gap we saw Lost Springs Station, distant apparently but a few hours' canter. Between us, however, lay the horrible salt plain,—a continuation of the low lands bounding the western edge of the Gt. S. Lake,—which the drainage of the hills over which we were travelling inundates till June.

After twelve miles over the bench we passed a dark rock, which protects a water called Reading's Springs, and we halted to form up at the mouth of Deep Creek Kanyon. This is a dangerous gorge, some nine miles long, formed by a water-course which sheds into the valley of the Gt. S. Lake. Here I rode forwards with " Jim," a young express rider from the last station, who volunteered much information upon the subject of Indians. He carried two Colt's revolvers, of the dragoon or largest size, considering all others too small. I asked him what he would do if a Gosh-Yuta appeared. He replied, that if the fellow were civil he might shake hands with him, if surly he would shoot him ; and at all events, when riding away, that he would keep a " stirrup eye" upon him : that he was in the habit of looking round corners to see if any one was taking aim, in which case he would throw himself from the saddle, or rush on, so as to spoil the shooting —the Indians, when charged, becoming excited, fire without effect. He mentioned four red men who could " draw a bead " against any white, usually, however, they take a minute to load, they require a long aim, and they stint their powder. He pointed out a place where Miller, one of the express riders, had lately been badly wounded, and lost his horse. Nothing, certainly, could be better fitted for an ambuscade than this gorge, with its caves and holes in snow cuts, earth-drops, and lines of strata, like walls of rudely piled stone ; in one place we saw the ashes of an Indian encampment ; in another a whirlwind, curling, as smoke would rise, from behind a projecting spur, made us advance with the greatest caution.

As we progressed the valley opened out, and became too broad to be dangerous.   Near the summit of the pass the land is well lined with white sage, which may be used as fodder, and a dwarf cedar adorns the hills.   The ground gives out a hollow sound, and the existence of a spring in the vicinity is suspected. Descending the western watershed, we sighted, in Deep Creek Valley, St. Mary's County, the first patch of cultivation since leaving Gt. S. Lake. The Indian name is Aybá-pá, or the Clay-coloured Water; pity that America and Australia have not always preserved the native local terms.   It is bisected by a rivulet in which three streamlets from the southern hills unite; like these features generally, its course is northward till it sinks : fields extend about one mile from each bank, and the rest of the yellow bottom is a tapestry of wire grass and wheat grass.   An Indian model farm had been established here; the war, however, prevented cultivation, the savages had burned down the house, and several of them had been killed by the soldiers.   On the west of the valley were white rocks of the lime used for mortar : the hills also showed lias and marble-like limestones.   The eastern wall was a grim line of jagged peaks, here bare with granite, there black with cedar; they are crossed by a short cut leading to the last station, which, however, generally proves the longest way, and in a dark ravine Kennedy pointed out the spot where he had of late nearly left his scalp.   Coal is said to be found there in chunks, and gold is supposed to abound; the people, however, believing that the valley cannot yet support extensive immigration, conceal it probably by " counsel."

At 4 P.M. we reached the settlement, consisting of two huts and a station-house, a large and respectable-looking building of unburnt brick, surrounded by fenced fields, watercourses, and stacks of good adobe.   We were introduced to the Mormon station-master, Mr. Sevier, and others.   They are mostly farm labourers, who spend the summer here and supply the road with provisions : in the winter they return to Grantsville, where their families are settled.   Amongst them was a Mr. Waddington, an old Pennsylvanian, and a bigoted Mormon. It is related of him that he had treasonably saved 300 Indians by warning them of an intended attack by the Federal troops.   He spoke strongly in favour of the despised Yutas, declared that they are ready to work, and can be led to anything by civility.   The anti-Mormons declared that his praise was for interested motives, wishing the savages to labour for him gratis, and I observed that when Mr. Waddington started to cut wood in the kanyon, he set out at night, lest his dust should be seen by his red friends.

The Mormons were not wanting in kindness ; they supplied us with excellent potatoes, and told us to make their house our home. We preferred, however, living and cooking afield. The station was dirty to the last degree : the flies suggested the Egyptian plague, they could be brushed from the walls in thousands, but though sage makes good brooms no one cares to sweep clean. This I repeat is not Mormon but Western : the people, like the Spaniards, apparently disdain any occupation save that of herding cattle, and will do so till the land is settled. In the evening Jake the Shoshone came in, grumbling loudly because he had not been allowed to ride ; he stood cross-legged like an African, ate a large supper at the station, and a second with us. No wonder that the savage in civilisation suffers, like the lady's lap-dog, from " liver." He was, however, a first-rate hand in shirking any work except that of peering and peeping into everything ; neither gospel nor gunpowder can reform this race. Mr. R——, the English farrier and Lothario, left us on this day, after a little quarrel with Kennedy. We were glad to receive permission to sleep upon the loose wheat in an inner room : at 8 A.M. the thermometer had shown 59° F., but on this night ice appeared in the pails.

The next day was a halt ; the stock wanted rest and the men provisions. A " beef "—the Westerns still retain the singular of " beeves '—was killed, and we obtained a store of potatoes and wheat. Default of oats, which are not yet common, this heating food is given to horses :—12 lbs. of grain to 14 of long forage, and the furious riding of the Mormons is the only preventive of its evil effects. The people believe that it causes stumbling by the swelling of the fetlock and knee joint ; similarly every E. Indian ghorewalla will declare that wheaten bread makes a horse tokkar khana—"eat trips." The *employés* of the station were quiet and respectable, a fact attributed by some of our party to the want of liquor, which is said to cause frequent fights. Our party was less peaceable ; there had been an extensive prigging of blankets, the cold now made them valuable, and this drove the losers " fighting mad."

The severity of the last night made us active, the appearance of deep snow upon the mountains and of ice in the valleys was an intelligible hint that the Sierra Nevada which lay before us would be by no means an easy task. Despite, therefore, the idleness always engendered by a halt, and the frigid blasts which poured down from the eastern hills, where rain was falling in torrents, we hitched up, bade adieu to our Mormon host, and set out about 4 P.M. Antelope Springs, the next station, was 30 miles distant; we resolved therefore to divide it, after the fashion of Asia and Africa, by a short forenoon march.

The road runs to the south-west down the Deep Creek Valley, and along the left bank of the western rivulet. Near the divide we found a good bottom with plenty of water and grass; the only fuel was the sage bush, which crackled merrily, like thorns, under the pot, but tainted the contents with its medicinal odour. The wagons were drawn up in a half-circle to aid us in catching the mules, the animals were turned out to graze, the men were divided into watches, and the masters took up their quarters in the wagons. Age gave the Judge a claim to the ambulance, which was admitted by all hands; I slept with "Scotch Joe," an exceedingly surly youth, who apparently preferred anything to work. At 8 P.M. a storm of wind and rain burst upon us from the S.W.: it was so violent that the wagons rocked before the blast, and at times the chance of a capsize suggested itself. The weather was highly favourable for Indian plundering, who on such nights expect to make a successful attack.

We awoke early in the frigid S.-W. wind, the thermometer showing 39° F. After a few hundred yards we reached "Eight-Mile Springs," so called from the distance to Deep Creek. The road, which yesterday would have been dusty to the hub, was now heavy and viscid; the rain had washed out the saleratus, and the sight and scent, and the country generally, were those of the environs of a horse-pond. An ugly stretch of two miles, perfectly desert, led to Eight-Mile Spring Kanyon, a jagged little ravine about 500 yards long, with a portalled entrance of tall rock. It is not, however, considered dangerous.

Beyond the kanyon lay another grisly land, if possible more deplorable than before; its only crops were dust and mud. On the right hand were turreted rocks, around whose base ran Indian trails, and a violent west wind howled over their summits. About 1.30 P.M. we came upon the station at Antelope Springs; it had been burned by the Gosh-Yutas in the last June, and had never been rebuilt. "George," our cook, who had been one of the inmates at the time, told us how he and his *confrères* had escaped. Fortunately the corral still stood: we found wood in plenty, water was lying in an adjoining bottom, and we used the two to brew our tea.

Beyond Antelope Springs was Shell Creek, distant thirty miles by long road and eighteen by the short cut. We had some difficulty in persuading Kennedy to take the latter; property not only sharpens the intellect, it also generates prudence, and the ravine is a well-known place for ambush. Fortunately two express riders came in and offered to precede us, which encouraged us. About 3 P.M. we left the springs and struck for the mouth of the kanyon, which has not been named; Sevier and Farish are the rival claimants. Entering the jagged fir and pine-clad breach we found the necessity of dismounting. The bed was dry it floods in spring and autumn — but very steep, and in a hole on the right stood water, which we did not touch for fear of poison. Reaching the summit in about an hour we saw below the shaggy foreground of evergreens, or rather everblacks, which cast grotesque and exaggerated shadows in the last rays of day, the snowy-white mountains, gloriously sunlit, on the far side of Shell Creek. Here for the first time appeared the piñon pine (*P. Monophyllus*), which forms the principal part of the Indian's diet; it was no beauty to look upon, a dwarfish tree, rendered shrub-like by being feathered down to the ground. The nut is ripe in early autumn, at which time the savages stow away their winter provision in dry ravines and pits. The fruit is about the size of a pistachio, with a decided flavour of turpentine, tolerably palatable, and at first laxative. The cones are thrown upon the fire, and when slightly burnt the nuts are easily extracted; these are eaten raw, or like the Hindu's toasted grains. The harvest is said to fail every second

year.   Last season produced a fine crop, whilst in this autumn
many of the trees were found, without apparent reason but
frost, dead.

We resumed the descent along a fiumara, which presently
"sank," and at 5 P.M. halted in a prairillon somewhat beyond.
Bunch-grass, sage-fuel, and water were abundant, but the place
was favourable for an attack.   It is a golden rule in an Indian
country never to pitch near trees or rocks that can mask an
approach, and we were breaking it in a place of danger.   However, the fire was extinguished early so as to prevent its becoming a mark for Indians, and the pickets placed on both sides of
the ravine were directed to lie motionless a little below the
crest and to fire at the first comer.   I need hardly say we were
not murdered ; the cold, however, was uncommonly piercing.

To " Robber's Roost," 5th October.

We set out at 6 A.M. the next morning, through a mixture of
snow and hail and howling wind, to finish the ravine, which was
in toto eight miles long.   The descent led us to Spring Valley,
a bulge in the mountains about eight miles broad, which a
sharp divide separates from Shell Valley its neighbour.   On the
summit we fell into the line of rivulet which gives the lowlands a name.   At the foot of the descent we saw a woodman,
and presently the station.   Nothing could more want tidying
than this log-hut, which showed the bullet marks of a recent
Indian attack.   The master was a Français de France, Constant
Dubail, and an ex-lancier : his mother's gossip had received a
remittance of 2000 francs from a son in California, consequently
he had torn himself from the *sein* of *sa pauvre mère,* and with
three others had started in search of fortune, and had nearly
starved.   The express riders were three roughs, of whom one
was a Mormon.   We passed our time whilst the mules were at
bait in visiting the springs.   There is a cold creek 200 yards
below the station, and close by the hut a warm rivulet, said to
contain leeches.   The American hirudo, however, has a serious
defect in a leech—it will not bite ; the faculty, therefore, are
little addicted to hirudination ; country doctors rarely keep the
villainous bloodsuckers, and only the wealthy can afford the per-
nicious luxury, which, imported from Spain, costs $12 per
dozen, somewhat the same price as oysters at Nijni Novgorod.

The weather, which was vile till 10 A.M., when the glass showed 40° (F.), promised to amend, and as the filthy hole — still full of flies, despite the cold — offered no attraction, we set out at 2 P.M. for Egan's Station, beyond an ill-omened kanyon of the same name. We descended into a valley by a regular slope, —in proportion as we leave distance between us and the Gt. S. Lake the bench formation on this line becomes less distinct,— and traversed a barren plain by a heavy road. Hares and prairie hens seemed however to like it, and a frieze of willow thicket at the western end showed the presence of water. We in the ambulance halted at the mouth of the kanyon; the stock and the boys had fallen far behind, and the place had an exceedingly bad name. But the cold was intense, the shades of evening were closing in, so we made ready for action, looked to the priming of gun and revolver, and then *en avant!* After passing that kanyon we should exchange the land of the Gosh-Yuta for those of the more friendly Shoshone.

An uglier place for sharpshooting can hardly be imagined. The floor of the kanyon is almost flush with the bases of the hills, and in such formations, the bed of the creek which occupies the sole is rough and winding. The road was vile, — now winding along, then crossing the stream,— hedged in with thicket and dotted with boulders. Ahead of us was a rocky projection which appeared to cross our path, and upon this Point Dangerous every eye was fixed.

Suddenly my eye caught sight of one fire — two fires under the black bunch of firs half-way up the hill-side on our left, and as suddenly they were quenched, probably with snow. Nothing remained but to hear the warwhoop, and to see a line of savages rushing down the rocks. We loosed the doors of the ambulance that we might jump out if necessary and tree ourselves behind it, and knowing that it would be useless to return, drove on at our fastest speed with sleet, snow, and wind in our faces. Under the circumstances, it was cold comfort to find when we had cleared the kanyon that Egan's Station at the further mouth had been reduced to a chimney stack and a few charred posts. The Gosh-Yutas had set fire to it two or three days before our arrival in revenge for the death of seventeen of their men by Lt. Weed's party. We could distinguish the pits from which the wolves had torn up the corpses, and one fellow's arm projected from the snow. After a hurried deliberation, in which Kennedy swore, with that musical voice in which the Dublin swains delight, that "shure we were all kilt,"—the possession of property not only actuates the mind, and adds industry to its qualities, it also produces a peculiar development of cautiousness,—we unhitched the mules, tethered them to the ambulance, and planted ourselves behind the palisade awaiting all comers, till the boys could bring reinforcement. The elements fought for us: although two tongues of high land directly in front of us would have formed a fine mask for approach, the snow lay in so even a sheet that a prowling coyote was detected, and the hail-like sleet which beat fiercely on our backs would have been a sore inconvenience to a party attacking in face. Our greatest disadvantage was the extreme cold; it was difficult to keep a finger warm enough to draw a trigger. Thomas, the judgeling, so he was called, was cool as a cucumber, mentally and bodily: youths generally are. Firstly they have their "*preuves*" to make; secondly, they know not what they do.

After an hour's freezing, which seemed a day's, we heard with quickened ears the shouts and tramp of the boys and the stock, which took a terrible load off the exile of Erin's heart. We threw ourselves into the wagons, numbed with cold, and forgot, on the soft piles of saddles, bridles, and baggage, and under heaps of blankets and buffaloes, the pains of Barahut. About 3 A.M. this enjoyment was brought to a close by arriving at the end of the stage, Butte Station. The road was six inches deep with snow, and the final ascent was accomplished with difficulty. The good station-master, Mr. Thomas, a Cambrian Mormon, who had, he informed me, three brothers in the British army, bade us kindly welcome, built a roaring fire, added meat to our supper of coffee and doughboy, and cleared by a summary process amongst the snorers places for us on the floor of " Robber's Roost," or " Thieves' Delight," as the place is facetiously known throughout the country-side.

Halt at " Robber's Roost," 6th October.

The last night's sound sleep was allowed to last through the morning. This day was perforce a halt: the old white mare and her colt had been left at the mouth of the kanyon, and one of the Shoshone Indian servants of the station had been persuaded by a bribe of a blanket and some gunpowder to return for them. About noon we arose, expecting a black fog, and looked down upon Butte Valley, whose northern edge we had traversed last night. Snow still lay there,—that bottom is rarely without frost,—but in the fine clear sunny day, with the mercury at 43° F. in the shade, the lowest levels re-became green, the hill cedars turned once more black, earth steamed like a garment hung out to dry, and dark spots here and there mottled the hills, which were capped with huge turbans of muslin-like mist. Whilst the Shoshone is tracking and driving the old mare, we will glance around the "Robber's Roost," which will answer for a study of the Western man's home.

It is about as civilised as the Galway shanty, or the normal dwelling-place in Central Equatorial Africa. A cabin fronting east and west, long walls thirty feet, with portholes for windows, short ditto fifteen; material, sandstone and bog ironstone slabs compacted with mud, the whole roofed with split cedar trunks, reposing on horizontals which rested on perpendiculars. Behind the house a corral of rails planted in the ground; the enclosed space a mass of earth, and a mere shed in one corner the only shelter. Outside the door — the hingeless and lockless back-board of a wagon, bearing the wounds of bullets — and resting on lintels and staples, which also had formed parts of locomotives, a slab acting stepping-stone over a mass of soppy black soil strewed with ashes, gobs of meat offals, and other delicacies. On the right hand a load of wood; on the left a tank formed by damming a dirty pool which had flowed through a corral behind the "Roost." There was a regular line of drip distilling from the caked and hollowed snow which toppled from the thick thatch above the cedar braces.

The inside reflected the outside. The length was divided by two perpendiculars, the southernmost of which, assisted by a half-way canvass partition, cut the hut into unequal parts. Behind it were two bunks for four men; standing bedsteads of poles planted in the ground, as in Australia and Unyamwezi, and covered with piles of ragged blankets. Beneath the framework were heaps of rubbish, saddles, cloths, harness, and straps, sacks of wheat, oats, meal, and potatoes, defended from the ground by underlying logs, and dogs nestled where they found room. The floor, which also frequently represented bedstead, was rough, uneven earth, neither tamped nor swept, and the fine end of a spring oozing through the western wall kept part of it in a state of eternal mud. A redeeming point was the fire-place, which occupied half of the northern short wall : it might have belonged to Guy of Warwick's great hall; its ingle nooks boasted dimensions which one connects with an idea of hospitality and jollity ; whilst a long hook hanging down it spoke of the bouillon-pot, and the iron oven of hot rolls. Nothing could be more simple than the furniture. The chairs were either posts mounted on four legs spread out for a base, or three-legged stools with reniform seats. The tables were rough-dressed planks, two feet by two, on rickety trestles. One stood in the centre for feeding purposes ; the other was placed as buffet in the corner near the fire, with eating apparatus — tin coffee-pot and gamelles, rough knives, " pitchforks," and pewter spoons. The walls were pegged to support spurs and pistols, whips, gloves, and leggings. Over the door in a niche stood a broken coffee-mill, for which a flat stone did duty. Near the entrance, on a board shelf raised about a foot from the ground, lay a tin skillet and its " dipper." Soap was supplied by a handful of gravel, and evaporation was expected to act towel. Under the board was a pail of water with a floating can, which enabled the inmates to supply the drainage of everlasting chaws. There was no sign of Bible, Shakspere, or Milton : a Holywell Street romance or two was the only attempt at literature. *En revanche*, weapons of the flesh, rifles, guns, and pistols, lay and hung all about the house, carelessly stowed as usual, and tools were not wanting — hammers, large borers, axe, saw, and chisel. An almost invariable figure in these huts is an Indian standing cross-legged at the door, or squatting uncomfortably close to the fire. He derides the whites for their wastefulness, preferring to crouch in parties of three or four over a little bit of fuel, than to sit before a blazing log. These savages act, amongst other things, as hunters, bringing home rabbits and birds. We tried our revolvers against one of them, and beat him easily : yet they are said to put, three times out of four, an arrow through a key-hole forty paces off. In shooting they place the thumb and fore-finger of the right hand upon the notch, and strengthen the pull by means of the second finger stretched along the bowstrings. The left hand holds the whipped handle, and the shaft rests upon the knuckle of the index.

From Mr. Thomas we heard an account of the affair which took place near Egan's Kanyon. In the last August, Lieut. Weed happened to be " on a scout," with seventeen mounted rifle-men, after Indians.   An express-rider from the West had ridden up to the station, which, being in a hollow, cannot be seen from afar, and found it surrounded by Gosh-Yuta Indians.   The fellows had tied up the master and the boy, and were preparing with civilised provisions a good dinner for themselves, to be followed by a little treat in the form of burning down the house and roasting their captives.   The Indians allowed the soldiers brought up by the express-rider to draw near, thinking that the dust was raised by fresh arrivals of their own people ; and when charged, at once fled.   The mounted riflemen were armed with revolvers, not with sabres, or they would have done considerable execution : as it was, seventeen of the enemy remained upon the field, besides those who were carried off by their friends.   The Indian will always leave a scalped and wounded fellow-tribesman in favour of an unscalped corpse.

In the evening the Shoshone returned bringing with him the white mare and her colt, which he had recovered *selon lui* from the hands of two Gosh-Yutas.   The weather still held up : we had expected to be snowed up in five days or so ; our departure therefore was joyfully fixed for the morrow.

To Ruby Valley, 7th October.

A frosty night was followed by a Tuscan day : a cold tramon-tana from the south, and a clear hot sun, which expanded the mercury at 10 A.M. to 70° F.   After taking leave of the hospi-table station-master, we resumed the road which ran up the short and heavy ascent, through a country here and there eighteen inches deep in snow, and abounding in large sage and little rabbits.   A descent led into Long Valley, whose northern end we crossed, and then we came upon a third ascent, where, finding a sinking creek, a halt was called for lunch.   The forma-tion of the whole country is a succession of basins and divides. Ensued another twelve miles' descent, which placed us in sight of Ruby Valley, and a mile beyond carried us to the station.

Ruby Valley is a half-way house, about 300 miles from Gt. S. L. City and at the same distance from Carson Valley.   It derives its name from the small precious stones which are found like nuggets of gold in the crevasses of primitive rock. The length of the valley is about 100 miles, by three or four broad, and springs are scattered in numbers along the base of the western mountains. The cold is said to be here more severe than in any place on the line of road, Spring Valley excepted. There is, however, excellent bench land for grazing. In this season the scenery is really pretty. The white peaks tower over hill-land black with cedar, and this looks down upon the green bottom scattered over with white sage—winter above lying by the side of summer below.

We were received at the Ruby Valley Station by Colonel Rogers, better known as " Uncle Billy." He had served in the troublous days of California as marshal, and has many a hair-breadth escape to relate. He is now assistant Indian agent, the superintendent of a Government model farm, and he lives *en garçon*, having left his wife and children at Frogtown. We were soon introduced to the chief of the country, Chy̆ŭkŭpĭchy̆ (the " old man"), a word of unpronounceable slur, changed by whites into Chokop, (" earth"). His lands are long to the north and south, though of little breadth. He commands about 500 warriors, and as Uncle Billy is returning to Frogtown, he is col-lecting a large hunting-party for the autumnal battue. In 1849 his sister was wantonly shot by emigrants to California. He attacked the train and slew in revenge five men, a fact with which we were not made acquainted till after our departure. His father and grandfather are both alive, but they have abdi-cated under the weight of years and infirmities, reserving their voices for the pow-wow.

We dined in the Colonel's stone hut, and then saw the lions feed ; after us, Chokop and five followers sat down with knife and fork before a huge tureen full of soft pie, amongst which they did terrible execution, champing and chewing with the noisi-ness of wild beasts, and eating each enough for three able-bodied sailors. The chief, a young man twenty-five years old, had little to denote the Indian, except vermilion where soap should have been ; one of his companions, however, crowned with eagle's feathers disposed in tulip shape, whilst the claws depended gracefully down his back, was an object worthy of Guinea. All were, however, to appearance, happy, and for the first time I heard an Indian really laugh outright. Outside

squatted the common herd in a costume which explains the
prevalence of rheumatism. The men were in rags, yet they had
their coquetry, vermilion streaked down their cheeks and
across their foreheads — the Indian fashion of the omnilocal
rouge. The women, especially the elders, were horrid objects;
shivering and half dressed in breech cloths and scanty capes or
tippets of wolf and rabbit skin: the existence of old age, however, speaks well for the race. Both are unclean; they use no
water where Asiatics would; they ignore soap, and rarely repair
to the stream, except, like animals, in hot weather.

We then strolled about the camp and called upon the two
Mistresses Chokop. One was a buxom dame, broad and strong,
with hair redolent of antelope marrow, who boasted of a "wikeap"
or wigwam in the shape of a conical tent. The other, much
her junior, and rather pretty, was sitting apart in a little bower
of bushes, with a newly born papoose in a willow cage, to
account for her isolation; the poor thing would have been driven
out even in the depth of winter, and were she to starve, she
must do without meat. As amongst the Jews, whenever the
Great Father is angry with the daughters of red men, they sit
apart; they never touch a cooking utensil, although it is not
held impure to address them, and they return only when the signs
of wrath have passed away. The abodes of the poorer clansmen
were three-quarter circles of earth, sticks, and sage bush to keep
off the southerly wind. A dog is usually one of the occupants.
Like the African, the Indian is cruel to his brute, starves it
and kicks it for attempting to steal a mouthful: " Love me,
love my dog," however, is his motto, and he quarrels with the
stranger that follows his example. The furniture was primitive. Upon a branch hung a dried antelope head used in
stalking concerning this sport Uncle Billy had a story of his
nearly being shot by being mistaken for the real animal: and
tripods of timber supporting cloths and moccasins, pans,
camp-kettles, stones for grinding grass seed, and a variety of
baskets. The material was mostly willow twig, with a layer of
gum, probably from the pine tree. Some were watertight like
the " Hán " of Somali land; others, formed like the Roman
amphora, were for storing grain, whilst others in giant cocked
hat-shape were intended for sweeping in crickets and the grass
seeds upon which these Indians feed. The chief gramineæ are

the atriplex and chenopodaceous plants.   After inspecting the
camp we retired precipitately : its condition was that of an
Egyptian army's last nighting place.

About two miles from the station there is a lake covered
with waterfowl, from the wild swan to the rail.   I preferred,
however, to correct my Shoshone vocabulary under the inspection
of Mose Wright, an express rider from a neighbouring station.
None of your "one-horse" interpreters, he had learned the
difficult dialect in his youth, and he had acquired all the into-
nation of an Indian.   Educated beyond the reach of civilisation,
he was in these days an oddity ; he was convicted of having
mistaken a billiard cue for a whip handle, and was accused of
having mounted the post supporting the electric telegraph wire
in order to hear what it was saying.   The evening was spent in
listening to Uncle Billy's adventures amongst the whites and
reds.   He spoke highly of his *protégés*, especially of their
affection and fidelity in married life : they certainly appeared
to look upon him as a father.   He owed something to leger-
demain ; here, as in Algeria, a Houdin or a Love would be great
medicine-men with whom nobody would dare to meddle.   Uncle
Billy managed to make the post pay by peltries of the mink,
wolf, woodchuck or ground hog, fox, badger, antelope, black-
tailed deer, and others.   He illustrated the peculiarities of the
Federal Government by a curious anecdote.   The indirect or
Federal duties are in round numbers $100,000,000, of which
$60,000,000 are spent, leaving a surplus of forty for the purpose
of general corruption : the system seems to date from the days
of the "ultimus Romanorum," President Jackson.   None but the
largest claimants can expect to be recognised.   A few years ago
one of the Indian Agents in —— was asked by a high official
what might be about the cost of purchasing a few hundred acres
for a government farm.   After reckoning up the amount of
beads, wire, blankets, and gunpowder, the total was found to be
$240.   The high official requested his friend to place the state-
ment on paper, and was somewhat surprised the next morning
to see the $240 swollen to $40,000.   The reason given was
characteristic : "What great government would condescend to
pay out of £8,000,000 a paltry £48 ; or would refuse to give
£8,000 ? "

CHAP. XIII.

TO CARSON VALLEY

BEFORE resuming the itinerary, it may be advisable briefly to describe the various tribes tenanting this territory.

We have now emerged from the Prairie Indians, the Dakota, Crow, Kiowa, Comanche, Osage, Apache, Cheyenne, Pawnee, and Arapaho. Utah Territory contains a total of about 19,000 souls of two great kindred races, the Shoshone or Snake, and the Yuta, called Uche by the Spaniards and Ute by the Anglo-American trappers. Like the Comanche and Apache, the Pimas, the Lipans, and the people of the Pueblos, they are of the Hispano-American division, once subject to the Conquistadores, and are bounded north by the Pánák* (Bannack) and the once formidable Blackfeet. The Shoshone own about one-third of the territory; their principal settlements lie north of the Gt. S. Lake, and on the line of the Humboldt or Mary River, some 400 miles west and 100 to 125 south of the Oregon line. They number about 4500 souls, and are wildest in the S. E. parts of their motherland. The Yuta claim the rest of the territory between Kansas, the Sierra Nevada, New Mexico, and the Oregon frontier. Of course the two peoples are mortal foes, and might be well pitted against each other. The Snakes would form excellent partisan warriors.

The Shoshone number fourteen tribes, regularly organised;

* The Panak is a small tribe of 500 souls, now considered dangerous: the greater part resides in Oregon, the smaller about ninety miles in the N. E. of the Territory, where they hunt the bison and the elk. For thirty years they have traded with Fort Bridger, and when first known they numbered 1200 lodges. "Horn" their principal chief, visited the place in April 1858. Mr. Forney, the late Superintendent of Indian affairs in U. T , granted them a home in the lands of Washaki, and they have intermarried and lived peaceably with the Shoshone.

the principal, which contains about 12,000 souls, is commanded by Washaki, assisted, as usual, by sub-chiefs, four to six in number. Five bands, numbering near 1000 each, roam about the mountains and kanyons of Gt. S. L. County, Weber, Bear, Cache, and Malad Valleys, extending eighty miles north from the Holy City. These have suffered the most from proximity with the whites, and no longer disdain agriculture. One band, 150 to 180 in number, confines itself to the N. Californian route from Bear and Malad Valleys to the Goose Creek Mountains. Seven bands roam over the country from the Humboldt River to 100 miles south of it, and extend·about 200 miles from east to west : the principal chief, Wanamuka, or " the Giver," had a band of 155 souls, and lived near the Honey Lake.

The Yuta claim, like the Shoshone, descent from an ancient people that immigrated into their present seats from the N.W. During the last thirty years they have considerably decreased according to the mountaineers, and have been demoralised mentally and physically by the emigrants : formerly they were friendly, now they are often at war with the intruders. As in Australia, arsenic and corrosive sublimate in springs and provisions have diminished their number. The nation is said to contain a total of 14,000 to 15,000 souls divided into twenty-seven bands, of which the following are the principal :—

The Pá-Yuta (Pey Utes) are the most docile, interesting, and powerful, containing twelve bands*; those in the west of the territory on the Humboldt River number 6000, and in the south 2200 souls ; they extend from forty miles west of Stony Point to the Californian line, and N. W. to the Oregon line, and inhabit the valley of the Fenelon River, which rising

---

* These are, 1. Wanamuka's; 2. San Joaquim, near the forks of that river in Carson Valley, numbering 170 ; 3. Hadsapoke, or Horse Stopper band, of 110, in Gold Kanyon on Carson River; 4. Wahi or Fox-band, on Big Bend of Carson River, 130 in number ; 5 and 6. Odakeo, "Tall man band," and Petodseka, "White Spot band," round the Lakes and Sinks of the Carson and Walker Rivers, numbering 484 men, 372 women, and 405 children ; 7. Tosarke, "Grey head band," their neighbours ; 8. Tonoziet, "Woman helper band," on the Truckee River below Big Meadows, numbering 280 souls ; 9. Torape, or "Lean man band," on the Truckee River near Lone Crossing, 360 souls ; 10. Gonega, the "Dancer band," 290 souls, near the mouth of the Truckee River; 11. Watsequendo, the "Four Crows," along the shores of Pyramid Lake, 320 souls ; 12. The second Wanamuka's band, 500 in number, along the shores of the Northern Mud Lake.

from Lake Bigler empties itself into Pyramid Lake.   The
term means Water-Yuta, that is to say those who live upon
fish which they take from lakes and rivers in wiers and traps
of willow, preferring that diet to roots, grass-seed, lizards, and
crickets, the food of the other so called Digger tribes.

Gosh Yuta or Gosha Ute is a small band, once *protégés* of the
Shoshone, who have the same language and limits.   Their principal chief died about five years ago, when the tribe was broken
up.   A body of sixty under a peaceful leader were settled permanently on the Indian farm at Deep Creek, and the remainder
wandered 40 to 200 miles west of Gt. S. L. City.   Through
this tribe our road lay ; during the late tumults they have lost
fifty warriors, and are now reduced to about 200 men.   Like the
Ghuzw of Arabia, they strengthen themselves by admitting the
outcasts of other tribes, and will presently become a mere
banditti.

Pavant or Paravan Yuta, are a distinct and self-organised
tribe, under one principal and several sub-chiefs, whose total is
set down at 700 souls.   Half of them are settled on the Indian
Farm at Corn Creek ; the other wing of the tribe lives along
Sevier Lake, and the surrounding country in the north-east
extremity of Fillmore Valley, fifty miles from the city, where
they join the Gosh Yuta.   The Pavants breed horses, wear clothes
of various patterns, grow grain, which the Gosh Yutas will not,
and are as brave and improvable as their neighbours are mean
and vile.

Timpenaguchyă*, or Timpana Yuta, corrupted into Tenpenny
Utes, who dwell about the kanyon of that name, and on the
east of the Sweetwater Lake.   Of this tribe was the chief Wakara,
who so called himself after Walker, the celebrated trapper ; the
notorious horse-stealer proved himself a friend to the L. D.
Saints.   He died at Meadow Creek, six miles from Fillmore city,
on the 29th January 1855, and at his obsequies two squaws, two
Pa Yuta children, and fifteen of his best horses composed the
" customs."

Uinta Yuta, in the mountains south of Fort Bridger, and in
the country along the Green River.   Of this tribe, which con
tains a total of 1000, a band of 500, under four chiefs, lately settled on the Indian reservations at Spanish Fork.

* In the Yuta language meaning " water among the stones."

Sampichyă, corrupted to San Pete Utas; about eighty warriors settled on the Indian Farm at San Pete. This and the Spanish Fork Farm number 900 inhabitants.

Elk Mountain Yutas, who are set down at 2000 souls, by some even 3000; they wander over the south-east portion of the Territory: and like the Uinta Yutas, are the most independent of white settlers.

Weber River Yutas are those principally seen in Gt. S. L. City; they are a poor and degraded tribe. Their chief settlement is forty miles to the north, and like the Gosh Yutas they understand Shoshone.

Amongst the Yutas are reckoned the Washo, from 500 to 700 souls. They inhabit the eastern slopes of the Sierra Nevada, from Honey Lake to the West Fork of Walker's River in the south. Of this troublesome tribe there are three bands; Captain Jim's, near Lake Bigler, and Carson, Washo, and Eagle Valleys, a total of 342 souls: Pasuka's band, 340 souls, in Little Valley, and Deer Dick's band in Long Valley, south-east of Honey Lake. They are usually called Shoshoko*, or " Digger Indians"— a term as insulting to a Shoshone as nigger to an African.

Besides the Parawat Yutas, the Yampas, 200 -- 300 miles south, on the White River; the Tabechyă, or sun-hunters, about Tête de Biche, near Spanish lands; and the Tash Yuta, near the Navajos; there are scatters of the nation along the Californian road from Beaver Valley, along the Santa Clara, Virgen, Las Vegas, and Muddy Rivers, to New Mexico.

The Indian Bureau of U. T. numbers one superintendent, six agents, and three to six farm-agents. The annual expenditure is set down at $40,000; the Mormons declare that it is iniquitously embezzled, and that the total spent upon the Indians hardly exceeds $1000 per annum. The savages expect blankets and clothing, flour and provisions, arms and ammunition : they receive only a little tobacco, become surly, and slay the settlers. It is understood that the Surveyor-General has recommended to the Federal Government the extinction of the Indian title— somewhat upon the principle of the English in Tasmania† and

---

* It is said to mean " one who goes on foot."

† Van Diemen's Land in the days of Captain Flinders (A.D. 1800, two generations ago) had a population of 100,000 souls, now well nigh annihilated by strong

New Zealand — to grounds in the U. T. and the establishment of a Land office for the sale of the two millions of acres already surveyed. Until the citizens can own their farms and fields under the existing pre-emption laws, and until the troublesome Indians can be removed by treaty to reservations remote from white settlements, the onward march of progress will be arrested. The savage and the civilised man, like crabbed age and youth, like the black and grey rat, cannot live together: the former starves unless placed in the most fertile spots, which the latter of course covets; the Mormons attempt a peace policy, but the hunting-grounds are encroached upon, and terrible massacres are the result. Here, as elsewhere, the battle of life is fiercely fought. It has been said —

> "Man differs more from man
> Than beast from beast."

Yet everywhere we trace the mighty resemblance.

The three principal farms which now form the nuclei of future reservations, are those at Spanish Fork, San Pete, and Corn Creek. The two latter have often been denuded by the grasshopper: the former has fared better. Situated in Utah Valley, under the shelter of lofty Nebo, it extends northwards within four miles of the Sweetwater Lake, and on the north-east is bounded by the Spanish Fork Creek, rich in trout and other fish. It was begun five years ago for the Yutas, who claim the land, and contains a total of 13,000 acres, of which 500 have been cultivated; 900 have been ditched to protect the crop, and 1000 have been walled round with a fence six feet high. Besides other improvements they have built a large adobe house and two rail corrals, and dug dams and channels for irrigation, together with a good stone-curbed well. Under civilised superintendence the savages begin to labour, and the chiefs aspire to erect houses. Yet the crops have been light, rarely exceeding 2500 bushels. San Pete Farm, in the Valley and on the Creek of the same name, lies 150 miles south of Gt. S. L. City; it supports, besides those who come for temporary assistance, a band of thirty souls; 200 acres have been planted with wheat and potatoes, two adobe

waters and corrosive sublimate. Neither man nor woman was safe in the vicinity of a native tribe; the Anglo-Scandinavian race thus found it necessary to wipe out a people that could not be civilised — a fair instance of the natural selection of species. And New Zealand now threatens to walk the path of Tasmania.

houses and a corral have been made, and irrigating trenches have
been dug.   Corn Creek Farm, in Fillmore Valley, was begun
about four years ago ; 300 acres have been broken up, several
adobe houses have been built for the Indians and the farm agent,
with the usual adjuncts, corral and fences.   The crickets and
grasshoppers have committed sad havoc amongst the wheat
corn and potatoes.   It is now tenanted by a Pahvant chief.
The Uinta Farm is near Fort Bridger.   Those lately opened in
Deep Creek and Ruby Valleys have this year lain fallow in consequence of Indian troubles ; the soil, however, is rich, and will
produce beets, potatoes, onions, turnips, and melons.   It is proposed to place the Pa Yutas and Washos in the Truckee Meadows, on the lands "watered by the majestic Kuyuehup, or
Salmon Trout River," where, besides fish and piñon-forests, there
are 15,000 acres fit for cultivation and herding.   The Indian
agents report that the cost will be $150,000 dollars, from which
the Mormons deduct at least two 0's.

The Yuta, though divided into many tribes and bands, is
a distinct race from its prairie neighbours, speaking a single
langue mère much diversified by dialect.   They are a superstitious brood and have many cruel practices—human sacrifices
and vivisepulture—like those of Dahomey and Ashantee.   Their
religion is the usual African and Indian fetissism, that germal
faith, which under favourable influences and amongst higher
races developed itself by natural means — or as explained
by a mythical, distinct, and independent revelation—into the
higher forms of Judaism, Christianity, and El Islam.   In the
vicinity of the Mormons many savages have been baptized, and
have become nominal Saints.   They divide white men into Shwop
or Americans and Mormons.   Their learned men have heard of
Washington, but like the French peasant's superstition concerning Napoleon, they believe him to be still alive.   They have a
name for the Book of Mormon, and have not learned, like their
more civilised eastern neighbours, to look upon it as the work of
Mujhe-Manitou, the bad-god, who, like Wiswakarma of the Hindus, amuses himself by caricaturing and parodying the creatures of the good-god.   They are not cannibals — the Wendigo
is a giant-man-eater of a mythologic type, not an actual anthro-
pophage — but like all Indians, especially those of New England, they "feel good" after eating a bit of the enemy, a natural

display of destructiveness : they will devour the heart of a
brave man to increase their courage, or chop it up, boil it in
soup, engorge a ladleful, and boast they have drunk the enemy's
blood. They are as liable to caprice as their Eastern neighbours.
A prisoner who has distinguished himself in battle is as often dis-
missed unhurt as porcupined with arrows and killed with cruel
tortures; if they yield in ingenuity of inflicting pain to the
Algonquins and Iroquois, it is not for want of inclination, but by
reason of their stupidity. Female captives who fall into their
hands are horribly treated ; I was told of one who, after all manner of atrocities, scalping included, escaped with life. They have
all the savage's improvidence; utility is not their decalogue.
Both sexes, except when clothed by a charitable Mormon, are
nearly naked, even in the severest weather ; they sleep in sleet
and snow unclothed, except with a cape of twisted rabbits' furs
and a miserable attempt at moccasins, lined with plaited cedar
bark ; leggings are unknown, even to the women. Their ornaments are vermilion, a few beads, and shell necklaces. They
rarely suffer from any disease but rheumatism, brought on by
living in the warm houses of the whites, and various consequences of liver complaint, produced by overgorging : as with
strong constitutions generally, they either die at once or readily
recover. They dress wounds with pine gum, after squeezing out
the blood, and their medicine-men have the usual variety of
savage nostrums. In the more desert parts of the Territory they
are exceedingly destitute. South of Cedar City, even ten years
ago, they had fields of wheat and corn of six acres each, and
supported emigrants ; some of them cultivate yearly along the
stream-banks peas, beans, sweet potatoes, and squashes. They
live upon the flesh of the bear, elk, antelope, dog, wolf, hare,
snake and lizard, besides crickets, grasshoppers, ants, and other
vermin. The cactus leaf, piñon-nut and various barks; the
seed of the bunch-grass and of the wheat or yellow grass, somewhat resembling rye ; the rabbit-bush twigs, which are chewed,
and various roots and tubers ; the soft sego-bulb, the rootlet of
the cat-tail flag, and of the tule, which, when sun-dried and
powdered to flour, keeps through the winter and is palatable
even to white men, conclude the list of their dainties. When
these fail they must steal or starve, and the dilemma is easily
solved, to the settler's cost.

The Yutas in the vicinity of the larger white settlements con-
tinually diminish ; bands of 150 warriors are now reduced to
thirty-five.   Some of the minor tribes in the southern part of
the Territory near New Mexico, can scarcely show a single squaw,
having traded them off for horses and arms ; they go about killing one another, and on kidnapping expeditions, which further
diminish the breed.   The complaint which has devastated the
South Sea Islands rages around the City of the Saints, and extends to the Rio Virgen.   In six months six squaws were shot
by red Othellos, for yielding their virtue to the fascinations of
tobacco, whiskey, and blankets ; the Lotharios were savage as well
as civilised. The operation of courting is performed by wrapping
a blanket round one's beloved ; if she reciprocates, it is a sign
of consent.   A refusal in these lands is often a serious business ;
the warrior collects his friends, carries off the recusant fair,
and after subjecting her to the insults of all his companions
espouses her.   There is little of the shame which Pliny attributes
to the " Barrus."   When a death takes place they wrap the
body in a skin or hide, and drag it by the leg to a grave, which
is heaped up with stones as a protection against wild beasts.
They mourn till the end of that moon, allow a month to elapse,
and then resume their lamentations for another moon : the inter-
val is gradually increased till the grief ends.   It is usual to
make the dead man's lodge appear as desolate as possible.

The Yuta is less servile, and consequently has a higher ethnic
status than the African negro ; he will not toil, and he turns at
a kick or a blow.   The emigrant who addresses him in the usual
phrase " d —— your eyes, git out of the road or I'll shoot you ! "
is pretty sure to come to grief.   Lately the Yutas demanded
compensation for the use of their grass upon the Truckee River,
when the emigrants fired, killing Wanamuka the chief.   After
the death of two or three whites, Mayor Ormsby, of the Militia
at Carson Valley, took the field, was decoyed into a kanyon by
Indian cunning, and perished with all his men.

To " Chokop" Pass, 8th October 1860.

The morning was wasted in binding two loose tires upon their
respective wheels ; it was past noon before we were *en route.*
We shook hands cordially with Uncle Billy, whose generosity —
a virtue highly prized by those who rarely practising expect it

to be practised upon them — has won for him the sobriquet of
the "Big-hearted Father." He had vainly, however, attempted
to rescue my silver pen-holder, whose glitter was too much for
Indian virtue. Our route lay over a long divide, cold but not
unpicturesque, a scene of light-tinted mountain mahogany,
black cedar, pure snowy hill, and pink sky. After ten miles we
reached the place where the road forks ; that to the right passing through Pine Valley falls into gravelly ford of the Humboldt
River, distant from this point eighty to eighty-five miles. After
surmounting the watershed we descended over bench-land into
a raw and dreary plain, in which greasewood was more plentiful
than sage-bush. "Huntingdon Valley" is traversed by Smith's
Fork, which flows northward to the Humboldt River ; when we
crossed it, it was a mere rivulet. Our camping ground was at
the farther end of the plain, under a Pass called after the chief
Chokop; the kanyon emitted a cold draught like the breathing
caves of Kentucky. We alighted at a water near the entrance,
and found bunch-grass, besides a little fuel. After two hours the
wagon came up with the stock, which was now becoming weary,
and we had the usual supper of dough, butter, and coffee.
I should have slept comfortably enough upon a shovel and a
layer of carpet bags, had not the furious south wind howled like
the distant whooping of Indians.

To the Wilderness again, 9th October.

The frosty night was followed by a thaw in the morning. We
hastened to ascend Chokop's Pass by a bad steep dugway : it lies
south of "Railroad Kanyon," which is said to be nearly flat-
soled. A descent led into "Moonshine," called by the Yutas
Pahannap Valley, and we saw with pleasure the bench rising
at the foot of the pass. The station is named Diamond Springs,
from an eye of warm, but sweet and beautifully clear water
bubbling up from the earth. A little below it drains off in a
deep rushy ditch, with a gravel bottom, containing equal parts
of comminuted shells : we found it an agreeable and opportune
bath. Hard work had begun to tell upon the temper of the
party. The Judge, who ever preferred monologue to dialogue,
aweary of the rolling prairies and barren plains, the bald and
rocky ridges, the muddy flats, saleratus ponds, and sandy
wastes, sighed monotonously for the woodland shades and the

rustling of living leaves near his Pennsylvanian home.   The
Marshal, with true Anglo-American impetuosity, could not
endure Paddy Kennedy's "slow and shyure" style of travel ; and
after a colloquy, in which the holiest of words were freely used
as adjectives, participles, and exclamations, offered to fight him by
way of quickening his pace.   The boys — four or five in number
— ate for breakfast a quarter of beef, as though they had been
Kafirs or Esquimaux, and were threatened with ration-cutting.
The station folks were Mormons, but not particularly civil : they
afterwards had to fly before the savages — which perhaps they
will be pleased to consider a "judgment" upon them.

Shortly after noon we left Diamond Springs, and carried on
for a stretch of seven miles to our lunching ground, a rushy
water, black where it overlies mud, and bluish-green where light
gravel and shells form the bottom : the taste is sulphury, and
it abounds in confervæ and animalculæ like leeches and little
tadpoles.   After playing a tidy bowie-knife, we remounted, and
passed over to the rough divide lying westward of Moonshine
Valley.   As night had closed in, we found some difficulty in
choosing a camping place : at length we pitched upon a
prairillon under the lea of a hill, where we had bunch-grass
and fuel, but no water.   The wind blew sternly through the
livelong night, and those who suffered from cramps in cold feet
had little to do with the "sweet restorer, balmy sleep."

To Sheawit Creek, 10th October.

At 6 A.M. the mercury was sunk only to 29° F. but the elevation and rapid evaporation, with the fierce gusty wind
coursing through the kanyon, rendered the sensation of cold
painful.   As usual on these occasions, "George," our chef,
sensibly preferred standing over the fire, and enwrapping himself with smoke, to the inevitable exposure incurred whilst
fetching a coffee-pot or a tea-kettle.   A long divide, with many
ascents and descents, at length placed in front of us a view of
the normal "distance"—heaps of hills, white as bridal cakes,
and, nearer, a sand-like plain, somewhat more yellow than the
average of those salt bottoms : instinct told us that there lay the
station-house.   From the hills rose the smokes of Indian fires :
the lands belong to the Tusawichya or White-Knives, a band of
the Shoshones under an independent chief.   This depression is

known to the Yutas as Sheawit or Willow Creek : the whites call it, from Mr. Bolivar Roberts, the Western agent, "Roberts' Springs Valley." It lies 286 miles from Capt. Floyd : from this point "Simpson's Road" strikes off to the S. E. and as Mr. Howard Egan's rule here terminates, it is considered the latter end of Mormondom. Like all the stations to the westward, that is to say, those now before us, it was burned down in the late Indian troubles, and has only been partially rebuilt. One of the *employés* was Mr. Mose Wright, of Illinois, who again kindly assisted me with correcting my vocabulary.

About the station loitered several Indians of the White-Knife tribe, which boasts, like the old Sioux and the modern Flat-heads, never to have stained its weapons with the blood of a white man. They may be a respectable race, but they are an ugly : they resemble the Diggers, and the children are not a little like juvenile baboons. The dress was the usual medley of rags and rabbit furs : they were streaked with vermilion ; and their hair — contrary to and more sensibly than the practice of our grandfathers — was fastened into a frontal pigtail, to prevent it falling into the eyes. These men attend upon the station, and herd the stock, for an occasional meal, their sole payment. They will trade their skins and peltries for arms and gunpowder, but, African-like, they are apt to look upon provisions, beads, and tobacco in the light of presents.

A long march of thirty-five miles lay before us. Kennedy resolved to pass the night at Sheawit Creek, and, despite their grumbling, sent on the boys, the stock, and the wagons, when rested from their labour, in the early afternoon. We spent a cosy, pleasant evening — such as I have enjoyed in the old Italian days before railroads — of travellers' tittle and Munchausen tattle, in the ingle corner and round the huge hearth of the half-finished station, with its holey walls. At intervals, the roarings of the wind, the ticking of the death watch, (a well known xylo-phagus,) boring a home in the soft cottonwood rafters, and the howlings of the Indians, who were keening at a neigh-bouring grave, formed a rude and appropriate chorus. Mose Wright recounted his early adventures in Oregon ; how, when he was a greenhorn, the Indians had danced the war-dance under his nose, had then set upon his companions, and after slaying them had displayed their scalps. He favoured us with a representation of the ceremony, an ursine performance,— the bear seems everywhere to have been the sire of Terpsichore,— whilst the right hand repeatedly clapped to his lips quavered the long loud howl into broken sounds :—" Howh ! howh ! howh ! ow ! ow ! ough ! ough ! aloo ! aloo ! loo ! loo ! oo !"   We talked of a curious animal, a breed between the dog and the bear, which represents the semi-fabulous jumard in these regions : it is said to be a cross far more savage than that between the dog and the wolf. The young grizzly is a favourite pet in the western hut, and a canine graft is hardly more monstrous than the progeny of the horse and the deer lately exhibited in London.   I still believe that in Africa, and indeed in India, there are accidentally mules bimanous and quadrumanous, and would suggest that such specimens should be sought as the means of settling on a rational basis the genus and species of "homo sapiens."

Mose Wright described the Indian arrow-poison.   The rattle-snake—the copperhead and the moccassin he ignored—is caught with a forked stick planted over its neck, and is allowed to fix its fangs in an antelope's liver.   The meat, which turns green, is carried upon a skewer when wanted for use : the flint head of an arrow, made purposely to break in the wound, is thrust into the poison, and when withdrawn is covered with a thin coat of glue.   Ammonia is considered a cure for it, and the Indians treat snake bites with the actual cautery.   The rattle-snake here attains a length of eight to nine feet, and is described as having reached the number of seventy-three rattles, which, supposing (as the theory is) that after the third year it puts forth one per annum, would raise its age to that of man : it is much feared in U. T.   We were also cautioned against the poison oak, which is worse than the poison vine east of the Mississippi. It is a dwarf bush with quercine leaves, dark coloured and prickly like those of the holly : the effect of a sting, of a touch, or, it is said, in sensitives of its proximity, is a painful itching, followed by a rash that lasts three weeks, and other highly inconvenient consequences.   Strong brine was recommended to us by our prairie doctor.

Amongst the _employés_ of the station was an intelligent young mechanic from Pennsylvania, who, threatened with consumption, had sought and soon found health in the pure regions of the Rocky Mountains.   He looked forward to revisiting civilisation, where comforts were attainable. In these wilds little luxuries like tea and coffee are often unprocurable; a dudheen or a cutty pipe sells for a dollar, consequently a hollowed potato or corn-cob with a reed tube is often rendered necessary; and tobacco must be mixed with a myrtaceous leaf called by the natives "timaya," and by the mountaineers "larb"—possibly a corruption of " l'herbe" or "la yerba." Newspapers and magazines arrive sometimes twice a year, when they have weathered the dangers of the way. Economy has deprived the stations of their gardens, and the shrinking of emigration, which now dribbles eastward, instead of flowing in full stream westward, leaves the exiles to amuse themselves.

To Dry Creek, 11th October.

We arose early, and found that it had not "frosted;" that flies were busy in the station-house; and that the snow, though thick on the northern faces, had melted from the southern shoulders of the hills — these were so many indices of the St. Martin's or Indian summer, the last warm glow of life before the cold and pallid death of the year. At 6 A.M. we entered the ambulance, and followed a good road across the remains of the long broad Sheawit Valley. After twelve miles we came upon a water surrounded by willows, with dwarf artemisia beyond; it grows better on the benches, where the subsoil is damper, than in the bottoms—and there we found our lazy boys, who, as Jim Gilston said, had been last night "on a drunk." Resuming our way, after three miles we reached some wells whose alkaline waters chap the skin. Twenty miles further led to the west end of the Sheawit Valley, where we found the station on a grassy bench at the foot of low rolling hills. It was a mere shell, with a substantial stone corral behind, and the inmates were speculating upon the possibility of roofing themselves in before the winter. Water is found in tolerable quantities below the station, but the place deserved its name, "Dry Creek."

A fraternal recognition took place between Long Jim and his brother, who discovered each other by the merest accident. Gilston, the *employé*, was an intelligent man: at San Francisco he had learned a little Chinese, and at Deep Creek he was studying the Indian dialects. He had missed making a fortune at Carson Valley, where in June or July 1859 the rich and now celebrated silver mines were discovered; and he warned us against the danger of tarrying in Carson City, where revolvers are fired even into houses known to contain " ladies." Col. Totten, the station-master, explained the formation of the gold diggings as beds of gravel, from one to 120 feet, overlying slate rock.

Dry Creek Station is on the eastern frontier of the western agency; as at Roberts' Creek, supplies and literature from Gt. S. L. City east and Carson City west are usually exhausted before they reach these final points. After a frugal feed, we inspected a grave for two, which bore the names of Loscier and Applegate, and the date 21st May. These men, *employés* of the station, were attacked by Indians — Panaks or Shoshones, or possibly both: the former was killed by the first fire; the latter, when shot in the groin, and unable to proceed, borrowed under pretext of defence a revolver, bade good-bye to his companions, and put a bullet through his own head: the remainder then escaped. Both these poor fellows remain unavenged. The Anglo-American, who is admirably protected by the officials of his government in Europe, Asia, and Africa, is systematically neglected — *teste* Mexico — in America. The double grave, piled up with stones, showed gaps where the wolves had attempted to tunnel, and bluebottle flies were buzzing over it in expectation. Col. Totten, at our instance, promised that it should be looked to.

The night was comfortably passed at Dry Creek, under the leeward side of a large haystack. The weather was cold, but clear and bright. We slept the sleep of the just.

To Simpson's Park, 12th October.

At the time of the cold clear dawn, whose grey contrasted strongly with the blush of the most lovely evening that preceded it, the mercury stood at 45° F. Shortly after 8 A.M. we were afield, hastening to finish the long divide that separates Roberts' Creek Valley from its western neighbour, which, as yet unchristened, is known to the b'hoys as Smokey Valley. The road wound in the shape of the letter U round the impassable part of the ridge. Crossing the north end of Smokey Valley, we came upon rolling ground, with water-willows and cedars " blazed " — barked with a gash — for sign-posts. Ensued a long kanyon, with a flat sole, not unlike Egan's, a gate by which the swift shallow stream had broken through the mountains: in places it was apparently a *cul-de-sac;* in others shoulder after shoulder rose in long perspective, with points and projections behind, which an enemy might easily turn. The granite walls were of Cyclopean form, with regular lines of cleavage, as in the Rattlesnake Hills, which gave a false air of stratification. The road was a mere path along and across the rivulet bed, and the lower slopes were garnished with the pepper-grass and the everlasting bunch-grass, so truly characteristic of the " Basin State." Above us, in the pellucid sky, towered the eagle in his pride of place; the rabbit ran before us from the thicket; the ground-squirrel cached himself in the sage bush; and where distance appeared, smokes upcurling in slow heavy masses told us that man was not far distant. A second divide, more abrupt than the former, placed us in sight of Simpson's Park — and such a park! a circlet of tawny stubble, embosomed in sage-grown hills, the " Hiré " or " Look-out," and others, without other tree but the deformed cedars. The bottom is notorious for cold; it freezes even in June and July ; and our night was, as may be imagined, none of the pleasantest.

The station-house in Simpson's Park was being rebuilt. As we issued from Mormondom into Christendom, the civility of our hosts perceptibly diminished ; the Judge, like the generality of Anglo-Americans, did unnecessary kow-tow to those whom republicanism made his equals, and the " gentlemen" when asked to do anything, became exceedingly surly. Among them was one Giovanni Brutisch, a Venetian, who, flying from conscription had found a home in Halifax : an unfortunate fire which burned down his house drove him to the Far West. He talked copiously of the old country, breathed the usual aspirations of *Italia una,* and thought that Garibaldi would do well " *se non lo molestano* "— a euphuism accompanied by a look more expressive than any nod. The station was well provided with good miniés, and the men apparently expected to use them ; it was, however, commanded by the neighbouring heights, and the haystacks were exposed to fire at a time of the year when no more forage could be collected. The Venetian made for us some good light bread of wheaten flour, started or leavened with hop-water, and corn bread " shortened" with butter, and enriched with two or three eggs. A hideous Pa-Yuta and surly Shoshone, whom I sketched, loitered about the station : they were dressed in the usual rabbit-skin cape, and carried little horn bows, with which they missed small marks at fifteen paces. The boys, who were now a-weary of watching, hired one of these men for a shirt—tobacco was not to be had, and a blanket was too high pay—to mount guard through the night. Like the Paggi or Ramoosee of W. India, one thief is paid to keep off many : the Indian is the best of wardens, it being with him a principle not to attack what the presence of a fellow tribesman defends.

To Reese River, 13th October.

Simpson's Park lies 195 miles from Carson City where we might consider the journey at an end.   Yet the cold of night did not allow us to set out before 10 A.M.   Our route lay across the park, which was dotted with wheat grass and broom-like reeds rising from a ground saupoudré like salt.   Presently we began to ascend Simpson's Pass, a long kanyon whose sloping sides and benches were dotted with the green bunch-grass. At the divide we found the "Sage Springs" whose position is too elevated for the infiltration of salt: they are consequently sweet and wholesome.   Descending by a rugged road we sighted everywhere on the heights the fires of the natives.   They were not symbols of war, but signals — for which smokes are eminently adapted — made by tribes telegraphing to one another, their being *en route* for their winter quarters.   Below us " Reese's River " Valley might have served for a sketch in the African desert : a plain of saleratus, here yellow with sand or hay, there black with fire, there brown where the skin of earth showed through her garb of rags, and beyond it were chocolate-coloured hills, from whose heads curled blue smokes of volcanic appearance.

Bisecting the barren plain, ran a bright little stream, whose banks, however, had been stripped of their "salt grass " : pure and clear it flows over a bed of gravel, sheds in a northerly direction, and sinks at a distance of about twenty miles.   From afar we all mistook the course, deceived as travellers often are, by the horizontality of the lines.   Leaving on the right the road which forks to the lower ford, we followed that on the left hand leading to the station.   There cannot be much travelling upon these lines : the tracks last for years, unaffected by snow :

the carcases of animals, however, no longer mummified as in the Eastern prairies, are readily reduced to skeletons.

The station-house in the Reese River Valley had lately been evacuated by its proprietors and burnt down by the Indians : a new building of adobe was already assuming a comfortable shape. The food around it being poor and thin, our cattle were driven to the mountains. At night, probably by contrast with the torrid sun, the frost appeared colder than ever : we provided against it, however, by burrowing into the haystack, and despite the jackal-like cry of the coyote and the near tramping of the old white mare, we slept like tops.

To Smith's Creek, 14th October.

Before 8 A.M. we were under weigh bound for Smith's Creek. Our path stretched over the remainder of Reese's River Valley, an expanse of white sage and large rabbit-bush which affords fuel even when green. After a long and peculiarly rough divide, we sighted the place of our destination. It lay beyond a broad plain or valley, like a huge white "splotch" in the centre, set in dirty brown vegetation backed by bare and rugged hills which are snow topped only on the north; presently we reached the "splotch" which changed its aspect from that of a muddy pool to a yellow floor of earth so hard that the wheels scarcely made a dint, except where a later inundation had caused the mud to cake, flake, and curl,— smooth as ice without being slippery. Beyond that point, guided by streams meandering through willow thickets, we entered a kanyon—all are now wearying of the name—and presently sighted the station deep in a hollow. It had a good stone corral and the usual haystack, which fires on the hill tops seemed to menace. Amongst the station folks we found two New Yorkers, a Belfast man, and a tawny Mexican named Anton, who had passed his life riding the San Bernardino road. The house was unusually neat, and displayed even signs of decoration in the adornment of the bunks with osier work taken from the neighbouring creek. We are now in the lands of the Pa Yuta, and rarely fail to meet a party on the road: they at once propose " shwop " and readily exchange pine-nuts for " white grub," *i. e.* biscuits. I observed, however, that none of the natives were allowed to enter the station-house, whereas, in other places, especially amongst the

Mormons, the savages squeezed themselves into the room, took the best seats near the fire, and never showed a symptom of moving.

To Cold Springs, 15th October.

After a warmer night than usual —thanks to fire and lodging —we awoke and found a genial south wind blowing. Our road lay through the kanyon, whose floor was flush with the plain; the bed of the mountain stream was the initiative of vile travelling, which, without our suspecting it, was to last till the end of the journey.   The strain upon the vehicle came near to smashing it, and the prudent Kennedy, with the view of sparing his best animals, gave us his worst, two aged brutes, one of which, in consequence of her squealing habits, had won for herself the title of " ole Hellion."   The divortia aquarum was a fine watershed to the westward, and the road was in V shape, whereas before it had oscillated between U and W W.   As we progressed, however, the valleys became more and more desert, the sage more stunted, and the hills more brown and barren. After a mid-day halt, rendered compulsory by the old white mare, we resumed our way along the valley southwards, over a mixture of pitch-hole and boulder, which forbids me to forget that day's journey.   At last, after much sticking and kicking on the part of the cattle, and the mental refreshment of abundant bad language, self-adhibited by the men, we made Cold Springs Station, which by means of a cut across the hills could be brought within eight miles of Smith's Creek.

The station was a wretched place half built and wholly un-roofed ; the four boys, an exceedingly rough set, ate standing, and neither paper nor pencil was known amongst them.   Our animals, however, found good water in a rivulet from the neighbouring hills and the promise of a plentiful feed on the morrow, whilst the humans, observing that a " beef" had been freshly killed, supped upon an excellent steak.   The warm wind was a pleasant contrast to the usual frost, but as it came from the south, all the weather-wise predicted that rain would result. We slept however, without such accident, under the haystack, and heard the loud howling of the wolves, which are said to be larger on these hills than elsewhere.

In the morning the wind had shifted from the south to a more
pluvial quarter, the south east — in these regions the westerly
wind promises the fairest — and stormy cirri mottled the sky.
We had a long stage of thirty-five miles before us, and required
an early start, yet the lazy b'hoys and the weary cattle saw 10
A.M. before we were *en route.*   Simpson's road lay to our
south, we could, however, sight about two miles distant from
the station the easternmost formation, which he calls Gibraltar
Gate. For the first three miles, our way was exceedingly rough ;
it gradually improved into a plain cut with nullahs, and overgrown with a chapparal, which concealed a few " burrowing
hares." The animals are rare ; during the snow they are said to
tread in one another's trails after Indian fashion, yet the
huntsman easily follows them.   After eight miles we passed a
spring, and two miles beyond it came to the Middle Gate, where
we halted from noon till 5·15 P.M.   Water was found in the
bed of a river which fills like a mill-dam after rain, and a plentiful supply of bunch grass, whose dark seeds it was difficult to
husk out of the oatlike capsules.   We spent our halt in practising what Sorrentines call *la caccia degl' uccelluzzi,* and in vain
attempts to walk round the uncommonly wary hawks, crows, and
wolves.

Hitching to as the sun neared the western horizon, we passed
through the Gate, narrowly escaping a " spill " down a dwarf
precipice.   A plain bounded on our left by cretaceous bluffs,
white as snow, led to the West Gate, two symmetrical projections like those further eastward.   After that began a long
divide broken by frequent chuckholes, which, however, had no
cunette at the bottom.   An ascent of five miles led to a
second broad basin, whose white and sounding ground, now
stony, then sandy, scattered over with carcass and skeleton, was
bounded in front by low dark ranges of hill.   Then crossing a
long rocky divide, so winding that the mules' heads pointed
within a few miles to N., S., E., and W., we descended by
narrow passes into a plain.   The eye could not distinguish it
from a lake, so misty and vague were its outlines : other senses
corrected vision, when we sank up to the hub in the loose sand.
As we progressed painfully, broken clay and dwarf vegetation
assumed in the dim shades fantastic and mysterious forms.   I

thought myself once more amongst the ruins of that Arab village concerning which Lebid sang,—

"Ay me! ay me! all lone and drear the dwelling place, the home —
On Mina, o'er Rijam and Ghool, wild beasts unheeded roam."

Tired out and cramped with cold, we were torpid with what the Bedouin calls El Rakl,—la Ragle du Désert, when part of brain sleeps whilst the rest is wide awake. At last, about 2·30 A.M. thoroughly "knocked up"— a phrase which I should advise the Englishman to eschew in the society of the fair Columbian — we sighted a roofless shed, found a haystack, and reckless of supper or of stamping horses, fell asleep upon the sand.

To Carson Lake, 17th October.

Sand Springs Station deserved its name. Like the Brazas de San Diego and other *mauvaises terres* near the Rio Grande, the land is cumbered here and there with drifted ridges of the finest sand, sometimes 200 feet high and shifting before every gale. Behind the house stood a mound shaped like the contents of an hour-glass, drifted up by the stormy S.E. gale in esplanade shape and falling steep to northward or against the wind. The water near this vile hole was thick and stale with sulphury salts: it blistered even the hands. The station house was no unfit object in such a scene, roofless and chairless, filthy and squalid, with a smoky fire in one corner, and a table in the centre of an impure floor, the walls open to every wind, and the interior full of dust. Hibernia, herself, never produced aught more characteristic. Of the *employés*, all loitered and sauntered about *desœuvrés* as cretins, except one, who lay on the ground crippled and apparently dying by the fall of a horse upon his breast bone.

About 11 A.M. we set off to cross the ten miles of valley that stretched between us and the summit of the western divide still separating us from Carson Lake. The land was a smooth saleratus plain, with curious masses of porous red and black basalt protruding from a ghastly white. The watershed was apparently to the north, the benches were distinctly marked, and the bottom looked as if it were inundated every year. It was smooth except where broken up by tracks, but all off the road was dangerous ground: in one place the horses sank to their hocks and were not extricated without difficulty. After a hot

FILST VIEW OF CARSON LAKE.

drive—the glass at 9 A.M. showed 74° F. — we began to toil up the divide, a sand formation mixed with bits of granite, red seeds, and dwarf shells, whose lips were for the most part broken off. Over the fine loose surface was a floating haze of the smaller particles, like the film that veils the Arabian desert. Arrived at the summit, we sighted for the first time Carson Lake, or rather the sink of the Carson River. It derives its name from the well known mountaineer whose adventurous roamings long anticipated scientific exploration. Supplied by the stream from the eastern flank of the Sierra Nevada, it is just such a lake as might be formed in any of the basins which we had traversed, a shallow sheet of water which, in the cloudy sky and mitigated glare of the sun, looked pale and muddy. Apparently it was divided by a long narrow ruddy line, like ochre-coloured sand; a near approach showed that water on the right was separated from a saleratus bed on the left by a thick belt of Tule rush. Stones imitated the sweep of the tide, and white particles the colour of a wash.

Our conscientious informant at Sand Springs Station had warned us that upon the summit of the divide we should find a perpendicular drop, down which the wagons could be lowered only by means of lariats affixed to the axle-trees and lashed round strong "stubbing posts." We were not, however, surprised to find a mild descent of about 30°. From the summit of the divide five miles led us over a plain too barren for sage, and a stretch of stone and saleratus to the watery margin which was troublesome with sloughs and mud. The cattle relished the water, although tainted by the rush; we failed, however, to find any of the fresh water clams, whose shells were scattered along the shore.

Remounting at 5·15 P.M. we proceeded to finish the ten miles which still separated us from the station, by a rough and stony road, perilous to wheel conveyances, which rounded the southern extremity of the lake. After passing a promontory whose bold projection had been conspicuous from afar, and threading a steep kanyon leading towards the lake, we fell into its selvage, which averaged about one mile in breadth. The small crescent of the moon soon ceased to befriend us, and we sat in the sadness of the shade, till presently a light glimmered under Arcturus, the road bent towards it and all felt "jolly." But,

"Heu, heu! nos miseros, quam totus homuncio nil est!"

A long dull hour still lay before us, and we were approaching civilised lands. " Sink Station" looked well from without; there was a frame house inside an adobe enclosure, and a pile of wood and a stout haystack promised fuel and fodder.   The inmates, however, were asleep, and it was ominously long before a door was opened.   At last appeared a surly cripple, who presently disappeared to arm himself with his revolver.   The judge asked civilly for a cup of water, he was told to fetch it from the lake which was not more than a mile off, though as the road was full of quagmires it would be hard to travel at night. Wood the churl would not part with ; we offered to buy it, to borrow it, to replace it in the morning ; he told us to go for it ourselves, and that after about two miles and a half we might chance to gather some.   Certainly our party was a law-abiding and a self-governing ; never did I see men so tamely bullied ; they threw back the fellow's sticks, and cold, hungry, and thirsty simply began to sulk.   An Indian standing by asked $20 to herd the stock for a single night.   At last, George the Cordon Blue, took courage, some went for water, others broke up a wagon plank, and supper after a fashion was concocted.

I preferred passing the night on a side of bacon in the wagon to using the cripple's haystack, and allowed sleep to steep my senses in forgetfulness, after deeply regretting that the Mormons do not extend somewhat farther westward.

To Fort Churchill, 18*th October*.

The b'hoys and the stock were doomed to remain near the Carson Lake where forage was abundant, whilst we made our way to Carson Valley — an arrangement not effected without excessive grumbling.   At last the deserted ones were satisfied with the promise that they should exchange their desert quarters for civilisation on Tuesday, and we were permitted to start. Crossing a long plain bordering on the Sink, we " snaked up " painfully a high divide which a little engineering skill would have avoided.   From the summit, bleak with west wind, we could descry, at a distance of fifty miles, a snowy saddle-back — the Sierra Nevada.   When the deep sand had fatigued our cattle, we halted for an hour to bait in a patch of land rich with bunch grass.   Descending from the eminence, we saw a gladdening sight : the Carson River, winding through its avenue of dark

cotton woods, and afar off, the quarters and barracks of Fort
Churchill. The nearer view was a hard tamped plain, besprin-
kled with black and red porous stones and a sparse vegetation,
with the ruddy and yellow autumnal hues; a miserable range of
low, brown sunburnt rocks and hills, whose ravines were choked
with white sand drifts, bounded the basin. The further distance
used it as a foil, the Sierra developed itself into four distinct
magnificent tiers of snow-capped and cloud-veiled mountain,
whose dissolving views faded into thin darkness as the sun disappeared behind their gigantic heads.

Whilst we admired these beauties night came on; the paths
intersected one another, and despite the glow and gleam of a
camp fire in the distance, we lost our way amongst the tall cottonwood. Dispersing in search of information, the marshal accidentally stumbled upon his predecessor in office, Mr. Smith,
who hospitably insisted upon our becoming his guests. He led
us to a farm-house already half roofed in against the cold,
fetched the whiskey for which our souls craved, gave to each a
peach that we might be good boys, and finally set before us a
prime beefsteak. Before sleeping we heard a number of
" shooting stories." Where the corpse is, says the Persian, there
will be the kites. A mining discovery never fails to attract
from afar a flock of legal vultures — attorneys, lawyers, and
judges. As the most valuable claims are mostly parted with by
the ignorant fortunate for a song, it is usual to seek some flaw
in the deed of sale, and a large proportion of the property finds
its way into the pockets of the acute professional, who works on
half profits. Consequently in these parts there is generally a
large amount of unscrupulous talent. One gentleman judge
had knived a waiter and shot a senator; another, almost as
" heavy *on* the shyoot," had in a single season killed one man
and wounded another. My informants declared that in and
about Carson a dead man for breakfast was the rule; besides accidents perpetually occurring to indifferent or to peace-making
parties, they reckoned per annum fifty murders. In a peculiar
fit of liveliness an intoxicated gentleman will discharge his
revolver in a ball-room, and when a " shyooting " begins in the
thin walled frame houses, those not concerned avoid bullets and
splinters by jumping into their beds. During my three days'
stay at Carson City I heard of three murders. A man " heavy

on the shoulder," who can " hit out straight from the hip," is a valuable acquisition.   The gambler or professional player, who in the Eastern States is exceptionably peaceful, because he fears the publicity of a quarrel, here must distinguish himself as a fighting man.   A curious story was told to illustrate how the ends of justice might, at a pinch, in the case of a popular character, be defeated.   A man was convicted of killing his adversary, after saying to the bystanders, " Stoop down while I shoot the son of a dog (female)."   Counsel for the people showed *malice prepense :* counsel for defence pleaded that his client was *rectus in curia,* and manifestly couldn't mean a man, but a dog.   The judge ratified the verdict of acquittal.

Such was the state of things, realising the old days of the Californian gold diggings, when I visited in 1860 Carson City. Its misrule, or rather want of rule, has probably long since passed away, leaving no more traces than a dream.   California has been transformed by her Vigilance Committee, so ignorantly and unjustly declaimed against in Europe and in the Eastern States of the Union, from a savage autonomy to one of the most orderly of the American Republics, and San Francisco, her capital, from a den of thieves and prostitutes, gamblers and miners, the offscourings of nations, to a social status not inferior to any of the most favoured cities.

Hurrah Again — in !   19*th October.*

This day will be the last of my diary.   We have now emerged from the deserts of the Basin State, and are debouching upon lands where coaches and the electric telegraph ply.

After a cold night at the hospitable Smith's, and losing the cattle, we managed to hitch to, and crossed, not without difficulty, the deep bed of the Carson River, which runs over sands glittering with mica.   A little beyond it we found the stationhouse, and congratulated ourselves that we had escaped a twelve hours' durance vile in its atmosphere of rum, kornschnapps, stale tobacco, flies, and profane oaths, not to mention the chance of being " wiped out" in a " difference" between a soldier and a gambler, or a miner and a rider.

From the station-house we walked, accompanied by a Mr. O., — who, after being an editor in Texas, had become a mail rider in U. T., — to the fort.   It was, upon the principle of its eastern neighbours, a well-disposed cantonment, containing quarters for the officers and barracks for the men. Fort Churchill had been built during the last few months: it lodged about two companies of infantry, and required at least 2000 men. Capt. F. F. Flint (6th Regt.) was then commanding, and Lieut.-Col. Thos. Swords, a deputy quartermaster-general, was on a tour of inspection. We went straight to the quartermaster's office, and there found Lieut. Moore, who introduced us to all present, and supplied us with the last newspapers and news. The camp was Teetotalist, and avoided cards like good Moslems: we were not, however, expected to drink water except in the form of strong waters, and the desert had disinclined us to abstain from whiskey. Finally, Mr. Byrne, the sutler, put into our ambulance a substantial lunch, with a bottle of cocktail, and another of cognac, especially intended to keep the cold out.

The dull morning had threatened snow, and shortly after noon the west wind brought up cold heavy showers, which continued with intervals to the end of the stage. Our next station was Miller's, distant 15 to 16 miles. The road ran along the valley of Carson River, whose trees were a repose to our eyes, and we congratulated ourselves when we looked down the stiff clay banks, 30 feet high, and wholly unfenced, that our journey was by day. The desert was now " done." At every few miles was a drinking "calaboose":* where sheds were not a kettle hung under a tree, and women peeped out of the log-huts. They were probably not charming, but, next to a sea voyage, a desert march is the finest cosmetic ever invented. We looked upon each as if

> " Her face was like the milky way i' the sky,
> A meeting of gentle lights without a name."

At Miller's Station, which we reached at 2·30 p.m., there really was one pretty girl — which, according to the author of the Art of Pluck, induces proclivity to temulency. Whilst the rain was heavy we sat round the hot stove, eating bread and cheese, sausages and anchovies, which Rabelais, not to speak of other honest drinkers, enumerates amongst provocatives to thirst. Then we started at

---

* The Spanish is Calabozo, the French Calabouse. In the Hispano-American countries it is used as a "common jail" or a "dog hole," and as usual is converted into a verb.

4 P.M. through the cold rain, along the bad road up the river bed, to "liquor up" was manifestly a duty we owed to ourselves. And finally, when my impatient companions betted a supper that we should reach Carson City before 9 P.M., and sealed it with a "smile," I knew that the only way to win was to ply Mr. Kennedy the driver with as many *pocula* as possible.

Colder waxed the weather and heavier the rain as, diverging from the river, we ascended the little bench upon which China-town lies. The line of ranches and frame houses, a kind of length-without-breadth place, once celebrated in the gold-digging days looked dreary and grim in the evening gloom. At 5·30 P.M. we were still fourteen miles distant from our destination. The benches and the country round about had been turned topsy-turvy in the search for precious metal, and the soil was still burrowed with shaft and tunnel, and crossed at every possible spot by flumes, at which the natives of the Flowery Land still found it worth their while to work. Beyond China-town we quitted the river, and in the cold darkness of night we slowly began to breast the steep ascent of a long divide.

We had been preceded on the way by a young man, driving in a light cart a pair of horses, which looked remarkable by the side of the usual Californian teams, three pair with the near wheeler ridden. Arriving at a bad place he kindly called out to us, but before his warning could be taken a soft and yielding sensation, succeeded by a decided leaning to the right, and ending with a loud crash, announced an overturn. In due time we were extricated, the pieces were picked up, and though the gun was broken the bottle of cocktail fortunately remained whole. The judge, probably and justly offended by my evil habit of laughing out of season, informed us that he had never been thrown before, an announcement which make us expect more " spills." The unhappy Kennedy had jumped off before the wheels pointed up hill; he had not lost a hoof, it is true, on the long march, but he wept spirits and water at the disappointing thought that the ambulance, this time drawn by his best team, and laden with all the dignities, had come to grief, and would not be fit to be seen. After 100 yards more another similar series of sensations announced a repetition of the scene, which deserved the epitaph,

" Hic jacet amphora vini."

This time, however, falling down a bank, we "came to smash," the bottle (eheu!) was broken, so was the judge's head, whilst the ear of the judgeling—serve him right for chaffing!—was cut, the pistols and powder flasks were half buried in the sand, a variety of small objects were lost, and the flying gear of the ambulance was a perfect wreck.   Unwilling to risk our necks by another trial, we walked over the rest of the rough ground, and, conducted by the good Croly, found our way to "Dutch Nick's," a ranch and tavern, apparently much frequented by the teamsters and other roughs, who seemed, honest fellows! deeply to regret that the accident had not been much more serious.

Remounting, after a time, we sped forwards, and sighted in front a dark line, but partially lit up about the flanks, with a brilliant illumination in the centre, the Kursaal of Mr. Hopkins, the local Crockford.   Our entrance to Penrod House, the Fifth Avenue of Carson City, was by no means of a triumphal order; Nature herself seemed to sympathise with us, besplashing us with tears heavier than Mr. Kennedy's.   But after a good supper and change of raiment, a cigar, "something warm," and the certainty of a bed combined to diffuse over our minds the calm satisfaction of having surmounted our difficulties *tant bien que mal.*

*   *   *   *   *   *

CONCLUSION.

The traveller and the lecturer have apparently laid down a law that whether the journey does or does not begin at home it should always end at that " hallowed spot." Unwilling to break through what is now becoming a time-honoured custom, I trespass upon the reader's patience for a few pages more, and make my final *salaam* in the muddy puddly streets, under the gusty, misty sky of the " Liverpool of the South."

After a day's rest at Carson City, employed in collecting certain necessaries of tobacco and raiment, which, intrinsically vile, were about treble the price of the best articles of their kind in the Burlington Arcade, I fell in with Captain Dall, superintendent of the Ophir mines, for whom I bore a recommendation from Judge Crosbie, of U. T. The valuable silver leads of Virginia City occupied me, under the guidance of that hospitable gentleman, two days, and on the third we returned to Carson City, *viâ* the Steamboat Springs, Washo Valley, and other local lions. On the 24th appeared the boys driving in the stock from Carson Lake; certain of these youths had disappeared; Jim Gilston, who had found his brother at Dry Creek Station, had bolted, of course forgetting to pay his passage. A stage coach, most creditably horsed, places the traveller from Carson City at San Francisco in two days; as Mr. Kennedy, however, wished to see me safely to the end, and the judge, esteeming me a fit Mentor for youth, had entrusted to me Telemachus, alias Thomas, his son, I resolved to cross the Sierra by easy stages. After taking kindly leave of and a last " liquor up " with my old *compagnons de voyage*, the judge and the marshal, we broke ground once more on the 25th of October. At Genoa, pronounce Ge-nóa, the country town built in a valley thirteen miles south of Carson, I met Judge Cradlebaugh, who set me right on grounds where the Mormons had sown some prejudices. Five

VIRGINIA CITY. (From the North-east.)

days of a very dilatory travel, placed us on the western slope of
the Sierra Nevada; the dugways and zigzags reminded me of the
descriptions of travellers over the Andes; the snow threatened
to block up the roads, and our days and nights were passed
amongst teamsters *en route*, and in the frame-house inn. On
the 30th November, reaching Diamond Springs, I was advised by
a Londoner, Mr. George Fryer, of the " Boomerang Saloon," to
visit the gold-diggings at Placerville, whither a coach was about
to start. At " Hang-town," as the place was less euphoniously
termed, Mr. Collum of the Cary House, kindly put me through
the gold washing and " hydraulicking," and Dr. Smith, an old
East Indian practitioner, and Mr. White, who had collected some
fine specimens of minerals, made the evenings pleasant. I
started on the 1st November by coach to Folsom, and there found
the railroad, which in two hours conducts to Sacramento : the
negro coachmen, driving hacks and wagons to the station, the
whistling of the steam, and the hurry of the train, struck me by
the contrast with the calm travel of the desert.

At Sacramento, the newer name for New Helvetia,— a capital
mass of shops and stores, groggeries, and hotels,— I cashed a
draught, settled old scores with Kennedy, who almost carried me
off by force to his location, shook hands with Thomas, and transferred myself from the Golden Eagle on board the steamer
Queen City. Eight hours down the Sacramento River, past
Benicia — the birth-place of the Boy — in the dark to the head
waters of the glorious bay, placed me at the " El Dorado of the
West," where a tolerable opera, a superior supper, and the society
of friends made the arrival exceptionably comfortable

I spent ten pleasant days at San Francisco. There remained
some traveller's work to be done ; the Giant Trees, the Yose-
mite or Yohamite Falls,— the highest cataracts yet known in
the world,— and the Almaden Cinnabar Mines, with British
Columbia, Vancouver's Island, and Los Angelos, temptingly near.
But in sooth I was aweary of the way; for eight months I had
lived on board steamers and railroad cars, coaches, and mules ;
my eyes were full of sight-seeing, my pockets empty, and my
brain stuffed with all manner of useful knowledge. It was far
more grateful to *flaner* about the stirring streets, to admire the
charming faces, to enjoy the delicious climate, and to pay quiet
visits like a " ladies' man," than to front wind and rain, muddy

roads, *arrieros*, and rough teamsters, fit only for Rembrandt, and the solitude of out-stations.   The presidential election was also in progress, and I wished to see with my eyes the working of a system which has been facetiously called " universal suffering and vote by bullet."   Mr. Consul Booker placed my name on the lists of the Union Club, which was a superior institution to that of Leamington; Col. Hooker of Oregon, and Mr. Tooney showed me life in San Francisco; Mr. Gregory Yale, whom I had met at Carson City, introduced me to a quiet picture of old Spanish happiness, fast fading from California; Mr. Donald Davidson, an old East Indian, talked East Indian with me ; and Lieuts. Macpherson and Brewer accompanied me over the forts and batteries which are intended to make of San Francisco a New World Cronstadt.   Mr. Polonius sensibly refused to cash for me a draught not authorised by my circular letter from the Union Bank.   Mr. Booker took a less prudential and mercantile view of the question, and kindly helped me through with the *necessaire* — £100.   My return for all this kindness was, I regret to say, a temperate but firm refusal to lecture upon the subject of Meccah and El Medinah, Central Africa, Indian Cotton, American politics, or everything in general.   I nevertheless bade my adieux to San Francisco and the hospitable San Franciscans with regret.

On the 15th November, the Golden Age, Commodore Watkins, steamed out of the Golden Gates, bearing on board amongst some 520 souls, the body that now addresses the public.   She was a model steamer with engines and engine rooms, clean as a club kitchen, and a cuisine whose terrapin soup and devilled crabs à la Baltimore will long maintain their position in my memory,—not so long, however, as the kindness and courtesy of the ancient mariner who commanded the Golden Age.   On the 28th we spent the best part of a night at Acapulco, the city of Cortez and of Doña Marina, where any lurking project of passing through ill-conditioned Mexico was finally dispelled. The route from Acapulco to Vera Cruz, over a once well worn highway, was simply and absolutely impassable.   Each sovereign and independent State in that miserable caricature of the Anglo-American Federal Union was at daggers drawn with all and every of its next door neighbours; the battles were paper battles, but the plundering and the barbarities—cosas de

Mejico!—were stern realities. A rich man could not travel because of the banditti; a poor man would have been enlisted almost outside the city gates; a man with many servants would have seen half of them converted to soldiers under his eyes, and have lost the other half by desertion, whilst a man without servants would have been himself press-gang'd; a liberal would have been murdered by the Church, and a church-man—even the frock is no protection—would have been martyred by the liberal party. For this disappointment I found a philosophical consolation in various experiments touching the influence of Mezcal-brandy, the Mexican national drink, upon the human mind and body.

On the 15th December we debarked at Panama; horridly wet, dull, and dirty was the "place of fish," and the "Aspin-wall House and its Mivart reminded me of a Parsee hotel in the Fort, Bombay. Yet I managed to spend there three plea-sant circlings of the sun. A visit to the acting Consul intro-duced me to M. Hurtado, the Intendente or Military Governor, and to a charming country-woman, whose fascinating society made me regret that my stay there could not be protracted. Though politics were running high, I became acquainted with most of the officers of the U.S. squadron, and only saw the last of them at Colon, alias Aspinwall. Messrs. Boyd and Power of the " Weekly Star and Herald," introduced me to the officials of the Panama R. R., Messrs Nelson, Center, and others, who, had I not expressed an aversion to " deadheadism " or gratis travelling, would have offered me a free passage. Last, but not least, I must mention the venerable name of Mrs. Seacole of Jamaica and Balaklava.

On the 8th December I passed over the celebrated Panama railway to Aspinwall, where Mr. Center, the superintendent of the line, made the evening highly agreeable with conversation aided by "Italia," a certain muscatel cognac that has yet to reach Great Britain. We steamed the next morning, under charge of Captain Leeds, over the Caribbean Sea or Spanish Main, bound for St. Thomas. A hard-hearted E.N.E. wind protracted the voyage of the Solent for six days, and we reached the Danish settlement in time, and only just in time, to save a week's delay upon that offensive scrap of negro liberty-land. On the 9th December we bade adieu with pleasure to the little dun-

geon-rock and turned the head of the good ship Seine, Captain
Rivett, towards the Western Islands. She played a pretty
wheel till almost within sight of Land's End, where Britannia
received us with her characteristic welcome, a gale and a pea
soup fog, which kept us cruising about for three days in the
unpleasant Solent and the Southampton Water.

IN THE SIERRA NEVADA.

APPENDIX I.

EMIGRANTS' ITINERARY,

Showing the distances between camping-places, the several mail-stations where mules are changed, the hours of travel, the character of the roads, and the facilities for obtaining water, wood, and grass on the route along the southern bank of the Platte River, from St. Joseph Mo. *via* Great Salt Lake City, to Carson Valley. From a Diary kept between the 7th August and the 19th October 1860.

No. of Mail.		Miles.	Start.	Arrival.	Date.

1.	Leave St. Joseph, Missouri, in N. lat. 39° 40′, and W. long. 94° 50′. Cross Missouri River by steam ferry. Five miles of bottom land, bend in river and settlements. Over rolling prairie 2000 ft. above sea-level. After 6 miles, Troy, capital of Doniphan Co. Kansas T. about a dozen shanties. Dine and change mules at Cold Spring — good water and grass.
	    Road from Fort Leavenworth (N. lat. 39° 21′ 14″, and W. long. 94° 44′) falls in at Cold Spring, distant 16 miles.
	    From St. Jo. to Cold Spring there are two routes, one lying north of the other, the former 20, the latter 24 miles in length.
		20— 24	A. M. 9.30	P. M. 3	Aug. 7

2.	After 10 miles, Valley Home, a whitewashed shanty. At Small Branch on Wolf River, 12 miles from Cold Spring, is a fiumara on north of road, with water, wood, and grass. Here the road from Fort Atchinson falls in. Kennekuk station, 44 miles from St. Joseph. Sup and change mules.	22— 23	P. M. 4	P. M. 8	Aug. 7
3.	Two miles beyond Kennekuk is the first of the three Grasshopper Creeks, flowing after rain to the Kansas River. Road rough and stony, water, wood, and grass. Four miles beyond the First Grasshopper is Whitehead, a young settlement on Big Grasshopper, water in pools, wood, and grass. Five and a half miles beyond is Walnut Creek, in Kikapoo Co. pass over corduroy bridge, roadside dotted with shanties. Thence to Locknan's, or Big Muddy Station.	25	P. M. 9	A. M. 1	Aug. 7, 8
4.	Seventeen miles beyond Walnut Creek, the Third Grasshopper, also falling into the Kansas River.				

No. of Mail.		Miles.	Start.	Arrival.	Date.
	Good camping-ground. Ten miles beyond lies Richland, deserted site. Thence to Seneca, capital of Nemehaw Co. A few shanties on N. bank of Big Nemehaw Creek, a tributary of the Missouri River, which affords water, wood, and grass.	18	A. M. 3	A. M. 6	Aug. 8
5.	Cross Wildcat Creek and other nullahs. Seven miles beyond Seneca lies Ashpoint, a few wooden huts, thence to "Uncle John's Grocery," where liquor and stores are procurable. Eleven miles from Big Nemehaw water, wood, and grass are found at certain seasons near the head of a ravine. Thence to Vermilion Creek, which heads to the N.-E. and enters the Big Blue 20 miles above its mouth. The ford is miry after rain, and the banks are thickly wooded. Water is found in wells 40—43 feet deep. Guittard's Station.	20	A. M. 8	NOON. 12	Aug. 8
6.	Fourteen miles from Guittards, Marysville, capital of Washington Co. affords supplies and a blacksmith. Then ford the Big Blue, tributary to Kansas River, clear and swift stream. Twelve miles W. of Marysville is frontier line between Kansas and Nebraska. Thence to Cottonwood Creek, fields in hollow near the stream.	25	P. M. 1	P. M. 6	Aug. 8
7.	Store at the crossing very dirty and disorderly. Good water in spring 400 yards N. of the road, wood and grass abundant. Seventeen and a half miles from the Big Blue is Walnut Creek, where emigrants encamp. Thence to West Turkey or Rock Creek in Nebraska T. a branch of the Big Blue: its approximate altitude is 1485 feet.	26	P. M. 6	P. M. 11	Aug. 8
8.	After 19 miles of rough road and mosquitos, cross Little Sandy, 5 miles E. of Big Sandy, water and trees plentiful. There Big Sandy deep and heavy bed. Big Sandy Station.	23	P. M. 12	A. M. 4	Aug. 9
9.	Cross hills forming divide of Little Blue River ascending valley 60 miles long. Little Blue fine stream of clear water falling into Kansas River, everywhere good supplies and good camping-ground. Along left bank to Kiowa.	19	A. M. 6	A. M. 10	Aug. 9
10.	Rough road of spurs and gullies runs up valley 2 miles wide. Well wooded chiefly with cottonwood and grass abundant. Ranch at Liberty Farm on the Little Blue.	25	A. M. 11	P. M. 3	Aug. 9
11.	Cross divide between Little Blue and Platte River, rough road, mosquitos troublesome. Approximate altitude of dividing ridge 2025 feet. Station at Thirty-two Mile-Creek, a small wooded and winding stream flowing into the Little Blue.	24	P. M. 4	P. M. 9	Aug. 9

No. of Mail.		Miles.	Start.	Arrival.	Date.
12.	After 27 miles strike valley of the Platte, along southern bank of river, over level ground, good for camping, fodder abundant. After 7 miles Fort Kearny in N. lat. 40° 38′ 45″, and W. long. 98° 58′ 11″: approximate altitude 2500 feet above sea level. Grocery, cloths, provisions, and supplies of all kinds are to be procured from the sutler's store. Beyond Kearny a rough and bad road leads to "Seventeen-Mile-Station."	34	P. M. 10·30	A. M. 8	Aug. 10
13.	Along south bank of Platte. Buffalo chips used for fuel. Sign of buffalo appears. Plum Creek Station on a stream where there is a bad crossing in wet weather.	21	A. M. 9·30	P. M. 1·15	Aug. 10
14.	Beyond Plum Creek, Willow Island Ranch, where supplies are procurable. Road along Platte, wood scarce, grass plentiful, buffalo abounds; after 20 miles "Cold Water Ranch." Halt and change at Midway Station.	25	P. M. 2·30	P. M. 8	Aug. 10
15.	Along Valley of Platte, road muddy after rain, fuel scarce, grass abundant, camp traces everywhere. Ranch at Cottonwood Station, at this season the western limit of buffalo.	27	P. M. 9	A. M. 1·45	Aug. 11
16.	Up Valley of Platte. No wood, buffalo chips for fuel. Good camping-ground, grass on small branch of Platte. To Junction House Ranch and thence to station at Frémont Springs.	30	A. M. 6·15	A. M. 11	Aug. 11
17.	Road passes O'Fallon's Bluffs. "Half-way House" a store and ranch, distant 120 miles from Fort Kearny, 400 from St. Joseph, 40 from the lower crossing, and 68 from the Upper crossing of the South Fork (Platte River). The station is called Alkali Lake.	25	NOON. 12	P. M. 5	Aug. 11
18.	Road along river, no timber, grass, buffalo chips, and mosquitos. Station at Diamond Springs near Lower Crossing.	25	P. M. 6	P. M. 10·15	Aug. 11
19.	Road along river. Last 4 miles very heavy sand, avoided by Lower Crossing. Poor accommodation at Upper Ford or Crossing on the eastern bank, where the mail passes the stream en route to Gt. S. L. city, and the road branches to Denver City and Pike's Peak.	25	P. M. 11	A. M. 3·15	Aug. 12
20.	Ford Platte 600 yards wide, 2·50 ft. deep, bed gravelly and solid, easy ford in dry season. Cross divide between North and South Forks along bank of Lodge Pole Creek. Land arid, wild sage for fuel. Lodge Pole Station.	35	A. M. 6·30	P. M. 12·45	Aug. 12
21.	Up Lodge Pole Creek over spur of table-land, then striking over the prairie finishes the high divide between the Forks. Approximate altitude 3500				

No. of Mail		Miles.	Start.	Arrival.	D te.
	feet. On the right is Ash-Hollow, where there is plenty of wood and a small spring. Station is Mud Springs, a poor ranch.	25	P. M. 3	P. M. 5·45	Aug. 12
22.	Route lies over rolling divide between the Forks, crossing Omaha, Lawrence, and other creeks where water and grass are procurable. Cedar is still found in hill-gullies. About half a mile north of Chimney Rock is a ranch where the cattle are changed.	25	A. M. 8	P. M. 12·30	Aug. 13
23.	Road along south bank of North Ford of Platte River. Wild sage only fuel in valley: small spring on top of first hill. Rugged labyrinth of paths abreast of Scott's Bluffs, which lie 5 miles S. of river in N. lat. 41° 48′ 26′, and W. long. 103° 45′ 02″. Water found in first ravine of Scott's Bluffs 200 yards below the road, cedars on heights. To Station.	24	P. M. 1·30	P. M. 5·30	Aug. 13
24.	Road along river, crosses Little Kiowa Creek, a tributary to Horse Creek, which flows into the Platte. Ford Horse Creek, a clear shallow stream with a sandy bottom. No wood below the hills.	16	P. M. 6·30	P. M. 8·30	Aug. 13
25.	Route over sandy and heavy river bottom and rolling ground, leaving the Platte on the right: cottonwood and willows on the banks. Ranch at Laramie City kept by M. Badeau, a Canadian, who sells spirits, Indian goods, and outfit.	26	A. M. 6	P. M. 10·20	Aug. 14
26.	After 9 miles of rough road cross Laramie Fork and enter Fort Laramie, N. lat. 42° 12′ 38″, and W. long. 104° 31′ 26″. Alt. 4519 feet. Military post with post-office, sutler's stores, and other conveniences. Thence to Ward's Station on the Central Star, small ranch and store.	18	P. M. 12·15	P. M. 4	Aug. 14
27.	Rough and bad road. After 14 miles, cross Bitter Cottonwood Creek, water rarely flows, after rain 10 ft. wide and 6 inches deep, grass and fuel abundant. Pass Indian shop and store. At Bitter Creek branch of Cottonwood the road to Salt Lake City forks. Emigrants follow Upper or South road over spurs of Black Hills, some way south of river to avoid kanyons and to find grass. The station is called Horseshoe Creek. Residence of road-agent, Mr. Slade, and one of the worst places on the line.	25	P. M. 5	P. M. 9·30	Aug. 14
28.	Road forks, one line follows Platte, the other turns to left, over "cut off;" highly undulating ridges crooked and deeply dented with dry beds of rivers; land desolate and desert. No wood nor water till end of stage. La Bonté River and Station, unfinished ranch in Valley, water and grass.	25	A. M. 10·45	A. M. 2·45	Aug. 15
29.	Road runs 6 miles (wheels often locked) on rugged				

No.of Mail.		Miles.	Start.	Arrival.	Date.
	red land, crosses several dry beds of creeks, and springs with water after melting of snow and frosts in dry season, thence into Valley of Platte. After 17 miles it crosses the La Prêle (Rush River), a stream 16 feet wide, where water and wood abound. At Box-Elder Creek Station good ranch and comfortable camping-ground.	25	P. M. 4	P. M. 9	Aug. 15
30.	Along the Platte River now shrunk to 100 yards. After 10 miles, at Deer Creek, a post office, blacksmith's shop, and store near Indian Agency. Thence a waste of wild sage to Little Muddy, a creek with water. No accommodation nor provisions at station.	20	A. M. 8 30	NOON. 12	Aug. 16
31.	After 8 miles cross vile bridge over Snow Creek. Thence up river valley along S. bank of Platte to lower ferry. To Lower Bridge, old station of troops. To Upper Bridge, where ferry has now been done away with.	18	P. M. 1·15	P. M. 4·15	Aug. 16
32.	Road ascends hill 7 miles long, land rough, barren. and sandy in dry season. After ten miles. red spring near the Red Buttes, old trading-place and post-office. Road then leaves Platte River and strikes over high, rolling, and barren prairie. After 18 miles "Devil's Backbone." Station at Willow Springs, wood, water, and grass, good place for encampment, but no accommodation nor provisions. On this stage mineral and alkaline waters dangerous to cattle abound.	28	A. M. 6 30	P. M. 12·50	Aug. 17
33.	After 3 miles, Green Creek, not to be depended upon, and Prospect Hill, a good look out. Then, at intervals of 3 miles, Harper's, Woodworth's, and Greasewood Creeks, followed by heavy sand. At 17 miles "Saleratus Lake" on west of road. Four miles beyond is "Independence Rock," Ford Sweetwater, leaving "Devil's Gate" on right. Pass blacksmith's shop. Sage only fuel. Plante or Muddy Station, family of Canadians, no conveniences.	33	P. M. 2·30	P. M. 9·15	Aug. 17
34.	Along winding banks of Sweetwater. After 4 miles, "Alkali Lake" S. of road. Land dry and stony, stunted cedars in hills. After 12 miles, "Devil's Post-Office," singular bluff on left of road and opposite ranch kept by Canadian. Mail Station "Three Crossings," at Ford No. 3, excellent water, wood, grass, game, and wild currants.	25	A. M. 7	A. M. 11	Aug. 18
35.	Up kanyon of Sweetwater. Ford river 5 times, making total of 8. After 16 miles, "Ice Springs" in swampy valley, and one quarter of a mile beyond " Warm Springs." Then rough descent and waterless stretch. Descend by " Lander's cut off" into fertile bottom. "Rocky Ridge Sta-				

No of Mail.		Miles.	Start.	Arrival.	Date.
	tion," at Muskrat Creek good cold spring, grass, and sage fuel.	35	A. M. 5·45	P. M. 12·45	Aug. 19
36.	Up bed of creek, and ascending long hills leave Sweetwater. After 4 miles, 3 alkaline ponds S. of road. Rough path. After 7 miles, "Strawberry Creek " 6 ft. wide, good camping-ground, willows and poplars. One mile beyond is Quaking Asp Creek often dry. Three miles beyond lies M'Achran's Branch 33 × 2. Then "Willow Creek" 10 × 2, good camping-ground. At Ford No. 9 Canadian ranch and store. Long table-land leads to "South Pass" dividing trip between Atlantic and Pacific, and thence 2 miles to station at " Pacific Springs," water, tolerable grass, sage fuel, and mosquitos.	35	A. M. 7·45	P. M. 3	Aug. 20
37.	Cross Miry Creek. Road down Pacific Creek, water scarce for 20 miles. After 11 miles, " Dry Sandy Creek," water scarce and too brackish to drink, grass little, sage and greasewood plentiful. After 16 miles, " Sublette's cut off," or the " Dry Drive," turns N. westwards to Soda Springs and Fort Hall : the left fork leads to Fort Bridger, and Gt. S. L. City. Four miles beyond junction is " Little Sandy Creek" 20 − 25 × 2, grass, timber, and good camping-ground. Eight miles beyond is " Big Sandy Creek," clear, swift, and with good crossing 110 × 2. Southern route best, along old road, no water for 49 miles. Big Sandy Creek Station.	33	A. M. 8	P. M. 12·50	Aug. 21
38.	Desolate road cuts off bend of river, no grass nor water. After 12 miles " Simpson's Hollow." Fall into Valley of Green River half a mile wide, water 110 yards broad. After 20½ miles, Upper Ford, Lower Ford 7 miles below Upper. Good camping-ground on bottom; at station in Green River grocery, stores, and ferry-boat when there is high water.	32	P. M. 1·45	P. M. 6·30	Aug. 21
39.	Diagonal ford over Green River, good camping-ground in bottom. Follow valley for 4 miles, grass, and fuel. Michel Martin's store and grocery. Road leaves river and crosses waterless, divide to Black's Fork 100 × 2, grass and fuel. Wretched station at Ham's Fork.	24	A. M. 8	NOON. 12	Aug. 22
40.	Ford Ham's Fork. After 12 miles road forks at the 2nd striking of Ham's Fork, both branches leading to Fort Bridger. Mail takes left hand path. Then Black's Fork 20 × 2, clear and pretty valley with grass and fuel, cottonwood and yellow currants. Cross stream 3 times. After 12 miles, " Church Butte." Ford Smith's Fork 30 ft. wide snd shallow, tributary of Black's Fork. Station at Millersville on Smith's Fork, large store and good accommodation.	20	P. M. 2	P. M. 5·15	Aug. 22

No. of Mail.		Miles.	Start.	Arrival.	Date.
41.	Road runs up valley of Black's Fork. After 12 miles, Fort Bridger in N. lat. 41° 18′ 12″, and W. long. 110° 32′ 23″, on Black's Fork of Green River. Commands Indian trade, fuel, corn, little grass. Post-office, sutler's store, grocery, and other conveniences. Thence rough and rolling ground to Muddy Creek Hill, steep and stony descent. Over fertile bottom to Big Muddy and Little Muddy Creek, which empties into Black's Fork below Fort Bridger. At Muddy Creek Station is a Canadian, provisions, excellent milk, no stores.	25	A. M. 8·30	P. M. 12·15	Aug. 23
42.	Rough country. Road winds along ridge to Quaking Asp Hill 7900 (8400 ?) feet above sea-level. Steep descent, rough and broken ground. After 18 miles Sulphur Creek Valley, stagnant stream, flowing after rain, ford bad and muddy. Station in fertile valley of Bear River, which turns northward and flows into E. side of Lake, wood, grass, and water. Poor accommodations at Bear River Station.	20	NOON. 12	P. M. 5·30	Aug. 23
43.	Road runs by Needle Rocks, falls into Valley of Egan's Creek. "Cache Cave" on right hand. Three miles below Cave is Red Fork in Echo Kanyon, unfinished station at entrance. Rough road, steep ascents and descents along Red Creek Station on Weber River, which falls into Salt Lake south of Bear River.	36	A. M. 8·15	P. M. 2·30	Aug. 24
44.	Road runs down Valley of Weber. Ford river. After 5¼ miles is a salt spring where the road leaves the river to avoid a deep kanyon and turns left into a valley with rough paths, trying to wheels. Then crosses mountain and ascending long hill descends to Bauchmin's Creek, tributary to Weber River. Creek 18 feet wide, swift, pebbly bed, good ford, grass and fuel abundant. Station called Carson's House; accommodations of the worst.	22	P. M. 4·30	P. M. 7·45	Aug. 24
45.	Ford Bauchmin's Creek 13 times in 8 miles. After 2 miles along a small watercourse ascend Big Mountain, whence first view of Gt. S. L. City, 12 miles distant. After 14 miles Big Kanyon Creek. Six miles further road leaves Big Kanyon Creek, and after steep ascent and descent makes Emigration Creek. Cross Little Mountain, 2 miles beyond Big Mountain, road rough and dangerous. Five miles from Emigration Kanyon to Gt. S. L. City. Road through "Big Field" 6 miles square.	29	A. M. 7	P. M. 7·15	Aug. 28

GREAT SALT LAKE CITY N. lat. 40° 46′ 08″
W. long. 112° 06′ 08″ (G.)
Altitude 4300 feet.

The variation of compass at Temple Block in 1849 was 15° 47′ 23″, and in 1860 it was 15° 54′, a slow progress towards the east. (In the Wind River Mts. as laid down by Col. Frémont in 1842 was E. 18°.) In Fillmore Valley it is now 18° 15′, and three years ago was about 17° east, the rapid progression to the east is accompanied with extreme irregularity, which the people attribute to the metallic constituents of the soil.

Total of days between St. Jo. and Gt. S. L. City   .   .   19
Total stages   45
Distance in statute miles   1136
From Fort Leavenworth to Gt. S. L. City   .   .   . 1168

ITINERARY OF THE MAIL ROUTE FROM GREAT SALT LAKE CITY TO SAN FRANCISCO.

No. of Mail.		Miles.	Start.	Arrival.	Date.
1 and 2.	Road through south of City, due south along right bank of Jordan. Cross many creeks, viz. Kanyon Creek, 4¼ miles, Mill Creek, 2½, First or Great Cottonwood Creek 2. Second ditto 4. Fork of road 1¼. Dry Creek 3½. Willow Creek 2¾. After 22—23 miles, hot and cold springs, and halfway house, the brewery under Point of the Mountain. Road across Ash Hollow or Jordan Kanyon, 2 miles. Fords river, knee deep, ascends a rough divide between Utah Valley and Cedar Valley 10 miles from camp, and finally reaches Cedar Creek and Camp Floyd.	44	10·30	9·30	Sept. 20
3.	Leaves Camp Floyd, 7 miles to divide of Cedar Valley. Crosses divide into Rush Valley, after total of 18·2 miles reaches Meadow Creek, good grass and water. Rush Valley Mail Station 1 mile beyond, food and accommodation.	20	10·30	9·30	Sept. 27
4.	Crosses remains of Rush Valley 7 miles. Up rough divide called Genl. Johnston's Pass. Spring often dry, 200 yards on right of road. At Point				

No.of Mail.		Miles.	Start.	Arrival.	Date.
	Look Out leaves Simpson's Road, which runs south. Cross Skull Valley, bad road. To bench on eastern flank of desert. Station called Egan's Springs, Simpson's Springs, or Lost Springs, grass plentiful, water good.	27	A. M. 9·30	4·30	Sept. 28
5.	New station, road forks to S.-E. and leads after 5 miles to grass and water. After 8 miles River Bottom, 1 mile broad. Long line over desert to Express Station, called Dugway, no grass, and no water.	20	P. M. 12	5·30	Sept. 29
6.	Steep road 2½ miles to summit of Dugway Pass. Descend by rough incline, 8 miles beyond road forks to Devil's Hole, 90 miles from Camp Floyd on Simpson's route, and 6 miles S. of Fish Springs. Eight miles beyond fork is Mountain Point, road winds S. and W. and then N. to avoid swamp, and crosses three sloughs. Beyond last is Fish Spring Station on bench, poor place, water plentiful but bad. Cattle here drink for first time after Lost Springs, distant 48 miles.	28	P. M. 6·30	A. M. 3·30	Sept. 29
7.	Road passes many pools. Halfway forks S. to Pleasant Valley (Simpson's line). Road again rounds swamp, crossing S. end of Salt Plain. After 21 miles, "Willow Creek," water rather brackish. Station "Willow Springs" on bench below hills at W. end of Desert, grass and hay plentiful.	33	A. M. 10	3·30	Sept. 30
8.	Road ascending bench turns N. to find Pass. After 6 miles Mountain Springs, good water, grass, and fuel. Six miles beyond is Deep Creek Kanyon, dangerous ravine 9 miles long. Then descends into fertile and well watered valley, and after 7 miles enters Deep Creek Mail Station. Indian farm.	28	A. M. 8	P. M. 4	Oct. 1
9.	Along W. Creek. After 8 miles, "Eight Miles Springs," water, grass, and sage fuel. Kanyon after 2½ miles, 500 yards long and easy. Then 19 miles through Antelope Valley to station of same name, burnt in June 1860 by Indians. Simpson's route from Pleasant Valley, distant 12·5 miles, falls into E. end of Antelope Valley, from Camp Floyd 151 miles.	30	A. M. 8	P. M. 4	Oct. 3, 4
10.	Road over valley for 2 miles to mouth of Shell Creek Kanyon, 6 miles long. Rough road, fuel plentiful. Descends into Spring Valley, and then passes over other divides into Shell Creek, where there is a mail station; water, grass, and fuel abundant.	18	A. M. 6	P. M. 11	Oct. 5
11.	Descends rough road. Crosses Steptoe Valley and bridged creek. Road heavy, sand or mud. After 16 miles Egan's Kanyon, dangerous for Indians.				

No.of Mail.		Miles	Start.	Arrival.	Date.
	Station at W. mouth, burned by Indians in Oct. 1860.	18	P. M. 2	P. M. 6	Oct. 5
12.	Pass divide, fall into Butte Valley, and cross its N. end. Bottom very cold. Mail Station half way up hill, very small spring, grass on N. side of hill. Butte Station.	18	P. M. 8	A. M. 3	Oct. 6
13.	Ascend long divide, 2 steep hills and falls. Cross N. end of Long Valley, all barren. Ascend divide and descend into Ruby Valley, road excellent, water, grass, and bottom, fuel distant. Good Mail Station.	22	A. M. 8	P. M. 1·45	Oct. 7
14.	Long divide, fuel plenty, no grass nor water. After 10 miles road branches, right hand to Gravelly Ford of Humboldt River. Cross dry bottom. Cross Smith's Fork of Humboldt River in Huntingdon Valley, little stream, bunch-grass and sage fuel on W. end. Ascend Chokop's Pass, Dugway and hard hill, descend into Moonshine Valley. Station at Diamond Springs; warm water but good.	23	A. M. 8	P. M. 1·45	Oct. 8, 9
15.	Cross Moonshine Valley. After 7 miles sulphurous spring and grass. Twelve miles beyond, ascend divide, no water, fuel and bunch-grass plentiful. Then long divide. After 9 miles, station on Roberts' Creek at E. end of Sheawit, or Roberts' Springs Valley.	28	A. M. 8	P. M. 1·45	Oct. 10
16.	Down Valley to west, good road, sage small, no fuel. After 12 miles, willows and water-holes, 3 miles beyond are alkaline wells. Station on bench, water below in dry creek, grass must be brought from 15 miles.	35	A. M. 6·30	P. M. 12·30	Oct. 11
17.	Cross long rough divide to Smokey Valley. At northern end creek called "Wanahonop," or "Netwood," i. e. trap. Thence long rough kanyon to Simpson's Park, grass plentiful, water in wells 10 feet deep. Simpson's Park in Shoshone country, and, according to Simpson's Itinerary, 348 miles from camp Floyd.	25	A. M. 8·15	P. M. 2·25	Oct. 12
18.	Cross Simpson's Park. Ascend Simpson's Pass, a long kanyon, with sweet, "Sage Springs," on summit, bunch-grass plentiful. Descend to fork of road, right hand to lower, left hand to upper, ford of Reese's River. Water perennial and good, food poor.	15	A M. 10	P. M. 2	Oct. 13
19.	Through remainder of Reese's River Valley. After long divide Valley of Smith's Creek, saleratus, no water nor grass. At last, station near kanyon, and hidden from view. Land belongs to Pa Yutas.	28	A. M. 7·20	P. M. 2·45	Oct. 14

No. of Mail.		Miles.	Start.	Arrival.	Date.
20.	Ascend rough kanyon, and descend to barren and saleratus plain. Towards south of valley over bench-land, rough with rock and pitch-hole. "Cold Springs Station" half built, near stream, fuel scarce.	25	A. M. 8·15	P. M. 4·15	Oct. 15
21.	At west gate 2 miles from station good grass. After 8 miles, water. Two miles beyond is middle gate, water in fiumara, and grass near. Beyond gate 2 basins, long divides, winding road, to "Sand Springs Valley," bad water, little grass.	35	A. M. 9·50	P. M. 2·30	Oct. 16
22.	Cross valley, 10 miles to summit, over slough inundations, and bad road. Summit shifting sand. Descend 5 miles to Carson Lake, water tolerable, tule abundant. Round S. side of lake to sink of Carson River Station, no provisions, pasture good, fuel scarce.	25	A. M. 11	P. M. 9	Oct. 17
23.	Cross long plain. Ascend very steep divide, and sight Sierra 50 miles distant. Descend to Carson River. Fort Churchill newly built. Sutler's stores, &c.	25	A. M. 9·30	P. M. 7·15	Oct. 18
24.	Carson City.	35	A. M. 11	P. M. 10·30	Oct. 19
	Carson City lies on the eastern foot of the Sierra Nevada, distant 552 statute miles, according to Captain Simpson, from Camp Floyd. The present itinerary reduces it to 544, and, adding 44 miles, to a total of 588 from Gt. S. L. City.				

ITINERARY

Of Capt. J. H. SIMPSON's Wagon Road from Camp Floyd to Genoa, Carson Valley, U. T. Explored by direction of General A. G. JOHNSTON, commanding the Department of Utah between the 2nd May to 12th June 1859.

Places.	Intermediate Distances. Miles.	Camp to Camp. Miles.	Total from Camp Floyd. Miles.	No. of Camp.	Wood.	Water.	Grass.
Camp Floyd, wood and grass in vicinity						W	
Meadow Creek	18·2	18·2	18·2	1			
Cross Meadow Creek (Rush Valley), mail station ¼ mile . .	1						
Spring ⅛ mile to right of Gen. Johnston's Pass, just after passing summit. This spring furnishes but little water, even in the spring, and in the summer would be most probably dry . . .	8·9	9·9	28·1	2	W	W	G

Places.	Intermediate Distances. Miles	Camp to Camp. Miles.	Total from Camp Floyd. Miles.	No. of Camp.	Wood.	Water.	Grass.
Simpson's Springs, mail station . . .	16·2	16·2	44·3	3	W	W	G
Summit, Short-cut Pass	21·6			{	Wil-low		
1·6 miles below summit	1·6	23·2	67·5	4	Sage		{ very little grass
Tolerable grass skirting low range of rocks } on right of road . . . . }	7·8						G
A little grass, sage in valley . . .	4·8				S		G
Devil's Hole, water slightly brackish . .	6·7					W	
Fish Springs, mail station	5·4	24·7	92·2	5	Ctw	W	G
Warm Springs	3·4				G W	W	G
Grass in considerable quantity of good } character . . . . . . }	26·4	29·7	12·19	6			G
Alkaline spring to right of road, water not } drinkable . . . . . }	1·						
Sulphur springs, water abundant and pa- } latable . . . . . . }	1·5	2·5	125·	7	W, S	W	G
Spring, Pleasant Valley, mail station	13·4	13·4	138·4	8	W	W	G
East side Antelope Valley		12·5	150·9	9	W	W	G
Spring Valley, good grass on west bench } and slopes . . . . . }	19·		169 9	10	G W	W	G
Cross marsh, road takes up a fine stream, } grass all along . . . . . }	3·5						
Leave Creek	3·5				W	W	G
Spring, copious, grass fine	2·8				W	W	G
East side Steptoe Valley, mail station .	1·3	11·1	181·0	11	W	W	G
Steptoe Creek; dry in summer . . .	6·5						
Mouth Egan Cañon	6·8	13·8	194·3	12	W	W	G
Spring, source of Egan Creek . . .	1·8				W	W	G
West side of Butte Valley. Mail station, } a very small spring, barely sufficient for } cooking purposes, near top of hill; grass } on N. side of same hill }	16·2	18·1	212 4	13	W	W	G
Spring 1 mile west side of summit of range .	12·	12·	224·4	14	W	W	G
Ruby Valley, mail station	9·2	9·2	233·6	15	G W	W	G
Smith's Fork, Humboldt R. Huntingdon's } Creek . . . . . }	14·4						
Small mountain stream	3·3	17·6	251·2	16	G W	W	G
Spring left of road	1·2				G W	W	G
Near west foot of Cho-kupe Pass . .	5·8	7·1	258·3	17	G W	W	G
Spring in Pah-hun-nupe Valley . . .	7·8						
Do. west side of Pah-hun-nupe Valley	5·6	13·3	271·6	18 {	S, W } G W	W	G
She-a-wi-te (Willow) Creek . . .	14·9	14 9	286·5	19	S, W	W	G
Bed of Nash R. water in pools, probably } not constant . . . . . }	11 6						
Small spring, grass on mountain side, 2 } miles off . . . . . . }	5·9	17·5	04 ·	20	S, W	W	G
Wons-in-dam-me, or Antelope Creek . .	7·	7·	311·	21	W	W	G
Creek	4·3				S, W	W	G
Creek west side of Valley	9 5	13·7	324·7	22	S, W	W	G
Wan-a-ho-no-pe (Netwood trap) Creek .	13·6						
Do. do. do. .	4·6	18·2	342·9	23	S, W	W	G
Simpson's Park, according to topographer, } Lt. Putnam and guide, Col. Reese . }	4·9	4·9	347·8	24	S, W	W	G

Places.	Intermediate Distances. Miles.	Camp to Camp. Miles.	Total from Camp Floyd Miles.	No. of Camp.	Wood.	Water.	Grass.
Small spring in Simpson's Pass (same authority)	3·						
Ford of Reese's River	8·2					W	G
Reese's River	2·6	13·8	361·6	25		W	G
Leave Reese's River	3·4					W	G
Small spring to left of road just before reaching summit of Pass	10						
Lt. J. L. Kirby Smith's Creek	7 8	21·2	382·8	26	G W	W	G
Englemanns "	1·6					W	
Lt. Putnam's "	8·6	10·2	393·	27	S, W	W	G
Do. South Fork "	2·7				W	W	G
Rock Creek	3·				W	W	G
Do.	3·1	8·7	101·7	28	W	W	G
Do. Sinks	1·7						
Spring water kegs shonld be filled for 2 days. Camp from this in alkaline flat	5·4					W	
Gibraltar Gate	0·6					W	
Creek joins Gibraltar Creek	4·2						
Middle Gate Spring	3·2	14·7	416·4	29	S, W	W	G
West Gate	3·5						
Dry wells, alkaline valley, very poor camp water and grass alkaline, and little of either. Rabbit bush fuel	21·0	24·5	440·9	30	Rab. bush	W	G
Creek connecting the 2 lakes of Carson. Road can be shortened some 8 or 10 miles by striking across head of Alkaline Valley after getting about 9 miles from camp 30, and then proceeding directly to shore of Carson Lake. It is not necessary to go so far north as the connecting creek referred to		16·6	157·5	31	Dry rush	W	R, G
Leave Carson Lake	9·7					W	R, G
Walker's River	21 5	01 2	488·7	32	W	W	G
Do. do.		10·	498·7	33	W	W	G
Do. North bend		6 3	505·	34	W	W	G
Small spring, not sufficient for large command, grass ½ mile south	14·1				S, W	W	G
Carson River	1·9						
Do. do.	3·0	19·0	524·	35	W	W	G
Pleasant Grove, cross Carson River and get into Old Emigrant Road. Mail station	9·0	9 0	533·	36	W	W	G
China town. Gold diggings	7·4					W	
Carson city. E. foot of Sierra Nevada	11·6	19 0	552·	37		W	G
Genoa Do. do. do.	12·9	12 9	564 9	38	W	W	G

To Brevt.-Major F. J. Porter,   (Signed)   J. H. Simpson,
    Assist.-Adj.-Genl.   Capt. Top. Engineers.
    Dept. Utah, Camp Floyd.